CW01021712

A CENTURY OF MODEL ANIMATION

A CENTURY OF MODEL ANIMATION

FROM MÉLIÈS TO AARDMAN

Ray Harryhausen and **Tony Dalton**

First published 2008 by Aurum Press Ltd,
7 Greenland Street, London NW1 0ND
www.aurumpress.co.uk

A catalogue record for this book is available from the British Library.

ISBN 978 1 84513 367 2

Book design by Ashley Western

Printed in China

PAGE 2
Detail of a bronze statue of the Beast featured in *The Beast from 20,000 Fathoms* (1952).

TITLE PAGE
Left, Willis O'Brien animating a dinosaur for *The Lost World* (1925).
Centre, Ray Harryhausen animating Medusa for *Clash of the Titans* (1981).
Right, Nick Park and the Aardman Animations team working on *Wallace & Gromit: The Curse of the Were-Rabbit* (2005).

CONTENTS PAGE
A clay maquette by Ray of a Cyclops for the unrealized *The Story of Odysseus* (1996-1998).

CONTENTS

Forewords

I met my boyhood hero Ray Harryhausen in 1971. It wasn't hard to do: all it took was nerve and a Los Angeles telephone book. The only Harryhausen listed was Ray's mother; and as luck would have it, he was over from London, visiting her, and he invited me to drop by – no doubt with some heavy-handed prompting. When he told me he was writing a book, I asked an entirely appropriate question for a tactless nineteen-year-old: 'Is it a memoir?' Ray was all of fifty and replied, with equal appropriateness, 'I *hope* not.'

Ray went on to make a few more movies ('Harryhausen movies', as we always called them; a fitting sobriquet given that he was their guiding artistic force). He also went on to write a few books: *Film Fantasy Scrapbook*, which was quite a bit more than the title implies; *An Animated Life*, a sort of autofilmography; and *The Art of Ray Harryhausen*, a Cyclops' treasure store of drawings and photos and behind-the-scenes revelations. You won't catch me calling any of them a memoir.

The last two were co-authored by Tony Dalton, with whom Ray has written this new book which you now hold in your hands: a history of stop-motion animation. It's the story of a unique art form, told from the perspective of its most beloved and respected practitioner.

Let's get one thing straight: Ray Harryhausen is so much more than solely an animator. He's a film-maker who conceives the stories and scenes and characters, designs and builds the characters, directs the scenes he's dreamed up, and executes the blending of live action with his magically moving puppets. And he's a master of all these disciplines, a genuinely unique creative voice.

The 'Harryhausen movie' was born in the 1950s, and arguably reached maturity in 1958 with *The 7th Voyage of Sinbad*. There had never been anything like it, ever. Stop-motion feature animation, under the guiding force of Willis O'Brien, had concentrated on bringing to life dinosaurs (and, with a forceful nudge from Merian C. Cooper, gorillas). Ray's first two forays into creature-creating similarly confined themselves to the realm of natural history – albeit very *imaginative* natural history – with a dinosaur (whose genus was Ray's own invention) and a giant octopus (technically not an octopus, but who's counting?). His next film brought a departure from form: a Venusian creature entirely born of Ray's fertile imagination. And then came a quantum leap: *The 7th Voyage of Sinbad*.

Audiences of today can only imagine the impact: *The 7th Voyage of Sinbad* had when it premiered fifty years ago. The monster movie genre was dominated by men in monster costumes, and photographically enlarged insects and lizards. Into this creative vacuum strode Sinbad, and believe me when I tell you that we kids knew the difference.

Here was an Arabian Nights tale come to thrilling life, with creatures hitherto realized only in storybook illustrations. Ray's fantasy creations captivated a whole generation; their bold designs put Arthur Rackham and Rene Bull (to say nothing of those giant tarantulas and iguanas) in the dust. Ray directed his wonderful cast of foam-rubber actors with wild invention, giving them fascinating things to do, wonderful choreography, and bits, and turns. The picture was remarkable because Ray himself was remarkable, and he was obviously driven by a passion to put onto the screen visions that had never been seen before, things that nobody else was doing, or could do. Due to his talent and taste and skill, he succeeded brilliantly. He was truly a voice in the wilderness.

He was so far ahead of his competition that I rather doubt Ray was really *aware* of his competition. The muse he followed was a demanding one, and stop-motion animation is solitary work. As a one-time member of this insular fraternity I can attest that standing on your feet, bending dozens of joints into hundreds of positions (each adjustment being just *so*), all day and often into the night is the bare minimum the job requires. Such isolation doubtless contributed to his success: he was pretty much answerable to only himself, unhampered by the helpful suggestions of colleagues or executives. But since the stop-motion animator lives such a 'lone wolf' existence, it's no wonder that some of the art's most significant figures are unsung.

This book does much to remedy that oversight. Ray was hugely influenced by *King Kong*, and was fortunate to meet, study under and work alongside the great Willis O'Brien, *his* boyhood inspiration. O'Brien's story is a fascinating, often frustrating and even tragic one, and I won't attempt to synopsize it here: Ray knew him and befriended him and can tell it far better than I. It is, however, a classic cautionary tale of artistic dreams thwarted by Hollywood realities, and in many ways can be viewed as the rule to Ray's exception. Anyone hoping for a career in the movie business should read it carefully. Twice.

When I was a boy, 'Harryhausen movies' were all I cared about, but they weren't the whole story of stop-motion, as I would eventually find out.

Ray made the sort of pictures which excited him, rather in the fashion of O'Brien. But there was a whole other kind of stop-motion film which had nothing to do with men battling monsters, and those films are examined here as well.

Ladislaw Starewicz, possibly a genius, created bizarre and engaging films which are unique and make for fascinating viewing, even today. Charlie Bowers was probably no genius (except perhaps by the standards of Hollywood, where anyone who doesn't breathe through his mouth eventually earns that appellation), but he produced some wacky little films which are wildly funny.

As to the art's more recent practitioners, Jim Danforth deserves all the praise anyone cares to heap upon him. Like Ray and Obie, he's a man of many remarkable talents and he certainly deserves a place on the dais among the greats.

Today, CGI has changed the film-making landscape, most obviously in the arena of the fantasy film. As with stop-motion, though, CGI is only as good as the artists and technicians who 'make it go'. Now it seems everybody's making 'Harryhausen movies'. Some are better than others, of course, but computer technology has enabled many scores of artists to take a whack at filling the screen with the sort of wonders which Ray once used to create alone. His voice in the wilderness has finally been joined by a chorus of new voices, which will sing new songs down through the generations. For my money, though, it was Ray Harryhausen who taught us all how to sing.

RANDALL WILLIAM COOK

The idea that the first man was created from clay is even older and more universal than the account in the Judeo-Christian Bible. In Egypt the ram-headed god Khnum was a potter who fashioned humans from the moistened dust. The Hawaiian creator deity Ku shaped the 'earth-formed woman' out of soft red clay. Yuma Indians tell of the twin-god Kokomaht reaching for a fistful of wet clay and forming the original man.

The image is irresistible: a human being rising out of the elemental cauldron of the earth itself, shaped by giant and loving hands, and then given the breath of life. The clay-man shakes off loose bits of mud, and then blinks, breathes, and takes a step.

In the eye of the imagination, that first step would appear quivering, halting, urgent with life. It would look like stop-motion.

The pioneers of stop-motion animation developed their craft from clay to foam latex and other materials of model animation, sometimes with sophisticated skeletons made from finely machined joints. The creators peopled their cinematic world not only with humans, but also with a whole menagerie of giant apes, dinosaurs, skeletons and talking raisins. The fact that all these creatures inhabit our imagination with such persistence is more than an accident of nostalgia for the pioneering days of film-making. There is something powerful and primordial about the way King Kong fights the prehistoric denizens of Skull Island in the groundbreaking 1933 film, or the way Mighty Joe Young wrestles the lions in the 1949 classic. Even from the viewpoint of our era of jaded expectations, those creatures manage to convince us that they are more than puppets. They seem like real creatures that move according to the dictates of their own thought.

The artists who have gravitated to stop-motion effects animation and stop-motion puppet films – people like Willis O'Brien, Ray Harryhausen, George Pal, Mike Jittlov, Will Vinton, Jim Danforth, Tim Burton, and Nick Park are a special breed. They are comfortable with working long hours alone. They are capable of dissecting and compressing time, and they're possessed of a rare mixture of patience and concentration. It took over four months of continuous effort for Ray Harryhausen to complete the sword fight sequence from the 1963 film *Jason and the Argonauts*. There was no room for correction or reconsideration. It was a work of inspiration and perspiration. And it was also a job completed with an eye to budget and to audience. As Ray modestly said about his work, 'We set out to entertain the public in a positive way.'

In 1993, I visited Ray at his studio, which he jokingly calls his 'den of iniquity'. He showed me many of the original models from his classic films, which were gathered together like ageing actors waiting to be called back onstage. I was thrilled to see the Medusa from the 1981 picture *Clash of the Titans*. I remembered her menacing gaze, with the twelve snakes writhing on her head – each with a head and a tail, each one moving independently – and that's not including her arms and her tail and the flickering firelight, all of which had to be controlled one frame at a time. I asked Ray how he remembered where each snake was heading, how he kept track of all those separate elements. 'How did you do it?' I asked.

He thought for a moment, closed his eyes, and smiled: 'I just did it,' he said.

James Gurney

Model animation has never been a *crowded* profession. It's always been a specialist area, very exclusive and slightly eccentric, populated by a handful of pioneers and geniuses. This book is an amazing and revelatory window onto their world.

Even today, when I'm sure there are more people working professionally in the field than ever before, they must still be numbered in hundreds rather than thousands.

It's a form of film-making which refuses to be mass-produced. In the early twentieth century 'classic' animation – the drawn kind – became big business precisely because people worked out how to industrialize the process, but model animation has always been a craft-based activity that won't be cloned. The joy of model animation – its whole *point* both for the animator and the viewer – has always been its intimacy. It's all about close focus – fingers, hands, touch. It's the feel of a puppet in the animator's hands – a unique blending of sculpture and performance. When an animated character is seen moving on screen, the animator is ever-present, everywhere in the shot, an invisible spirit transforming the puppet into a living being. Magically, the animated performance has much of the immediacy and vitality of a live one.

Like cinema itself, model animation has gone through an entire life-cycle in little more than a hundred years (depending of course on when you start counting). At the start of the last century audiences were more than happy to watch a few household objects move around by themselves – that was Entertainment! Seventy years later, model animation was at the very cutting edge of special effects in the highest budget films of the day. And today it's a mature and sophisticated technique, where directors have acquired the confidence to make films of any length in all kinds of styles from the highly traditional, to the almost abstract.

But the wonderful thing is that in all that history – from the very first discovery that it could even be *done* right down to the present – just two men link hands and carry the story of model animation from its stone age to the computer age – Willis O'Brien and Ray Harryhausen.

To have met Ray Harryhausen, and to have learned from him, as I've been lucky enough to do, is to learn from a man who learned from the man who virtually invented the art form. In literary terms it would be rather as if I could talk with Charles Dickens to discover that he in turn had chatted with Homer. Two degrees of separation span the entire history of model animation.

I never met Willis O'Brien – though in terms of chronology it would have been entirely possible – but of course I've known his work for ever. As a young animation enthusiast, I used to believe that model animation started with *King Kong*. That living, breathing, fighting, thinking ape seemed to appear from nowhere, fully formed and entirely miraculous. In due time I discovered Willis O'Brien's earlier film *The Lost World*, and later still realized – with much delight – that he'd started out making short animated comedies, on miniature stages, using all the language and techniques of live-action film just as I'd done with my colleague at Aardman, David Sproxton. It was exciting and humbling to realize that we'd confronted the same problems and made the same discoveries over sixty years apart.

Traditionally, if an art form as young as animation can have traditions, animators are literally an anonymous bunch. Most people recognize Mickey, Wallace, Daffy and Bart, and many people know the names of their original inventors. But the animators who brought them to life, hundreds of people who worked over decades, go largely unknown and unrecognized, except by their appreciative and long-suffering families.

But Ray Harryhausen has bucked the trend. Wonder of wonders, here's an animator (and designer and producer and creator and choreographer and all the rest of it), but here's an animator whose name is known! Here's a man, what's more, who pretty well invented an entire genre of film-making and then carried it by sheer talent and imagination for over forty years. His name is synonymous with the finest animation of fantasy creatures, and with a whole genre of film-making.

Famously, Ray's love affair with model animation began at the age of thirteen when he went to see *King Kong* at Grauman's Chinese Theatre on Hollywood Boulevard. Much less famously, my own enthusiasm caught fire at the age of nine when I went to see Ray's *Jason and the Argonauts* at the Orpheus on Northumbria Drive in Bristol. I realize it doesn't have quite the same ring to it, but the principle is exactly the same – great ideas spark great reactions, and the inspiration to create spreads like wildfire. This book records in wonderful detail, and with fabulous images, that exciting progress of ideas down the generations and across a hundred years.

And happily (for me and all my colleagues at Aardman, apart from anyone else) it's a story that continues with equal vigour today. It would be natural to assume that the art and craft of model animation would be under threat from its young and glamorous sibling – computer animation. Certainly there are a thousand times more people engaged with the new craft than with the old one. And yet model animation continues to inspire artists and grab the attention and love of audiences; not because it's an amazing special effect but because it's vital, alive and warm. Like hand-made furniture, or pottery or painting the spark of human contact still shines through the work as brightly as it did a hundred years ago.

PETER LORD

Introductions

Although it had originally been our intention to write a book about my mentor Willis O'Brien, the man who brought *King Kong* to life, as we began to assemble an outline we, and the publishers, realized that, if we were writing about O'Brien, then why not research and write a history of the origins of model animation with specific emphasis on the combination of live action and model animation, which I call Dynamation or dimensional animation. Beginning with the embryonic experiments and discoveries on the eve of the twentieth-century, which would lead to dimensional animation, we could then follow the progression of true innovators like O'Brien, and the development of techniques such as Dynamation. O'Brien, as will become apparent, was a major player in the development of the art but not the originator of model animation. So to get to Dynamation and beyond we felt that we needed to top and tail his life and career.

It was surprising to discover, as our research progressed, that there had been no previously published history of the art (although there is the excellent *Stop-Motion Filmography* by Neil Pettigrew that lists major films that combine stop-motion with live action), so we decided that our book should reflect the genius of as many of the artists and technicians as possible, past and present, which would gratifyingly include my own work. A hundred years of model animation is a long time, so this has to be a personal history of the individuals I respect and those whom I consider to be the innovators and the cornerstones of our peculiar profession. Sadly, there are far too many for us to mention them all in this book but to those people who are not included, be assured that your work is very much part of the history of the art.

We hope also that this book, along with our two previous collaborations, will prove to be an inspiration to new animators. If you are just such a potential film-maker, have no doubts that it is a lonely profession, at least it was when I worked on my pictures, but the loneliness, accompanied by much frustration and pain, was always outweighed by the excitement of seeing my creatures move in the same 'reality' as humans. That special exhilaration never ever left me. It is the thrill of breathing 'life' into one's own creations and at the same time giving them individual personalities that makes an animator's work so uniquely exciting and fulfilling.

Ray Harryhausen
England
2008

A Century of Model Animation has taken us nearly two years to research and collate and it should be seen as a companion piece to our two previous books, *An Animated Life* and *The Art of Ray Harryhausen*, but like the others should also, we hope, stand alone as a book on the history and art of this most delicate and loneliest of cinematic art forms.

Primarily, it is a book about model animation combined with live action, what Ray and producer Charles Schneer officially called Dynamation. The wording used to describe three-dimensionally animated films varies from country to country, or even animator to animator. In Europe the genre is called puppet or model animation, and in the US stop-motion animation (which is why the American edition has that title). For Ray and myself the phrase 'stop-motion' describes the process by which the animation is produced and can apply to both two-dimensional and three-dimensional animation, so the phrase is potentially inadequate. Ray calls his technique dimensional animation, which doesn't just refer to the three-dimensional aspect of the model but also to the fact that it is placed within a three-dimensional situation, normally live action. However, for the sake of simplicity, in this book we have adopted, for the most part, the term model animation.

To lead us up to the point in the art's history where animation was combined with live action, we needed to look at the beginnings. Therefore our first task was to document the often complex and obscure, but equally fascinating, early history of model animation, from its origins around1895 through to 1993 and the advent of *Jurassic Park*. The story begins with the early pioneers who used model stop-motion as a simple gimmick, a comedy tool or as a magician's trick. Although crude, their efforts played a vital part in the developments which led to the combining of live action with model animation. We began our first book *An Animated Life* with the French pioneer Georges Méliès. We have since been criticized on the basis that Méliès didn't actually carry out any stop-motion animation, which is not correct. He did dabble in animation, but as far as this book is concerned his place in stop-motion history is as the discoverer of what he called 'stop-action', stopping the camera and replacing or moving a person or an object, which as I have already pointed out is the basis of model animation, and so we believe this more than qualifies Méliès to be described as, at the very least, one of the art's primary originators.

Following on from those early innovators, we describe the life and career of *King Kong*'s creator, Willis O'Brien, who is credited with the idea and the first commercial use of a combination of live action with animation, or more specifically, combining humans with dinosaurs. After O'Brien we come to Ray himself and the impact of Dynamation, a simpler technique for combining humans with models than that used by O'Brien. We then discuss O'Brien and Ray's contemporaries and followers. To complete the circle we have looked at the demise of Dynamation and the advent of Computer Generated Imagery (CGI), but we also show that, far from dying, the art of model animation is in fact currently reaching out for new horizons.

Many films today, certainly most fantasy features, use CGI when combinations of humans and creatures are called for. These features will not generally be included in this book as they depend, not on stop-motion animation but on representations of a three-dimensional objects or creature produced on a computer. This seemingly creates a three-dimensional creation but in essence it is only two-dimensional, although the process that leads up to the CG image is often achieved by means of models. Whenever Ray and I find ourselves talking about model animation (which is often) and CG we use the word 'fantasy' a lot. It would seem to me that what is lacking in many CG-led contemporary features is the all-important element of fantasy. What CGI does is to make everything, whether it is the historical reality of dinosaurs or the mythology of dragons, too realistic and therefore often misses out on fantasy - the one reason, more often than not, for the story. This is not to say that these films are not good, they are; but for Ray and myself they are not always as enjoyable as what we consider to be fantasy. The art of model animation often possesses the heart, soul and personality of the individual or dominant animator, so that the model usually has a character that, in turn, somehow provides the creature with a unique slant towards fantasy. Compare the 1933 and the 2005 versions of *King Kong*. In the first film the ape displays arrogance, love, anger and pathos but in the remake there is only spectacle. Although a good film, the remake is just that, a remake, and sadly loses the fantasy element of the original by allowing the dinosaurs and the ape to seem *too* real. Perhaps the public demands more realism today, but for Ray and myself this often tends to kill the fantasy.

As Ray points out, this is a personal history of the art and we know and regret that there are films and technicians which have perforce been left out. If we were to write a complete history of the art it would probably fill ten volumes, so we were restricted to what we were allowed to put in. It was a hard process.

Personally I would like to thank all the animators and technicians who have helped with this book and Ray, without whom, a lot of the aforementioned animators and technicians would have perhaps become plumbers!

Tony Dalton

TONY DALTON
ENGLAND
2008

May 25 Cents

Science and Invention

IN PICTURES

EXPERIMENTER PUBLISHING COMPANY, NEW YORK, PUBLISHERS OF
RADIO NEWS - SCIENCE & INVENTION - THE EXPERIMENTER - MOTOR CAMPER & TOURIST

CHAPTER ONE

BASICS

'Animation is to evoke life'

EADWEARD MUYBRIDGE

'an-i-ma-tion (n): The act, process or result of imparting life, interest, motion, or activity'

DICTIONARY.COM

14 Science and Invention for May, 1925 | Science and Invention for May, 1925 15

"The Lost World"

Trick Photography Involving Complicated Hand Moved Miniature Models Explained in Detail.

By EDWIN SCHALLERT and J. K. BURLEIGH

Photos 1 and 3 show close-ups of jungle scenes which in reality were built in studio.

Drawings 2 and 4 above illustrate the methods by which the photos 1 and 3 were taken. A large studio tank was built in which tropical plants and houses were placed.

THE film story entitled "The Lost World," written by A. Conan Doyle and presented by First National, presents some of the greatest surprises and the best examples of trick photography of the cinema season. The story deals with the discovery of a land at the headwaters of the Amazon River in South America inhabited by gigantic prehistoric animals. The methods used in taking these photographs with miniature models of the animals are illustrated on this and the two succeeding pages.

In the photographing of the various scenes in this picture, two main miniature settings were required. One of these was the ground below the plateau pictured in various illustrations on these pages, and the other was the ground on the top of the plateau. Of course, there were minor miniature sets as well, such as the one depicting the street scene in London. In these miniature scenes the animals used were made up of a rubber-like composition veined throughout with wires. The result was that the models were extremely pliable yet would stay in whatever position they were placed. In all of the action photos the strip of film was taken two frames at a time with what is known as a stop motion camera. With this device one turn of the crank exposes one frame of film. Between the exposure of each two frames, the models were moved to their next position by hand.

FLYING DRAGON (MINIATURE SUSPENDED BY INVISIBLE WIRES)

TO SHOW RELATIVE SIZE

Above: The prehistoric animal ambling down the city street was taken with the stop motion camera mentioned at the right. When the falling building effect was produced, the miniature set was pulled apart by wires.

Fig. 7 above gives an idea of the relative sizes of the miniature models of prehistoric animals used in this film.

EFFECT ON SCREEN

WIRE

Fig. 8 above shows the miniature animal swimming out to sea. The model was inflated with air so as to float and pulled through the water by means of a wire. A miniature ship completed the effect.

Fig. 9 above shows the ape-man employed in this picture who was really an actor with a realistic costume. Fig. 10 above shows how effect of height was obtained. Girders did not show in film.

In plateau scene above, animal appears to push log.

In Fig. 11 log is removed with wire. In Fig. 12, miniature figures seem to climb rope ladder. Close-ups are taken as in Fig. 10.

The photograph of an animal in the same picture with human actors was accomplished by double exposure. Part of the lens was masked as the photo of the animal was taken and the other part masked while the actors were being filmed.

INVISIBLE WIRES

The miniature model manipulated by hand ambled along the bridge and suddenly decided to head back for South America. He crashed through the side of the miniature bridge, being pulled by invisible wires as above.

Using the stop motion camera, the animal models were placed in position by hand as illustrated above in Fig. 16. Even the motions of eating were taken two frames at a time, the mouth being opened or closed between each two frames. The effect of saliva in the mouth was produced by shellac and the blood in the fight scenes was a thick dark liquid.

While in London, the beast thrust its head into a clubroom. The interior scene was taken as above, a full sized model of the head being used.

The volcano scene was taken as in Fig. 19. During part of this scene, many of the prehistoric animals were shown running across the land. Red fire and smoke added to the effect.

In close-ups of some of the animals, the audience could see them appear to actually breathe. This effect was produced by means of a pump and a bladder as shown above, the bladder being rythmically inflated and deflated. The rubber tube was either hidden by scenery or else not included in the photograph as in Fig. 18.

In the London scene, the tail of the animal knocked down several people. A full sized tail of canvas was made for this scene and caused to switch around, producing the desired effect.

Today there are many sources available to those who want to know how films, and particularly special effects, have been created, although most now usually focus on Computer-Generated Imagery (CGI). There are magazines, books and internet sites completely devoted to effects and special 'making of' DVD documentaries, all of which are usually extremely accurate in their content. But in the early and middle 1930s, when Ray, then a fourteen- or fifteen-year old budding film-maker, wanted to try to recreate some of the prehistoric creatures which featured in *King Kong* (1933) there were only a handful of obscure sources that imparted any clues as to how either *King Kong* or its predecessor, *The Lost World* (1925), had been made. Ray realized that the same techniques must have been used in both pictures to bring long-dead creatures back to life on the screen, but he didn't know how it was done. Determined to find out he made a journey to his local library and discovered several magazine articles that provided some insight.

The first, 'Trick Photography Involving Complicated Hand Moved Miniature Models Explained in Detail', had appeared *Science and Invention* back in May 1925, the year in which *The Lost World* had been released. The authors describe the principles of model animation with reasonable accuracy, though, as Ray would later realize, they did make some mistakes. One was to describe the animated models as being constructed around armatures which had a 'rubber-like composition veined throughout with wires'; another was to state that, 'In all the action photos the strip of film was taken two frames at a time with what is known as a stop-motion camera.' He got the name of the camera right, but the film was, of course, shot one frame at a time.

Another article that Ray saw had been published in 1933 in *Popular Science* and was about the making of *Kong*. It was entitled 'Latest Wonder Movie is Technical Marvel' and it was almost totally inaccurate. It began well enough by stating that the effects had been achieved by 'animating beasts by moving limbs etc between exposures' but then reproduced an illustration of a life-sized creature resembling a man in ape costume. It went on to say that the 'image of the girl… is cut and placed in Ape's hands, each frame individually photographed to show progress of action, as moving arms etc. This is known as animation.' Not too bad, until you look at the accompanying illustration which shows a pair of scissors and a human hand seemingly pasting a cut-out picture of the girl in position which was, as we shall see, almost wholly misleading. Only five years later, in 1938, would *Look* magazine publish a clear and accurate account of the making of *Kong*; in the meantime Ray had to proceed on the basis of the sparse information he had and a process of trial and error.

16 Science and Invention for May, 1925

"The Lost World"

(Continued from page 15)

Above: The complete assembly of painted, life-size and animal sets.

Fig. 26 above is one of the most gripping scenes in the whole photoplay. Depending on the principle of perspective, the miniature model and scenery were placed in the foreground and the actors in the background.

Above: A photograph produced by a combination of Figs. 23, 24 and 25.

Above: One of the miniature animal models.

To produce the photo in Fig. 21, a miniature scene was painted on glass as in Fig. 23, a full size set made as in Fig. 24 and a model as in Fig. 25 were used. They were all arranged as shown in Fig. 22, the full sized set in the background.

In the scene above, a complete miniature set moderately lighted occupied the foreground, while the actors strongly lighted were in the background. In the result, both sets appeared to be equally distant from the camera.

In the photograph shown in Fig. 28, where the two prehistoric animals are engaged in mortal combat, the same principle of perspective described above was brought into play as in Fig. 31. Figs. 29 and 30 detail this part of the filming. The extreme background was a painted scene, while the foliage in the foreground consisted of miniatures.

Above in Fig. 32 is illustrated another scene wherein the models and human figures appear on the same picture. A complete description of how these animal models were made and photographed appeared in the August, 1922, issue of this magazine.

PREVIOUS SPREAD
Left, the cover of the May 1925 edition of *Science and Invention*, showing an artist's rendition of the brontosaurus from *The Lost World* rampaging through London.
Right, a detail of an illustration, circa 1925, showing how the animator moved the model of the brontosaurus for *The Lost World* and, behind, how it moved from frame to frame. Although crude and exaggerated, this is extremely accurate.

LEFT
Pages from *Science and Invention* revealing how *The Lost World* (1925) had been made. The explanation is very accurate considering the stop-motion technique was so obscure.

OVERLEAF
'Latest Wonder Movie is Technical Marvel'. Unlike the illustrations on the left, this magazine spread about the making of *King Kong* is almost entirely inaccurate. The figure at the bottom left is obviously a man in an ape suit and is actually described as a 'man in ape costume' at the top of the facing page.

As it turned out, by the time he began his experiments Ray had succeeded, after a little help from his father's friends in the film business, in grasping the basics of model animation. Essentially, these were that a model had to be photographed one frame at a time with its pose being adjusted between frames and that this required that the model should be flexible but at the same time capable of holding a position whilst it was photographed. Of course, it took many hours of practice and experimentation before Ray learned how to achieve realistic movement on the screen. But as soon as he began to manipulate and shoot his first models he realized that he loved the process, a feeling that was heightened ten-fold when his first reels of film were returned from the laboratory and he watched the models come to life on the screen. In short, he was smitten. Of course, the models' movements were jerky because the 16mm camera which he had borrowed from a friend did not have a single-frame facility; he had to tap the start button as quickly as possible, hoping to expose no more than one frame of film. Inevitably, sometimes two or even three frames were exposed, and the movement of the models became jerky, but it was movement. Fluidity would come with experience and better equipment.

In this chapter we shall describe the basics of stop-motion model animation. This will not only enable readers to understand the principles of the art but also demonstrate how inventive the animator has to be.

First of all, what is stop-motion model animation? Two-dimensional stop-motion animation refers to animated artwork, namely a drawing or graphics. Three-dimensional stop-motion animation relates to the same process, but with a three-dimensional object, usually a model of some kind. Although both processes have one factor in common – the use of stop-frame or stop-motion animation to create the illusion of movement – it is, with some exceptions, acknowledged that the model animator is able to introduce more individuality into this subjects because they are themselves three-dimensional and can be filmed in a three-dimensional setting. Most models are human- or animal-like in form, and this encourages the animator to instill into them some personal elements in the form of actions and reactions based on experience and observation. This is an essential component in the art of stop-motion model animation, which we will come to later.

The basic principal of stop-motion technique is that to make an object move you have to photograph each stage in that movement on successive frames on a strip of film. For most feature films the gauge of the film is 35mm, although 16mm is sometimes used for short film subjects. The film is made up of individual pictures or frames, and each second of 35mm screen time requires 24 frames.[1] No matter

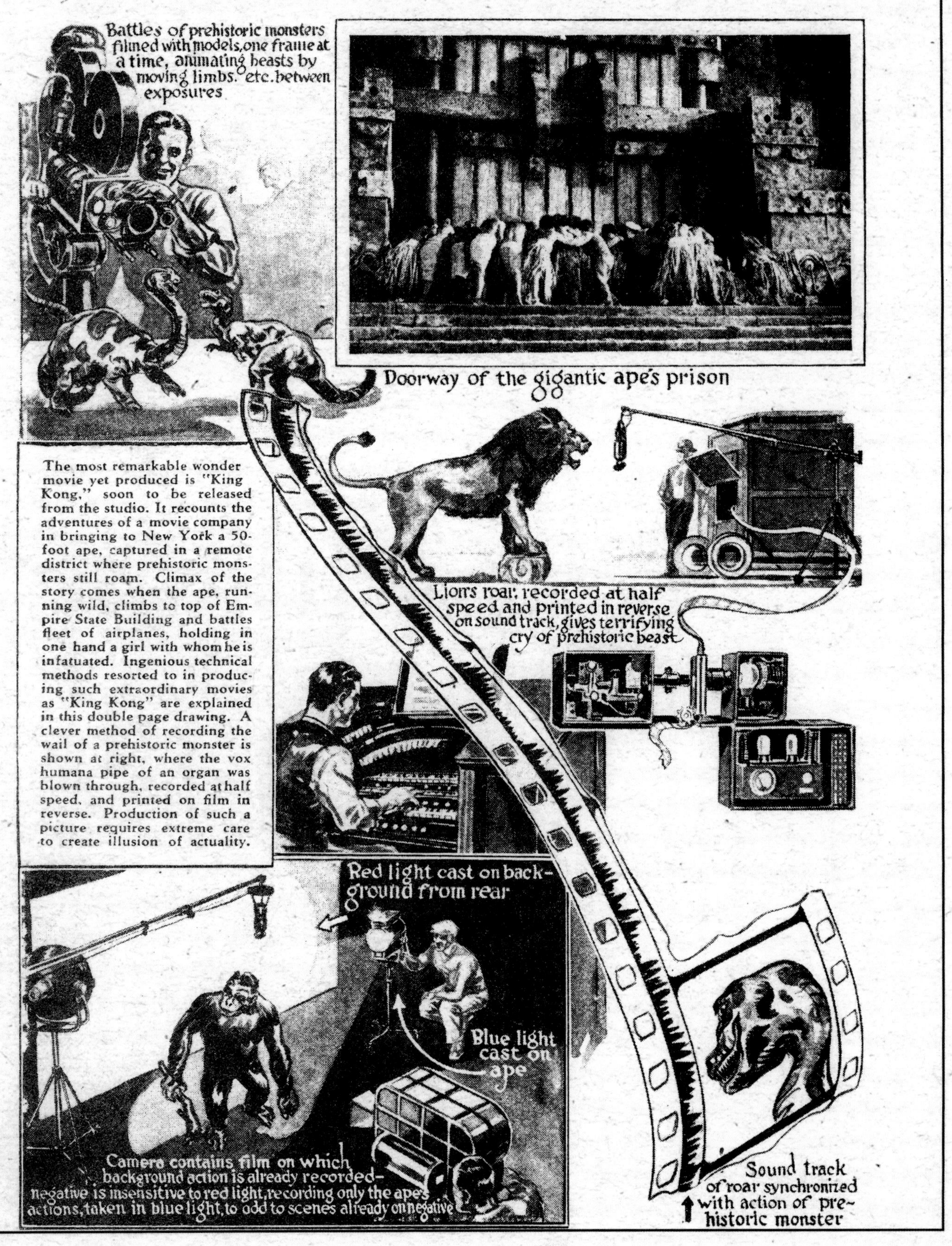
Latest WONDER MOVIE
Battles of prehistoric monsters filmed with models, one frame at a time, animating beasts by moving limbs, etc. between exposures
Doorway of the gigantic ape's prison
Lion's roar, recorded at half speed and printed in reverse on sound track, gives terrifying cry of prehistoric beast
Red light cast on background from rear
Blue light cast on ape
Camera contains film on which background action is already recorded—negative is insensitive to red light, recording only the ape's actions, taken in blue light, to add to scenes already on negative
Sound track of roar synchronized with action of prehistoric monster
The most remarkable wonder movie yet produced is "King Kong," soon to be released from the studio. It recounts the adventures of a movie company in bringing to New York a 50-foot ape, captured in a remote district where prehistoric monsters still roam. Climax of the story comes when the ape, running wild, climbs to top of Empire State Building and battles fleet of airplanes, holding in one hand a girl with whom he is infatuated. Ingenious technical methods resorted to in producing such extraordinary movies as "King Kong" are explained in this double page drawing. A clever method of recording the wail of a prehistoric monster is shown at right, where the vox humana pipe of an organ was blown through, recorded at half speed, and printed on film in reverse. Production of such a picture requires extreme care to create illusion of actuality.

is TECHNICAL MARVEL

How 50-foot Ape is shown climbing Empire State Building— Model built on studio floor, man in ape costume photographed apparently crawling up face of building

Filming skyline of New York to get results shown in Fig. 1

Fighting planes projected on screen from rear,—size reduced to give ape 50ft proportions

Camera shoots through glass on which is New York skyline—getting effect shown in Fig. 5

Normal size actor in ape costume

Girl whose clothing is torn by Ape on top of tower, photographed to get small image shown in Fig. 6.

Photographing planes in flight, as in Fig. 2— we now have two units ofthe composite scene as in Fig. 3

Image of girl, as in Fig. 6, is cut and placed in Ape's hands, each frame individually photographed to show progress of action, as moving arms, etc. "This is known as 'animating'"

On the Screen the 50-foot Ape is shown on top of Emvire Siate Building struggling girl in hand, airplanes attacking him, with New York in background

Photographing "animated" frames

saunders

whether it is live action or animation that has been filmed, each individual frame captures a slightly different split second of the action, so that when projected those 24 frames give the illusion of movement. If 24 frames amounts to only one second of screen time, it follows that a minute requires 1440 frames and an hour 86,400 frames.

If you are photographing a live-action film then the number of frames is relatively unimportant, but for an animator that number will determine how much time will be required to complete any given scene or sequence. To create the illusion of life in a model or models is a much, much slower process than filming live actors. The process is painstaking and repetitive: the animator has first to place his model into the required position, then stand aside and operate a foot or hand switch which operates the camera, move back to the model and slightly adjust it, expose another frame, and so on until the sequence is completed. When successive frames are projected at normal speed the model appears to be moving of its own accord. He has to do that 24 times to produce one second of screen time and 1440 times to achieve a minute.

To take an example of the time involved in animating a sequence let us attempt to examine one of Ray's greatest achievements, the skeleton fight in *Jason and the Argonauts* (1963). The entire sequence, including cutaways of the actors, runs approximately 4 minutes and 37 seconds, of which there is approximately 3 minutes and 40 seconds of animation.[2] There are seven skeleton models, each with basically five appendages (one head, two arms and two legs) making 35 appendages in all. Of course, not all the skeletons appear on the screen at the same time and not all the shots showed the full skeleton, but for

BELOW
Behind the scenes in Ray's hobby house studio circa 1953 during the making of *The Story of King Midas* (1953). The photograph shows the detailed miniature set with Midas sitting and counting his money in his underground vault. In the foreground is the 16mm Cine Kodak Special (the only model available at the time that had a stop-motion facility motor recess as well as a stop-motion facility if hand wound). Ray still has this camera in his extensive collection. The stop-motion motor on the right of the camera is attached to it by a shaft and was made by Ray's father.

RIGHT
A close-up of the Kodak Cine Special as it is today. The recess for the stop-motion motor shaft can be seen just in front of and below the winding handle.

FACING PAGE FROM TOP RIGHT
A sequence of seven images showing Ray manipulating the original armatured model of Medusa that featured in *Clash of the Titans*(1981) in a sequence which sees her raising her bow to shoot.

CINÉ-KODAK
· SPECIAL ·
CLOSED
¼ OPEN
½ OPEN
OPEN
SINGLE FRAME

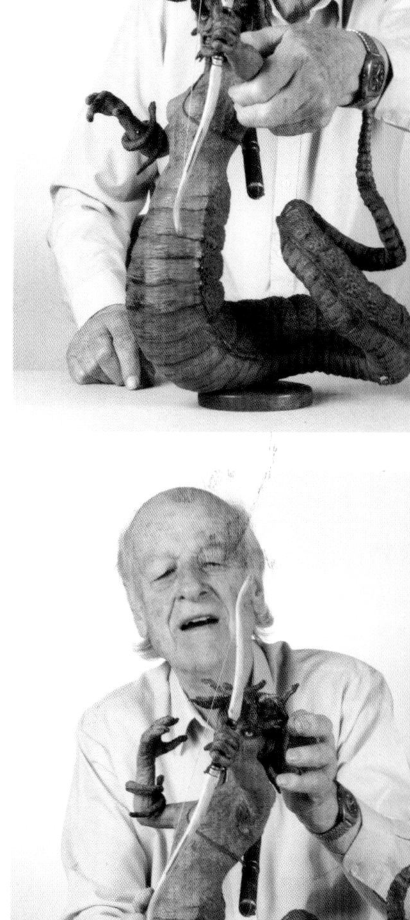

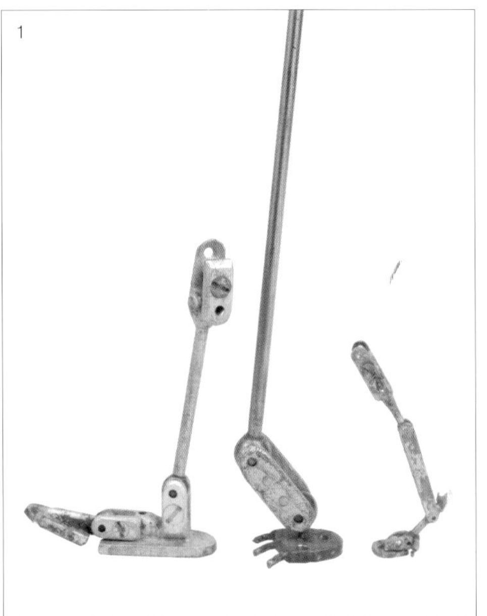

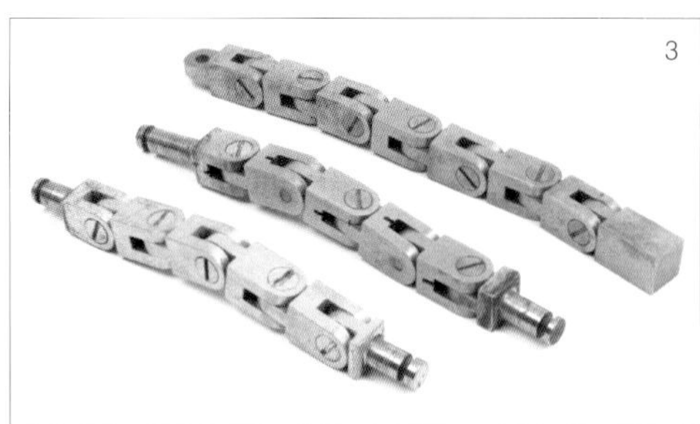

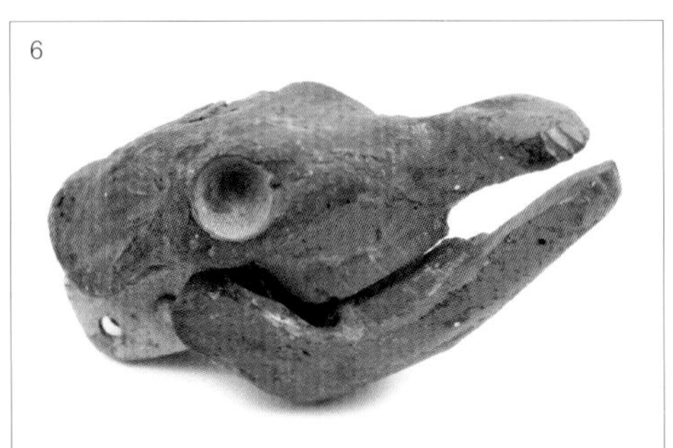

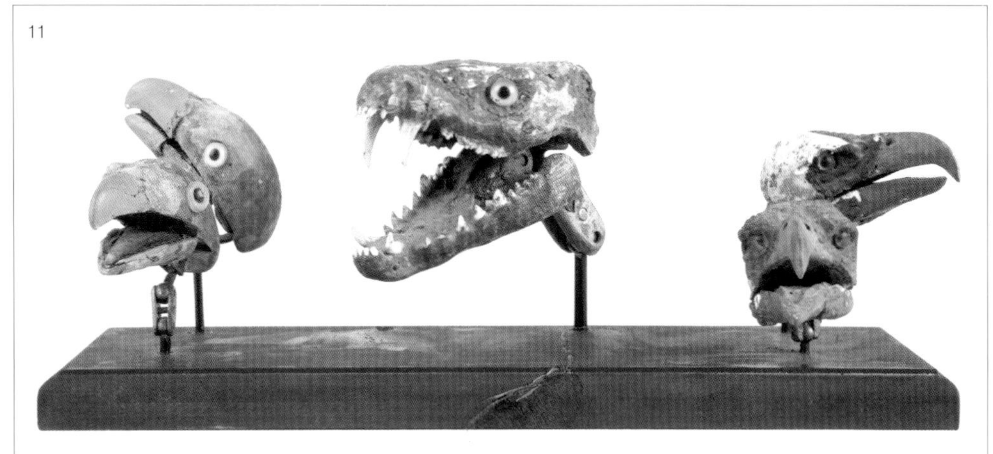

1 An assortment of lower leg and foot armatures.
2 One of Ray's earliest armatures, a triceratops.
3 Three hinge joints used for backbones and tails.
4 A section of a ball-and-socket armature designed with lugs to be fixed directly to the animation table.
5 The crab from *Mysterious Island*, showing the exposed armature.
6 A plesiosaurus head made for *Evolution of the World*.
7 The jig made by Ray's father to ensure that Ray could drill a hole in the dead centre of a ball bearing.
8 All that now remains of the Beast from *The Beast From 20,000 Fathoms*.
9 The Jupitarian, an even earlier armature from 1936/37.
10 Armatures of the tiger for *Sinbad and the Eye of the Tiger* and a homunculus for *The Golden Voyage of Sinbad*.
11 Heads of creatures from *The 7th Voyage of Sinbad*. From the left, two heads of the baby Roc, the dragon and the mother Roc.

BELOW
The original armature for Medusa which featured in *Clash of the Titans* (1981). Aside from the Hydra in *Jason and the Argonauts* (1963), this was one of the most complex armatures that Ray designed. Note the lugs on the bottom of the armature for securing the model to the animation table. Ray took this picture of the armature which he placed on his garden wall.

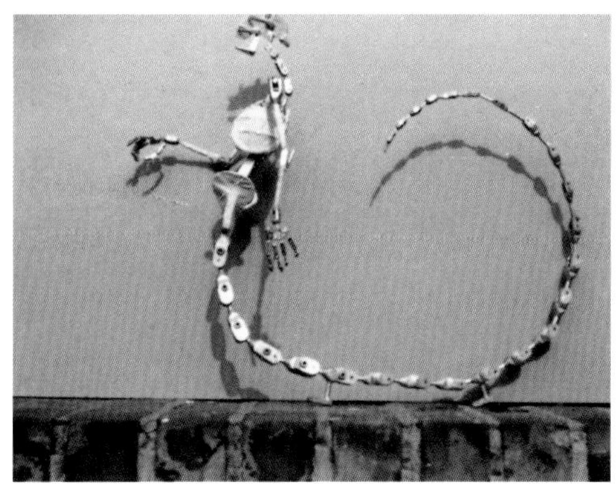

simplicity's sake, let us say Ray animated all the appendages throughout the sequence. So if all 35 appendages had to be moved between each frame, one second of action (24 frames) would have involved Ray making 840 movements. The total of 3 minutes and 40 seconds (220 seconds) of animation therefore required a staggering total of 184,800 movements! Now that is high, too high, because we must again remember that not all the skeletons were in each scene – although in a number of shots Ray had to animate the skeletons bending and crouching, using their hip joints, which meant that there were more than five appendages. Let us therefore generously reduce that total by 100,000, which leaves us with 84,000 movements! Admittedly the skeleton scene is an extreme example, but whatever the final number of movements was the work clearly required tireless dedication. Ray took four and half months to shoot this one sequence, working on his own almost seven days a week.

So in basic and general terms, animation is the illusion of movement created by shooting one frame of film at a time and moving a model or object between each frame so that they appear to move of their own accord when the finished film is projected. Now we need to concentrate on the key tools of the art.

There is a world of difference between the puppets used today by Aardman Animations (the creators of *Wallace and Gromit* amongst other things) and in Tim Burton's films (*The Nightmare Before Christmas*, *James and the Giant Peach* and *Corpse Bride*) and the models used by Willis O'Brien and Ray and their contemporaries for their films. The puppets used by Aardman and Burton, and much earlier by George Pal for his *Puppetoon* series, are stylized caricatures whereas the models used by O'Brien and Ray were interpretations of once-living or mythical creatures and the aim was to convince viewers, even if only for the duration of the film, that they were watching real creatures in a real world.

There are also major differences in the way the models are constructed. Potentially they can be made of any pliable substance. Today, Aardman Animations use Plasticine (albeit very sophisticated Plasticine) which was also occasionally used by some of the early pioneers, who also used articulated toys of one kind or another. But to achieve the degree of sophistication we see in *King Kong* and in Ray's films the models have to be built on different principles.

When the animation pioneer Willis O'Brien ('Obie') began his early experiments he constructed his models from cloth, rubber and clay over simple, jointed wooden skeletons. But as his expertise matured he developed steel skeletons, or internal armatures, articulated with steel ball-and-socket joints and, later, hinge joints. The armatures were then covered with layers of latex rubber shaped to provide the models with a muscular structure. Depending on the kind of

ABOVE
Medusa in action in *Clash of the Titans*.

LEFT
The impressive Cyclops from *The 7th Voyage of Sinbad* (1958).

BELOW
All that is left of the Cyclops, which is now missing one leg (cannibalized for a subsequent model).

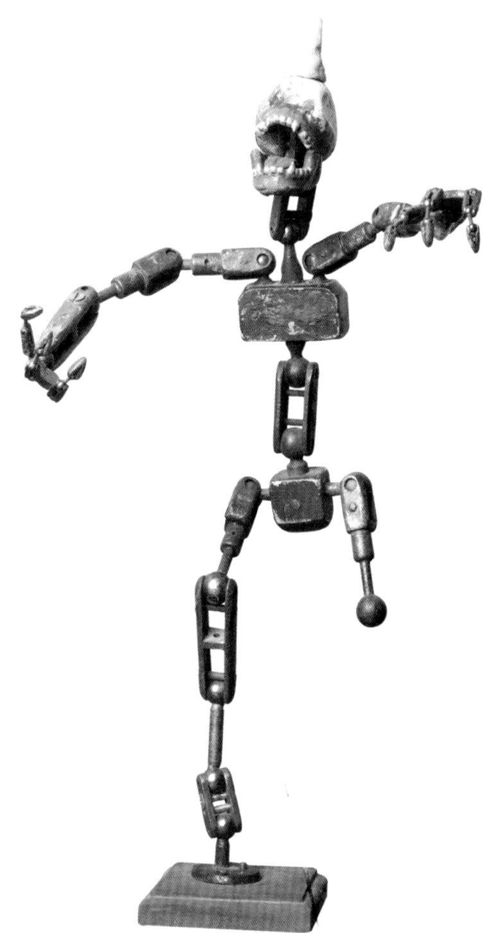

creature being made, the latex body might either be painted or covered in an appropriate choice of fur. Years later, while learning the techniques of model animation, Ray had to find his own method of model construction. It was a slow and sometimes frustrating learning curve. For his early model brontosaurus, Ray used the 'gooseneck' of an old wooden flexible lamp for the long neck and tail of the creature. The body was made of papier-mâché and for the hip joints he adapted ball-and-socket joints from rear-view mirrors purchased at Pep Boys Auto Stores. The neck, tail and legs were then built up with either foam rubber or cotton wool. The skin was made of pieces of old silk stockings and then covered with a thin layer of liquid latex. Like Obie, Ray soon learned that the joints in wooden armatures slipped, so that it was difficult to keep the models in a fixed position which prevented smooth animation. Again following in Obie's pioneering footsteps, Ray concluded that the only solution was to use full metal armatures.

Internal armatures are the starting point for building any model and they can be either very simple or extremely complex. For example, the metal ball-and-socket armature used for Medusa that appeared in *Clash of the Titans*, incorporated a total of 150 joints. At the other extreme, the snakes on Medusa's head and the one wrapped around her arm contain only a single copper wire with the latex moulded around it. Steel ball-and-socket and hinge joints both allow a wide range of movement, but the ball-and-socket construction is usually used for delicate joints – knees, hands, legs etc while the stronger hinge joint is used for the backbone of large creatures, such as an allosaurus or tyrannosaurus rex, or occasionally for torso joints. A ball-and-socket joint consists of a metal ball which fits into curved recesses in two rectangular pieces of metal which are clamped on either side so that the whole arrangement can be tightened or loosened by turning one or two screws. Although extremely

ABOVE
Three examples of clay maquettes designed and sculpted by Ray. Left, a Cyclops for an unrealized project to be called *The Story of Odysseus* (1996-1998) to be produced by Carrington & Cosgrove Hall Productions. The horn that Ray had used for the 1958 version of the creature was replaced by fangs and a rather distinguished beard. Centre, the Sphinx that was to have featured in another unrealized production called *Force of the Trojans* (1984). It was a mixture of many creatures. Right, one of the creatures for another unrealized project that was to have been directed by Michael Winner and called *People of the Mist* (1983).

BELOW LEFT
An early clay maquette of the upper torso and head for the Kraken featured in *Clash of the Titans* (1981).

BELOW
In the centre of the picture is a clay maquette of Medusa and on the left is a detailed plaster rendition of her head, minus the snakes.

ABOVE
A clay maquette of a satyr designed and sculpted by Ray as an experiment for what was to have been *Daphnis and Chloe* (circa 1939).

TOP LEFT
The stand-in for the triceratops from *One Million Years BC* (1966), made of hard rubber, with resin horns. Dimensions: 19"(L) x 7"(H) x 7"(W).

CENTRE LEFT
The original armatured giant walrus with resin horns featured in *Sinbad and the Eye of the Tiger* (1977). Dimensions: 20"(L) x 10"(H) x 10"(W).

BOTTOM LEFT
The original armatured brontosaurs which featured briefly in *One Million Years BC*. It is in almost perfect condition after forty-two years because it didn't have to perform under lights for too long, the tail is however in need of some tightening. Dimensions: 20"(L) x 15"(H) x 7"(W).

TOP
Two views of an early experiment for the tiger in *Sinbad and the Eye of the Tiger*. Made of hard rubber and partially covered in a fur. Note the ribs showing through the cast body, a detail that would not have been seen on the fully fur-covered model.

CENTRE LEFT
The original armatured model of the two-headed Dioskilos featured in *Clash of the Titans*. Dimensions: 15"(L) x 9"(H) x 6"(W).

CENTRE RIGHT
Detail of the armatured tiger featured in *Sinbad and the Eye of the Tiger*. There was only one model but it was designed and made in such detail that Ray was able to photograph it in close-up. Dimensions; 11"(L) x 7"(H) x 4"(W).

LEFT
The armatured Gryphon featured in *The Golden Voyage of Sinbad*. The model has undergone some restoration, primarily on the wings, but otherwise he isn't looking too bad. Dimensions: 16"(L) x 26"(H) including wings x 9"(W).

RIGHT
A wooden template that Ray used to wind the wire for the ribcages of the skeletons for *Jason and the Argonauts*. Ray carved this himself to enable him to make sure that all the ribcages had the same dimensions. You can clearly see where he has marked the positions of the ribs onto the wood.

FAR RIGHT
Detail of one of the seven armatured skeletons used in *Jason and the Argonauts* showing the ribcage.

BELOW
One of Ray's original creations made in 1938. It is the mammoth made for *Evolution of the World* (1938-1940). The tusks were made of wood and painted to resemble ivory and the fur is Siberian goat. Considering his age (seventy years) he is still in extremely good condition.

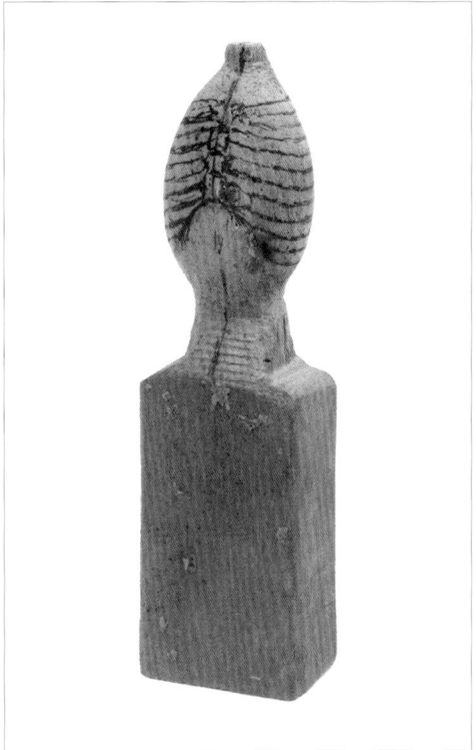

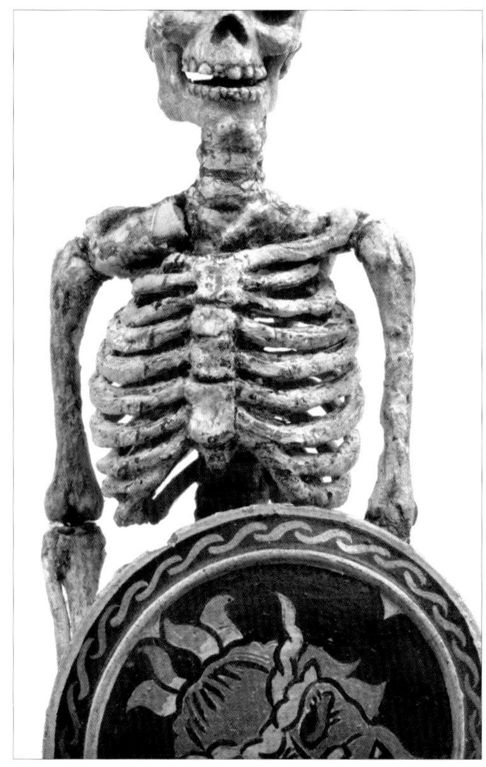

flexible, the joint can also stand up to brutal animation. Ray would often make these joints himself. Beginning with an ordinary ball bearing, he would heat it up so that it was tempered and would then drill it exactly in the centre using a special jig that his dad had made for him to hold it in position When that was done he would use silver solder to fix a short shaft into the hole. The hinge joint is just that, two or more pieces of metal each attached to its neighbours by a hinge. It is stronger and less prone to wear, hence its use for bigger models to bear the weight. Ray was extremely fortunate in that he had a father who was a machinist and it was he who turned and constructed all of Ray's armatures up to and including those used for *First Men in the Moon* (1964). He also taught his eager son all he knew about machining and construction, which was to prove invaluable in subsequent years when Ray was working on his own and facing technical problems.

In the case of some creatures, for example Kong, Joe in *Mighty Joe Young* and the baboon and Trog featured in *Sinbad and the Eye of the Tiger*, single wires, or very small ball-and-socket joints, were placed in the face of the model during construction to allow the animator to produce facial expressions such as a raised eyebrow or a snarl. These little refinements helped the animator to instill an element of personality into the model.

During the gruelling process of animation the models may be moved hundreds of times, sometimes leading to wear and tear which causes joints to become loosened, necessitating a

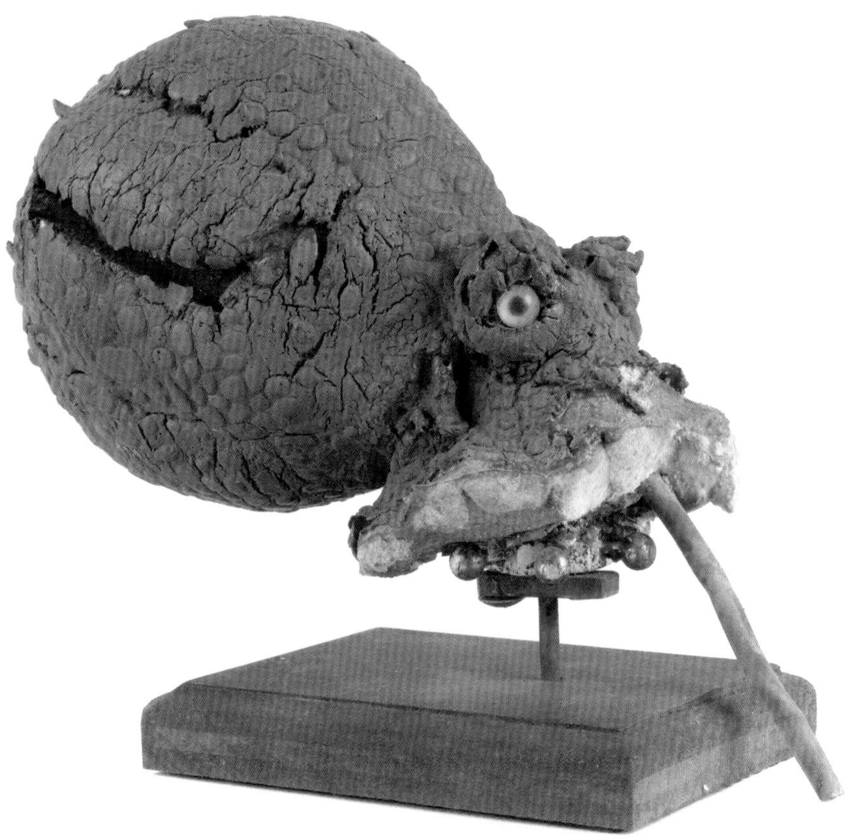

quick maintenance job, either on the spot or more usually overnight. Ray's method of repair was very straightforward. Because he had designed the armature and so knew exactly where each joint was, he would use a screwdriver to push through the outer covering of latex and tighten the screw or screws that held the joint in place and then simply pull the screwdriver out again letting the latex resume its original shape. Sometimes the latex required a little touching up if the joint was especially troublesome, but more often than not the incision would be undetectable.

Once the armature or skeleton has been designed and constructed it had to be given 'flesh'. There were two methods of doing this. The first was the 'build-up' method and the second the 'casting' method. The build-up method used layers of sponge rubber fixed in position around the metal armature with glue and then trimmed into shape with scissors. Additional layers of muscle could be added using cotton wool and more sponge rubber. The potentially quicker 'casting' method began with a wax or clay model from which a plaster mould was cast. The metal armature was then wrapped with tape and/or rubber dam (a very thin rubber sheeting) which held it in a more or less central position in the mould and also prevented the liquid latex from sticking to the metal and causing rust. Following that a solution of liquid latex would be whipped up to create an aerated foam liquid and then poured into the mould. On occasions, the armature might 'wander' inside the mould which meant that the foam rubber had to be removed and the process started all over again. When a successful casting had been produced it was then baked in an oven. Ray would more often than not carry out this task in his kitchen oven but when Diana, his wife, eventually complained of the smell, Ray was forced to build a special baking oven in his garage. Sometimes, when the liquid latex mixture wasn't exactly right, the whole concoction was liable to fall like a bad soufflé. Once an acceptable result had been achieved the model would then be cleaned up to remove any superfluous pieces of latex, after which the glass eyes and teeth were inserted and the whole model painted or covered with fur.

In Obie's *The Lost World*, and in a number of Ray's pictures, some of the creatures visibly 'breath'. This simple but effective trick was developed by Obie using medical bladders, called Orsop bags (Obie would also sometimes use football bladders), which were inserted inside the armature ribcage before the sponge and latex covering was applied. To inflate and deflate the bladder the animator would use a small rubber hand pump that was attached to a rubber tube that exited the model roughly where the anus would have been. The tube was always placed so that it was hidden from the camera, or at least disguised in some way. To make the creature breath in the animator would squeeze the pump

ABOVE LEFT
The original armatured head of the octopus featured in *It Came From Beneath the Sea* (1955). It is in a poor condition and the sack is split revealing the Orsop bag inside, which Ray used to make it 'breath'. The tube used to inflate and deflate the bag seen hanging out the front, would have originally hung down between the six tentacles (an octopus actually has eight, but to save costs Ray reduced these to six as not all were ever seen at the same time). The tentacles have been lost, recycled to make tails for subsequent creatures.

ABOVE
An inflatable medical bag from Ray's collection (this example is called an Accoson) which was inserted into the chest of a creature and slowly pumped up and then deflated during animation.

RIGHT
Two photographs of the original armatured Kali featured in *The Golden Voyage of Sinbad*. Kali spent a great deal of time under the hot studio lights and this is reflected by the deterioration in the condition of the model. The hands, arms and feet have suffered the worst (the latex has fallen away to reveal the metal armature) as they were animated almost throughout the sequence. It is not only the appendages which have suffered, the entire latex covering has shrunk and the metal armature is now visible at the base of the spine.

once, close a valve on the rubber tubing, expose the next frame, and then repeat the process between five and ten times. To make the model breath out the air was gradually released, frame by frame, until the bladder was deflated. When the footage is projected at the correct speed the creature looks as though it is breathing.

Even though the models were built to be tough, a particularly demanding scene or even the weather (the cool mornings were usually okay but the afternoon heat was sometimes a problem) could lead sweaty human fingers to make the paint on a model shiny, and Ray would sometimes have to wear white cotton editors gloves whilst animating to avoid leaving any marks on the models.

Lighting on miniature sets could be intense and damaging to the models' rubber latex skins, which can degenerate rapidly. To reduce the time that the articulated models were under the lights, Obie and Ray usually used stand-ins whilst the set was being lit. It helped reduce the amount of touching up required. Obie would use wooden stand-ins but Ray's were usually made of solid rubber and cast from the same mould as the armatured version. Their dimensions and details were exactly the same (they were painted the same colours) and when placed in the set they would allow it to be lit accurately before they were replaced by the armatured model.

The equipment used for film animation has changed radically over the last twenty-five years or so and what is described here are the items Ray would have used on most, if not all, of his films up to 1980. Some of the most basic items would not have changed since Obie photographed *The Lost World* in 1924/25. These are the tools of the Dynamation animator, not necessary the puppet animator, although a number of pieces of equipment remain the same for any stop-motion technician.

To begin with, the animator's camera is no ordinary camera. A normal cinematographer's camera will photograph or process a reel of celluloid once the camera is operated by a button or trigger, not stopping until the camera operator wants it to. An animator's camera is equipped with a stop-motion facility, which means that the animator can shoot one frame at a time. When Ray worked with George Pal on the *Puppetoons* series in the early 1940s, they were using Bell & Howell cameras with colour wheels attached to the front of the lens. The wheels each held three coloured gelatins, red, blue and yellow. Each frame was shot three times, once through each of the gelatins, and later in the laboratory the three frames were printed as one. The rushes would come back the next day in beautiful Technicolor. Later on, when working on *Mighty Joe Young*, Ray used a Mitchell rack over camera, which possessed a precise registration mechanism, an essential requirement for any animator shooting with celluloid. Ray used the same Mitchell camera for filming *It Came From Beneath the Sea* and subsequent films until the completion of *Clash of the Titans*, but as the camera was the property of Ameran Films (producer Charles Schneer's production company), it had to be returned to them and was subsequently sold off. Its fate is unknown.

To operate the stop-motion facility a remote control button was used, usually operated by the animator's foot, which saved time as there was no need to walk back to the camera after each exposure. In the early days Ray built his button controls of wood with a metal contact but they were later made of metal alloy.

The camera rackover is a viewfinder mechanism. When Ray was ready to shoot a frame he would move (rackover) the camera mechanism so that when he looked through the viewfinder he saw the scene exactly as it would appear through the lens, the right way up and without the parallactic displacement that affects cameras without the rackover mechanism because the viewfinder is slightly to one side of the lens. When Ray was satisfied, the viewing mechanism would be racked back ready for the next frame to be photographed. During the filming of the roping scene for *The Valley of Gwangi* , when Ray was matching the live action ropes to the miniature ropes, he had to rack the camera over before each frame was exposed to ensure that the positions of the real and miniature ropes corresponded and then rack the mechanism back. There were, understandably, occasions when he would forget to rack it back which would result in a blank frame. On *Mighty Joe*

ABOVE
Ray posing with his Mitchell camera and wooden tripod along with the large armatured figure of the Kraken from *Clash of the Titans*.

ABOVE RIGHT
One of Ray's three wooden tripods with one of the camera mounts. The tips of the legs were fastened to the animation floor (Ray always insisted on a false wooden animation floor) with chains or, sometimes, nailed wooden batons, as were the lights and almost anything else that was liable to move.

BELOW
Three animation switches. The two on the left were improvised wooden foot switches that operated the camera and the rear projector simultaneously and the one on the right was designed and used on *Clash of the Titans*. The first two show how inventive, but at the same time economical, Ray had to be.

Young the cameras had small switches on the side so that they would only record a frame if the rackover was in the shooting position. Today this is not necessary as modern cameras have a digital imager, normally available through the same lens system.

To achieve exact registration the camera and its tripod, as well as all other equipment including lights and stands had to be firmly secured to a special wooden animation floor to avoid any movement that may effect the animation. Ray would often use sandbags and on occasions bolt the tripod to the floor to secure his camera tripod.

Two of the key items of equipment for combining animation with live action are the rear projector and the rear-projector screen. Rear projecting a still or moving image onto a rear screen dates from 1913 when Norman O. Dawley used the process for the first time on a western called *The Drifter*. The idea was to bring a real location into the controlled environment of the studio so that actors could perform in front of it. However, for model animation the screen is much smaller than that used for actors. The technique was adopted to some extent by Obie for *King Kong*, and then taken up by Ray and his contemporaries, for rear-projecting live action with actors to enable the models to 'react' to them.

The stop-motion projector is, of course, modified, like the camera, to move the film one frame at a time. Ray still has a number of projectors, two of which were made for *Mighty Joe Young* (there were originally four made for the production), one of these was bought before making *The Beast From 20,000 Fathoms* and the second he bought later. The reason that more than one projector was required was to allow the animator to have a second setup (or in the case of *Mighty Joe Young* four setup's) available when waiting for the rushes of the previous setup to come back from the processing laboratory. Ray also has a third rear projector bought from Darlyne O'Brien (Obie's second wife), which Obie had used on *King Kong*.

The rear-projector screen onto which the live action is projected, is made of a translucent material so that the image can be clearly seen, with little deterioration of quality, on the side that appears at the rear of the animation table and model, which is the side to be photographed by the camera. The main dilemma with any rear-projection screen is

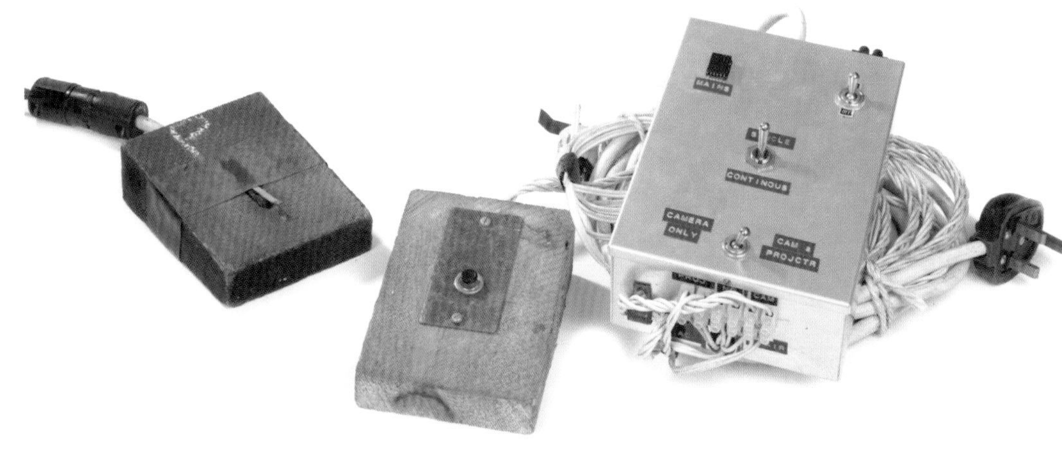

RIGHT
Ray with the Mitchell camera which he used to photograph so many of his feature films. Sadly, he no longer has it as it was the property of his producer Charles Schneer's company and had to be returned when they ceased making films. Its present whereabouts are unknown.

FAR RIGHT
A rear projector (the lens is not original) dating from the early 1930s Note the lamp housing on the back and the two blowers at the rear of the film gate, which enabled the frames of celluloid to be kept cool. Ray purchased it from Darlyne O'Brien after Obie's death in the early 1960s. It was used on *King Kong* in 1932/3 and was still in use for *Clash of the Titans*, forty-eight years later. Ray also has two camera/rear projector motors that he used whilst making *Mighty Joe Young* (1949) which were originally made for *King Kong*.

BELOW
One of two Cunningham rear projectors in Ray's collection. It is one of four that were beautifully constructed by Harry Cunningham for use on *Mighty Joe Young*.

grain. During the making of *The 7th Voyage of Sinbad*, grain was a huge problem because Ray was using colour stock for the first time and the grain on the screen was very apparent, especially in certain scenes where he was shooting very close to the screen. The close proximity would mean that the camera picked up the grain of the screen's texture. The only way he could solve this problem was by using a technique Obie developed in 1930 and first used on *King Kong*. An electric motor was used to drive an eccentric cam which vibrated the screen in an irregular circular movement which meant that the screen's texture blurred, so removing most of, if not all, the grain.

The animation table can be any size. It depends on the scene required. An extreme example would be *The Lost World* (1925) where one of the tables was one hundred and fifty by seventy-five feet because Obie wanted to show a huge plateau with herds of dinosaurs. However this was unusual. At the other extreme one of the tables on which Medusa was animated was only a few feet square. Depending on the shot the average animation table is perhaps four or five feet across and about two feet deep and is usually about the height of the animator's hips to allow easy and comfortable access to the model. The table was also usually positioned about eight to twelve inches away from the rear-projection screen. Ray had special sturdy metal stands made for his tables, which could be adjusted up and down or even tilted.

The surface of the table depends on how the animator plans to fix the model. If the table surface is not to be seen, then the tabletop can consist of pegboard, each peg hole an eighth of an inch in diameter. These holes are used to allow the model to be secured by means of a bolt, wing nut or wire below the table so that it doesn't move whilst being photographed. When the model is designed and constructed the animator incorporates a threaded recess in the bottom of the foot or paw (this can also be a threaded bolt, a wire or a screwed peg), through which a bolt can be screwed, which in turn is tightened by a wing-nut underneath the animation table. In the case of the giant crab in *Mysterious Island* wire had to be used because a crab has naturally pointed ends to its legs so Ray had to drill tiny holes in the points which were then treaded with wire that could be secured beneath the animation table.

To prevent the peg holes from being seen the animator would sometimes shoot at an angle to avoid showing the surface but when this was unavoidable a false surface for the animation tabletop was used to disguise these holes. Obie would usually use a layer of thin sponge rubber but in Ray's early short films he would work out exactly where the model's feet would make contact with the surface of the animation table and then drill holes in the surface, which he would then fill with wide-headed nails. The head of the nail would cover the hole and, when painted the same colour as the surface, would be impossible to see. During the animation process, when the foot was coming down to make contact with the nail head, Ray would take out the nail and in the next frame or two, when the foot had touched the surface, he would insert a bolt up through the hole and tighten it. The reverse would take place when the foot left the surface of the table.

In the case of Medusa Ray built her armature with two plates or lugs in the base, where the snake body meets the floor, to enable him to secure her to the table. These were disguised by the latex covering but could easily be accessed so that he could fix a bolt into them during animation. With all such models, especially where movement is unusual, the animator has to anticipate how the creature will move before the armature is designed and built, otherwise the plate or fixing point may not be in the correct place. The mooncalf in *First Men in the Moon* also had special securing lugs in its armature as did

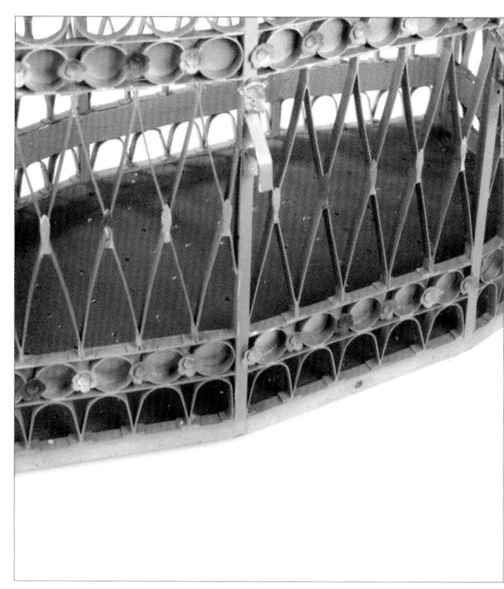

the snake woman in *The 7th Voyage of Sinbad*, but if it was an animal or humanoid creature the securing point would be in the base of the foot. Various methods of fixing have been experimented with over the years. For the 1954 feature production called *Hansel and Gretel: An Opera Fantasy*, in which the characters were called 'Kinemins', animator Michael Myerberg constructed the animation table of metal and gave the puppets metal feet, which were magnetized. Although ingenious, its practicality was limited because the models could still be accidentally moved.

In some cases, when the surface has to be seen, Ray would add a small section of miniature surface into the scene. A good example of this is sections of the Kali sequence in *The Golden Voyage of Sinbad*. Ray glued a layer of sand to the animation table on which the model of Kali stood to match the look and colour of the surface of the floor in the live action. Anything can be used to achieve such a surface, including sawdust, styrofoam or plaster, although of course it all has to be secured so that it doesn't move during animation.

Sandwiched between the animation table and the camera is a wooden frame to hold the matte glass onto which a matte is painted.[3] A matte glass is an essential part of the split-screen process which enables the animator to 'insert' a model or models into a live-action scene. It is a transparent sheet of glass on which an area or areas are painted black so that the corresponding area on the frame of film remains unexposed. When the film is rerun through the camera the matte is replaced by a counter glass, a sort of negative version of the original, so that the previously unexposed parts of the film are now exposed while the previously exposed areas remain unaffected. The line which divides the matted out parts of the frame from the exposed areas is called the matte line.

This wooden frame, which Ray first developed for *The Beast From 20,000 Fathoms*, held the glass firmly in place as well as registering the glass in exactly the correct position when inserted.[4] To determine where the matte line should be drawn Ray would rackover the camera and, looking through the viewfinder at the rear-projected live action, use a long wooden pole with a grease pencil fixed to the end to draw the matte line on the glass. The matte line would have

ABOVE LEFT
One of two animation table stands used for tilting.

ABOVE CENTRE
The feet of the ornithomimus featured in *The Valley of Gwangi* (1969). This unusual view of a Dynamation model clearly shows the recesses in the base of the feet into which bolts were screwed through the animation table.

ABOVE RIGHT
The floor of the large cage (there were two, the second one was much smaller) used for the baboon in *Sinbad and the Eye of the Tiger*. Note the peg holes in the base of the cage through which the screws were inserted from below to secure the feet of the model baboon.

RIGHT
A test to match the foreground with the background for the skeleton fight in *The 7th Voyage of Sinbad*. The rear-projection screen showing Sinbad (Kerwin Mathews) was about twelve inches away from the animation table. Again, the peg holes can be clearly seen beneath the skeleton model.

LEFT
A view of the underside of the archelon from *One Million Years BC*. Again, the holes used to secure the model, in this case its flippers, are clearly visible.

been predetermined during the live-action photography and would usually follow a natural line or a line around rocks. Rarely, if ever, was a straight line across sand or ground ever used because the line would then be likely to become more obvious. The positioning of the matte line also had to consider the need to keep the surface of animation table hidden.

Once the matte line had been drawn, the glass would be taken out of the frame and placed on a lightbox.[5] Using black matt paint Ray would then carefully trace the grease pencil line and paint out the area it delineated. When the paint was dry he would then place the counter glass on top and, still working over the lightbox, paint the 'negative' version. He would have two pieces of glass which were 'positive' and 'negative' versions of each other. Before animation photography was begun Ray would make a test to ensure the matte line wasn't visible and, if it was, he would have to scrape off a little of the paint until he achieved a perfect match between the two elements. When he was ready to begin animation he would take the first piece of glass and place it back into the wooden frame. The model was then animated to correspond with the live action on the rear-projection screen, following which the background plate and the camera would be wound back to the starting point. The animation table was removed and the second piece of glass would then be inserted into the wooden frame and the rear-projection footage would be then re-photographed by the camera for what is called a second pass. When the rushes came back the next day the animated model could be seen right in the middle of the live action.

The lighting is of course an integral part of animation especially where split screens were involved. Ray had to spend a great deal of time matching the lighting, and therefore colour, with the live action on the rear-projection plate otherwise the model would have not appeared to match the live action. If one of the lamps blew out, he would of course have to replace it with new one, which meant that he then had take a light reading and place filters over the lamp because a new lamp would be more intense than the old one.

Depending on the animator, a gauge, or surface gauge, may be required for registration purposes. What we call a gauge is actually a machinist's tool made from metal. It consists of a solid, heavy base on which is mounted a thin vertical rod. An adjustable clamp is used to secure a pointed horizontal rod to the vertical one. Using the gauge involved putting the point of the horizontal rod on a carefully chosen part of the model before manipulating it. The gauge allowed Ray to see exactly how much he had moved the model and, if placed in the same position on the animation table after each frame, enabled him to accurately pace a piece of animation. The gauge would be used when the model had to move excessively slowly, when the timing of a movement was critical or when the model was especially complex. The octopus in *It Came From Beneath the Sea* (1955) and the nautilus in *Mysterious Island* (1961) were both required to make minute movements, sometimes half a millimetre, sometimes two millimetres, and for these movements a gauge was invaluable. To animate the seven Hydra's heads in *Jason and the Argonauts*

Ray used two or three gauges each pointing to a particular point on the head, for example the tip of the nose, or quite often he would insert a tiny steel pin in the head away from the camera where it couldn't be seen. There have been occasions when one of these pins was inadvertently shown, one appears in the test Ray made for his unrealized project *War of the Worlds* (1949). In it the Martian is seen crawling out of the spaceship and the pin can be seen shining in the top of the head for two or three frames when it passes through a dark shadow.

However, when the model wasn't too complex or the movements were bold, Ray found that he didn't require such accurate registration, he would just use his eye. This ability came with experience. Obie never used a gauge during the animation for *King Kong*, something that is apparent as sometimes the model 'wanders' to the right or the left. The models for Kong were much bigger than those used later by Ray for *Mighty Joe Young* (1949) so Obie probably felt that he didn't need a visual register and it must also be remembered that, in 1932, this kind of animation and its accompanying techniques were all experimental.

The aerial wire brace, as it is now called, is another essential piece of equipment when animating models that have to be suspended above the animation table. It allows the animator to manoeuvre a model in any direction. The design is essentially based on the puppeteer's control, or as it is sometimes called, a marionette control, which is basically two short pieces of wood fixed together in the middle like a cross, attached to which are the strings that operate the mannequin, although sometimes the leg controls are separate. When Ray built his first 'aerial brace' for his *Evolution of the World* project (1938/9) it was made of two pieces of thin wood each about ten inches long and firmly secured by glue in the middle, with his model suspended from thin wires attached to each of the four ends. In the late 1940s and early to mid-1950s, Ray used recording wire (wire used for recording music etc before magnetic tape came in), which later was replaced by plastic fishing line. The wires would be attached to the model and

ABOVE
A simple example of the split-screen or Dynamation process. The live action was shot in such a way as to enable Ray to draw a matte line along the top of the warehouse on the left across the top of the black lower half of the container ship and the sea horizon. This allowed him to 'insert' the animated tentacle and the miniature railway car into the action.

BELOW LEFT
A wonderful old rheostat, a device that is used to vary the strength of an electrical current, which resembles something out of an old Frankenstein movie. Ray used it to adjust the light on the rear projector and it was a vital piece of equipment on all his features right up to, and including, *Clash of the Titans*.

BELOW CENTRE
A small example of a frame used to hold a painted matte glass that would matte off an area of the rear-projected image. To ensure the glass was always slotted into the frame in exactly the same position each time a registration pin was used, which can be see in the bottom left-hand corner.

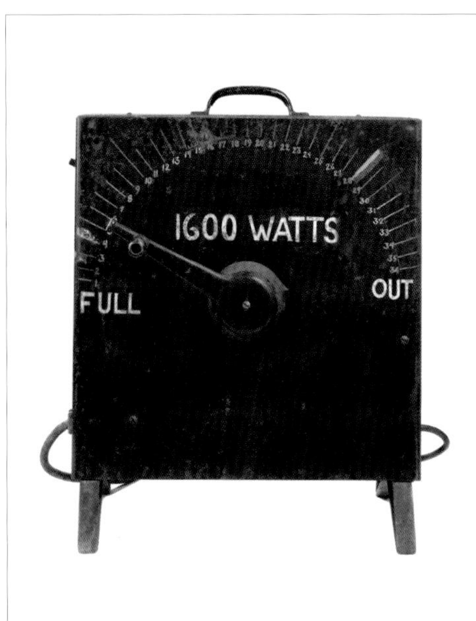

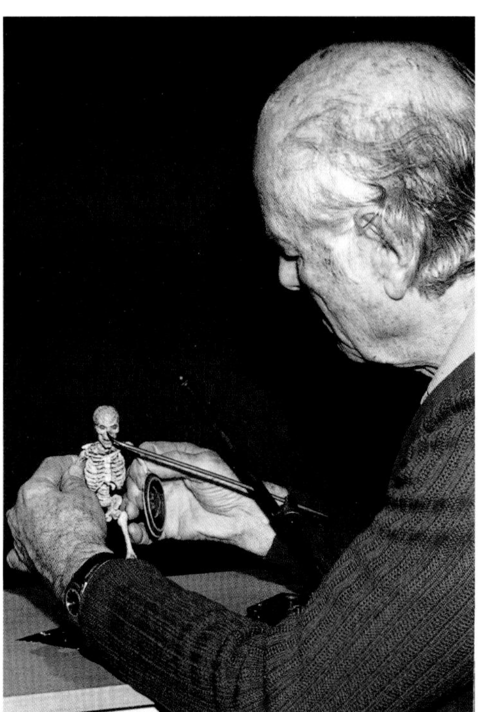

the whole brace attached to an overhead wooden frame or, on occasions, a small gantry.

As we discovered recently, Ray has three surviving aerial braces. One was an early device and although made of metal it has only the basic four arms. The remaining two are much more sophisticated devices that are made of light alloy and incorporate gears to allow more refined movements such as hovering, moving horizontally, vertically and diagonally or dipping and diving. These were used to allow the aerial models more freedom of movement in such films as *Earth Vs the Flying Saucers*, *One Million Years BC* and *The Valley of Gwangi*. Ray would also use a brace when a model was required to leap or jump off the ground. There are several good examples of this in the skeleton sequences in *Jason and the Argonauts*; another is the ceratosaurus which jumps on the back of the triceratops in *One Million Years BC*. Animating a creature leaping is more complicated that it might appear. The arc which the creature follows through the air has to be exactly calculated to correspond with live action or the movements of another creature; and if the movements are not evenly spaced it can easily appear to falter in mid-air.

As an experiment we re-attached one of the original eight-inch flying saucers from *Earth Vs the Flying Saucers* to one of the geared braces. It took us a total of twenty minutes to lace the device correctly using some original recording wire that Ray had used for the film, making sure that the four wires were attached to the geared system at one end and the nodules on the underside of the saucer. If Ray had had to do that each time he wished to change an angle with a brace that did not have gears then it would have taken him months to complete one sequence, hence the introduction of gears, which were designed by Ray and his father.

FACING PAGE, BOTTOM RIGHT
An unused and non-armatured model of the Kraken constructed for pre-publicity for *Clash of the Titans*. We found this long-lost model in the back of one of Ray's many cupboards in 2006. The frame in front of the model holds a distortion glass which was usually positioned about twelve inches from the camera to avoid showing the wooden frame. The entire frame with its glass would be mounted on a threaded gear which moved it about a millimeter from one side to the other in order to create the illusion of water. Ray used this trick many times, not only for the Kraken but also for the Beast and the octopus.

TOP LEFT
A Martian appearing from its projectile in the test footage for the unrealized *War of the Worlds* (1949). The shot shows a registration pin used to determine how much a model has to be moved when used in conjunction with a surface gauge. The metal pin can be seen almost between the eyes of the creature and should have not have been visible.

CENTRE LEFT
Ray animating one of the skeletons used to illustrate his animation process for a British documentary on his life called *Working With Dinosaurs* (1999). This is a rare instance of Ray using a surface gauge as he was rarely, if ever, photographed using one.

BELOW
Two rare photographs taken during the animation of the flying saucers in *Earth Vs the Flying Saucers* (1956). They show the geared aerial wire brace (top and centre of both pictures) used to support the model saucers during animation.

In a number of Ray's early films (*Evolution* and several of the *Fairy Tales*) there are scenes where small birds can be seen flying across the set. These birds became something of a trademark for Obie as they can be seen in many of his films and Ray had become fascinated with them and included them in his own early work. Ray made them of carved wood with copper wings and they were mounted on stretched wire so they could be easily animated when flying horizontally across the screen.

Because of the weight of model of the flying horse Pegasus in *Clash of the Titan*, and because the creature had to gallop, for most of the aerial shots, although not all, Ray utilized another device, which for want of a better description, Ray's calls the 'Pogo stick'. This was a rigid vertical metal rod or shaft attached to the model on the side away from the camera. The rod was mounted on a horizontal five-foot screwed lathe track, borrowed from the Pinewood Studios machine shop, which gave horizontal movement for the model, with vertical movement being achieved by manually moving the model up and down the rod and securing it with a locking device. To hide the rod a V-shaped mirror was used to reflect the blue screen behind the model. When the sky was added later onto the blue screen by an optical printer, the rod simply disappeared.

There are, of course, many other items of animation equipment, but the above are the key and basic elements for creating a moving model and integrating it with live action. However, the equipment is not everything. As will become clear in the following chapters, especially in Chapter 4, there is much more to animation, any type of model animation, than just possessing the technical knowledge. Animating creatures like those that appear in Ray's films require three basic laws, laws of Dynamation – **imagination**, **dedication** and **patience**. The first doesn't necessarily mean that you are required to think up incredible flights of fantasy, although that does help; it means that the animator is required to observe and interpret actions, movements and situations that will be reflected in the animation. The second requires the animator to be 'married' to the art. It has to be a passion, an obsession or a calling. Finally, patience. This is perfectly illustrated by the analysis of the skeleton fight in *Jason and the Argonauts* earlier in this chapter. The sequence took over four months to calculate and animate which doesn't include the pre-planning. Whenever we talk about patience, Ray always recalls that when he was a youngster, learning his trade, he lost his temper and in his anger threw a hammer across his workshop. As soon as it had left his hand he regretted the action and watched with horror as it bounced off the concrete floor and smashed through a glass painting, which had taken him weeks to complete. From that day onwards he never lost his temper again, at least not in an animation studio.

All animators have to abide by these three laws,and possibly many more, if they want to successfully pursue their time-consuming but rewarding art, and in the last century of so there have been many great model animation artists.

ABOVE
An early example of the use of an aerial wire brace, in this case to suspend a leaping model allosaurus above a doomed brontosaurus in a test for *Evolution of the World*.

BELOW LEFT
The geared rigid rod mount, nicknamed the 'pogo stick', which was used for Pegasus in most of the aerial scenes. This was strong enough to support the heavy model, making the task of animating it a great deal easier and less time-consuming than would have been the case if aerial wires had been used - although wires were used on the smaller models.

BELOW RIGHT
The small armatured model of Bubo suspended on aerial wires.

RIGHT (MAIN PHOTOGRAPH)
This photograph, taken in 2007, shows Ray adjusting one of his aerial wire braces which supports one of the original eight-inch saucer models used in *Earth Vs the Flying Saucers*. When filming it was usual to stabilize the saucer by attaching another wire to its base from which a sandbag would be suspended.

RIGHT TOP
Reels of the recording wire used to suspend models from the aerial braces.

RIGHT BOTTOM
Detail of the gears on one of Ray's aerial braces. The gears allowed the wires supporting a model to be lengthened or shortened in order to tilt the model or make it ascend or descend. This is one of two geared braces made by Ray's father.

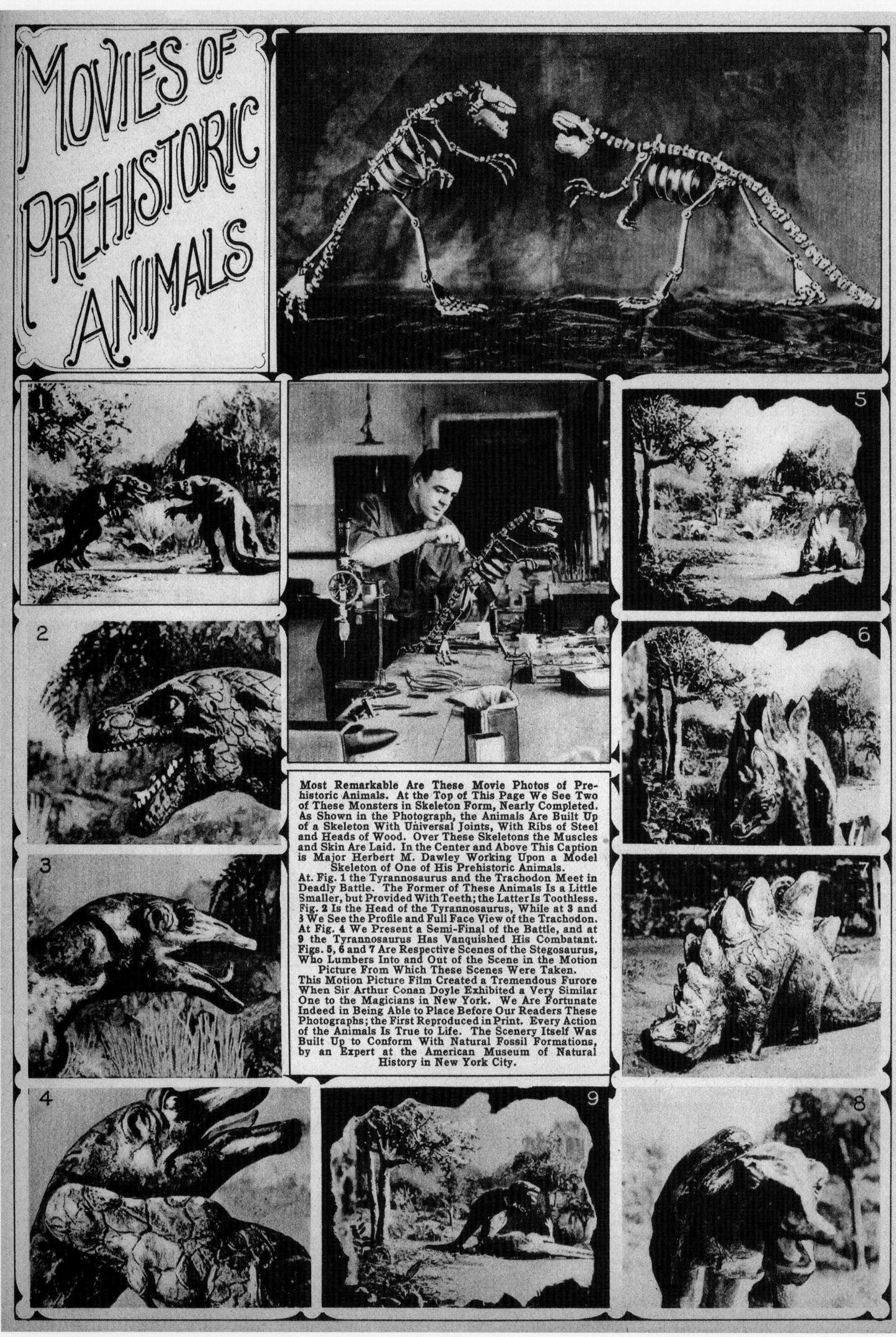

MOVIES OF PREHISTORIC ANIMALS

1

2

3

4

5

6

7

8

9

Most Remarkable Are These Movie Photos of Prehistoric Animals. At the Top of This Page We See Two of These Monsters in Skeleton Form, Nearly Completed. As Shown in the Photograph, the Animals Are Built Up of a Skeleton With Universal Joints, With Ribs of Steel and Heads of Wood. Over These Skeletons the Muscles and Skin Are Laid. In the Center and Above This Caption is Major Herbert M. Dawley Working Upon a Model Skeleton of One of His Prehistoric Animals.

At. Fig. 1 the Tyrannosaurus and the Trachodon Meet in Deadly Battle. The Former of These Animals Is a Little Smaller, but Provided With Teeth; the Latter Is Toothless. Fig. 2 Is the Head of the Tyrannosaurus, While at 3 and 3 We See the Profile and Full Face View of the Trachodon. At Fig. 4 We Present a Semi-Final of the Battle, and at 9 the Tyrannosaurus Has Vanquished His Combatant. Figs. 5, 6 and 7 Are Respective Scenes of the Stegosaurus, Who Lumbers Into and Out of the Scene in the Motion Picture From Which These Scenes Were Taken.

This Motion Picture Film Created a Tremendous Furore When Sir Arthur Conan Doyle Exhibited a Very Similar One to the Magicians in New York. We Are Fortunate Indeed in Being Able to Place Before Our Readers These Photographs; the First Reproduced in Print. Every Action of the Animals Is True to Life. The Scenery Itself Was Built Up to Conform With Natural Fossil Formations, by an Expert at the American Museum of Natural History in New York City.

CHAPTER TWO

THE BEGINNINGS OF MODEL ANIMATION 1895-1930

PREVIOUS SPREAD
Left, a remarkable magazine layout from the August 1922 edition of *Science & Invention* showing (centre) Herbert Dawley at work on an armature of a tyrannosaurus rex and surrounded by scenes from *Along the Moonbeam Trail* (1920). Some of the creatures featured are a duckbill dinosaur, a stegosaurus and a tyrannosaurus rex. Willis O'Brien was generally thought to have animated all the creatures for this film, although we do not know who designed them, but this central image and the one on page 45 clearly show Dawley at work on the models. However it is possible that the photographs were taken as part of a publicity setup as the article was published in response to *The Lost World* lawsuit that was filed in June 1925.
Right, the wonderful pioneer fantasy filmmaker, Georges Méliès (1861-1938), circa 1930s. Méliès is usually credited with the discovery of the technique of stop-motion.

ABOVE
The Vanishing Lady(1896) showing Méliès performing the old stage trick by means of replacement, or substitution, stop-motion.

Like a great many cinematic techniques, model animation took many years to realize its true potential and to find the genre for which it was ideally suited. It is generally considered that the period of experimentation culminated in 1925 with the release of *The Lost World*. It was from that point on that model animation became an established art. In the thirty years or so before 1925 the early pioneers did little more than dabble with the potential of the idea, it took a truly visionary individual, Willis O'Brien, to recognize that potential and realize it. However, the early pioneers, with their short innovative films, played an indispensable role in developing the technique to the point at which it was ready to burst upon a wider audience. Many of those whose work is discussed here are all-but forgotten but they all deserve recognition for the part they played, whether by accident or intention, in the development of model animation.

The story begins at the end of the nineteenth century with the discovery that if the operator of one of the newly invented moving-picture cameras stopped turning the handle (the early cameras were all manually operated), paused, and then restarted the results could be both intriguing and potentially useful. Like the invention of cinema itself, the true origins of this form of stop-motion, now known as stop-motion replacement, are shrouded in the mists of time, but the individual generally credited with the discovery is the French ex-conjurer and film pioneer Georges Méliès.

This remarkable man was responsible not only for making the first fantasy films but also for many innovations in cinematic technique, including double exposures, fades and dissolves. In 1896 he happened upon the phenomenon of 'stop-action', as he called it, whilst he was filming a Paris street scene for his film *Place de l'Opéra*. He had set up his camera, which had the habit of jamming and tearing the film stock, on the side of the road facing across the street to the opera house and had commenced filming when his camera jammed again. After a minute or so he managed to get the problem sorted out and recommenced filming. When the film was processed he was amazed to discover that one set of vehicles and people appeared to be substituted for another as if by magic. Relating the incident later, in 1907, he said, 'I suddenly saw a Madeleine-Bastille omnibus change into a hearse and men into women.' Being a magician by trade, he immediately saw the potential and began using the trick in some of his films. The first of these was *Escamotage d'une Dame Chez Robert Houdin* [*The Vanishing Lady*] (1896) where a woman (Jehanne d'Alcy) is seated looking at the camera and Méliès (who played a magician in the film) makes her disappear by stopping the camera and removing her from the set and recommencing filming, so making it appear she has disappeared into thin air. Then a skeleton appears in the chair which Méliès covers with a cloth. When the cloth is removed the woman has returned. That's the entire story of the picture. A simple cinematic version of an old magician's trick.

However, since writing *An Animated Life* in 2002 we have come across what appears to be an even earlier example of stop-motion replacement. Although we haven't had the opportunity to see the film, the evidence allegedly occurs in Thomas Edison's 1895 film *The Execution of Mary, Queen of Scots*. In his excellent book *The Emergence of Cinema: The American Screen to 1907*, Charles Musser states, '*The Execution of Mary, Queen of Scots* used "stop-motion substitution" to show the decapitation of Mary (played by Robert Thomae, secretary and treasurer of the Kinetoscope Company): just before the beheading took place, the camera stopped, Thomae was replaced by a dummy, and the filming resumed. When the two takes were spliced together, the interruption was not evident to the spectator and appeared as one continuous shot.'[1] This description clearly seems to show that there was a scene incorporating a substitution or replacement that took place between two consecutive frames of film and tricked the audience into believing that the action was continuous. Even if Musser is correct in suggesting that this was achieved by splicing two bits of film together, rather than simply a pause in the filming, it would still seem that Edison, or someone working for Edison, had used the technique a year before Méliès discovered it whilst making the 1896 film.

However, it is very unlikely that Méliès even knew of Edison's film and we feel it is right that the main credit for the innovation should have been awarded to him. He used the stop-motion replacement technique in many of his subsequent subjects, including *The Haunted Castle* (1896), *The Astronomer's Dream* (1898) and, most notably, *Cinderella* (1899) in which he transformed a pumpkin into a coach.

Stop-motion replacement, although an ingenious and effective trick, does not, of course, involve animation. But Méliès clearly saw the possibilities of manipulating the same object between frames rather than simply replacing it with another object, for he did just that in a short advertising film (the name of which has been lost) that he made in 1897. This first appearance of what we would now call stop-motion model animation was hardly earthshaking – a set of children's wooden alphabet blocks appear to assemble themselves to spell out the advertiser's name – but it did mark the point at which a new technique was truly born.

Given that he was chiefly known for his films of fantasy subjects, it is surprising that Méliès did not, apparently, see the potential for applying the new technique to this genre. Instead the credit for making that inventive leap must go to a

BELOW LEFT
James Stuart Blackton (1875-1941) the pioneer film-maker who really began the art of stop-motion animation with *The Humpty Dumpty Circus* (1898).

BELOW CENTRE
Two frames from *The Enchanted Drawing* (1900) showing Blackton in front of a drawing that appears to produce, by means of stop-motion replacement, a bottle of wine and a glass amongst other items.

BELOW RIGHT
Edwin Stanton Porter (1869-1941) the pioneer and film-maker responsible for *The 'Teddy' Bears* (1907).

British-born film-maker, James Stuart Blackton who, while working in America in 1897, made what is believed to be the first example of animated film using models, in his case toys. Blackton had been born in 1875 in Sheffield, Yorkshire but at the age of ten had accompanied his parents when they emigrated to America. When he was nineteen he met Albert Edward Smith, a fellow Briton with whom he performed in a Vaudeville act, and the two men later went into business together. Blackton's interest in film-making was first sparked in 1896 when, while working for the *New York Evening World* newspaper, he met Thomas Edison and soon afterwards he and Smith began making short pictures. Later, along with Smith and William T. Rock, Blackton became one of the founders of the American Vitagraph motion picture company.

In 1897 Blackton and Smith were filming a short, Méliès-like subject on the roof of the Morse Building in New York which involved stopping the camera on several occasions. When they viewed the processed film they saw that wisps of steam from a vent in an adjoining building appeared to suddenly change shape and immediately recognized that they had accidentally discovered a new technique. Being of an inventive turn of mind, the two men began experimenting to see how they could exploit what they saw as a new gimmick. They soon hit on the idea of filming inanimate objects which were moved between frames to achieve movement and in 1898 they released *The Humpty Dumpty Circus*, a short film made for Vitagraph, which featured tricks performed by articulated wooden toy animals and acrobats belonging to Blackton's small daughter. It was Blackton who carried out the animation whilst Smith directed. Regrettably, little more is known of the film as, like so many of those early movies, it has long since been lost to us. However, it seems likely that *The Humpty Dumpty Circus* was the first film to tell a story using animated three-dimensional objects and, as such, it must be seen as a landmark.

That a few of the early model animation films have survived is thanks to the George Kleine Collection, the Paper Print Collection and the Richard Marshall Collection, all preserved in the Library of Congress in Washington DC, and it was largely with the help of these collections that we have been able, at least in part, to piece together the early history.

Two years after *The Humpty Dumpty Circus* Blackton made *The Enchanted Drawing* (1900), which is in essence a cartoon short. It not only shows Blackton himself as the artist who produces the drawing in question but also features a few stop-frame replacement tricks. For example, Blackton draws a bottle and a glass that magically become real. Filmed in Edison's pioneering 'Black Maria' studio in New Jersey, the film illustrates the origins of both graphic and three-dimensional animation techniques.

In the same year Blackton and Smith made *Visit to the Spiritualist* which, according to the Edison exhibitors' catalogue for 1900, was

'acknowledged by exhibitors to be the funniest of all moving magical films'. The catalogue goes on to describe the storyline which featured 'a countryman who visits a spiritualist following which he sees funny things'. Several scenes involve stop-motion animation, including one in which a handkerchief grows larger and larger and then dances around the floor. The 'countryman' then sees a ghost, 'and throws off his hat and coat which immediately fly back on his body. He repeatedly throws them off and they as often return.' The end sequence concludes with 'numerous ghosts and hobgoblins appearing and disappearing before the eyes of the frightened countryman, who finally leaves the room in great haste'.

The pioneers of three-dimensional animation were by no means confined to America. Elsewhere other early film-makers took up the technique and developed it in their own style. In Britain the substitution trick had been exploited-ed by various pioneer film-makers amongst them George Albert Smith who played a key role in the development of British film production and was a leading member of the group of film pioneers based around the town of Brighton on England's south coast. Smith used a number of trick techniques including replacement in several of his films including *Santa Claus* (1898). Another such early pioneer Robert William Paul, (who became known as the man who began the British film industry), was not only a film-maker but also the inventor of the Paul-Acres camera, which he developed with another pioneer, Birt Acres. Paul became associated with magician David Devant (his real name was David Wighton) and together they made a number of films using the replacement technique including *The Mysterious Rabbit*, *The Egg Laying Man* and *Objects Produced from Paper* all made in 1896. Perhaps Paul's greatest film was *The ? Motorist* (1906) in which a car travels to the moon and onto the rings of Saturn in true Melies/Jules Verne style.

However, in Britain the potential of three-dimensional animation was first truly recognized by the film-maker and producer Arthur Melbourne-Cooper who also had the distinction of being the first to use the close-up. Melbourne-Cooper had at one time been an assistant to Birt Acres, who had dabbled in cartoons, or quick-draw animation. It was these experiments that had inspired Melbourne-Cooper so that when he branched out on his own he concentrated on three-dimensional animation, coming up with some very innovative ideas of his own. He called his creations 'trick films' or 'stop-and-start films'. His first 'trick film', *Matches Appeal* [aka *Matches: An Appeal*], made in 1899 used animated matchsticks. It was primarily a government propaganda film encouraging public donations to be sent to Bryant & May (a match company) who would then send matches to the soldiers fighting in the Boer War in South Africa. The short film showed animated matchstick puppets writing on a black wall: 'For one guinea [one pound and one shilling in old currency] Messrs Bryant & May will forward a case containing sufficient to supply a box of matches to each man in a battalion with the name of the sender inside.' The film was shown at The Empire Theatre in London in 1899 and was so popular that Melbourne-Cooper followed it up with a series of short films featuring animated models that included *Dolly's Toys* (1901), a combination of live action and puppet animation in which the toys of four children come to life when their owners go to bed.

Between 1904 and 1909 Melbourne-Cooper worked with Robert Paul, continuing his experimentation with model animation, live action and fantasy. Their work included *The Enchanted Toymaker* (1904), *The Fairy Godmother* (1906) and *Dreams of Toyland* (1908). The last of these again featured toys coming to life in a boy's dream and showed up to fifteen animated models in the same shot of a wide miniature street set. This multi-animation was extremely complex and illustrates just how innovative and far-seeing Melbourne-Cooper was. In 1908 he made *Noah's Ark* in which a girl dreams that Noah and his animals come to life and his last film with Paul was a semi-sequel called *Tales of the Ark* (1909). Paul retired in 1910 but Melbourne-Cooper continued to make films such as *Cinderella* (1910), *Wooden Athletes* (1912) and *The Toymaker's Dream* (1913). Arthur Melbourne-Cooper is one of the key figures in the history of model animation not only because he experimented with various ideas such as multi-model animation, but also because he was the first to recognize that rather than just being a gimmick, the technique had the potential to become a genre in its own right and to realize that potential insofar as the practices of the industry at time allowed.

Also working in England around 1908 was Edward Rogers who made the first stop-motion puppet film in colour called *War in Toyland*. We know nothing else about the film, the man or whether he made any more animated films, but it is likely that the colour process was Kinemacolor, which was used in England between 1908 and 1914.

Back in America, another film pioneer, Edwin Stanton Porter, better known for the 1903 classic *The Great Train Robbery*, made a one-minute film called *Fun in a Bakery Shop* (1902), which used clay for its 'lightning sculpture' sequence. The simple story concerns a baker's assistant who hurls some dough at a rat and misses, and then sculpts various faces and shapes into the dough. Porter must have seen the commercial possibilities of stop-motion because in 1906 he made a short seven-minute film for the Edison Company entitled *Dream of a Rarebit Fiend*, which was based on *Rarebit Fiend*, Winsor McKay's popular comic strip of the time. The story, though again very simple, used trick effects to show the title character dreaming and to show his bed dancing around the room, which were achieved in part by stop-motion. *Dream of a Rarebit Fiend* although only 470 feet in length, took very nearly two months to complete but sold 192 copies, a considerable number at the time, during its first year of release.

In 1907 Porter went on to make *The 'Teddy' Bears*, a thirteen-minute tinted film, loosely based on *Goldilocks and the Three Bears* but also making reference to a popular news story of the time about President 'Teddy' Roosevelt shooting a mother bear and capturing her cub, an incident which was the origin of the 'Teddy' bear. The film contains one key ninety-second

FACING PAGE
Three frames from Arthur Melbourne-Cooper's *Dreams of Toyland* (1908). Notice the impressive number of animated toys in the set-pieces.

BELOW
Nine frames showing the inventiveness of the animation in Edwin S. Porter's *The 'Teddy' Bears*. In several frames one of the 'teddy' bears is whirling in the air, and we can only suggest that Porter used aerial wires; possibly the first time they were ever used.

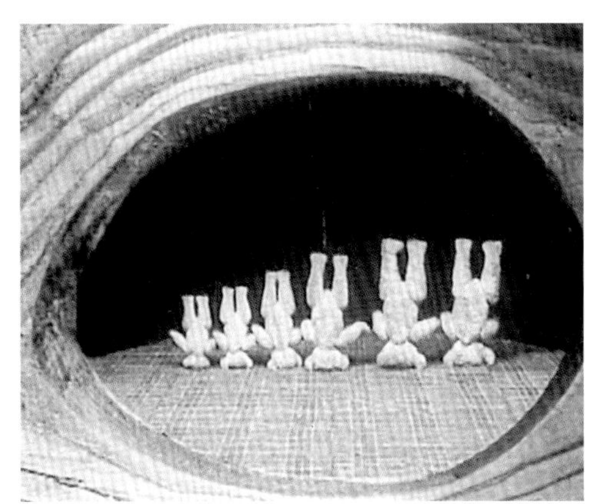

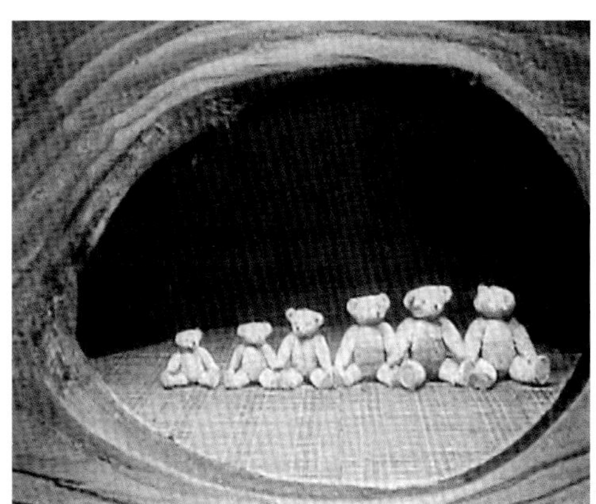

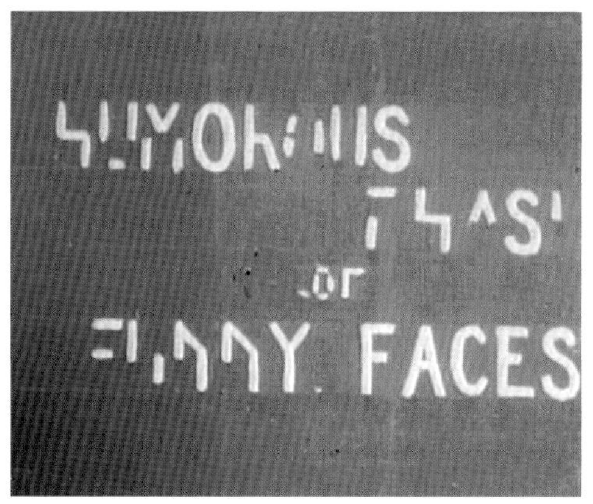

stop-motion animation sequence that is preceded by a shot of Goldilocks peering through a knothole in a door in the bears' house. We see the action from her point of view, framed by the edge of the knothole, as a family of six animated teddy bears of varying heights dance and perform acrobatic tricks. In one shot the tallest of the bears stands on his head and whirls around on the spot. Porter took seven days to shoot the sequence, working eight hours a day, and it stands as another important landmark in the history of model animation. But although the animated sequences are intercut with shots of Goldilocks reacting to the bears' performance they never appear in the same frame. We are still some time away from combining animated models with live actors or indeed other live elements.

Blackton reappears in our story in 1906 with a cartoon short, *Humorous Phases of Funny Faces*, which is mainly graphic animation but is interesting because it combines this with three-dimensional animation in the opening sequence where lines appear to eventually spell out the name of the film. In 1907 Blackton followed this up with *A Mid-Winter Night's Dream* and *The Haunted Hotel* (Albert Smith was the photographer on the latter) for Vitagraph, both of which utilized three-dimensional animation. The first featured animated toys and the second saw inanimate objects becoming ghostly tools for spirits, a wine bottle apparently pouring itself into a glass, slices of bread being cut and a table being set by invisible hands. Then, in 1909, Blackton produced and directed another landmark film, *Princess Nicotine*, sometimes known as *The Smoke Fairy*. It is a five-minute film that features matches, cigarettes and a pipe jumping into a box, followed by a flower breaking down into petals, the petals changing into tobacco which then assembles itself into a cigar, all achieved by animation and shot by Blackton. *Princess Nicotine* was the most celebrated trick film of its day, praised in an article in *Scientific American* and warranting a whole chapter in the 1912 book *Motion Pictures: How They Are Made and Worked*. Blackton, a prolific film-maker up to 1927, became an expert in both graphic and three-dimensional animation which are used in many of his films and he is seen today as one of the leading innovators in both fields.

There were several key stop-motion animators working in France at the beginning of the twentieth century. Most notable of these was Émil Cohl, known as 'The Father of the Animated Cartoon' because of the huge number of cartoons and animated shorts he produced. He had developed his artistic skills while working for the political caricaturist André Gill and was part of the 'Incoherent' movement, which promoted absurdism, naive art and images based on nightmares. In 1907, when he was fifty years of age, he turned his attention to film-making, joining Gaumont where he worked on animation with a vertically-mounted camera, turning out three or four sequences a month for insertion into live-action comedy films.

In 1908 Blackton's 1906 film *The Haunted Hotel* was released in Paris where it enjoyed both popular and financial success. According to legend, Gaumont director Etienne Arnaud told his studio staff to work out how the trick photography was accomplished and Cohl, after studying the film and carrying out some experiments, realized that the secret lay in stop-motion techniques. Cohl's first complete film was a cartoon short called *Fantasmagorie* made in 1908, and although he is now best remembered for his work in graphic animation, he did make a huge contribution to the art of model stop-motion animation through his use of crude puppets or stick figures. To save having to draw separate new frames, or cells, for his cartoons, he cut out the drawings of his characters, and animated the cut-outs. Amongst the films he made during this period are Le *Cauchemar du Fantoche* [*The Puppet's Nightmare*], *Les Allumettes Animées* [*Animated Matches*] – the first of three films featuring animated matchsticks – and *Un Drame chez les Fantoches* [aka *A Puppet Drama* or *The Love Affair in Toyland* or *Mystical Love-Making*] all of which were completed in 1908.

In 1910 Cohl made *Le Songe d'un Garçon de Café* [aka *The Hasher's Delirium*] for Société des Etablissements L. Gaumont to illustrate the dangers of drug-taking. It shows a man watching as lines of a unknown material is animated to spell out the names of various sinful substances and these words in turn are animated into evil faces. Later the same year Cohl left Gaumont for Pathé where he made the *The Automatic Moving Company* about which little is known, although we do know that it showed pieces of furniture moving on their own accord out of a lorry and up the stairs of a house before neatly arranging themselves in various rooms. The following year, 1911, Cohl produced his second and last film for Pathé called *The Idler* before leaving again to join the Eclipse film company. None of the films he made for Eclipse survive today but we do know that some, including *Campbell Soup*, featured animated objects of one kind or another. By the start of the First World War Cohl's star had waned and one of his last model animation films was *Les Allumettes Ensorcelées* [aka *Bewitches Matches*], the

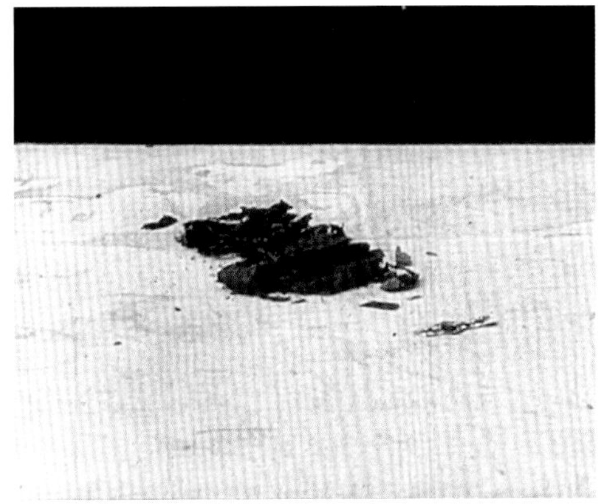

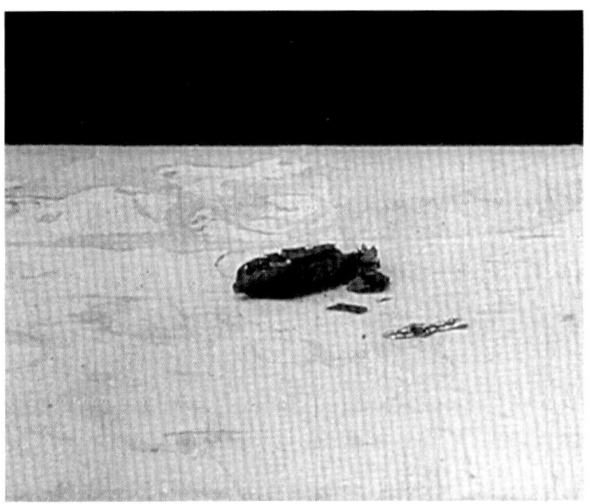

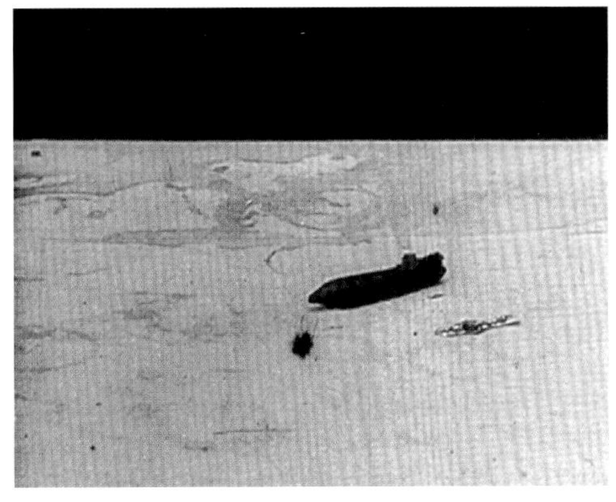

TOP LEFT
Two frames from Blackton's *Humorous Phases of Funny Faces* (1906) showing how he filled in the gaps for the title page with a paintbrush. Blackton's hand can be seen in the second frame on the extreme left of the picture.

BOTTOM LEFT
Three stop-frame sequences from Segundo de Chomón's *Hotel Electrico* (1908) showing a bag opening on its own, a shoe brush cleaning a shoe and Chomón himself being shaved as though by magic.

ABOVE
Six frames from Blackton's very innovative and entertaining *Princess Nicotine* (1909). In the first frame we see cigarettes jumping into a cigarette box and in the subsequent frames the animated progression by which a pile of tobacco leaves is transformed into a rolled cigar.

only one of his several animated match films to have survived. Sadly, his final film, *Fantoche Cherche un Logement* [*Puppet Looks for an Apartment*], passed almost unnoticed on its release in April 1921. The fad for model animation had apparently passed, at least in France.

Among those working in Europe at the same time as Cohl was the Spanish film director Segundo de Chomón who made a trick film called *Satán se divierte* in 1906 and then, in 1908, *Hotel Electrico* [aka *El Hotel Eléctrico*] which used a storyline and techniques similar to those of Blackton's *The Haunted Hotel*. In the film baggage moves around a room and one of the bags contains paintbrushes that also begin to move. Later we see a man (played by Chomón) whose boots begins to unbuckle of their one accord, the same character is shaved by a stop-motion razor and the hair of a woman (played by Julienne Mathieu) ties itself up into a bun. Although crude, the animation is very inventive. Chomón went on to make many other short films including the stop-motion *El Teatro Eléctrico de Bob* (1908) and in 1914 worked on the epic *Cabiria* in Italy and then, in 1927, on Abel Gance's classic *Napoleon*.

Returning again to the American continent, Biograph, another American production company, produced *Dolls in Dreamland* in 1907. Sadly we don't know the name of the film-maker. The story again features a boy who dreams that his new toys come to life, a popular scenario for incorporating animated objects that had been pioneered by Melbourne-Cooper in Britain. It featured dancing dolls, a teddy bear, dolls driving cars, toys fighting with a toy policeman and a bus crash, all delivered in model animation. Also released in the same year was a short entitled *Bobby's Daydream* (1907) made for the Vitagraph company, which contained animated objects but other than that little else is known about it.

The following year saw the release of *A Sculptor's Welsh Rarebit Nightmare* [aka *The Sculptor's Nightmare*] made by Wallace McCutcheon (nicknamed 'Old Man' McCutcheon) and photographed by legendary cinematographer Billy Bitzer who did his most important work with director D.W.Griffith and was responsible for such photographic innovations as the fade-out, soft focus, filming with artificial lighting and matte photography. The film was one of the earliest examples of clay animation. The story concerns a sculptor who is commissioned by a political club to sculpt a bust of each of the members. After taking the money, he becomes inebriated and, while in jail, has a nightmare in which he sees himself creating clay busts of various American politicians. Sadly, we again know very little about another clay animation film called *Modelling Extraordinary* (1912) except that it was made by the Natural Colour Kinematograph Company. Animated clay cropped up again in 1916 in the first of Willie Hopkin's 54 episodes of *Miracles in Mud* and in that year the first woman animator, Helena Smith Dayton, an artist, author and playwright, began experimenting in New

York with clay figures dressed in dolls' clothes and possessing human hair. She released her first film, *Romeo & Juliet*, in 1917 followed by a number of other short films based on classical literature. Again her films are regrettably lost to us.

In Argentina, beginning in 1915/16, an Italian-born political film-maker, Quirino Cristiani, was making cartoon animation films but also shooting stop-motion animation using cardboard cut-outs. Having watched Émile Cohl's 1908 film *Animated Matches* Cristini made a one-minute film called *La Intervencion en la Provencia de Buenos Aires* (*Intervention in the Province of Buenos Aires*), about the ousting of Buenos Aires governor Marcelino Ugarte for dishonesty, using stop-motion cut-outs.

On the other side of the world, there were a number of major animators working in Eastern Europe and Russia who had found many original uses for model animation. One of the most interesting of these was a Pole whose name was Wladislaw Starewicz (or, as he and others have variously spelled it, Ladislav Starevich, Wladyslaw Starewicz, Ladislaw Starewicz or Starewitch, the last being the name he used when living in France). The record of Starewicz's early life and career, like the spelling of his name, is somewhat vague and contradictory, but we have pieced together what is known of how he came to make three-dimensional animated films. He was born in 1882 in Moscow of Polish parents but brought up in Kaunas, which is today in Lithuania. As he grew up he became interested in drawing, writing and entomology (the study of insects). At the age of twenty-seven he became involved with the Museum of Natural History in Kaunas (some reports say that he was one of its founders and the first director) where he made three natural history live-action documentaries. In 1909 he began planning another short film that was to be about stag beetles, specifically a stag beetle fight. But how to film it? Most such creatures become lethargic and even die under photographic lights. However, whilst he had been planning his first films he, too, had seen *Les Allumettes Animés (Animated Matches)* by Émil Cohl and after working out how it had been done, decided to film the stag beetle film in stop-motion. This momentous decision would begin a life-long involvement with the animation of insects and. later, model animals.

When he began he knew nothing of models with metal skeletons so he used real beetles for *The Battle of the Stag Beetles* (1910). The beetles were killed and their shells preserved, but the legs and mandibles were removed and then re-attached by wires fixed to the thorax by means of sealing wax, so creating an articulated puppet. The film was released by the Aleksandr Khanzhonkov Studio in Moscow and was an immense success, so much so that in 1911 the studio offered him a job making similar films. Between 1911 and 1918 Starewicz made over thirty films for the company, the most distinguished and inventive of which were *The Cameraman's Revenge* (1911) a film of jealously, infidelity and revenge, *The Ant and the Grasshopper* (1911), which was so well received in Russia that Starewicz was decorated by the Tsar himself and *The Beautiful Leukanida* (1912) a fairy tale about beetles, which was widely acclaimed. The animation was sufficiently life-like to convince one London newspaper that 'the insects were alive, trained by an unidentified Russian scientist'. Other outstanding titles were a 41-minute featurette *The Night Before Christmas* (1912), *The Four Devils* (1913), *Christmas Eve* (1913), *A Terrible Revenge* (1913) which won a Gold Medal at an international festival in Milan in the following year, *Ruslan and Ludmila* (1915) and *On the Warsaw Highway* (1916). Viewed today, the animation in Starewicz's early films seems basic and even naive but they still possess a dark and grotesque quality which makes them fascinating to watch.

Over the years Starewicz developed his techniques by constructing models with steel ball-and-socket armatures padded out with sponge which was then covered with light felt and leather. This gave his puppets endurance (the real insects had not lasted long under lights) and the illusion of reality. He also developed his animation techniques, creating motion-blur to suggest rapid movement by mounting the models on wires which were lightly touched before each frame was shot so that they vibrated and slightly 'blurred' the image.

In 1918, in the aftermath of the Russian Revolution, Starewicz left Moscow for the safer cities of Odessa and Yalta before eventually leaving Russia altogether for Italy and then France where he finally settled in 1919. Working with other Russian émigrés in Georges Méliès' old studio he began by making *The Scarecrow* (1921). When many of his compatriots left France for Berlin and Hollywood, Starewicz moved out of Paris to Fontenay-sous-Bois where he would spend the rest of his life and career. At the end of the silent era he directed several innovative films including *Love in Black and White* (1923) which satirized Hollywood, featuring puppets of Chaplin, Mary Pickford and Tom Mix, and also *The Voice of the Nightingale* (1923) which received a Hugo Riesenfiels medal, as 'the most novel short subject motion picture in the USA during the year 1925'.

The 1930s saw Starewicz produce even more original films, with sound and then colour. Amongst these were *The Lion and the Fly* (1932), *The Old Lion* (1932) and the first in the *Mascot* series, *The Mascot* (1934), about a toy dog's search for an orange to give to a dying girl in which live action was combined with rear-projection images.

In 1929-30 Starewicz made his first and only feature film called *The Tale of the Fox*, which is perhaps the best known and widely seen of his films. It was his most ambitious project, which took him ten years to prepare and eighteen months to photograph. Because of financing and soundtrack problems it did not receive its premiere in Berlin until April 1937. The satirical story was based on a medieval fable about Renard the Fox and is set in the kingdom of animals where Master Fox makes a living out of tricking the other animals. The ruler of the kingdom, the Lion King, listens to complaints about the Master Fox and has him arrested and brought before the throne to answer for his misdeeds. The characterization of the animals, especially the fox, is superb and shows extraordinary subtlety, with each puppet possessing an individual and distinctive personality. This is the film in which one feels Starewicz best expressed his own character. Allegedly the final crowd scene featured one hundred models, all simultaneously animated, with the three-minute sequence necessitating 273,000 movements.

Over the years Starewicz made some 47 films and was working on another, *Like Dog and Cat*, when he died in 1965. Ray remembers seeing one or two of these films (the ones made later in France) and being fascinated by them. Although Starewicz's style was not one that he would have chosen himself, there is no doubt that Ray's career, and those of his contemporaries, was hugely influenced by Starewicz's work. Even

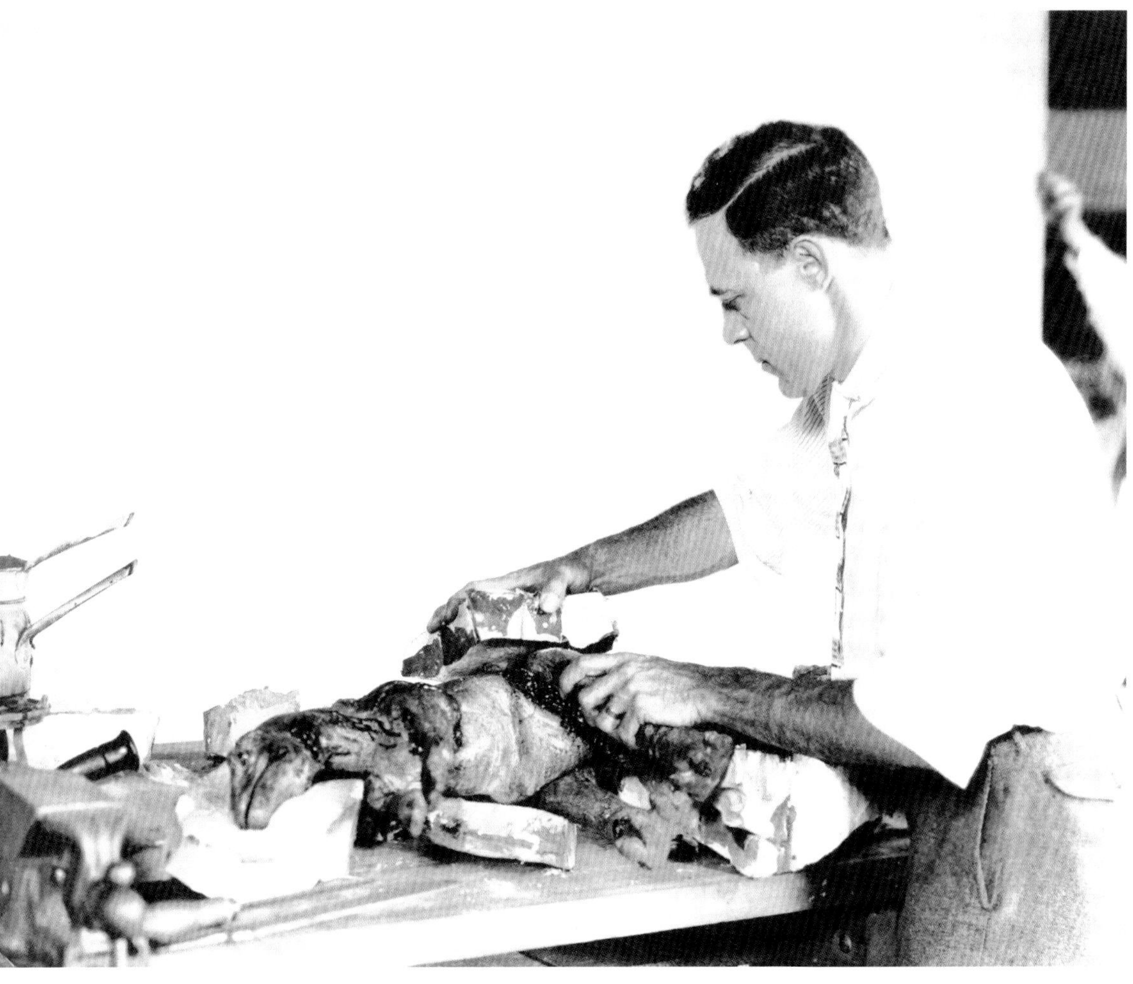

BELOW LEFT
Two scenes from Howard S. Moss's *Mary & Gretel* (1917). In the first a fairy appears to the lost characters of the title and in the second a white rabbit watches drunken gnomes. Note how the gnome on the right is leaning forward; even considering that he is intoxicated, the angle is very precarious.

ABOVE
A rare photo of Herbert Dawley removing a piece of a mould from a casting of a duckbill dinosaur taken for *Along the Moonbeam Trail* (1920). The mould suggests that it was made from a waxy clay and the double-pot on a gas ring at the back of the bench, confirms that a substance (probably liquid latex) was poured into the mould.

BELOW RIGHT
A hand-painted glass slide advertising the forthcoming *Along the Moonbeam Trail* (1920).

today, although his films are not exactly popular, one feels that they have continued to exert an influence on films such as Tim Burton's *The Nightmare Before Christmas* (1993), *James and the Giant Peach* (1996) and *Corpse Bride* (2006).

A more obscure figure is the American film-maker Howard S. Moss who worked in Chicago where he wrote, animated and directed a number of shorts and features, several of which we know used animated puppets. Although little is known about Moss we are aware of at least five titles, two of which utilized animation. These were *Mary & Gretel* (1917) made for the Peter Pan Film Corporation and *Cracked Ice* (1922) made for Rialto Productions. The first (called the 'Motoy' puppet series) used basic articulated toys such as a large white rabbit, a fairy, Rip Van Winkle, several gnomes and two little baby female dolls in a surreal short that resembles a conglomeration of *Alice in Wonderland* and several fairy tales. The film is extremely crude and somewhat dull but it does feature a number of these characters being animated at the same time, sometimes up to four. It is obvious that the puppets are simply dolls (probably bought from a toy shop), which almost certainly did not have internal armatures but wire joints. The characters move extremely awkwardly, waddling rather than walking, and on occasions the gnomes are seen to lean dangerously forward when walking. The second film, *Cracked Ice*, we sadly know nothing about.

Another American, Major Herbert M. Dawley, began his film career in New York in 1918 when he met legendary pioneer Willis O'Brien (see Chapter 3). Dawley had dabbled with animation for some time but was primarily a sculptor who became interested in film-making when he saw O'Brien's *The Dinosaur and the Missing Link* (1915). For a time Dawley and O'Brien communicated by letter which led to Dawley commissioning O'Brien to make *The Ghost of Slumber Mountain* (1919), an original idea by O'Brien that would feature 'living' and realistic dinosaurs. Although the two men parted company (by most accounts not on the best of terms, as we shall see) shortly after the film was released to enormous success, Dawley followed it up with *Along the Moonbeam Trail* (1920), which is believed to have utilized out-takes filmed by O'Brien for the earlier film, although animator and palaeontologist Stephen Czerkas has recently seen a rediscovered copy of the film and has suggested that the animation is not up to O'Brien's standard.[2] Dawley then teamed up with Tony Sarg who was one of America's foremost puppeteers, to make the animated series of 'Shadowgraph' shorts called *Tony Sarg's Alamanac* (1921-23), which used silhouette cut-outs. Only the first three titles are known to us – *The First Circus*, *The Tooth Carpenter* and *Why They Love Cavemen*. As far as we are aware the series was Sarg's only excursion into movies but Dawley went on to make a number of fantasy films, now mostly lost, that are reputed to have featured either cartoon or three-dimensional animation.

The 1920s saw the arrival on the animation scene of a curious and extremely eccentric American film-maker by the name of Charley Bowers (Charles R. Bowers). Better known for his cartoon animation, he had once been in partnership with Raoul Barré, a Canadian pioneer cartoon animator who had also dabbled in model animation. However, from 1912 to 1925 Bowers worked independently as a cartoon animator but increasingly concentrated on animat-

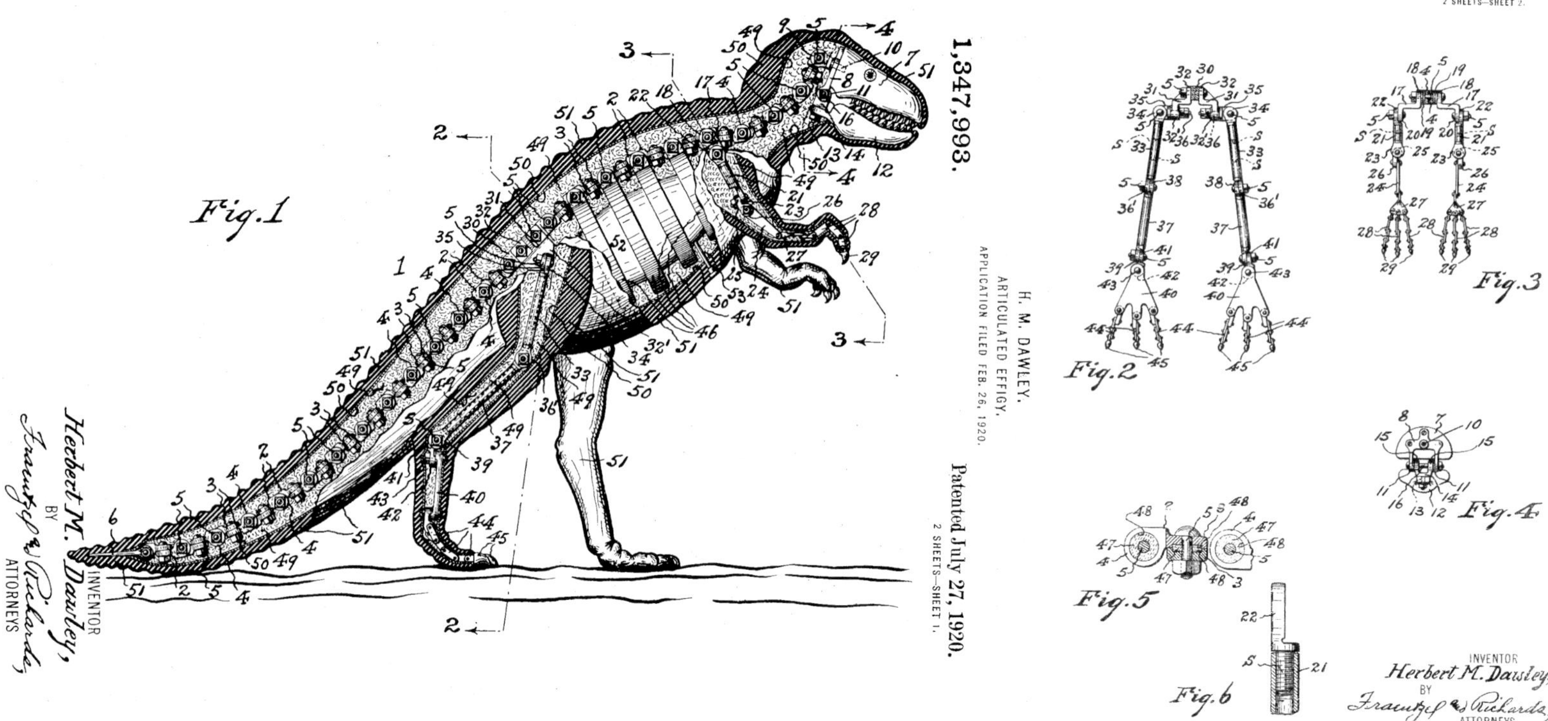

ed clay, toys and puppets. He grandly described his work as The Bowers Process'. He produced most of his films at his Astoria studio in New York and then moved to Los Angeles. Between 1926 and 1928 he made eighteen two-reelers, the most distinctive of which were *Now You Tell One* (1926) and *There It Is* (1928). They are truly bizarre in content, a cross between the zany humour of the Goons and the Road Runner cartoons. *Now You Tell One* featured a straw hat seemingly growing whilst on a man's head, a cat growing from a plant and a mouse firing a gun. *There It Is*, made by the Bowers Comedy Corp, directed and photographed by H. L. Muller and produced by Bowers, is an even weirder film. The central character is a Scottish detective called Charley MacNeesha, played by Bowers, who is summoned to solve strange goings on in an old dark house. The film begins with a cook cracking open an egg, from which grows a fully developed chicken. The intermediate section, between the egg and the chicken, was achieved by stop-motion. MacNeesha also has an assistant called MacGregor, a tiny animated creature who lives in a matchbox and resembles a strange looking bug attired in a kilt. The film contains other animated sequences including a parcel unwrapping itself and a cuckoo in a cuckoo clock being eaten by a cat. The animation in these films is on occasions excellent, there is even a shot that shows MacGregor jumping out of his matchbox that was probably achieved with aerial wires. Bower's work only survives today because of the George Eastman Collection and the Toulouse Cinémathèque. The latter apparently uncovered a pile of rusty reels once owned by a travelling gypsy exhibitor, which turned out to include a great deal of Bowers' work.

In 1923 Buster Keaton made his first feature film called *The Three Ages*, directed by Keaton and Eddie Cline. The opening section of the film was set in the Stone Age and shows Keaton standing on the back of a crudely built animated brontosaurus. The film was made at Metro Pictures but we don't know who was responsible for the construction of the brontosaurus and a small model of Keaton himself, but it is likely to have been Keaton's technical adviser Fred Gabourie. The stop-motion work was executed by two-dimensional animator Max Fleischer, who would later become famous for the *Betty Boop* and *Popeye* cartoons. We do know that he had seen O'Brien's *The Ghost of Slumber Mountain* because he used clips from it in his 1923 film *Evolution*, and it may have been this that led him to experiment with model animation but as far as we are aware he made no other films using models.[3]

Around the same time, in 1922/23, British sculptor Virginia May produced a short film for Pathe News in London for their Pathe Review, labelled 523 and called *Monsters From the Past.* The first caption reads, '10 million years ago, when the world was young, giant reptiles ruled the earth. These mighty beasts were busy writing their own history in the sands of time.' The first creature we see is a kind of brontosaurus although it also seems to owe something to con-

ABOVE
Two illustrations of the 'Articulated Effigy' submitted by Herbert Dawley and his attorney to the US patent office on 26 February 1920 and officially patented on 27 July 1920. The patent is extremely detailed, showing the internal armature for a carnivorous dinosaur model. It was this patent that Dawley invoked when threatening the producer of *The Lost World*.

TOP RIGHT
Six scenes from Charley Bowers *There It Is* (1928). Five show the strange animated bug creature MacGregor, in the last one he is seen with with his 'wife' and 'children'. Scene four shows a toy cart disappearing into the wall, an effect that can only have been created with stop-motion. We can only surmise that the cart was cut into sections and these were added between camera exposures and then the whole sequence was reversed to make it seem as if it was disappearing.

BOTTOM RIGHT
An intriguing few frames from Major Johann Georg Hand Ewald's *Aus der Urzeit der Erde* [*From Primordial Times*]. They show dimetrodons (or stegosaurus), two carnivorous dinosaurs fighting and two smaller dinosaurs eating a large dead beast.

temporary ideas about the Loch Ness monster. The film continues with a caption, 'And the sands reveal another chapter' before showing the bones of a tyrannosaurus rex, a triceratops and a brontosaurus being released from the sand by means of animation. All the creatures were modelled in clay and based on fossilized bones. Towards the end of the film we see Virginia May herself modelling in clay, but the action is reversed so that she appears to start with a complete model of an allosaurus which she then reduces to a lump of clay. The major set piece in the film is a reasonably well animated fight between a tyrannosaurus rex and a triceratops. The proportions of the models are good and the fight itself inventive; even the tails flick and whip with excitement and at one point the triceratops is seen scratching the ground with its front foot. Less successful was May's attempt to have her tyrannosaurus make a small leap, the action is undoubtedly crude, probably accomplished by supporting it from the side away from the camera.

Still in Europe, but this time in Germany, Major Johann Georg Hand Ewald had become involved with three-dimensional animation in 1918. In 1924 he set up Ewald Film GmbH. in Berlin and, supported by his sons, produced the educational short *Aus der Urzeit der Erde* [*From Primordial Times*] which was released in 1925 and was probably inspired by O'Brien's *The Lost World*. The film was photographed using tabletop animation showing rubber dinosaurs walking and fighting in prehistoric settings. Judging by the few feet of film that have survived in the German Bundesarchiv / Filmarchiv, which features a brontosaurus, a fight between two dimetrodons (or they may perhaps be stegosaurs) beside a lake, and two small carnivorous dinosaurs eating a larger one. Although the models are somewhat crude the loss of most of this film, and any subsequent ones made by Ewald, is greatly to be regretted.

On the other hand, we have probably not lost much of interest with the disappearance of most of three animated film series made in the late 1920s by the Kinex Studios in Hollywood called *Snap the Gingerbread Man* , *Chip the Wooden Man* and *Daffy Doings in Doodlebugville*. Little is known about them except that each was approximately eight minutes long, but from what we have seen it appears that their style was that of comic cartoons, but using animated models. All seem to have been aimed at a younger audience, and all feature crude humanoid and animal puppets and even cruder animation.

There is one other key pioneer, an American called Joseph Leeland Roop. Sadly, not enough is known about him even though he worked on sections of the animation for *The Lost World* (1925) (see Chapter 3) alongside Willis O'Brien. Born in 1869 in Louisville, Kentucky, Roop was a sculptor, photo-engraver and photographer who became fascinated with cinema as early as the 1880s when he invented a version of the lantern slide projector which apparently used a roll of celluloid film stock that could be hand-cranked through the projector. During the early 1900s he established his own studio and began experimenting with sculpting and building models for animation. In

1913 he submitted designs for a moving picture and projecting device to the US patent office. He was not only an inventive man when it came to the mechanics of cinema, but was also, according to his grand-daughter, Rena-Beth Smith, a prolific film-maker, working on as many as 700 films. This claim may be somewhat exaggerated but the evidence is that he was certainly involved with quite a number of films although not credited, as was usual in those early days. In 1916, according to his grand-daughter, after years of experimenting with moulds and models for animation,

> *....he formulated a secret composition to allow figures to bend in different positions, bit by bit, each time photographed to produce movement. His creations of miniature sets portraying animals, people, destruction of buildings, or whatever needed, were shot and reproduced to life-size on the screen. His animation from the miniatures were a great success in such movies as* The Great Glory, Black Cyclone, Tarzan's Return, The Gorilla Hunt ... [4]

In 1917, while in Dayton, Ohio, he made the models and animated *The Birth of Christ* for the International Bible Students; and then moved to California. Around 1922 he made a series of animated shorts called *Tom and Jerry* which utilized models of a boy (Tom) and a mule (Jerry).

We can glean a little further information about Roop and his work from an article in the May 1924 edition of *Popular Mechanics*. The author calls him 'a Los Angeles producer' and suggests that he made educational, scientific and comedy shorts, using puppets and stop-motion animation. The article goes on to say that

> *'The special features which characterize Mr Roop's work in this line and which overcome the serious limitations which have existed heretofore, include the use of a special rubber composition, with flexible steel framework or skeleton. The figures are first made of clay and from them molds are made, from which in turn are cast the final figures.'*

At this time Roop's contemporary, Willis O'Brien, was making his models using the build-up process but the account of Roop's casting methods shows that he and O'Brien were both innovating, working on different lines with the same objectives in mind. The article goes on: 'The advantages of the flexible manikins and animals go even further,

BELOW
Roop himself leans over a miniature street model showing some of his *Tom & Jerry* characters. Jerry the mule is on the extreme right and Tom is standing in front of the jail with a banjo. Note the name O'Brien on the store front in the middle.

TOP RIGHT
A rare photograph of Joseph Leeland Roop's miniature animation setup for one of his *Tom & Jerry* short films, which Roop called 'animated cartoons'. The camera is on the right (with its side open) and we can see just how elaborate his miniature sets were.

BOTTOM RIGHT
Roop putting the finishing touches to a clay maquette of Jerry the mule, whilst models of Tom and others look on. The *Tom & Jerry* films were shown at the California Theatre on Main and 8th in Los Angeles.

marked changes in facial expressions being possible. The jungle lion actually acts out his roar with a mouth that opens wider and wider, while the eyes bulge fiercely and his mane stands erect.' The next passage is particularly interesting:

> *In conjunction with the use of these figures is the special stage. It is equipped with numerous overhead wires running in various directions. The figures of the actors are suspended from these in most instances by invisible threads. This rather complicated overhead construction is invaluable to proper spacing of moving figures, thus assuring the accurate register of the actor's motions.*

This suggests that to stabilize his models while they 'walked' Roop suspended them from some kind of overhead aerial brace rather than fixing them to the animation table.

In 1924 Roop became part of the team working on *The Lost World* and it seems that he animated several sequences, including scenes that featured the baryonyx (a duck-billed or crocodile- headed dinosaur). The animation in these sequences is nowhere near as smooth as O'Brien's work, probably because Roop was not

BELOW
Roop with a full-sized model of a dragon-like dinosaur. The creature would seem to be made out of oil-based clay. Note the models or maquettes on the bench.

used to animating such creatures in the same way as O'Brien was. There is also evidence from various sources, including a letter from the palaeontologist Charles Gilmore from whom Roop was seeking advice on construction, that Roop made other dinosaur models after his work on *The Lost World*. There are also photographs showing some of these models and they appear to be articulated, or at least the diplodocus does, as it is pictured in slightly different positions. Whether these models were made for a movie is not known. What we do know is that in 1926 Roop made a short called *The Lost Whirl*, a film inspired by, but not based on, *The Lost World*, which allegedly featured more of his own dinosaur effects. Roop died in 1932 in California on his sixty-third birthday and although he has been a lost figure in the history of model animation it is obvious that his work was very much part of that history and it is therefore sad that none of the films he made or contributed to, aside from *The Lost World*, seem to have survived.

Like Roop, many of these film-makers discussed in this chapter are little known and most of their films are now irrevocably lost to us. The individuals and films we have mentioned are those that we know of and which we feel have a significant place in the history of three-dimensional animation. It seems certain that there are many more people who played a part in the development of the art and we hope that one day these pioneers and their films will come to light and will receive the credit due to them.

In the first decade or so of the twentieth century most of these pioneer films were aimed at children, or at least family audiences, perhaps

because the obvious items to use for animation were articulated children's toys which readily lent themselves to imitating human actions in a comic manner. Although crude, these short subjects achieved a great deal of success at the time and were crucial to the realization and development of three-dimensional animation techniques. However few of the pioneers, apart perhaps for Blackton and Roop, seem to have visualized the importance and potential of what they were producing and they rarely continued to make films using the process. It should also be remembered that these films only featured sections of stop-motion as a novelty item within a live-action film. No one had yet made the all-important step of combining animated models with live action in the same frame. Part of the problem was that no one had found the ideal subject for combining the two elements.

LEFT
A rare photograph of Roop animating a baroyonyx for *The Lost World* (1925).

BELOW
A creature chasing antelopes or horses. Like the full-size construction on page 50 the creature seems to match nothing in the known dinosaur world so it can only be assumed that it is an 'imaginary dinosaur-like dragon'. He seems to have built a number of such imaginary creatures, although for what purpose we do not know. It is possible that as these are models that they might be armatured with a latex covering but again we don't know for what purpose they were constructed.

KING KONG
A MERIAN C. COOPER and ERNEST B. SCHOEDSACK PRODUCTION
Radio Pictures

CHAPTER THREE

VISIONARY AND STAR-MAKER – WILLIS O'BRIEN

'Out of the uncharted, forgotten corner of the world, a monster...surviving 7 million years of evolution... crashes into the haunts of civilization... onto the talking screen... to stagger the imagination of man.'

KING KONG SOUVENIR PROGRAMME

Willis O'Brien, or Obie as he was known, would change three-dimensional animation from a children's novelty into an art form. Today he is recognized as being the genius who created the 'star' of *King Kong* (1933) and that film established his reputation as the father of fluid model animation and the visionary who saw the potential of combining animated models with live action in the same frame.

Willis Harold O'Brien was born in Oakland, California on 2 March 1886 to William Henry O'Brien and Minnie Gregg O'Brien. Two older brothers (Gregg and Douglas), an older sister (Dorothy) and a younger brother (Meredith) survived into adulthood; another younger brother was killed when he fell from a wagon. Sadly, although Obie greatly admired his older brother Gregg, he never considered himself close to his other siblings. He was a very good-looking young boy with 'expressive liquid blue eyes' (as Darlyne, his second wife, describes them), which reflected every emotion. Obie loved San Francisco and spent much of his time there, even as a young lad. Darlyne recalled that he 'lived in a very colourful era'. 'He had many memories of the old Barbary Coast and of the earthquake of 1906 and he often spoke of how nice people were to each other after the earthquake.'[1]

The young O'Brien was always a restless boy and at the age of thirteen he left his parents and spent four years drifting from job to job. These included working on a chicken farm and trapping in southern Oregon, where he befriended a Native American from the Modoc tribe. 'He became very expert with the rope and knew his horses thoroughly, which is why be could draw and paint them so beautifully, with perfect action.'[2] Whilst in Oregon he heard of the opportunity to act as a guide for a group of scientists from the University of Southern California who wanted him to take them to Crater Lake in search of fossils. The scientists found a skeleton from the *felidae* family (probably what we know today as a sabre-toothed tiger) and whilst they excavated this and other fossilized bones Obie watched, rapidly becoming fascinated by the study of prehistoric life, especially dinosaurs.

In 1903, aged seventeen, he returned home and found employment as an office boy with a company of architects where he quickly became a qualified draughtsman. It was during this time that he became passionate about cinema, visiting the local Nickelodeons whenever time and money allowed. Still a restless soul, he found an outlet for his artistic talents (he was a natural but untrained artist) at the *San Francisco Daily World* newspaper where he got a job as a sports cartoonist, specializing in boxing, a sport he loved. Not satisfied with being on the periphery of sport, he decided to try and become a jockey. But, for all his efforts to lose weight by exercising at the local gym, it became apparent that he was just too substantially built to achieve this ambition and he turned to boxing, entering nine local bouts as Willis 'Shamus' O'Brien and winning all of them. After his ninth bout, however, he realized that his physique was not robust enough for the profession (although he had strong wrists his hands were too small) and the wanderlust struck again.

In an effort to settle his son down in a more prestigious profession, William O'Brien arranged for him to take a job with the Southern Pacific Railroad as a brakeman. Although Obie knuckled down to the job for several years and worked his way up to become a surveyor for the railroad, he was still not satisfied with the prospect of an orthodox career and at the age of twenty-nine returned to San Francisco to work as a sculptor in a marble shop. After learning the trade, which he managed to do extremely quickly, Obie won a competition to design the fireplace of a millionaire's home and assisted the head architect of the forthcoming 1915 San Francisco World's Fair.

It was in that small marble shop that Obie finally realized his destiny. The year was 1914 and in a moment of idleness the young O'Brien modelled several clay figures. Seeing what he was doing, a colleague called Stenberg challenged him to a tabletop mock fight with the figurines. At first it was just a piece of fun but Obie began to speculate how the figures might be made to 'move' with the aid of film, much like the characters he had seen in cartoon films at the picture houses. He had read somewhere that such cartoons were made by filming a series of drawings, each showing a different stage in the progression of the action. If that technique could be applied to models (and why not?), by the same process of shooting one frame and then moving the models very slightly before shooting another, it might be possible to produce a convincing illusion of movement. As Obie later put it in an interview with the *New York Times* (published on 11 November 1962, the day after his death), 'Out of this came the idea of movies with animated models.' By accident he had stumbled on the work to which he would devote the rest of his life, a life which would see him progressively develop the art of three-dimensional animation to a level of near-perfection.

To succeed in the field which Obie had now taken up it is not enough to be a good animator; the art also requires thorough training in drawing and model-making and, perhaps even more importantly, a vivid and active imagination. Obie possessed all these assets and many, many more. But his greatest achievement was that he hit on the idea of using model animation in a very specific way. As well as his interest in moving pictures he continued to be fascinated by the dinosaurs and other prehistoric creatures which had first captured his imagination back in Oregon all those years before. Obie could see that dinosaurs

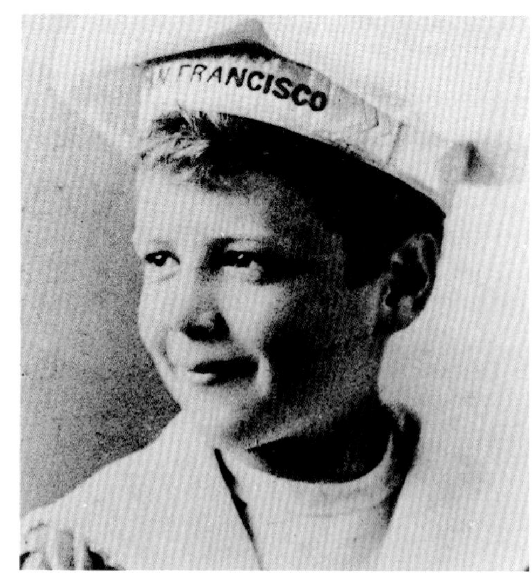

were the perfect subjects for an animator. If he was able to bring them to life then the cinematic possibilities were endless; and dinosaurs would become the distinctive trademark of all his work.

But how could Obie test his idea of using stop-motion to animate his creations? In 1914, using some of the money that he had saved whilst working in the marble shop, he rented a small shed on the roof of the Bank of Italy building in San Francisco. There he began to experiment and eventually constructed a brontosaurus from modelling clay moulded over a crude wooden armature (he had realized that the model would require an internal skeleton so that it would hold a position whilst he photographed it). We don't know the dimensions of this model but the arma-

PREVIOUS SPREAD
Left, a page of the special brochure given away with *The Hollywood Reporter* prior to the release of *King Kong* in 1933. It was beautifully designed and was covered in a copper cover (see page 84).
Right, Willis O'Brien circa 1920s. The photograph is signed although we are unable to recognize the name.

LEFT
Portrait of O'Brien as a child, taken in 1893 when he was aged seven years.

BELOW LEFT
Two cartoons drawn and painted by O'Brien. He was a good artist and an excellent, if eccentric, cartoonist. These were done in his later years when he was making *Mighty Joe Young* (1949).

BELOW
Eight scenes from *The Dinosaur and the Missing Link* (1915).

Top, the first three images.
The 'missing link', Wild Willie, which O'Brien called 'Kong's ancestor'.

Top, fourth image.
The strange looking phororhacos, or 'desert quail'.

Bottom, from left to right.
Theophilus Ivoryhead being eyed up by the phororhacos; Theophilus on a lake in a boat with the brontosaurus-like creature having a drink; Wild Willie fighting the brontosaurus; Theophilus has his foot on the ape pretending he has killed it.

ture was built of wooden struts held together with bolts and wing nuts which could be tightened to hold the model in a pose. Next, he hired a 35mm camera and employed the services of a newsreel cameraman to produce a one-minute test of the brontosaurus walking across a painted miniature prehistoric background. The clay covering of the model was extremely malleable and progress was painfully slow because the model needed attention after every frame was shot in order to remove the marks and indentations left by Obie's fingers as he manipulated it. Although crude in the extreme, the film was promising enough to convince Obie that the technique would work and that his dream of breathing life into these lost creatures was practical and likely to be commercially viable. Gradually over the next few weeks, by trial and error, he learned how best to animate the model, and began to develop his own style and to give his model a basic but reasonable fluidity of movement. It is sad that this first film and the records of his other experiments have not survived.

Obie's next step was to look for finance to make a longer film. His father was not encouraging, telling his son in no uncertain terms that there could be no possibility of a future in movies, and especially not of a career working with models. Obie asked around and following a number of unsuccessful meetings met with San Francisco exhibitor (owner of the first post-quake Nickelodeon) and sometime producer, Herman Wobber. Wobber was intrigued and impressed by Obie's artwork and test films, seeing the commercial possibilities of the process. He immediately formed a company to finance the making of a movie and is reputed to have advanced Obie a extremely generous $5,000 to make an animated model film that he could exhibit and/or sell. What proportion of that figure was for the hire of a basement room in the Imperial Theater on Market Street where the film was shot, and for the construction of the models, scenarios and the animation work itself, and what proportion was for Obie, is lost in the mists of time. Thrilled that he had at last found finance for his venture, Obie sat down and wrote a basic outline and from that produced a number of sketches and drawings for a one-reeler 'caveman comedy', which he called *The Dinosaur and the Missing Link* (1915).

Set in the Stone Age, the film featured four human characters, all played by animated puppets: three suitors, named Duke, Stonejaw Steve and Theophilus Ivoryhead who are competing for the attentions of a pretty young cave girl called Araminta Rockface. The 'missing link' of the title is Wild Willie, an ape-like creature which Obie called 'Kong's ancestor'. The plot is simple. After Willie steals the supper that Araminta and her suitors are preparing to eat the three suitors are despatched to find more meat and fish. In the course of his quest one of the men comes across what looks like a phororhacos (a prehistoric chicken-like creature, called a 'desert quail' in the titles, which would have to wait forty-six years to be animated again in Ray's *Mysterious Island*). Meanwhile Willie gets into a fight with a brontosaurus (at least it is called a brontosaurus although it has very un-brontosaurus-like spikes

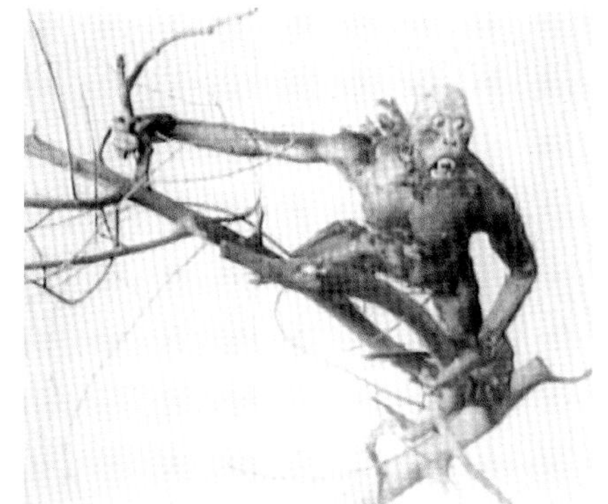

or lumps on its back) and Willie looses. As the dinosaur plods off the screen Theophilus arrives and, seeing Araminta on her way to find out what has happened to supper, puts his foot on Willie's body (a gesture, derived from Obie's days as a boxer, that he would use in subsequent films) pretending that he has killed it. Of course he wins the day and the girl.

As suggested above, the concepts for the dinosaurs were not exactly accurate although even at this point in his career Obie was aware of the work of American wildlife artist Charles R. Knight, whose anatomical renditions of dinosaurs were seen at the time as definitive. But much more important was the fact that Obie had found ways of dramatically improving his models. Instead of using clay moulded around a wooden armature he had experimented and found more flexible, practical and permanent substitutes for both elements. First, he replaced the wooden armature with a metal ball-and-socket skeleton, which he learned how to machine and assemble himself. Although crude, this new armature gave a model the flexibility he required while at the same time allowing it to retain a position indefinitely. Next he searched for a more practical covering, one that would not mark when manipulated. He looked at many possible options, amongst them using cotton wool covered with a rubber skin, but that didn't give him the form that he required. Keeping the cotton-wadding interior he layered the outside of the models with sections of rubber, sealing the joints with a latex solution. In the case of Wild Willie, the 'missing link', he also covered the model with sections of rabbit fur.

The entire five-minute film took a total of two months to shoot and the results were spectacular, although of course crude by today's standards. Obie was captivated with his creation, as was Herman Wobber who watched the film in his Nickelodeon. Wobber decided to test the one-reeler out with an audience and again the reaction was favourable, better than either Wobber of Obie could have hoped for. Encouraged by this response, Wobber cabled The Edison Company, at that time one of the leading film distributors, and sent them a copy of the film. A year later Edison bought the film for $525 and went on to exhibit it across the country. One reviewer in *The Moving Picture World* said of the film, '*The Dinosaur and the Missing Link* is startling and amusing at the same time. The grotesque manikins are curiously human in their movements, and will excite the interest of the entire family.' The film proved popular and in the best traditions of film producers 'cashing in' on a success, Edison released the picture again in 1917 under the title *The Dinosaur and the Baboon*.

While Obie was waiting for Wobber to sell *The Dinosaur and the Missing Link* he photographed a second five-minute film, called *Birth of a Flivver* (1915), about two cavemen who invent the wheel and then try to harness a brontosaurus to it but finally decide that the invention is not worth anything and discard it. Following the success of *The Dinosaur and the Missing Link* Edison also bought this second film and, through Conquest Pictures (the name the Edison company would use for Obie's films), offered him a job in their New York studios, which were at 2826 Decatur Street in the Bronx. It was proposed that he should make a series of ten five-minute one-reeler comedies using his model animation process and that he should be paid one dollar for every foot of film he produced.

Obie moved to the East Coast in 1915. William O'Brien accompanied his son to the train station and Darlyne recollected that, 'As Obie and his father stood at the station, his father took off his heavy overcoat and handed it to Obie.' At the New York studios he was allocated a small working area, which the other

ABOVE LEFT
O'Brien in his Edison Studio workshop circa 1917 making one of his 'Manikin Productions'.

ABOVE
The New York Edison Studio about the time O'Brien was working there.

RIGHT
A colourful poster for *The Ghost of Slumber Mountain* (1919). The creatures are a little out of proportion but it is interesting to note that it was the dinosaurs that were the stars.

employees nicknamed 'Manikin Productions'. As with *The Dinosaur and the Missing Link* and *Birth of a Flivver*, he wrote the stories, built the models, constructed and painted the sets and then directed and photographed each film. The first was *R.F.D 10,000 B.C.* (1916) about a prehistoric mailman called Henry Saurus (a typical Obie joke), whose post cart is pulled by a brontosaurus and who is vying with Johnny Bearskin for the affections of Winnie Warclub on Valentine's Day. This was followed in quick succession by *Morpheus Mike* (1917) about a dreamer who sees himself eating in a Stone Age café and is served by a mastodon, then came *Prehistoric Poultry* (1916) about a Neanderthal family and their pet dinoris (an ostrich-like dinosaur). A press release put out by the Edison Studios in 1916 states rather grandly:

> *Willis O'Brien, whose mannikin comedies are the comic features of the Edison Conquest program of moving pictures, is an artist, a sculptor, a moving picture director, a cameraman, an anatomist, a pattern maker, an inventor and an expert in the analysis of animal movements. In addition he devises miniature stage settings, designs the costumes, and... but why go on. The little actors whose antics have helped greatly in the success of Conquest Pictures are anatomically correct mannikins, no longer that a baby's doll but built to exact measurements. Each mannikin has every joint that a man has. The dinosaurs and mammoths used in Mr O'Brien's 'stone age' stories are built precisely in accordance with the structure of these prehistoric animals as shown by their skeletons in the American Museum of Natural History. The hands of any of these little actors are little larger than your thumbnail, yet each of the tiny fingers has three joints, just like a finger of a flesh-and-blood actor. Every hand or foot is constructed of nineteen delicate little castings. Although Mr O'Brien himself makes the patterns for them, the castings alone cost him just $16.50 for every hand.*

The release also claimed that Obie 'worked eighteen or twenty hours a day' but became coy when it described the animation – 'Just how they are made to do it, however, is Mr O'Brien's secret.'[3] Although interesting, it has to be remembered that it was a publicity announcement, and some of the information it purports to divulge is possibly inaccurate. Obie went on to make *Curious Pets of Our Ancestors* (1917), *In the Villain's Power* (1917) and *The Puzzling Billboard* (1917), which was part of the series *Sam Loyd's Famous Puzzles* in which Obie animated letters on a billboard.

Sadly, the Edison Company fell into difficulties because of its heavy involvement with the Motion Picture Patents Company, which had been dissolved as it had been judged to be a monopoly. As a result it had to make some stringent cut-backs, which meant that some of the films in production and some that had been completed, were shelved, including the last three films made by Obie.

All of Obie's films to date had used models, even for the human characters, but in the autumn of 1917, during the last few months that Obie was at the company, he took another very important step forward. His final job was to design and animate a series of shorts called *Mickey's Naughty Nightmares* [aka *Nippy's Nightmares*], for which he used a live-action boy in conjunction with his animated models. The boy and the animation were filmed separately and then cut together and so did not appear in the same frame. Even so, the film anticipated the future of the art, combining animated models and live actors in a way which allowed them to interact with each other.

Because of the cutbacks Obie soon found himself without a job and left New York to return to Oakland where he reflected on what he had accomplished. The Edison films had demonstrated the potential of model animation but they were all light-hearted comedies. What Obie really wanted to do was drop the comedy and make films that 'starred' dinosaurs, rather than films that featured them. His chance came in 1918 when another model animator and sculptor, Major Herbert M. Dawley, who had been impressed with Obie's films for Edison, contacted him to ask if he would like to participate in a possible project. Dawley's experimentations in animation had been much cruder than Obie's but Obie thought that at least he would be working with someone who had an idea of what animation was all about. Dawley gave him a three-month contract and so Obie returned to New York to work in Dawley's New Jersey studio in Chatham. The project that materialized there was based on an idea Obie had had for some time, which they called *The Ghost of Slumber Mountain* (1919).

The film is a fantasy adventure which starts with Jack Holmes (played by Dawley) telling his nephews a story that begins with his ascent of Slumber Mountain. During the climb he and a companion come across a cabin which had been the home of a long-deceased hermit affectionately called Mad Dick (who Darlyne always claimed was definitely played by Obie). The mysterious cabin is 'filled with bones and books about prehistoric animals' to quote the on-screen caption. That same evening Jack falls asleep and dreams that he meets Mad Dick who reveals to him, with the aid of a magical box-shaped telescope, life on the mountain forty

million years ago. Jack is able to see a brontosaurus walking into a lake (the water was gelatine), a huge bird known as a diatrmya preening its feathers and eating a snake, two triceratops locking horns and finally a fight between a triceratops and what looks like an allosaurus, which ends in the death of the triceratops. Breaking away from eating his prey the allosaurus looks directly at Jack and then chases him. Jack manages to fire several shots with his pistol (the creature is seen bleeding from a gunshot wound, making it the first dinosaur to be shot by modern man although it would be by no means the last) but it still keeps coming. Just as the creature catches up with him and is about to devour him, Jack wakes up. A simple story but one that adequately accomplished what Obie had always wanted, to combine live action with model animation in a dramatic way, although the final step of combining both in the same frame was yet to be taken.

Dawley advanced Obie $3,000 for the proposed 25-minute project and for the next three months Obie again worked as writer, designer, modeller, painter, animator, photographer and director, occasionally assisted, we believe, by Dawley. To ensure authenticity Obie based the designs of the dinosaurs on concepts by Charles Robert Knight, some of which were displayed at the American Museum of Natural History in New York, where Obie had seen them when he was working at the Edison studio. Knight had been the first artist to try to portray dinosaurs as they might actually have looked in the flesh, basing his pictures on their fossilized remains. His stunning and vibrant artwork would continue to be a major influence on Obie's subsequent pictures, including *King Kong*, and on the work of a long line of other model animators, including Ray. When Obie returned to the east coast to work on *The Ghost of Slumber Mountain* he met Knight in order to discuss how his models should look and the artist recommended Dr Barnum Brown, the resident vertebrate palaeontologist at the American Museum of Natural History, as a source of information and advice. It was Brown who advised Obie on how to plan the anatomy, movements and characteristics of the prehistoric creatures featured in the film.

Obie was continually trying to improve the construction of his models and he had realized, during the making of the Edison films, that the metal ball-and-socket armatures solved the problem of building models that were flexible while remaining rigid enough to hold a pose during animation. So he used them again in the models for the new film, covering them with layers of cotton wool and rubber to build up the models' muscles and give them texture and detail. Along with the featured dinosaurs – an allosaurus, two triceratops, the dymtryx and a brontosaurus – Obie also built several others, including a tyrannosaurus rex, a baryonyx and a stegosaurus. Although he did photograph several scenes featuring these latter models, none appeared in the final film because it was Dawley's opinion that audiences would become bored with too much animation!

The animation contained in the brief dinosaur sequences is often jerky, sometimes static and erratic but always inventive. It included some of the trademark scenes that would be repeated in future films featuring dinosaur animation. There is, for example a scene showing the triceraptops and the allosaurus manoeuvring for position before their fight, and another in which the allosaurus licks its lips after feasting on its prey. In addition there is a scene which features a triceratops looking off camera to the left and this is followed by the camera panning to the left to reveal another triceratops. The remarkable thing is that the first triceratops is still being animated as the camera pans. This was a notable innovation on Obie's part and illustrates his continuing passion for experimentation.

When completed, *The Ghost of Slumber Mountain* was sold by Dawley to World Cinema Distributing Company and thanks to its originality – 'living' dinosaurs were a fascinating novelty for the cinema-going public – it was an enormous success, equivalent to one of today's blockbusters. The film was seen by no less than half a million people during its Broadway engagement and grossed an incredible $100,000. All of which should have given model animated films, and certainly Obie, an immense boost when it came to financing similar projects. However, following the New York premiere, Obie's name was eliminated from all the publicity material and Dawley took all the kudos resulting from its success; his screen credit read, 'Produced by Herbert M. Dawley' which suggested, in the absence of Obie's name, that the film had been conceived and made entirely by Dawley, much to Obie's frustration and anger.

In an article, 'Making Actors of Prehistoric Animals' by Charles W. Person, which appeared in *Illustrated World* dated November 1919 Dawley

LEFT
Six frames from *The Ghost of Slumber Mountain*.

Top, from left to right. Herbert Dawley, playing Jack, looks at one of the dinosaur model (probably made by O'Brien) in the cabin of the dead Mad Dick, the hermit; two frames showing Jack being confronted accusingly by the ghost of Mad Dick (played by O'Brien in a long white wig and beard).

Bottom, from left to right. The triceratops; the allosaurus; the allosaurus and the triceratops fighting to the death.

TOP LEFT
An advertisment in *The Moving Picture World* magazine dated 5 April 1919 for *The Ghost of Slumber Mountain* in which the distributor, World Pictures, proudly announce it as 'The Greatest Triumph of the Motion Picture' and indeed it was. Note that it is only Herbert Dawley's name that appears so that the phrase 'But he accomplished the impossible' would suggest that it only refers to Dawley.

TOP RIGHT
The brontosaurus that is only briefly seen in *The Ghost of Slumber Mountain*.

ABOVE
Herbert Dawley who appears as Jack in the opening scenes of *The Ghost of Slumber Mountain*.

appears to take all the credit for the concept as well as the construction and animation of the creatures. Nowhere in the article is Obie's name mentioned and it is clear that Dawley was the writer's only source. The article claims that:

> *He [Dawley] laid in a supply of lumber, cloth, paint, clay and other materials with which to construct his million-year old animals. He first prepared a rugged wooden skeleton, finished it off with a covering of clay to express the muscles, tendons and bones of the living animal, and over this placed a skin-like covering of cloth painted a dark brown color. After building several animals - one of them seventeen feet high - he was ready to make them act for the camera.*

It seems unlikely that the journalist would have included so many inaccuracies – wooden skeletons, clay and cloth coverings, a model seventeen feet high – unless he had been quoting directly from Dawley. The article goes on,

> *In order to make the film a success it was necessary to have his creatures move about from one place to another, raise their ponderous legs, lift their heads, open their mouths, swish their tails, and even amble through mud and water! How did he make them do this? The answer is evident to every student of the motion-picture laboratory methods. By utilizing what is technically known as the motion-stop process – so laborious and time-consuming that it is practically abandoned in these days of quick production – he made thousands of exposures of his animals in thousands of different attitudes, with the result that when the film was run through the projecting machine it gave the impression that these wood, clay and cloth figures were actual animals, alive and moving.*

Although the basic principle of stop-motion [not motion-stop] is correctly described the author, or more likely Dawley, again veered off into fantasy when explaining how the models were animated:

> *In addition to placing the legs in the proper posture each time an exposure was made, he had to change the position of the neck, the trunk, and the tail each time a new step was taken. This is comparatively easy to do when the model is small, but when it is seventeen feet high, it requires an effort and patience that few men would care to exercise.*

The article concludes: 'Mr Dawley was able to take something like twenty feet of film a day - that is, on days he worked hard and consistently.'

Without Obie's input (although Obie may well have executed designs for the models) Dawley made a follow up picture called *Along the Moonbeam Trail*, which was released in 1920. The story told of two small boys who have a strange dream in which a pterodactyl chases them to another plane where they see the Earth as it was ten million years ago. There they encounter various other prehistoric creatures, a tyrannosaurus rex, a stegosaurus and a trachodon. For many years it was alleged that Dawley used Obie's unused animation cut from *The Ghost of Slumber Mountain* but photos published to coincide with the release of *Along the Moonbeam Trail* suggest that the film may have been entirely Dawley's own work. They show him posed beside a model, apparently about to animate it, and opening a mould that contains what appears to be a model baryonyx (Obie at this time wasn't using the casting process as depicted in the Dawley photo although as a sculptor Dawley may well have used this method). Although these are likely to be publicity stills taken specifically to promote the film new evidence has come to light that Dawley may well have animated the models himself.[4]

By the time the offensive *Illustrated World* article was published Obie was beyond either frustration or anger; he was simply disappointed and dejected. He didn't pursue the matter as far as we are aware, perhaps because the prospect of legal fees was as daunting then as it would be to anyone faced with the same dilemma today. Or perhaps it was because he didn't like confrontation. He was a gentle man, prone to taking the easy way out and causing as little fuss as possible. Either way, in the not to distant future he would come to regret that decision.

It would seem to have been a simple matter for Obie to prove that he had played a part in the development of model animation prior to meeting Dawley and that he had worked on the *The Ghost of Slumber Mountain.* Of course, we know nothing of Dawley's side of the case, and whatever the truth of what happened between the two men, it is now lost to us. We are only able to tell the story based on what we know about Obie the man, the film itself (there is a lot of Obie in the animation), the recollections of Darlyne O'Brien and of people who had worked with Obie, such as Ray. But based on the evidence we have, such as it is, it is no wonder Obie never really got over what Dawley had done to him. Darlyne O'Brien told Don Shay in 1963, 'Obie was very bitter towards Mr Herbert Dawley for having tried to take credit for his work.' Ray, too, is adamant that Obie was a bitter man when it came to discussing *The Ghost of Slumber Mountain,* which he was always very reluctant to do. However, one thing is not in dispute, Dawley did commission Obie to make *The Ghost of Slumber Mountain* and it was that film that not only allowed him to further develop his art but also gave him his breakthrough into feature films. Without *The Ghost of Slumber Mountain* there might never have been a *Kong,* at least not the *Kong* we know.

The next few years saw Obie continuing to refine and improve his animation techniques and the accompanying visual aids (miniature sets, glass paintings etc), refinements that would allow his creations more and more realism. However, he still had that ongoing dream – to combine his models with live-action in the same frame. All his preparation would lead him to a project that would set the seal on how all three-dimensional animation feature films would be produced for the next twenty-five years. All he needed was to find someone who could share his vision and finance such a project. And in 1919 such a man was near at hand.

In 1919 Obie went to work with Watterson R. Rothacker who was the West Coast manager of the entertainment magazine *Billboard* and founder of the Industrial Motion Picture Company. Rothacker had seen Obie's early shorts and also *The Ghost of Slumber Mountain* and had been very impressed and, through his association with *Billboard,* was aware of Obie's problems with Dawley. Rothacker made a press announcement in August 1919, which not only recognized Obie's achievements but took a side swipe at Dawley in the process. Referring to *The Ghost of Slumber Mountain* , the announcement read, 'When this picture was presented at The Strand (New York), Mr O'Brien was given full credit for its production, but since then an attempt has been made to create the impression that the work was done by him [Dawley], which, of course, is contrary to the facts in the case. Mr O'Brien is constantly improving his unique process, which *we control.*'

Ever since its publication in 1912, Obie had been obsessed with an adventure novel written by Sir Arthur Conan Doyle called *The Lost World.* Doyle's story told of a group or explorers, led by Professor Challenger, who discover a lost plateau in the South American rain forests, which is inhabited by dinosaurs. On their return to London they exhibit a pterodactyl, which escapes and terrorizes the city. The story, especially the final section, was so original in 1912 that it caused a sensation. Nearly a century after its publication the idea of a prehistoric animal at liberty in a modern city has been copied in numerous movies, perhaps because there is something visually fascinating to film-makers about a dinosaur running amok in a well ordered city. It seemed to Obie as though it had been written with his work in mind.

Ostensibly, Obie was contracted to make a series of stop-motion shorts and did start work on preparing a number of 'novelty pictures' although none were ever put before a camera. But Obie had in mind a much more ambitious project. He knew that Rothacker controlled the rights to film all of Conan Doyle's literary work, including *The Lost World,* and he soon set about persuading his new employer that he could film the story using animated dinosaurs. Obie was a fine artist and possessed a unique ability to visualize cinematic scenes on paper, so he worked on a number of drawings and sketches illustrating key episodes from the novel and also made a test sequence with an allosaur fighting a brontosaurus on the edge of the plateau. Obie was also aware that he would need to combine live action with model animation in order to deliver the all-important illusion of reality to the improbable story. He proposed to achieve this primarily by means of mattes. A matte is basically a mask that allows an area in each frame of film to remain unexposed, the film can then be run through the camera for a second time, with the previously exposed part of the frame masked by a counter-matte, so that two different subjects appear in the same frame. This technique had been used by film-makers as far back as the 1890s and Méliès himself had made use of it in several of his films. The process had also been utilized in several landmark American films, perhaps most famously in Edwin S. Porter's *The Great Train Robbery* (1903). Obie intended to use mattes to 'insert' human actors into his prehistoric settings so that they would appear to be interacting directly with his animated dinosaurs. Over the following years this process would be refined and improved and in *King Kong* whole areas were masked off to allow the tiny humans to interact with Kong and the other creatures in the film.

Armed with all these elements Obie presented his idea to Rothacker who gave it his immediate and very enthusiastic approval. The courage it took to make such a decision should not be underrated. To embark upon a project that 'starred' dinosaurs using a process that had only been tested on short films was, at the time, a daring and innovative move by both Obie and Rothacker. The next move was for Rothacker to approach First National Pictures to co-finance and produce the project; with the help of Obie's artwork and other preparations that showed how it could all be done, he rapidly got the go-ahead for the production to begin.

The Lost World was to be photographed at First National's Brunton Studios in Burbank, California with Earl J. Hudson in charge of production and it was to be directed by Harry Hoyt. The stars, apart from the dinosaurs, were Wallace Beery, Bessie Love, and Lewis Stone, Lloyd Hughes and Arthur Hoty. In his small studio away from the main stages, Obie began work on designing the effects, working with Fred W. Jackson (the head of the studio's special effects department) and with Ralph Hammeras and Marcel Delgado. Hammeras had been employed by Earl Hudson as a matte painter and was to work on the matte paintings, glass paintings and miniature sets. In an interview in *Cinefex* edited by Don Shay in January 1984, Hammeras recalls,

> *Mr Hudson told me that he had a man by the name of Willis O'Brien, who did the most unusual things – like making prehistoric animals come to life on the screen. He said he thought that we would make a good combination in working on a picture he was going to make called* The Lost World. *The next day, I met O'Brien for the first time. Mr Hudson told us to get together. For the next two weeks, O'Brien showed me film clips of tests he had made and also explained how he constructed his prehistoric animals – the precision machine work so he could animate the anatomy, the football bladder he used for making it breathe and the material for the skin texture. He was definitely a pioneer in what he was doing.*

In 1919 and early 1920 Obie had attended sculpture classes at the Otis Art Institute (now the Otis College of Art and Design) in Los Angeles,

First National Pictures Inc. presents
The Lost World
Sir Arthur Conan Doyles
stupendous story
By arrangement with
Watterson R. Rothacker
Research and technical director
Willis H. O'Brien
With
Bessie Love
Lewis Stone
Wallace Beery
Lloyd Hughes
FIRST NATIONAL PICTURES
A First National Picture

shortly after it had opened to students. It was there that he met the twenty-year-old Mexican Marcel Delgado who was working by day in a grocery shop but studying in the evening to be a sculptor. Obie realized this young man was extremely talented and asked if he would like to work in motion pictures, to which Delgado said no, he wanted to be an artist. But Obie knew his man and asked Delgado to visit the studio. Once there, the sculptor was smitten and accepted Obie's offer, so beginning an association that would last for over twenty-five years. Delgado recalled that, 'I had the studio room all to myself – a beautiful studio room all decorated with Charles Knight drawings on the walls and statues that O'Brien [had] made…'.[5]

In all, the pre-production, which involved experiments on effects scenes, mattes and the models, took two years. Live-action photography all took place in the studio and was closely overseen by Obie to ensure that it would match up with the animation scenes when the two were combined.

The Lost World featured a wide range of prehistoric creatures all of which were based on Charles Knight's paintings. They included allosaurs, a baryonyx, a brontosaurus, anchiceratops, pterodactyls and triceratops along with other prehistoric species. A total of fifty models were utilized in the film (a huge number, both then and now) most of which averaged twenty inches in length although that figure also includes smaller models that were used for long shots. Some of the publicity stills also feature creatures that do not appear in the final cut, or at least, what is left of it today (there has been substantial restoration of the film in recent years but the full release print is still lost to us). We can only assume that these were either not used or were cut from the final release print. Perhaps First National thought, like Dawley, that the public could only take in so much animation.

Before Delgado began work on the models Obie designed more technically advanced ball-and-socket armatures made of aluminium, which improved on his previous designs, allowing for smoother animation and better rigidity during photography. Delgado made clay models of the main creatures based on Obie's drawings to work from and began to construct the bodies on the armatures. He started by placing rough rubber muscles on various parts of the armature (if a bladder was to be used this would of course be inserted first) which would stretch and change shape realistically when the joints were moved to different positions. He then stuffed the metal ribcage and the outer area of the armature with cotton, forming the basic shape of the animal which was then covered in latex rubber. Finally,

PREVIOUS SPREAD
The very impressive poster for *The Lost World* (1925). It portrays an allosaurus rampaging through a city, rather than a brontosaurus as in the film, but the impression of size and the promise of cinematic spectacle are both enhanced by the use of a carnivorous beast.

LEFT
A rare photograph of O'Brien working on *The Lost World*. It shows him moving what appears to be either a centrosaurus or a monoclonius in a miniature set.

ABOVE LEFT
The lakeside scene in *The Lost World* showing a group of brontosaurus in the foreground.

ABOVE RIGHT
Two technicians (sadly we have been unable to identify them but the blurred image on the left might be O'Brien) working through an animation access slot that was normally hidden by the camera's perspective and the miniature foliage.

the models were painted in colours that would 'reflect' best in black and white photography. Although relatively crude by today's standards the models were state of the art in the early 1920s and today still have a quality of innocence and charm. Further refinements, apart from the bladders that enabled some of them to 'breath', were a varnish which Obie used to make them appear to salivate, dark chocolate for blood (remember it was black and white) and the extensive use of aerial wires, which allowed the pterodactyls to fly and other creatures to leap into the air. Delgado worked on maintaining the models throughout the animation: 'During the course of production, after the days work was over, these puppets had to be restored, groomed, repaired if broken. They had to be in perfect condition for the next day. Many times they were torn down completely to overhaul the steel skeleton when it was worn out. This happened frequently and it was quite a chore to maintain them in animating condition.'[6]

Following the completion of the film some of the models were donated to the Museum of Arts and Sciences at Exposition Park in Los Angeles where they were exhibited for several years. In the 1930s a young, very impressionable lad called Ray Harryhausen haunted the museum, always visiting the basement room, which was devoted to film-making. In that magical room were displayed artwork and the test footage from *Creation* (1930/1) together with clips and artwork from *King Kong* (1933) and an eighteen-inch wood carving of Kong which, rather bizarrely, held a carved daisy in one of its hands. Obie had had the latter made as a lighting stand-in for the latex model. Ray also recalls a miniature military airplane (he doesn't know what it was from although we do know that it wasn't one of those used at the end of *King Kong*, so it may have been for the doomed *Creation*), which was clearly marked as being donated by Willis O'Brien. There was also a big black book that Obie had had made up of hand tests from *Son of Kong*. However, the stars of the exhibition were the armatured models featured in *The Lost World*. Ray remembers marvelling at the brontosaurus that had terrified London and what looked like a styracosaurus. Eventually the models deteriorated to a point where they had to be withdrawn and stored. Many years later, when a new wing was added to the museum, the remains of the models were accidentally walled up between the old building and the new. In recent years Ray revisited the museum and the staff showed him several reclaimed models which had been rescued from incarceration. Ray inspected an allosaurus and a triceratops although, as he pointed out at the time, he didn't remember these as ones that he had seen on exhibition. So perhaps somewhere, deep in the walls of the museum, rest the crumbling remains of the models from *The Lost World*. What a time capsule!

The miniature sets constructed by Hammeras and his crew were mostly about six feet across by five feet deep, and approximately three and half feet from the ground to allow Obie ease of access to the models. Hammeras recalled that, 'The miniature sets also had to be built shallow in depth, so that O'Brien could reach into the set without disturbing any of the foliage while animating.'[7] Other sets were built which could be accessed from the side or below, which involved incorporating a hill or other landscape feature that would hide a slot through which Obie could reach to the very back of the set or animate a model from the side away from the camera. The miniature set for the eruption of the volcano, in which dozens of prehistoric creatures flee the conflagration, was a massive seventy-five by one hundred and fifty feet. Again, impressive even by today's standards. Lighting the miniature sets was a particular problem.

Obie used a bank of Cooper-Hewitt mercury vapour lights suspended five or six feet above the sets, which supplied a steady illumination without any flickering. Hammeras recalled that after the lights were installed, '…we sowed Red Top grass seed wherever grass was called for. This was a low-growing variety, and in about ten days it would be full-grown.'[8] These miniature sets where then boxed in by Hammeras and his crew: 'A wall was put all around to keep anybody from disturbing the concentration O'Brien needed so that he could remember every move he made of the feet, neck or head of his dinosaurs.'[9] Although the walls helped Obie to concentrate Delgado also suggested that he wanted to 'keep the process secret'.[10]

Although he would later use a form of peg board covered by foam rubber to ensure that the models were firmly fixed in place during photography, for this film Obie carefully worked out the direction and length of each step a creature would take then pre-drilled holes in the animation table. These holes were plugged and when the model's foot, or claw, needed to come down he would remove the plug and insert a bolt which was screwed into a threaded hole in the base of the foot. This had been the method he had used for most, if not all, of his previous films.

Unlike sound film, 35mm silent film was usually projected at a rate of sixteen frames per second or sixty feet per minute. This meant that Obie had to shoot 960 frames to produce one minute of screen time and, working up to thirteen hours a day, he was only able to achieve a maximum of 35 feet a day (480 frames), which would last a little over thirty seconds on-screen. Ralph Hammeras again recalls, 'At the end of the day's shooting, he [Obie] would come with about thirty-five feet of film. Of course, that varied a bit because the amount of footage he was able to shoot in a day depended upon the number of characters in the scene and how difficult the action was. Most of the finished shots were about a hundred feet long.'

Nothing like it had been seen before. Obie was on new and untried ground but he knew it could be done. Considering the film is over eighty years old, the standard of animation is excellent although some movements do seem a little crude and there are times when the models 'pause' at the beginning and end of a scene as though waiting for further instructions. Obie did most of the animation himself although he was assisted by several other technicians, including Hammeras or Delgado, when there were multiple models involved, such as in the sequence in which the creatures flee from the erupting volcano. In an interview in 1973 with Don Shay, Delgado mentioned the name of William, or Bill, Fox whom he thought had also assisted with animation; unfortunately there is no record of such a man. We do, however, know the name of another animator, Joseph Leeland Roop He is little known today, even by experts and enthusiasts, but some basic notes, scrapbooks and photographs survive in the Natural History Museum of Los Angeles County which give us some insight into his background and his involvement on *The Lost World* (see Chapter 2). We know, for example, that he probably animated, at least in part, sequences that featured the baryonyx. Sad to say, it is these scenes that seem the crudest and certainly not nearly as good as the fight between the allosaurus and the brontosaurus, which we do know was animated by Obie.

The first creature we see in the film is a crudely animated pterodactyl, which glides, not flies, over the plateau carrying a dead animal in its beak. In long shot, it lands on the pinnacle of rock (a miniature section of a glass painting by Ralph Hammeras) near the edge of the plateau. The pterodactyl model is a touch too large in proportion to the surrounding landscape but when seen in close-up (Obie would have used a larger model) the detail is excellent.

Once the adventurers are on the plateau a grazing brontosaurus is seen which then turns and plods off to investigate the newly arrived humans. The model used in this scene was perhaps 20 inches in length and about 10 inches high, but a smaller model (approximately 3 inches high and 8 inches long with a basic ball-and-socket armature, designed to match the scale of the miniature set), was used for the scene of the same creature at the edge of the plateau looking at the log bridge. The explorers are trapped when the brontosaurus takes a dislike to the log and pushes it over the edge. The log was animated on aerial wires so that it appears to plummet down the side of the miniature set and into the jungle below.

The next key scene is a fight between an allosaurus and a baryonyx (a duck-billed or crocodile-headed dinosaur), both carnivorous species. Although Obie's allosaurus is somewhat taller and lankier than we now perceive them to have been the design is still impressive. The allosaurus manages to kill the baryonyx by biting its neck and blood – in reality thick, dark chocolate – begins to flow from the wound. Throughout the battle we can see both creatures 'breathing', which had to be animated in addition to the action itself, but as already mentioned the style and movements are not perhaps the best in the film.

For both of us the next scene, showing a triceratops defending her offspring when another allosaurus attacks, is one of the best in the film. Obie animated the action in which the mother pushes her baby out of harm's way whilst she takes on the aggressor. The push with her snout is tender and protective and is a good example of the way in which Obie managed on occasions to give his creatures real character.

RIGHT
Selected images from *The Lost World* (1925).

Top row, from left to right. Clapperboard showing that the animation for scene 636 was to be done by Joseph Roop. Clapperboard, again for take 636, but this time showing that the animator was to be Willis O'Brien. An allosaurus attacking a baryonyx, watched by two brontosaurus, possibly mother and young.

Second row, left to right. Publicity still showing a brontosaurus and in the lower left Wallace Beery, Arthur Hoyt, Lewis Stone and Bessie Love. The allosaurus attacking the explorer's camp. Allosurus with the 'burning' log in its mouth.

Third row, left to right. An allosaurus attacking a triceratops. A triceratops fatally injuring an allosaurus and another allosaurus getting the better of a baby triceratops, note the edge of the miniature sets in both pictures. An allosaurus in a miniature set threatens the explorers. This latter picture was either a missing scene from the film (as are the last two images) or a publicity photograph.

Bottom row, left to right. A close-up of the brontosaurus snarling. A close-up of the allosaurus snarling. The brontosaurus begins to fall over the cliff watched by the allosaurus.

LOST WORLD
JacKman — O'Brien
SCENE ROOP TAKE
636
1

LOST WORLD
JacKman, OBrien.
SCENE TAKE
636
Take
Evans
2
I

In following scenes we see what appears to be another allosaurus attacking the explorers' camp at night. The wide establishing shot shows a clear static matte line below which the actors are sitting beside a fire and above which we see the allosaurus and miniature jungle set. For the second time in movie history men shoot at a dinosaur, wounding it in its snout and drawing blood. This, quite understandably, infuriates the creature. In another attempt to frighten it off, one of the explorers grabs a flaming log from the fire and throws it at the beast, which catches it in its mouth. The man is seen throwing the log in a medium shot and the scene then cuts to the allosaurus with the log in its mouth. We believe the log in the animated shot was a tiny miniature with pointed pieces of metal, resembling flames, fixed to either end. These minuscule pieces of metal, which were animated along with the allosaurus, simulate flickering flames. The whole idea of having the flaming log caught by the dinosaur is such an ingenious touch that it is likely that it was conceived by Obie who wanted his animated dinosaurs to appear to interact with the humans. The image of the allosaurus towering over the group around the campfire, which must have seemed quite sensational in 1925, was a trick that Obie would use many times in the future.

In subsequent scenes we see three triceratops, one of which is attacked and killed by another allosaurus that leaps onto its back. The leap, of course, was accomplished with the aid of aerial wires. Then, as it feasts on the dead triceratops, the allosaurus manages to catch a passing pterodactyl which is rash enough to venture too close. This latter action comes as a complete surprise to the audience, as was intended. Obie, like Ray, revelled in surprising his audience.

In the next scene Wallace Beery and Arthur Hoty appear in the foreground looking at a grazing brontosaurus in the distance. Ray surmises that this scene, and perhaps other similar ones, were filmed in the following manner. The lower part of the set, on which the actors performed, would have been built on the back-lot and the brontosaurus, surrounded by its miniature set, placed in front of it. To film the live action they would have turned off the lights on the miniature set and shot the live actors who would have been shown by the director, or more likely Obie, how to mime their reactions to the creature. When the live action was complete they would have run the film back, darkened the full-size set and illuminated the miniature one, and then animated the model's reactions to the actors. Although it would have taken two or three days this ingenious perspective photography would have been worth the effort.

Next comes what is, as already mentioned, one of the movie's classic scenes – the fight between an allosaurus and a brontosaurus on the edge of the plateau. We see close-ups of both creatures, their mouths curling in aggressive snarls (achieved by means of wires in the mouths of the models) and their teeth bared. This is another touch that is pure Obie. Showing the close-ups of the beasts, snarling like boxers at the start of a fight, was one of the ways in which he could provide them with a degree of personality. In this scene there are several other Obie tricks. He applied rubber cement to the mouths as he was animating to make it look like saliva and the creatures' tails whip and curl to indicate anger and defiance. The way in which the creatures circle each other, manoeuvring for a position from which to attack, also illustrates how Obie drew upon his knowledge of boxing. The only weakness in the scene is the lack of movement in the body of the brontosaurus, which sometimes remains static while the neck alone moves, a compromise that was presumably adopted in order to save the amount of time taken in animation. The fight ends with the poor old brontosaurus falling over the edge of the plateau and plunging down into a lake of mud. The whole scene from start to finish is extremely dramatic, even by today's standards, and must have greatly impressed audiences, which included a five-year-old Ray Harryhausen. It is his favourite scene in the film.

There is one other scene that is nothing short of spectacular, especially when viewed on a large screen. During the eruption of the plateau's volcano we are treated to a wide shot showing a plain full of herds of fleeing dinosaurs, including stegosaurus and triceratops. Although the models' movements are basic there is so much animation that it seems inconceivable that there isn't any split-screen trickery, but there

BELOW LEFT
The impressive stampede of the dinosaurs after the volcano has erupted in *The Lost World*. If you look carefully it is evident that there are far more creatures in the frame than the group of triceratops in the foreground.

BELOW RIGHT
The brontosaurus terrifies London. Ray saw this model in a diorama in the Museum of Arts and Sciences at Exposition Park in Los Angeles.

RIGHT
A diagram from the patent application for a 'composite picture' setup, which O'Brien lodged with the US patent office in 1928 and which was officially patented on 14 February 1933.

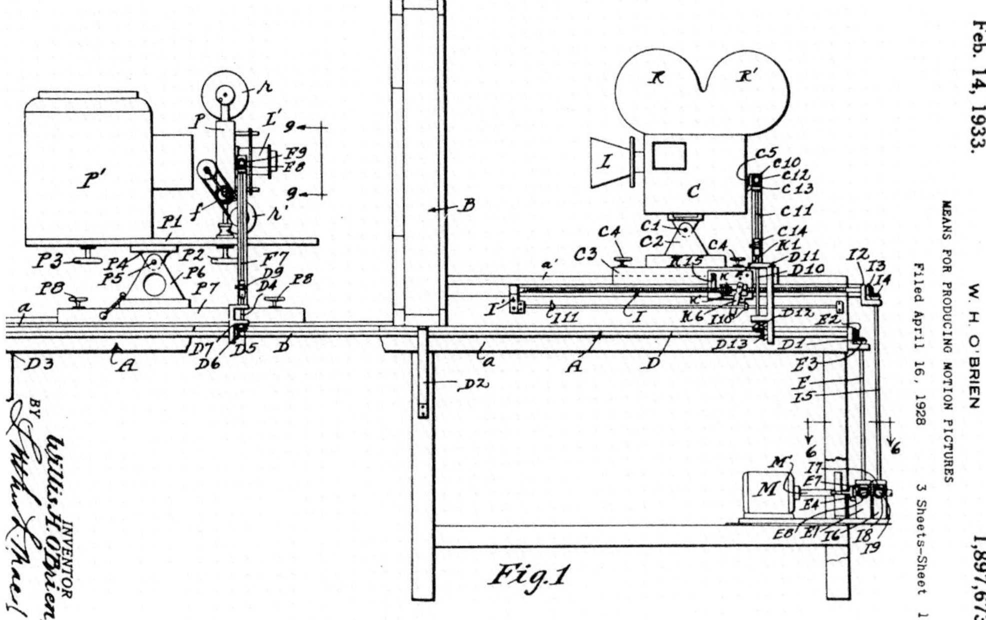

isn't. In another, slightly later, scene there are at least eight or nine models, all moving around a lake (made of mirrored glass). To produce these sequences Obie and his team would have accessed the miniature set from below by means of the slots in the animation table, which would have been just large enough to allow the animators to pop up and make adjustments to the models for the next frame. Miniature trees and small hills in the set disguised these access slots.

The finale of the film departs from the story in Doyle's novel. In the book Doyle had a young pterodactyl escape from the Queen's Hall where Professor Challenger is presenting his findings to his scientific colleagues, but in the film it is the brontosaurus, recovered from the mud lake and transported back to London, that escapes. Incidentally, in the building where the scientists meet we are shown a skeleton of a brontosaurus on exhibition and Ray remembers seeing that very same skeleton when he made a visit to the First National back-lot (which was taken over by Warner Bros), when he was about ten years old.

In the film, news of the brontosaurus' escape reaches Challenger during his presentation, following which he rushes off. We see the colossal beast calmly sauntering down various London streets with people fleeing in front of him(achieved by double printing); destroying a statue (the destruction was achieved by the use of aerial wires); pushing over the side of a building (again the crumbling sections of wall and falling bricks were all animated on wires) and falling through the roadway of Tower Bridge (it is Tower Bridge, not London Bridge). One has the feeling that Obie was in his element during the filming of these scenes, developing, sometimes for the first time, optical effects that allowed him to show the model brontosaurus and real people in the same frame; the only downside is that Obie neglected to put enough actions into the brontosaurus' tail, which gives the beast a rather dull and plodding appearance. That aside, the sequence is still spectacular and exciting.

Regrettably, the production of *The Lost World* was delayed by two hiccups. The first was due to Obie's old partner on *The Ghost of Slumber Mountain*, Herbert Dawley, who took out a lawsuit against Watterson Rothacker, threatening to sue him for $100,000 for infringement of patent rights, claiming that he had invented the basic design for the animated models they were using on *The Lost World*. In 1920 Dawley had patented a design for an animation model (which he had called an 'Articulated Effigy'), something that Obie had neglected to do. Dawley told the press that,

> *An employee of mine who learned the process by working in my office has been claiming, as employees sometimes do, that he did all the work and that the idea belongs to him and that sort of thing. I have received no notice whatsoever, before reading about it today, that it was contemplated to use my work in this fashion, and I shall certainly consult my lawyer at once and seek an injunction against the production of* The Lost World.

The 'employee' Dawley was referring to was, of course, Obie. It must have been a relatively easy matter to show, from the evidence of *The Dinosaur and the Missing Link* and the short films Obie had made for Edison, that Obie had been familiar with the stop-motion process and the use of armatured models before he became involved with Dawley. Faced by this irrefutable evidence, Dawley dropped the case, but not before production on *The Lost World* had been held up for a costly few weeks. Moreover, because neither he nor Obie had taken out a patent and to avoid any further problems, Rothacker decided to make a settlement with Dawley, the terms of which were never disclosed.

Little was heard of Dawley after that. His career as a film producer and animator appears to have ended in 1925 with a film called *Jack the Giant Killer*, perhaps because the film industry knew what he had done or because the settlement had been large enough to retire on. The last thing we know about Dawley is that he patented a stage effects technique which created 'supernatural spirits' live on stage in 1928, about the same time as he founded a theatre in Chatham, New Jersey, where he lived. But the effects of the lawsuit haunted Obie. Darlyne recalls that when he returned to California after completing *The Lost World*, 'He actually had to get affidavits from friends stating that he was the one who had done the work, in order to get a job.'[11]

The experience did, however, teach Obie a valuable lesson and when he invented a miniature rear-projection set-up he registered the details with the US patents office on 16 April 1928 and the process was subsequently utilized in *King Kong*. Obie also registered patents on four other 'Motion Picture' inventions – a 'Film Holder' in 1918, a 'Composite Picture' set-up in 1933, a 'Method of Producing Color Effects in Photography' in 1936 and finally, in 1950, a method, which is described in the patent as a means by which

> *a single model figure may be successively photographed in different aspects of animation or a series of separate models, each representative of a different aspect of animation, and may be successively photographed before a suitable*

background and set and in which the facial expression and animation of such facial expression may be provided without requiring any change of facial expression upon the model to be photographed.

In simple terms this means that Obie had come up with the idea of projecting facial expressions on to models. Although an interesting concept, it would have been impractical. This last patent was lodged by Obie but later assigned to producer Edward Nassour.

The second hold-up on *The Lost World* arose from financial problems at the production company, First National. The firm decided to close down most of its production on the West Coast and move everything to the old Biograph Studios in the Bronx, New York so Obie and all his crew had to up stakes and recommence filming on the other side of the country.

One of the tributes to Obie's superb work on the film came from Conan Doyle himself. During the production Rothacker had kept Doyle informed of the film's progress and in April 1922, following the completion of the animation of the fight between the allosaurus and the brontosaurus, Rothacker sent a reel of the footage to the author (who was then just preparing to set off for America to deliver a series of lectures on spiritualism, a subject that had come to fascinate him) to illustrate how they were bringing his dinosaurs 'alive'. Doyle was transfixed by what he saw, so much so that when he was invited by his friend Harry Houdini to attend a meeting of the Society of American Magicians in New York, he replied that he would be there but that he wanted to show the best of American magicians something that would make all their tricks seem tame. On the night, Doyle introduced the film by announcing, 'These pictures are not occult, but they are psychic because everything that emanates from the human brain is psychic.' No one in the audience, including a *New York Times* reporter, had any idea how the fantastic images were created and, knowing of Doyle's passion for the subject, assumed that they were seeing something produced from a spiritualist source. The newspaper announced next day that Doyle's '...monsters of the ancient world or the new world which he has discovered in the ether, were extraordinarily life-like. If fakes, they were masterpieces.' When Doyle saw the article he gave a press conference to explain exactly how the creatures had been 'given life'. Marvellous publicity for the film and a triumph for Obie.

After fourteen months of animation the $1,000,000, two-hour film was released in 1925 and from that point on the art of model animation would go from strength to strength. The film was a phenomenal success, due mainly to the real stars of the picture, the dinosaurs. Obie told Ray many years later that the screenwriter, Marian Fairfax, had approached him during his work on the animation and said that, in case the dinosaurs didn't work, she had written the screenplay in such a way that they could be left out! What is extraordinary about the story is that Fairfax was perfectly serious. To film *The Lost World* without the dinosaurs would have been like making *Gone with the Wind* without Scarlet O'Hara.

Obie's personal life and career were never easy, it was always either feast or famine, and although *The Lost World* was a box-office success and he received a good wage plus a bonus of $10,000 (which he spent in six months), the First National executives were extremely slow to realize the commercial potential of Obie's techniques, probably because they could only see the time and costs that had been involved. However, the studio did consider a number of new projects. The first was an untitled sequel to *The Lost World* (Ray thinks this might have been tentatively called *Return to The Lost World*) which production manager Earl Hudson announced late in 1925. Then in 1926 came a project provisionally titled *Atlantis* in which it was planned to include a sea serpent and a herd of mastodons. This was followed by an adaptation of H.G.Wells' *Food of the Gods*. Obie's pet project, though, was a film of Mary Shelley's *Frankenstein* which was proposed in 1928 and for which he planned to animate the monster, but *Frankenstein* and the other projects were all dropped for one reason or another and in 1930 Obie left First National when it was taken over by Warner Brothers.

Almost immediately he went over to RKO (Radio-Keith-Orpheum) Pictures to work on another idea of his, which had the working title of *Creation* and which was also earmarked to be directed by Harry Hoyt. The story tells of a yachting party and the crew of a Chilean submarine who are all shipwrecked by a typhoon on an island in the Pacific and subsequently discover that it is the remnant of a massive extinct volcano. The island has somehow preserved prehistoric life alongside evidence of a lost pre-Incan civilization. In essence it was another, although perhaps more sophisticated, version of *The Lost World*.

Obie, along with two of the studio artists, Byron L. Crabbe and Mario Larrinaga, worked on detailed drawings for the key sequences and linked these with intricate and precise storyboards so that no aspect of the film was left to chance. Obie had definite ideas as to how the fantasy locations in the film would look. He had photographic copies of a number of drawings by the nineteenth-century artist Gustave Doré, specifically from his works *Paradise Lost*, *The Bible* and *The Divine Comedy*. Obie had 'discovered' Doré whilst studying at the Otis Art Institute and thought his work extremely cinematic. Doré's paintings depicted fantastic landscapes in which features were dramatically illuminated, often against contrastingly sombre foregrounds and backgrounds. It was this combination of light, depth and fantasy that Obie was looking for when designing *Creation*. At the same time as he was collaborating with the studio artists he was also working with Delgado (who had left First National with Obie) on the design and construction of the models. The steel ball-and-socket armatures were machined at the studio to Obie's specifications and Delgado then filled out the interiors with layers of sponge and latex slowly sculpting the muscles and adding details like wrinkles and folds of skin. Their methods of modelling were becoming more lifelike and, along with the interior skeletons, more sophisticated and refined.

After nine months Obie and his crew shot two test sequences to show the front office what the picture might look like. The first was

LEFT

The cast and crew of *The Lost World* lined up outside Stage 6 at First National. It is difficult to identify anyone except Bessie Love (sitting left on the neck of the brontosaurus skeleton) and Leeland Roop who is standing fourth from left. But it is likely that O'Brien is in there somewhere.

ABOVE

Four drawings for *Creation*.

Top left. Sketches for the triceratops and what looks like a map, or a trail, showing various triceratops, probably drawn by O'Brien.

Top right. The drawing by Mario Larrinaga of the island on which the yacht and the submarine are shipwrecked.

Bottom left. A very dramatic image of an arsinotherium attacking the sailors.

Bottom, right. A mother triceratops and her young. This and the previous drawing were executed by Byron Crabbe and O'Brien.

a miniature yacht struggling to keep afloat amid the violence of the storm and the other, part of which still survives, shows one of the survivors of the shipwreck, a character called Hallett (played by Ralf Harolde), shooting a young triceratops and then being chased through the dense jungle by the mother. The test concluded with the huge triceratops pushing a tree trunk onto Hallett and then goring him to death. The sequence is an exciting taste of what might have been. Sadly, though, RKO was in financial trouble and productions were being halted and even cancelled throughout the studio. After a year of pre-production work, costing $120,000, Obie knew that *Creation* was in jeopardy.

In September 1931 a new executive, David O. Selznick, was appointed executive vice-president in charge of production in an effort to stave off bankruptcy. Realizing he would need help with the assignment Selznick asked Merian C. Cooper, a producer he had met whilst making *The Four Feathers* (1929), to sort out the studio's finances and production schedules, especially RKO's large investment in O'Brien's animation project. Cooper (or Coop as he was known) had been a World War I pilot, an adventurer and finally a film-maker whose films included *Grass* (1925), *Chang* (1927) and *The Four Feathers*, which had all been filmed in remote locations such as Russia, Persia, Siam, the Sudan and Portuguese East Africa.

Whilst making *The Four Feathers* it is said that Cooper became fascinated with gorillas and wanted to make a film about a real gorilla and giant Komodo dragons but nobody was interested because of the location costs. However, when Cooper looked over *Creation* and viewed the test reel, he dismissed the story and script, but was hugely impressed with Obie's

technical effects and it occurred to him that it might be possible to film his gorilla idea without incurring the huge expense of shipping crews out to Africa and other locations. He met with Obie and outlined his idea for a film about a huge ape and Obie responded by telling Cooper that he could make an ape do anything and appear as large as he wanted, just as he had done with the triceratops and the live actor in the test. Cooper was intrigued and asked Obie if he could produce a drawing of a huge ape attacking an explorer. It was at this moment that Obie knew that *Creation* was lost but he enthusiastically agreed to do what Cooper wanted. Working with studio artist Byron Crabbe, he made a preliminary sketch and then produced an oil painting, 'which depicted a half-naked cave woman and a modern clad explorer (complete with rifle and pith helmet) being menaced by a ferocious twenty-foot-tall gorilla. Obie painted the gorilla and left the rest to Crabbe.'[12] Obie wanted the picture to be cinematic and so showed the simian in an excessively aggressive pose – drooling and holding a large club-like branch.

Once again Cooper was impressed and sat down with director Ernest B. Schoedsack, with whom he had worked previously, to write a basic outline for the story. When both were satisfied with all the elements Cooper took the outline, along with the drawing and the test for *Creation*, to Selznick. Although slightly less

ABOVE
A black and white copy of the original colour painting by Willis O'Brien and Byron Crabbe of an early impression of Kong charging a hunter/explorer and a half-naked native girl. On the left Kong is brandishing a branch. Note how O'Brien perceived Kong as a mutant human/ape with vicious teeth and a drooling mouth.

TOP RIGHT
An atmospheric Doré-influenced drawing by Byron Crabbe and Willis O'Brien of the fight between Kong and the tyrannosaurus rex.

RIGHT
Drawings of the three artists - Willis O'Brien, Mario Larrinaga and Byron Crabbe - featured in *The Hollywood Reporter* souvenir brochure.

enthusiastic than Cooper, Selznick could see the originality of the dramatic adventure that Cooper and Schoedsack had sketched out as well as its box-office potential. Again, it is hard to imagine today just how original this project was in the early 1930s. Not even *The Lost World* had come anywhere near what was proposed for this production. Biting the bullet, Selznick gave Cooper the go-ahead to develop the storyline and film a suitable test reel, which Selznick would then present to the RKO New York executives.

Cooper, Schoedsack and British mystery writer Edgar Wallace (according to Cooper and Selznick, Wallace's contribution was minimal, if not non-existent, as he died of pneumonia in February 1932) sat down to write a treatment and to decide on a title for the project. Legend has it that Wallace suggested they call it 'King Ape' and although Cooper liked the 'King' element of the title he wasn't keen on calling something so large an ape. It was Cooper who came up with 'Kong', which in the language of East Indian natives, means gorilla. Some accounts credit the title to David Selznick but, although Cooper was notorious for trying to take the credit where little credit was due, it seems likely that in this case his claim was justified as Selznick doesn't mention this in any of his famous published memos. As the storyline was being gradually hammered out in script conferences (attended by Cooper, Schoedsack, Schoedsack's screenwriter wife Ruth Rose and Obie), Obie produced scores and scores of sketches and storyboards. In conversations with Val Warren in 1964, Darlyne O'Brien recounted how Obie worked:

Whenever Obie set up his drawing board he would pace the floor trying to come up with an idea. Most of the time he would be so tense and earnest that it was difficult for him to allow his mind to think as freely as he would have liked. Immediately he would have three of four drinks mixed with Schenley's, which would relax him and release the wildest imaginings of his creative mind. Thus, whenever anyone observing his work would ask him where he got all his ideas from, he would answer, 'Out of a bottle of Seagrams Bourbon.'[13]

Aside from dreaming up ideas and producing preliminary sketches he did very little work at home, 'He would lay out paintings and sketches but would finish them at the studio.'[14] Based on the preliminary sketches, Obie, Crabbe and Larrinaga would render beautifully detailed pre-production drawings of key or primary scenes. Larrinaga recalled the happy times he had working with Obie, 'Obie would stand back of us as we were painting and sing to us what we came later to adopt as a sort of theme song – "I'll Get By – As Long As I Have You!".'[15] It soon became apparent that two scenes stood out as best representing how the film would look as a whole. The first was a fight between Kong and a tyrannosaurus rex over a girl and the second was what would become known as the log sequence in which Kong shakes sailors from a huge tree that had fallen across a ravine. It was decided that both these scenes would be shot for the demonstration test reel. So Obie began to make plans.

Obie again showed everyone working on the production examples of Gustave Doré's artwork and whilst the backgrounds were being designed by Obie, Crabbe, Larrinaga and other artists - Ernest Smythe, Duncan Gleason, Leland Curtis and Jack Shaw – Delgado began work on designing non-armatured prototypes for Kong, the tyrannosaurus rex and the human figures. Obie told Ray a story about the design for Kong. Cooper had definite ideas about this and talked in great detail with Obie and Delgado. When he left, Obie told Delgado to build a model ape that was more human than ape. Delgado went away and came back with a design that had human elements but looked in essence like an ape, which pleased Obie. However, when Cooper saw the model he didn't like it at all and told Delgado that he wanted it more ape-like and more terrifying. The second prototype model was again rejected. In frustration Cooper sent a telegram to the Curator of Zoology at the Natural History Museum in New York asking for the dimensions of a male gorilla, the larger the better. The curator gave exact measurements and although these didn't establish the size of the gorilla for the film, the proportions were dictated by that telegram. At a subsequent meeting Obie was convinced that the gorilla should be more human than ape but Cooper insisted it must be more ape. Obie stormed off but came back after he had calmed down and told Delgado to produce what Cooper wanted. As a result the third prototype was much more ape than human (the most obvious concession to its

LEFT
Artwork for *King Kong*.

Top left. A drawing by O'Brien and Byron Crabbe showing Kong shaking the sailors from the log bridge. Note the depth: the foreground is dark and foreboding whilst the action is bathed in light. It's another good example of the Doré effect that O'Brien always insisted on.

Top right. A beautiful drawing by Mario Larrinaga of Kong crossing the log bridge with the girl.

Second row left. A drawing by Byron Crabbe that was one of those used by Merian Cooper to sell the idea of Kong to the RKO front office. It shows the sailors' boat being capsized by a submerged brontosaurus. In the final film the boat would be replaced by a raft constructed by the sailors.

Second row right. Kong breaks through the great gates, a drawing by an unknown studio artist.

Third row left. A drawing by Mario Larrinaga showing Kong fighting the elasmosaurus inside the cave.

Third row right. A preliminary sketch, we think by O'Brien, which was in Marcel Delgado's possession. It shows one of the spiders attacking a sailor who has fallen into the ravine.

Bottom left. A drawing by Byron Crabbe of Kong fighting the pteranodon.

Bottom right. A sketch/cartoon by O'Brien showing Kong and what looks like an allosaurus or a tyrannosaurus rex in the background.

TOP RIGHT
An exact copy of Kong's skull.

TOP FAR RIGHT
One of the internal metal armatures for Kong designed by O'Brien.

BOTTOM RIGHT
Victor and Marcel Delgado working on a full-scale Kong hand.

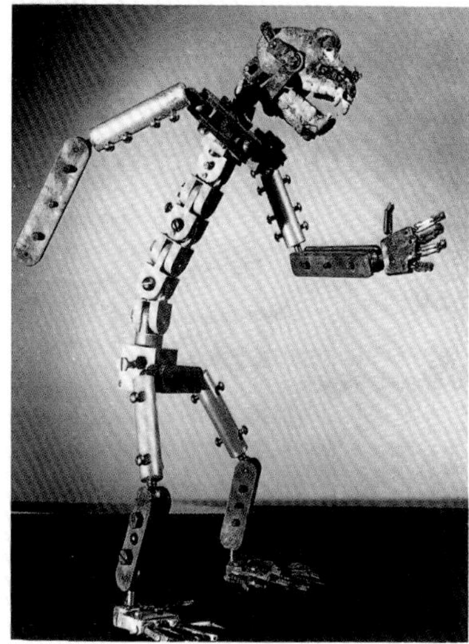

"KING KONG" AN RKO RADIO PICTURE

humanoid side was the paunch and rump) and to Obie's and Delgado's relief, it was accepted and it is this version that we see on the screen.

Obie's involvement with almost every aspect of the design and look of the film was considerable. He designed the smallest details of the metal armatures on which Delgado constructed the bodies. For *Kong* Delgado again used his own 'build-up method' of construction, which he had gradually improved since *The Lost World*. It still involved building up the musculature by means of sections of rubber but for the *Kong* dinosaurs he added warts and folds, which he cut from strips of rubber and then pasted on. Joined by his brother Victor, Delgado constructed two eighteen-inch high Kong models based on the prototype, each weighing almost ten pounds. The highly tempered steel armatures (again machined in the RKO workshops) were extremely detailed, allowing every part of Kong's body to be animated with precision, including all his tiny fingers and toes. His mouth could be opened and closed and his eyes could be made to blink. Finally, the models were covered in very fine rabbit fur that looked entirely realistic in relation to their size. That fur would cause Obie some sleepless nights. There is a story that when he received the first developed footage for the test he was horrified to see that, because his fingers had disturbed the creature's coat when he animated it, the fur appeared to move. Reportedly Obie was afraid that when the time came to screen the footage for Cooper he would be replaced for making such an obvious error. However, when Cooper saw the footage he was delighted to see how realistic the animation was and asked how Obie had managed to make the fur seem as if it was blowing in the breeze! Whether this story is true or not, the moving fur did become a feature of *King Kong* and added something to the creature's fantastic and distinctive personality.

Working on the animation with assistants Fred Reefe (a studio expert on mechanical devices who secured the models beneath the animation table) and E.B. Gibson, it took Obie nearly three months to film the two scenes. The test reel was then shown to studio executives, together with the triceratops scene from *Creation* and the key drawings of the other scenes that were planned. The reception was overwhelmingly favourable; so much so that the executives immediately gave the production the final green light allocating it the title *King Kong: The Eighth Wonder of the World* and the production number 601.

Work began immediately. In addition to the Kong models already constructed, there were small detailed human models, a brontosaurus, a triceratops, a pterandon, a stegosaurus, spiders and lizards (both for a pit sequence which was later cut from the final film), small birds and a variety of other prehistoric species. After testing the possibility of casting the models Obie decided to stick with the 'build-up' method because he felt that this gave him the best results. In each case Delgado would begin with a clay model of what he wanted and from that the armature would be designed and constructed. He then 'stuffed' and padded out the armature with sponge and cotton, which gave him the rough shape of the model required. He would then add rubber 'muscles' which would move with the articulated legs and head, giving the models' movements an even greater degree of realism. He then applied a 'skin' of liquid latex rubber, which he sculpted into details such as scales, wrinkles and folds of skin. These models were far more sophisticated and therefore far more liable to damage than those for either *The Lost World* or indeed *Creation*. Artist Mario Larrinaga, who had the dubious distinction of being 'Kong's personal make-up man', recalled, 'He [Kong] had to be retouched every night and put away in a safe place so that he would be ready to come on the scene early the next morning. You see, he got a lot of manhandling under the hot lights all day long.'[16]

When asked how he tackled animation Obie would say,' Experience is the only teacher. Each new set is an individual problem and requires separate treatment. There is no set rule or method by which you can classify all miniatures.' For most of the time there were just two people involved on the animation, Obie and his assistant E.B.'Buzz' Gibson, who had originally been an RKO studio grip but whom Obie trained in the art of animation. He had assisted and observed Obie whilst he was filming the fight with the tyrannosaurus rex for the test and later, when production was under way, Obie allowed him to

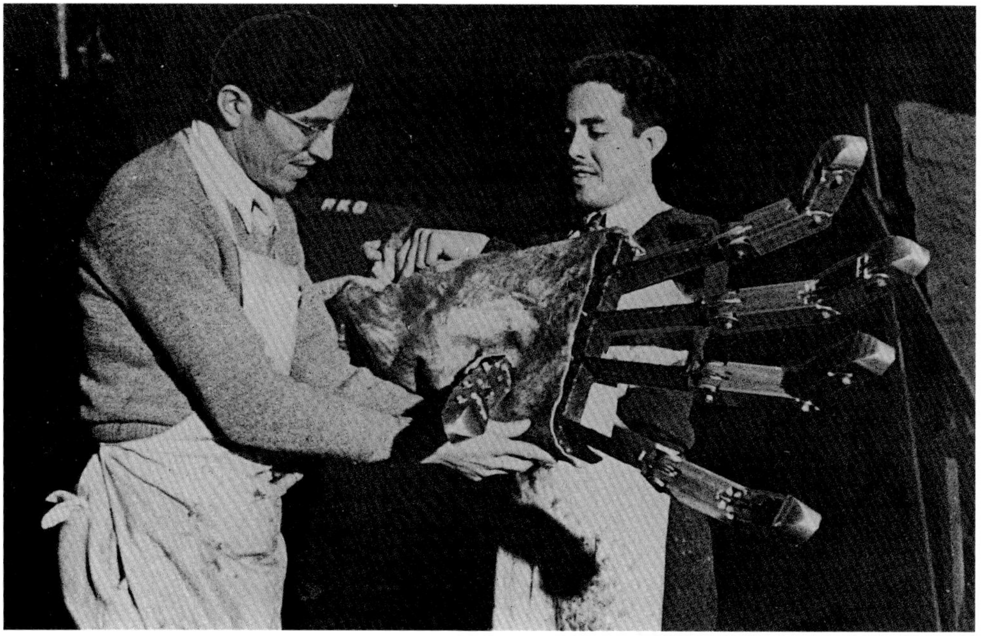

recreated in detail, and jungle settings on a tropical island. Mario Larrinaga and Byron Crabbe made the sketches and later painted the backings and glasses for the sets after the miniatures were drawn up and put to work. Besides these men, others were necessary for the actual working of the miniature.

This was typical of Obie in that he was always generous in giving credit where credit was due, perhaps because he remembered how Dawley had robbed him of the credit that was due to him all those years before.

All of the animation was executed on tabletop sets with bases made from two-inch pine. The surfaces of the tables were about three-quarters of an inch thick and drilled with a grid of eighth-inch holes to accommodate the pegs that were located in the feet of the models' metal armatures. When the pegs were secured with wires from below this gave the models the stability that was vital during animation. These holes are never visible as either the camera was on the same level as the tabletop or they were concealed by a glass painting or miniature set. When necessary, perhaps when only one foot was actually on the 'ground', steel rods were fixed to the models on the side that was, concealed from the camera, so that they were held steady whilst being manipulated.

Before the animation of a scene began Obie made sure that all lamps illuminating the miniature sets were replaced because a blown lamp would have had terrible consequences for a scene

animate various scenes, including Kong's climb up the Empire State Building. But Obie's preference was for working alone, especially when it came to shots that necessitated what Obie called 'delicate actions', mostly involving Kong.

Nevertheless, in a rare interview called 'Miniature Effects Shots' in the *International Photographer* dated May 1933, Obie, always a modest man, paid tribute to his staff.

The miniature technician cannot bring his set to the screen single-handed. It is fundamentally an artist's conception but requires the united efforts of many craftsmen, its success depending entirely upon the combination of artistic, photographic and mechanical effects, each person being a specialist in his field but also having a general knowledge of the whole. When making King Kong *it is necessary to have a large staff of experienced men to carry on the work. A group of men were kept busy building and repairing the animals or executing any mechanical necessity that was required. Another group built the miniatures, which included a New York Elevated Railway*

TOP LEFT
Two models from *King Kong* in a mock battle. On the left is a styracosaurus, not used in the final film (it would appear in *Son of Kong*) and on the right is the tyrannosaurus rex used in the film.

BOTTOM FAR LEFT
Two wide-shot images showing the insertion of Fay Wray and the altar pillars into the miniature jungle set by means of the Dunning Process.

BOTTOM LEFT
A closer shot with the altar in the foreground. A studio technician acts as a stand-in for a test that will allow the altar and the girl to be composited into the miniature jungle background.

TOP RIGHT
A larger model of the head and neck of a brontosaurus (seen in the rear projection) attacking a doomed sailor who has sought sanctuary in a tree.

BELOW
The test shot of the stegosaurus in its miniature jungle set. Note the pegboard on which it stands. It was secured in position through the holes in the pegboard during animation; the camera angle ensured that the board did not appear on screen.

if it was half finished; the intensity of a new bulb would never match that of the one it replaced. The large incandescent lamps were sometimes known to blow up, an effect triggered when the temperature changed as someone exited or entered the studio, so once animation had begun no one was allowed on or off the set. All facilities, including toilets, were on site and enough food and drink were brought in to last the day, no matter how long that day was likely to be.

Kong's first spectacular appearance in the film is preceded by a gradual but necessary build-up. We see trees and shrubs being shaken and know something big is on its way to seize poor Ann Darrow (Fay Wray). Then he appears. The planning for the scene was superb. They had thought about how Kong was to take the girl without hurting her, and Obie had decided that her arms would be secured by ropes which could be released by turning a stick. So Kong releases one arm and then she is seen freeing the other. The shots in which Kong and Fay Wray appeared together were created by means of the Dunning Process, an optical system for combining images of a live actor with backgrounds that were shot later on a different set. Fay, together with the altar and its pillars, were photographed under an orange light, Kong and the miniature trees were shot separately and the two elements were put together in the laboratory using an optical printer. The sequence was in fact filmed a total of sixteen times. Cooper and Schoedsack didn't like the first take which they felt lacked the right

effect. Only after fifteen further attempts had been made, with a range of variations, did Cooper opt for the first take after all.

As a thirteen year-old, Ray was fascinated and impressed with Kong's first, spectacular appearance: 'I knew it wasn't real and yet it looked real.' His limited knowledge of cinema told him that it wasn't a full-scale model but if not how was it that this gigantic creature could be in the same frame as a real woman? Ray also loved the huge wall and gates, though he occasionally and very jokingly (because he never wants to be seen to criticise the film) asks why it is that, if the ancients who had built the wall and gate hadn't wanted any of the creatures who lived behind it to escape, then why build the gate so large? Of course the answer is cinematic spectacle. It would have been boring if the gate had been six feet high. The gates had originally been constructed as the entrance to the great temple of Jehovah for Cecil B. deMille's 1927 production of *King of Kings* but when Cooper saw them on the back-lot, he knew that they had to be adapted for the Skull Island gates.

In pursuit of Ann and Kong, Carl Denham (Robert Armstrong) the hero John Discoll (Bruce Cabot) and sailors from the ship which brought them to the island, encounter and kill a stegosaurus. Ray has, from the very first time he saw the picture, been impressed with the texture and muscular elements of the model and also with the way it was animated, especially during its death throes when the tail creates a wave or ripple effect, finally ending in a 'death rattle'. The animation for the sequence was shot first and then rear-projected on to a large screen so that the real actors were able to react to the creature. The scene is also one of the best examples of Obie's obsession with Gustave Doré. The viewer's eye is focused on the brightly lit creature which is framed by vegetation painted on a series of glass screens.

While the sailors are rowing across a lake in the island's interior they encounter a brontosaurus which is first seen in the water and a non-armatured model was used for this shot which involved the use of high-speed photography to slow down the model's motion on-screen. But when the creature emerges from the water

LEFT
A picture spread from *The International Photographer*. The central image shows O'Brien posing with the full-scale bust of Kong on the back lot at RKO. However, the other four images are, we think, tests etc for *Son of Kong*. Note the styracosaurus in the bottom two images.

BELOW LEFT
A hand test showing Kong and a model of a man on the log bridge.

BELOW
A paste-up by Ernest Bacharach showing Kong shaking the sailors off the log. Ray saw the original when visiting Bacharach in his office at RKO. Note the head of a styracosaurus on the extreme right. This creature never appeared in the final film.

TOP RIGHT
Kong fights the tyrannosaurus rex. This was again a paste-up by Bacharach, as in the film Kong is not shown levering the t. rex's mouth open with a branch.

TOP FAR RIGHT
Above, Kong fights the t. rex. Note the depth of the image, the dark foreground and lighter central action. Below, Kong celebrates his victory over the t. rex by beating his chest.

BOTTOM RIGHT
Kong fights the elasmosaurus, a snake-like creature, in the 'Doré' cave. Note that Fay Wray is rear-projected in on the far left and the man standing looking up on the left of the cave is double-printed in.

BOTTOM FAR RIGHT
O'Brien in the process of animating the elasmosaurus and Kong. In the foreground, behind O'Brien's back, is the glass painting of the foreground of the cave.

to chase one of the unfortunate sailors up a tree, an animated model was used. At various points a model is also substituted for the sailor in long shot or, later, when he is in contact with the creature. For the close shot of the creature attacking the man from behind the tree Obie used a separate armatured model consisting only of the neck and head. In homage to *The Lost World* there is a close shot of the brontosaurus curling its mouth and snarling.

There are quite often tiny birds flying across scenes, which are probably archaeopteryxes (flying dinosaurs from the Jurassic period). These models were about one-and-a- half inches across and carved from wood with copper wings and animated on stretched wires. These flying birds impressed Ray so much that in his amateur films and the 'Fairy Tale' series similar birds often appear flitting across the miniature set.

Whilst the sailors are struggling with the brontosaurus Kong is making his way to his lair and we see him cross a ravine via a huge fallen tree which Ray calls the Doré log because it was influenced by the artist's wonderful illustration for *Atala*. This is another scene which had a significant influence on some of Ray's films. When the remaining sailors arrive in pursuit, Kong shakes the log so that they fall into the ravine. The actors were shot on a full-sized log in the studio and Obie would have had a print made of the action so that he could analyze it in detail and then animate Kong's movements to

match up with the movements of the full-size log. The animation was subsequently double-printed into the picture.

One of the key sequences in the film is the fight between Kong and the tyrannosaurus rex which demonstrates 'King' Kong's domination of all the island's creatures. What you see today is the test sequence that Obie shot for Cooper and the RKO executives. In effect, the remainder of the picture was shot around this and the log sequence. The titanic fight remains one of the best sequences in the entire film, not only because it is action-packed, but also because of Kong's human-like reactions when he has finally killed the t. rex. Throughout the sequence there are actions that are obviously based on the boxing and wrestling manoeuvres familiar to Obie. For example, the preliminary circling by the two creatures, especially Kong, and the arm holds with which the ape immobilizes the dinosaur. Further human-like characteristics are evident when the tyrannosaurus rex is dead. Kong lifts its head, opening and closing its jaws to make sure it is no longer a threat. This is probably a post-battle reaction that Obie improvised at the last minute and is almost reminiscent of a hunter prodding his prey with a stick to make sure he is safe. Finally, as Obie had done all those years before in *The Dinosaur and the Missing Link*, he had Kong put one foot on the tyrannosaurus rex whilst pounding his chest in triumph. Years later, Obie's second wife Darlyne, said, 'Obie's personality shone through in everything he made *King Kong* do. I could see his sense of humour in everything Kong did. I am absolutely certain no one will be able to put into a picture what Obie did.'

In the process of making his way to the top of Skull Mountain, Kong enters a cave. It is a cavern with an extremely Doré-like atmosphere; there are bright shafts of light and dark, threatening corners enhanced with wisps of steam (achieved by double or triple exposure) creating wraith-like columns. Deep inside Kong puts Fay Wray gently down and we see her try to crawl away. As soon as she is on the ground the real Fay Wray takes the place of the model that had been in Kong's hand, an effect achieved by means of miniature rear projection. During the

girl's temporary escape Kong fights an elasmosaurus (a creature shown here with a thin snake-like body, although in reality they possessed long, thin necks like a snake but their bodies were much bigger with large fins, giving the impression of 'Snakes threaded through the bodies of turtles' (as the nineteenth-century English palaeontologist Dean Conybeare put it). It is a sequence that contains a great deal of mood and action; the slimy elasmosaurus winds itself around the body of Kong like a malevolent force that wants to corrupt and destroy the strength and innocence of Kong. The animation shows Obie at his best, manipulating both models as they fight for supremacy over each other. Kong's reaction when the creature wraps itself around his neck it is a typical example of the animator imagining what he would do if he found himself in the same situation. In the end Kong pulls the creature away and slams it down on the floor of the cave like a wrestler, so killing it. As with the t. rex, Kong looks at the body to make sure it is dead and then performs two chest thumps in triumph. This sequence again fascinated Ray. The image of the creature wrapping itself around Kong's body made such an impression that throughout Ray's career he wanted, not to copy it exactly, but to emulate it; hence the images of the snake-woman in *The 7th Voyage of Sinbad*, the *hydra* in *Jason and the Argonauts* and others for movies that remained unrealized such as the giant snake wrapping itself about a Cyclops intended for *The 7th Voyage of Sinbad* and another encircling a carnivorous dinosaur in *King of the Geniis* (which was to become *The Golden Voyage of Sinbad*).

Kong eventually gets Fay Wray outside the cave, on a high and wide open ledge where he settles down to study his 'conquest', carefully pulling off various items of her clothing. Despite the size difference, it is a strangely tender moment. There is nothing threatening about the way he removes the clothes; his curiosity is childlike as he wonders what they are and what lies beneath. For this sequence Fay Wray sat in a full-scale version of Kong's hand and technicians pulled wires attached to her clothes. This shot was then miniature rear-projected into the miniature set, just behind the model of the rest of Kong's body. The model was situated in front of the screen with its right arm concealed by the torso so that it looked as if the full-size hand was attached to the model.

Kong is next faced with the challenge of fighting off a pterodactyl or a pterandon that sees Ann Darrow as a tasty morsel. The creature's wings are perhaps more accurate than those later given to similar creatures in Ray's movies (Ray gave his pterodactyls bat-like wings which he felt looked cinematically better) but they seem rather ordinary even though the creature isn't required to fly that much in the scene. According to Obie, the fight with the pterodactyl was the most difficult sequence to film, presumably because of the complex aerial brace work that would have been required. In all, it took a total of nearly eight weeks to shoot the entire sequence.

Although there are other animation sequences that follow the fight with the pteradon, including Kong's pursuit of Ann Darrow through the gates,

LEFT
A test of Kong on the side of a mountain holding a model of Fay Wray. This was never used in the final film.

TOP RIGHT
The pteranodon sees the hapless Fay Wray as a tasty morsel. This was a hand test to determine lighting.

TOP FAR RIGHT
Kong intervenes, again a hand test to determine lighting.

RIGHT
Kong grabs the pteranodon which has a model of Fay Wray in its claws. This sequence was one of the most complex in the entire film because of the large amount of laborious aerial work. The background painting can be seen behind and along the top a wooden beam in which is a nail that supported one of the wires holding the model.

we will now turn our attention to the first of two main sequences that take place in New York. The elevated railway sequence was the last to be completed and was not originally intended to be in the picture at all. Legend has it that after the first rough cut of the film Cooper was told that it ran to thirteen reels (these would have probably been ten- minute reels) which, as Cooper was fiercely superstitious, he thought was a bad omen. The production assistant, Archie Marshek, however, told it differently, explaining that: 'He really wanted an excuse to film another sequence he had in mind.'[17] For this scene Obie and his team created one of the film's most elaborate sets that included not just the elevated railway track and train but apartment blocks and a complex painted backdrop.

At the beginning of the scene there is a simple action, which goes almost unnoticed. It occurs when Kong pulls himself up to look over the top of the tracks and, whilst balanced there, swings his left leg into the air in an almost child-like gesture. When Obie looked at the scene on paper he must have known that it would be dull without something to provide it with a lift and, although we don't know this for certain, it seems likely that Obie animated that leg on the spur of the moment, thus enhancing the shot with an apparently incidental movement that in fact transforms the scene and its character. As Kong is looking over the edge of the rails he sees an approaching train. The train has one glaring light, which Kong sees as a rival beast that he must eliminate, as he would have done on Skull Island. We next see Kong looking over the edge of the track from the train driver's point of view. This was achieved by mounting the camera on the miniature rails and slowly animating it along the tracks towards the waiting Kong.

The scene of Kong on the top of the Empire State Building is one of the iconic moments in the history of model animation, if not in the history of cinema itself. The composition, technical inventiveness and sheer excitement of the sequence are as fresh and spectacular today as they must have been in 1933. Obie was always proud of what he man-

TOP LEFT
Another paste-up, probably by Ernest Bacharach, of Kong on the top of the Empire State Building fending off the planes.

ABOVE
E.B.'Buzz' Gibson animating Kong up what will, when a shot of the real building is matted in, be the side of the Empire State Building. Note the holes which Gibson used to attach the model's hands and feet during animation. Ray remembers Gibson as a 'nice fellow'.

BELOW LEFT
A promotional paste-up illustrating Kong's size, as he appeared on screen, in comparison to what would be eight full-sized gorillas.

TOP RIGHT
A test of Kong in a detailed miniature set overlooking the ravine.

RIGHT
The brontosaurus chasing one of the sailors. Note the dark area in the bottom section of the photograph. This was a matted-out area into which flowing water would be added.

aged to accomplish in the way of action and pathos in this sequence. The first we see of Kong on the building is his slow climb up the side. The image of the building is the real Empire State but with a matte line along the right edge where Kong is climbing. Kong himself is a smaller model than elsewhere, in scale with the overall size of the structure. The tiny planes that appear from the top right-hand corner are animated and matted into the picture, as are the planes in the next shot where Kong has reached the summit. These models were suspended on piano wire by means of wooden braces. To simulate the point of view from the diving planes as they try to shoot Kong, Obie needed to track the camera forward one frame at a time at the same rate as he was animating the model of Kong. For this he built a 24-foot wooden ramp along which the camera moved on a dolly track. The dolly could be secured by tightening a nut and after each frame was shot it was moved the required distance down the ramp and secured again for the next frame. The complex scenes of Kong swatting at the planes as though they are large flies, would have taken Obie a great deal of time to shoot, probably one or two weeks. The movements of Kong had to be coordinated with those of the planes which would have been suspended on aerial wires (some scenes have planes flying in front of Kong and some behind). In this sequence there are several close-up shots of the aviators in one of the planes. The pilot is actually Merian Cooper and the gunner is director Ernest Schoedsack.

Originally the intention was to use a rear-projected image of the real New York shot from the top of the building for the cityscape seen in the background during this sequence, but it became apparent that the image wouldn't be as detailed as required. Remarkably, what you see in these shots are paintings, executed by Mario Larrinaga, his brother Juan and Byron Crabbe on three planes to create the illusion of depth.

Kong's slow and painful death is full of pathos and emotion. He holds on to the building with one hand and with the other touches his shoulder to see the blood (coloured glycerine) and we see an expression on his face that suggests he cannot comprehend what is happening to him. He then lovingly looks down at the girl and, again, what we seem to see in that look is regret. It is all pure Obie. As any good animator would have, he put himself in Kong's place and asked: 'What would I think and what would I do?' The movements and the character of the dying creature are probably Obie's finest piece of animation. Finally, a plane fires a last burst at Kong and he totters and falls to his death. It is an extremely moving scene and even though you know it is only a model you can't help feeling sorry for him. Diana Harryhausen always cries when he falls and Diana must have seen the picture almost as many times as Ray.

Throughout the filming, the scale of Kong was a major consideration. All the scenes on Skull Island were designed on a basic one-inch-to-one-foot scale, making the full-size Kong eighteen feet high but for the New York scenes Cooper ordered that Kong's size be increased hoping that the difference wouldn't be noticed. It wasn't. Schoedsack observed that, 'We realized we'd never get much drama out of a fly crawling up the tallest building in the world,' and so it was decided to increase Kong's stature

LEFT
The section that was cut from the final release print of *King Kong*. Here we see one of the menacing spiders that occupied the floor of the ravine into which the sailors fell after they were shaken from the log bridge. The model would probably have been given extra support by means of aerial wires. To Ray's knowledge, Ray Bradbury is the only person to have seen this sequence. Ray himself has never seen it.

BELOW
Ernest B. Schoedsack, left, and Merian C. Cooper look at a publicity artist's depiction of Kong in New York.

RIGHT
A production photograph with some of the native actors in front of the great gates set. Seated, from left to right, Merian C. Cooper (Producer/Director), Willis O'Brien (Chief Technician), Fay Wray (who plays Ann Darrow) and Ernest B. Schoedsack (Producer/Director).

to twenty-four feet. In fact, Kong's size fluctuates through the film to achieve the right proportional effect.

The technical progress made between *The Lost World*, released in 1925, and *King Kong*, released in 1933, was enormous. Those eight years had seen Obie perfect not only the smoothness of his animation and sophistication and agility in his models, but also the use of optical mattes and glass paintings to achieve a 3-D effect. Obie had used the latter to some extent on *The Lost World* but in *Kong* the technique was perfected. Glass paintings had for many years been used to add 'false' sections to landscapes or buildings in order to save the cost of constructing complete sets. But Obie used them to 'sandwich' the models and miniature vegetation on the animation table, which not only gave the scenes depth but also a fantasy atmosphere that captured his favoured Doré style. The paintings were done on iridescence-free plate glass in tones of opaque grey and were between eight and twelve feet across. Sometimes up to three sheets of glass would be used in a scene, each mounted in a wooden frame which was secured to a wooden stand fixed to the floor. The paintings were so finely detailed that they were works of art in their own right. On *King Kong* (and later for *Mighty Joe Young*) the sheet of glass nearest the camera was generally eighteen to twenty inches in front of the animation table, leaving little room for the animator to slide in to carry out his intricate work and there could be other problems. Ray

recalls that while working on *Mighty Joe Young* there were several occasions when things got too hot on the miniature sets and one of the paintings suddenly cracked right across. When this happened everybody was extremely disheartened because it meant that everything would have to be done all over again, including the animation. No matter how accurate and good a new painting was, it would never exactly match the one that had cracked. Fortunately this problem didn't occur too often.

Whenever possible, Obie always shot from a low angle and used wide-angle lenses; this not only created an illusion of height but also had a practical purpose. Framing the action from a low position meant that the surface of the animation table with its peg holes would not be visible. When a view of the surface couldn't be avoided Obie would cover it with a layer of sponge rubber about an eighth of an inch thick. Ray recalls that they used the same method when making *Mighty Joe Young* but with an additional refinement. George Lofgren (one of the assistants and also a gifted taxidermist and maker of props and miniatures) would stick hairs from a lion's mane (obtained from a taxidermist) into the sponge rubber to simulate clumps of grass.

Obie liked to do as much of the optical work as possible in the camera; partly because if he sent it to other departments they would likely take credit for it and partly because processing shots through an optical printer involved producing a dupe, whereas producing a composite picture of various sections of the frame by photographing one section, then matting that out and running the camera back to shot another section, was all done on the original negative. The mattes played a vital part in determining the final look of the film as they provide the main means by which animation was combined with live action in the same shot. Obie used the static matte. This meant that a section of the glass matte was painted out by the artist with black paint and when the animation shot was photographed through the glass, the painted, or matted out, area, of each frame remained unexposed. To 'insert' the humans into the picture a counter matte was painted (the area that had been unexposed before was left and the rest of the glass, was painted out with black matte paint), and the human action was then photographed. When the entire film was developed the two areas would blend and hopefully appear to have been photographed simultaneously. For the miniature settings, mostly jungle, Obie used a combination of elements. Some of the trees were miniature versions of the real thing, for example genista (a virtually leafless leguminous shrub of the genus *Genista*) the stems of which were wired to keep them upright. The use of succulents gave a rain forest effect and roots from discarded grape vines were used for gnarled ancient trees and exposed roots. However, most of the plant life was sculpted in Plasticine over wood and wire, covered with toilet tissue, then covered in shellack (resin) and finally painted. Other trees, such as palms and ferns, were cut-outs made of copper. All had to remain securely in place as the animation was photographed. There were, of course, some problems. Whilst photographing the test reel of the fight between Kong and the tyrannosaurus rex, Obie discovered that if a scene was not completed in one go the projected film could show drastic changes in the live plants, which could grow, change colour and in some cases even die, overnight. One example of this was when a primrose was used (the large long leaves were a perfect size in relation to the models) and during a long sequence of animation nobody noticed that it had almost come into flower under the heat of the lights. The entire sequence had to be scrapped and re-shot.

Another problem with continuity was that lamps would not have the same intensity if they were switched off and then switched on again after an interval, so if a scene was started then it had to be finished in one go. A great deal of time was spent setting up the miniature sets to make sure all the elements were exactly right and there would be many photographic tests before they were considered animation-ready. There is a story about one such set that included a complex array of miniature flora and three painted glass sheets. Having satisfied themselves that everything was exactly right, Obie and his crew went off to lunch but whilst they were eating there was a slight earthquake and when they returned Obie realized that there had been subtle changes so the entire set-up had to be realigned and re-lit.

RKO paint technician Sidney Saunders invented a special cellulose acetate rear-projection screen, which measured sixteen by twenty feet, for which he won an American Academy Award®. This was introduced just as work was to begin on the test reel and was first used in the scenes in which Fay Wray is seen in the foreground whilst Kong fights the tyrannosaurus rex in the background. Another of the innovations developed for the film was miniature rear projection. This is a process that involves incorporating a very small rear-projection screen into a miniature set. Finding a suitable surface onto which to project tiny images was a big problem because of grain. After experimenting with many materials, including cloth, tracing paper and even cellophane they discovered that rubber sheets (they were actually condoms) stretched over a small wooden frame produced a high-quality image, free of grain. The one disadvantage of using such thin rubber was that it deteriorated extremely quickly when exposed to the heat of the projected image and the studio lights and had to be replaced on a regular basis. A good example of the use of miniature rear projection is the scene where Kong is searching for the hero, Driscoll (Bruce Cabot), at the edge of the ravine after Kong has toppled the other men from the log. Cabot is shown hiding in a cave in the wall of the ravine, just below the edge, and Kong tries to find him by feeling around with his hand.

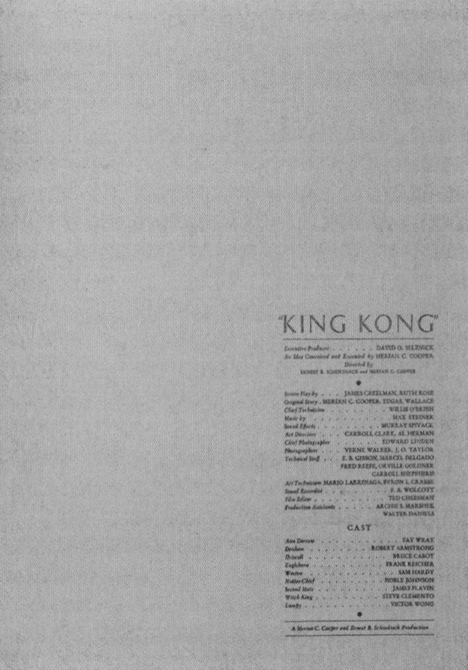

"KING KONG"

Executive Producer . . . . . . DAVID O. SELZNICK
An Idea Conceived and Executed by MERIAN C. COOPER
Directed by
ERNEST B. SCHOEDSACK *and* MERIAN C. COOPER

Screen Play by . . . JAMES CREELMAN, RUTH ROSE
Original Story . MERIAN C. COOPER, EDGAR WALLACE
Chief Technician . . . . WILLIS O'BRIEN
Music by . . . . MAX STEINER
Sound Effects . . . . MURRAY SPIVACK
Art Direction . . . CARROLL CLARK, AL HERMAN
Chief Photographer . . . . . . EDWARD LINDEN
Photographers . . . VERNE WALKER, J. O. TAYLOR
Technical Staff . . . E. B. GIBSON, MARCEL DELGADO
FRED REEFE, ORVILLE GOLDNER
CARROLL SHEPPHIRD
Art Technicians MARIO LARRINAGA, BYRON L. CRABBE
Sound Recordist . . . . E. A. WOLCOTT
Film Editor . . . . TED CHEESMAN
Production Assistants . . . . . ARCHIE S. MARSHEK
WALTER DANIELS

CAST

Ann Darrow . . . . FAY WRAY
Denham . . . . ROBERT ARMSTRONG
Driscoll . . . . BRUCE CABOT
Englehorn . . . . FRANK REICHER
Weston . . . . SAM HARDY
Native Chief . . . . NOBLE JOHNSON
Second Mate . . . . JAMES FLAVIN
Witch King . . . . STEVE CLEMENTO
Lumpy . . . . VICTOR WONG

A Merian C. Cooper and Ernest B. Schoedsack Production

ABOVE LEFT
One of the two beautiful art deco copper pages from *The Hollywood Reporter* souvenir brochure. Ray has always been upset that the lead actor in *King Kong*, Robert Armstrong, was never pictured in this brochure, even though everyone else was, including the key technicians.

ABOVE CENTRE
The cast and credits from the souvenir brochure.

ABOVE
One of the many poster designs for *King Kong*.

RIGHT
Two other poster designs.

Cabot's performance, choreographed by Obie, was filmed and then back-projected, one frame at a time, onto a tiny screen set into the back of the miniature cave while the model of Kong was animated to grope around inside it.

One regret is that several sequences were axed from the film. The most famous, or infamous, was to have followed the scene in which the sailors are toppled from the log into the ravine. At the bottom of the ravine the men were to have been attacked and killed by giant spiders, man-eating plants with long slimy tentacles and carnivorous lizards. It was photographed but was cut at a very early stage, partly because Cooper thought (quite rightly) that it slowed the action down and partly because he worried that it might be a little too terrifying for audiences. Marcel Delgado described some of the creatures he devised for this scene: 'We used a couple of lizard-like monsters, of my own imagination. These creatures consisted of a long lizard-like body, with thorny spikes all along the back, a ferocious parrot-beaked head and a pair of strong, muscled forearms.'[18] Another scene that was cut was to have featured a triceratops protecting its baby from Kong, which was very reminiscent of a similar scene in *The Lost World*. According to Mario Larrinaga, 'The triceratops sequence, I believe, was cut from the picture because of the animal's natural stiffness, which would hinder its smooth animation in miniature which was an inch to the foot scale.'[19] Finally, there is a scene where the original conception was completely changed. This was the one in which Kong is displayed to the public in a theatre, which was shot at the Shrine Auditorium in Los Angeles; the original plan had been to have him exhibited in the Yankee Stadium.

As we have been at pains to point out, all animators instill into their creations a little, or in some cases a lot, of their own personalities. There is a great deal of Obie in *King Kong*. Discussing his work on *King Kong* Obie was quoted in the *International Photographer* magazine in May 1933:

> *Experience is the only teacher of the various treatments required to obtain the desired effects. Each new set is an individual problem and requires separate treatment. There is no common rule or method by which you can classify all miniatures. The miniature of today is a much more convincing and effective medium that it was a few years ago. The introduction of real people into the miniature (by process, matte or projection) and the addition of sound have all helped considerably. Miniatures and so-called trick shots are not a medium used to fool the public, but rather a means of obtaining a better or otherwise impossible angle to further the completeness of the story and often are used as the only possible solution to get the desired effects.*

The effects were 55 weeks in production and following the addition of sound effects and music the film was premiered in New York on 2 March 1933 at two theatres, the New Roxy and the Radio City Music Hall, giving a total seating capacity of 10,000 and earning a staggering $89,931 in four days (seats then cost $0.15). This was followed by an opening at Grauman's Chinese Theatre in Hollywood on Friday 24 March. The world and Ray Harryhausen have never been the same since. Produced at a cost of $672,000 the film went on to become the biggest grossing picture of the year. The success of the project enabled RKO to stay in production and made Merian Cooper, Fay

Wray and Willis O'Brien household names. It guaranteed the first two life-long careers, but for Obie it was to be his pinnacle, a triumph from which the only path was downwards.

In the wake of the phenomenal success of *King Kong*, Cooper, Schoedsack and RKO rushed a sequel into production (nothing has changed). Initially this was called *Jamboree*, a working title bestowed by Cooper to keep the journalists guessing, but inevitably, in the true tradition of sequels, it ended up as *Son of Kong* (1933). Whereas the first picture had taken a total of three years, *Son of Kong* took just nine short months to complete and cost just $250,000, with $50,000 of that being allocated for the effects. The story tells of the return of Carl Denham (Robert Armstrong repeating his role) to Skull Island accompanied this time by Hilda Peterson (Helen Mack) in search of a lost treasure. But instead of the treasure he finds a smaller, cuddlier, white-furred version of the great Kong. There follows a variety of animation scenes, including a battle with a triceratops (the model made for the first film), a styracosaurus (also made for the first film), a sea creature, a cave bear and a rather silly dragon-like creature. Three models of little Kong were built by Marcel Delgado using the armatures constructed for the original Kong; Delgado also constructed the other new creatures including the dragon, which he also designed.

Sadly, both the storyline and the dialogue in *Son of Kong* are truly awful, perhaps because the emphasis is on the comic angle rather than the spectacle. This new Kong is too cuddly, too human and certainly too small; he is, in short, a shadow of his huge, impressive dad. The film also has little drama, excitement or fantasy.

LEFT
Son of Kong (1933). Kong's son fights the dragon-like creature in front of the temple watched by Robert Armstrong and Helen Mack.

BELOW
Helen Mack and Robert Armstrong see baby Kong for the first time. Mack and Armstrong are standing in a full-sized set with Kong rear-projected onto a full screen.

Overall, it is as far from the original *Kong* as the film-makers could possibly have made it. To make matters worse, the animation is far from smooth and on occasions even jerky- a word that most animators fear above all others. There are only two scenes that really warrant any mention. The first is the appearance of little Kong, which occurs nearly 35 minutes into the picture when Denham and his companion, Peterson, find him trapped and struggling in a quagmire. Although it is rather a dull introduction to the creature, the scene is moving and effective. The other sequence is the finale in which little Kong saves Denham. During a volcanic eruption Skull Island begins to sink and just as it is about to completely disappear beneath the waves the brave little Kong holds Denham above the encroaching water in his raised hand so he can escape in a boat with the other three survivors. Finally, as the boat sails away, we see little Kong succumb to the waves. This sequence is both spectacular and exciting, the first scene in the movie that could claim any such qualities.

Obie hated the whole project and although he attempted to instill some depth and quality into the venture at an early stage of the production, Cooper and Schoedsack were set on making a quick buck on the back of the success of the original picture. Obie, as always, made many drawings and sketches to illustrate how a quality

RIGHT
The awful sea monster which was mechanically operated not animated. O'Brien hated it.

BELOW
A smiling Willis O'Brien. Soon tragedy would strike.

BELOW RIGHT
Baby Kong rear-projected whilst Mack and Armstrong react. The armatures used for the models in *King Kong* were stripped down and reused for the 'son' models.

film could be produced but his ideas were dismissed and, indeed, he was generally ignored throughout the production. Although he went into the studio to pick up his pay cheques, he took little or no part in the production and it was 'Buzz' Gibson who completed the animation, an act that Obie viewed as disloyal. When Ray later asked Obie about the film, he would always seem very despondent about it and on one occasion he said that the film really was not his in any way. After the success of the first film and the vindication of his life's work he viewed *Son of Kong* as an insult. Darlyne O'Brien commented that,

> *Cooper and Schoedsack let O'Brien work pretty much without interference on* King Kong *because they knew very little about the then 'recent animation techniques'. But while making* Son of Kong *they considered themselves experts on the process and assumed that they weren't entirely dependent on O'Brien's ideas. Since they didn't try to conceal their attitude towards him, Obie washed his hands of the entire matter and let them run the whole show without once contributing his creative genius to the production.*[20]

Obie's lack of enthusiasm for the project may have also been aggravated by a dreadful personal tragedy that occurred in his private life. During the production of *Son of Kong*, in October 1933, his first wife, Hazel Collette, shot and

killed their two teenage sons and then turned the gun on herself. Obie would never truly get over this appalling event, although a few months after the tragedy he was introduced to Darlyne and they were married a year later, on 17 November 1934. Darlyne would prove to be not only a good wife but also a companion who was able to understand her husband's unique creativity. Speaking of his first marriage, years later, she said, 'He was a dreamer and a creator and could not fit into the conventional pattern of a husband and father.'[21]

Although Obie requested that his name be taken off the credits for *Son of Kong*, Cooper refused, well aware of its value; indeed, Obie's

This new Kong is too cuddly, too human and certainly too small; he is, in short, a shadow of his huge, impressive dad.

Left. O'Brien adjusting the styracosaurus model and a human figure. There is great sadness in his eyes. According to Jim Aupperle, he was told by Darlyne O'Brien that the picture was taken just after O'Brien's first wife shot and killed their two sons. The picture was damaged when O'Brien tore it up because it reminded him of the tragedy.

Top. Willis O'Brien Jr. posing with the white-furred son of Kong. This was taken shortly before his mother shot and killed him along with his brother.

Above. The other brother, William O'Brien. William was blind and the older of O'Brien's two sons from his first marriage to Hazel O'Brien.

Various production shots from *Son of Kong*.

Top left. E.B.'Buzz' Gibson animating the styracosaurus.

Top centre. Willis O'Brien adjusting the styracosaurus in the miniature set watched by artist Byron Crabbe.

Top right. Mario Larrinaga 'touching up' the rear end of the styracosaurus watched by Crabbe. Larrinaga and Crabbe had to constantly make sure the paint finish on the models was always perfect.

Second row left. O'Brien, second from left, directing the mechanical sea monster sequence.

Second row centre. O'Brien, in the middle foreground, watching the crew whilst the sea monster is photographed in the tank.

Second row right. O'Brien quietly watching the filming of the sea monster. He hated the use of mechanical models.

Third row left. Mario Larrinaga (left) and Byron Crabbe (right) laugh whilst finishing a glass painting. Perhaps Obie had been singing 'I'll Get By – As Long As I Have You!'.

Third row centre. O'Brien, second from left, inspects the styracosaurus, with animator E.B. 'Buzz' Gibson (with pipe). Byron Crabbe and Mario Larrinaga are still smiling in the background.

Third row right. A rare smile at the camera from O'Brien whilst filming the sea monster sequence. O'Brien hated *Son of Kong*, believing it to be a cheap and rushed sequel, which of course it was.

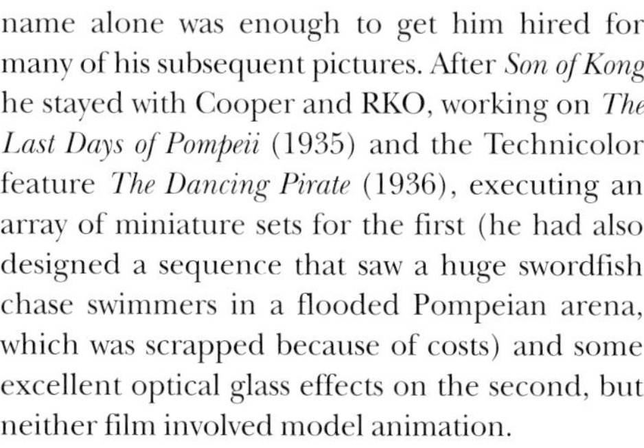

name alone was enough to get him hired for many of his subsequent pictures. After *Son of Kong* he stayed with Cooper and RKO, working on *The Last Days of Pompeii* (1935) and the Technicolor feature *The Dancing Pirate* (1936), executing an array of miniature sets for the first (he had also designed a sequence that saw a huge swordfish chase swimmers in a flooded Pompeian arena, which was scrapped because of costs) and some excellent optical glass effects on the second, but neither film involved model animation.

On the 21 October 1935 Obie was put under contract to Cooper and his new Pioneer Pictures (Cooper left RKO in 1935 to head the independent company). The contractual paperwork makes interesting reading. Pioneer Pictures refers to Obie's work as 'special photographic operations, including so-called "miniature shots", glass shots and/or "trick shots",' and the title the picture Obie is likely to work on is given as 'Willis O'Brien Productions; for example *The Last Days of Pompeii*, *She* and *Kong*.' The contract was for 'one year, two months and eleven days, or until the completion of the said Willis O'Brien Production is completed'. He was to be paid $200 per week during the preparation of a project and $400 when actually working on a project. The agreement goes on to say, 'We also agree to pay you a bonus of $5000.00 upon completion by you of all services.' Less generously, the contract also states that Obie has to sign away rights to any innovations and techniques that he might devise during the production of a 'Willis O'Brien Production'.

In 1938 he began pre-production on a Cooper/Schoedsack project that looked though it might be a worthy successor to *Kong* and which would require a great deal of model animation. Called *War Eagles*, it was based on an original story devised by Merian Cooper and was set amidst a lost Viking civilization thriving in the Arctic, where people travel around their ice-bound realm on giant eagles and live alongside huge carnivorous dinosaurs. As usual, Obie's first task, working with artist Duncan Gleason, was to prepare sketches and key sequence drawings for the various ideas that had been discussed at script meetings attended by Cooper, Schoedsack, Obie and Cyril Hume, the screenwriter. In all Obie produced over three hundred sketches, thirty detailed drawings and even several oil paintings, a great many of which Ray was fortunate enough to see when he visited Obie for the first time at the MGM studios where the film was to be produced.

Obie welcomed Ray by calling him Harry (from that day onwards Ray was known to his mentor as Young Harry) and showed the teenager the *War Eagles* artwork, which covered several walls. Ray was particularly impressed by two of the paintings. One showed the Statue of Liberty with gigantic eagles perched on the spikes of her helmet and the other depicted a dirigible flying over the New York skyline and surrounded by soaring eagles. Ray never forgot those images but sadly they are now lost to us. Ray's first impression of Obie was of a man who enjoyed

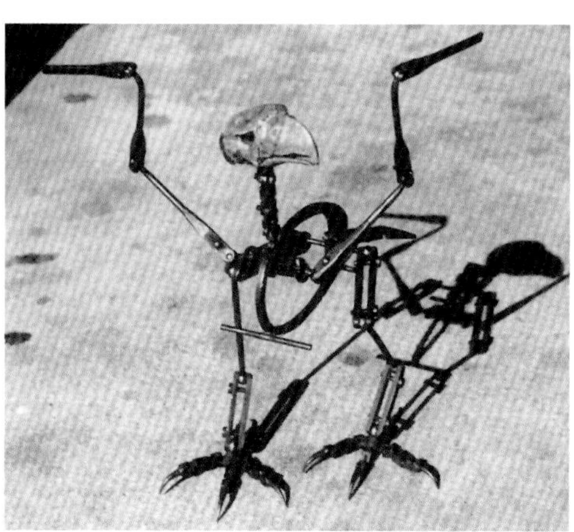

ABOVE LEFT
O'Brien posing with a fishing rod and the swordfish constructed by Marcel Delgado for *The Last Days of Pompeii* (1935). The swordfish was to have been used in a scene that was never filmed which would have shown the arena flooded and swordfish unleashed on slaves.

ABOVE CENTRE
A test (shot in colour) for the unrealized *War Eagles* (1939) showing an allosaurus and one of the Vikings' war eagles.

ABOVE
An armature originally designed for one of the Vikings that would have been used for the test animation for *War Eagles*. It is six and half inches high with a resin head. It was re-used for long shots of Jill in *Mighty Joe Young* (1949) when she is playing the piano. The image at the top right of page 97 shows Pete Peterson animating Joe whilst he supports the piano and the model of Jill.

BOTTOM LEFT
One of the eagle armatures for *War Eagles*. Ray remembers that O'Brien brought one in during the making of *Mighty Joe Young*, along with the human armature seen above.

TOP RIGHT
Willis O'Brien at his drawing board. Behind him is a rendition for the unrealized *Gwangi* (1941) painted on hardboard. Ray recalls that it was one of the highlights during his visit to Obie at his home.

TOP FAR RIGHT
Three tyrannosaurus rex models made by Marcel Delgado for *Gwangi*. The one on the left of the photograph is a plaster copy, the middle one is the finished articulated model and the original clay maquette is on the right. Rather embarrassingly, when Ray visited Obie at home he was shown the armatured model but accidentally broke one of the legs. Obie didn't seem to mind at all but Ray was devastated.

BOTTOM RIGHT
Another scene from the test for *War Eagles* showing the allosaurus.

what he was doing and who most certainly enjoyed life, an observation that was confirmed by special effects technician Ralph Hammeras, who worked with Obie several times, and described him as 'a happy-go-lucky guy – very easy to get along with' and as someone who didn't try to impress.[22]

Once the script for *War Eagles* was approved Obie and his team set about designing and building a selection of models for a test reel. In all, there were six model eagles, an allosaurus and several tiny human figures, all made by Marcel Delgado who was assisted by George Loftgren. Ray recollects that when he was working on *Mighty Joe Young*, Lofgren still had several of the eagles together with a small figure (featured as Jill playing the piano in *Mighty Joe Young*) which incorporated an armature that had started life as an eagle-rider in the test reel for *War Eagles*. The 400-foot test reel was shot in colour and showed a sequence in which eagle-mounted Vikings attack an allosaurus.

Obie told Ray years later that the project had faced a massive amount of antagonism from the staff at MGM. The studio at that time was very insular, almost a city within a city, and the presence of outsiders was resented, even if they were talented specialists. Obie was thwarted at every turn. When Ray visited, Obie was just beginning the photography for the test in the pre-production offices, but, unbeknownst to Ray, had just been advised that, as studio space was at a premium, he would have to work and shoot the test in a makeshift tent.

After a year of preparation and tests the production was halted when Hitler marched into Poland and Cooper re-enlisted in the Army Air Corps. The 'postponement' of *War Eagles* was a massive blow for Obie who considered that the project offered him the opportunity to improve some of the technical visuals that included colour mattes and miniature rear-and foreground projection, and believed that, if successful (and he had no doubts that it would be), it would inevitably lead to further productions involving model animation. He continued to hope that the project would be resurrected after the war, but by 1946, when Cooper returned, the world had moved on and the story was considered dated.

The years between 1939 and 1947 were perhaps the worst that Obie had experienced. In 1941 he began work at the Pathe Studios in Culver City on *Gwangi*, a story and a project of his own devising, which was to have been produced by John Speaks back at his old stamping ground, RKO. It was a story close to his heart, involving an allosaurus, called *Gwangi* by Native Americans, which is discovered in a hidden valley by a group of cowboys. For Obie, a story which included both horses and his beloved dinosaurs was perfect. Aside from the allosaurus, the film was to have included a pterodactyl, a herd of tiny horses (eohippos) and a triceratops, all designed by Obie and built by Marcel Delgado. Again, he produced hundreds of sketches, a number of oil paintings, nearly thirty key drawings and a complete storyboard. Ray recollects that Obie told him that he had produced many glass paintings, dozens of dioramas (cardboard scene set-ups to show where the rear projection was to be and where the live action was to take place in relation to the effects), and an armatured model of Gwangi, which Ray saw in his apartment. Ray remembers that the model had a wonderfully detailed skin texture but had not been painted. All this work again went for nothing. *Gwangi* was shelved because the studio found itself in financial difficulties and began the inevitable restructuring of its front office to try and solve the problem. Once again Obie found himself out of work with no prospects. Darlyne said of this period, 'Obie did what he had to, to pay the bills.'

In 1942 he worked for a year and a half in Chicago at the Wilding Studios on Argyle Street (formerly the S&A Studio)[23] for the United States Navy on orientation films for the war effort, and when he returned to Los Angeles in late 1943 he was reduced to executing a matte painting for an RKO production, which he then had to smuggle through a picket line outside the studio. It seemed that there was no producer or studio interested in Obie's type of picture, either because of the war or perhaps because his techniques were expensive. All he could do was take menial jobs to keep the wolf from the door. It was a tough time for him and it was beginning to tell physically.

But things did improve, if only briefly. In 1945 he received a call from Cooper to say that he was developing another ape picture and that he wanted Obie to design and execute all the effects. It was to be called *Mr Joseph Young of Africa* and was the story of a ten-foot gorilla, Joe, which is brought to America by entrepreneur Max O'Hara (played by Robert Armstrong, who had played the similar character of Carl Denham in *King Kong* and *Son of Kong*). Also slated to star were Ben Johnson and Terry Moore. Obie

was very excited and saw this project as a means of resuscitating his declining career, especially as Cooper was to be involved and the production was backed by John Ford and RKO. Cooper asked Obie if he could work on the designs and visualizations from his home; meanwhile Cooper, with Schoedsack and Ruth Rose, would develop the script so that he could present it to RKO for approval. Obie readily agreed, even though there was very little money available for the extensive pre-production visualization work. He also realized that he would need help.

He had stayed in touch with 'Young Harry', whose enthusiasm and talent he admired, through the war years and knew that Ray had all the right qualifications to help him in this new project. So in late 1945 he contacted Ray to ask if he would like to be involved; Ray's response was a very swift and excited 'Yes'. Over the following year Ray observed Obie at work while helping out with a wide range of jobs; cutting frames for drawings, copy typing, cutting mattes for production drawings, mounting storyboards and even sharpening pencils. Ray always found Obie to be a patient, cheerful man who rarely seemed to get depressed. As Ray's participation increased Obie asked his enthusiastic student to sculpt two clay busts showing what Joe would look like, which were later used for reference during pre-production. Unbeknown to Obie, Ray also executed two drawings of his own, which he never showed Obie because he was anxious that his mentor's reaction to them would not be favourable.

The production received the final go-ahead in late 1946 with a healthy budget of $1.5 million and soon after the 47-strong effects team moved onto Stage One at RKO's Pathé lot in Culver City. There were in total six models of Joe, all constructed by Marcel Delgado; four were 15 inches high, one 8 inches and one 4 inches; under Obie's close supervision Ray designed the intricate ball-and-socket armatures for all six of them. These were made of duralumin (a light but very hard alloy of aluminium and copper) and each was made up of approximately 150 articulated components (the two hands alone required over 60) and were machined and assembled by Harry Cunningham in the RKO metal shop. Delgado designed armatures for the other models, which included the lions (for a nightclub sequence), horses and a few small human figures for various shots in the nightclub and for the finale which took place in an orphanage. The other materials used in the model construction were the same as for the Kong models – foam rubber, cotton and dental dam covered with latex rubber and sculpted to give the creature a natural and flexible shape. But whereas Kong's fur had been rabbit, which was easily marked by the animator's fingers, Joe was covered in the skin of unborn lamb, which didn't have the same problems because George Loftgren had invented a treatment for rubberizing the wool, so enabling the animators to operate the model without disturbing the covering.

Animation on the film was begun in late 1947 and it fell to Ray to execute around ninety per-

LEFT
O'Brien at his drawing board, taken whilst he was making *Mighty Joe Young*.

RIGHT
Artwork by Willis O'Brien for *Mighty Joe Young* (1949).

Top left. The survivors of a plane crash are protected by Joe from the escaped lions. This idea was never used in the final film.

Top right. A wonderful action sequence for the nightclub breakout. We see Joe hanging on a vine whilst swinging a lion by its tail.

Middle left. Jill visits Joe in the jungle. Another unrealized scene. O'Brien would produce three or four hundred pre-production sketches and drawings of which only about twenty percent would be integrated into treatments and the script.

Middle right. Joe attacks the lion's cage.

Bottom left. A comic sequence that was again dropped from the final script and was rendered originally in colour. We see Joe swathed in bandages after his fight with another gorilla on a cable car – another unrealized sequence.

Bottom right. The lion escapes from the cage. It was this drawing, together with the one shown above it, that led to the lion cage sequence seen in the film.

LEFT

A watercolour on illustration cardboard by Willis O'Brien showing his original idea for Joe's stage appearance. Although extremely implausible and prohibitively expensive to film, this is a beautifully executed painting that illustrates O'Brien's cinematic vision. The number of mattes this scene would have necessitated is truly staggering.

BELOW

Another watercolour on illustration cardboard by O'Brien showing Joe knocked out after his escapade in the nightclub.

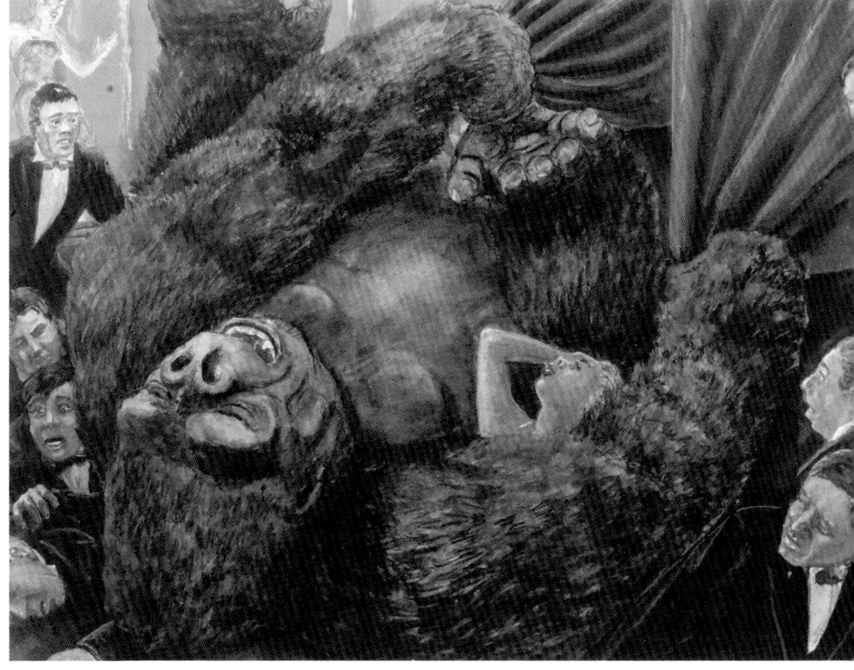

cent of the work, which he did with very few retakes, earning himself the nickname 'one-take Harryhausen'. Obie had so much faith in Ray's ability to deliver the goods that Ray was never told what to do by anyone, including the master himself. He was just allocated a sequence and left to his own devices. The other animator was newcomer Pete Peterson who completed another five percent of the film. Peterson had originally been a grip at the studio, where he started in the 1940s, and had become fascinated by the animation process, sitting and quietly watching Ray at work. His interest was so great that he began experiments at home, photographing real people with tape pasted to their arms and legs so that he could study movement. Eventually he summoned up the courage to ask Obie to try him out and Obie allocated him a small corner of the animation stage in which to work. Obie's faith in Peterson was justified; everyone was surprised at just how quickly he mastered the art of achieving fluid movements and gestures.

Obie himself only managed to animate a small number of scenes, including part of the roping sequence and the orphanage scene. Most of his time was taken up in organizing the planning and set-ups. Ray remembers that he would sometimes surreptitiously observe Obie's animation style even though he was deeply involved on the same or an adjacent scene set-up. But by then Ray was animating at least as well as Obie, probably better. The student had caught up with the master and was developing his own style. Delgado worked on a few short scenes, including long shots of Joe's climb up the tree to save the orphan girl trapped in the burning building, and Scott Whittaker also tried his hand at animation but none of the footage was ever used. Likewise when 'Buzz' Gibson and his brother were brought in by Cooper in an attempt to speed up animation, they left after six weeks and none of the footage they had shot was ever used either.

Joe's personality was quite well-developed. He had to 'act' and display emotions in a way that would allow an audience to empathize with him. However, he was never going to be another Kong. True, he was given some Kong-like behaviour, such as pounding his chest (animated by Ray) – an action that had originally been devised by Obie as far back as *The Dinosaur and the Missing Link*. But, leaving such tribute actions aside, Joe was more human than ape. This is evident when, for example, he is required to drink alcohol and exhibit the symptoms of drunkenness, or in his

BELOW LEFT

O'Brien adjusting a miniature wagon for *Mighty Joe Young*. Behind him is George Lofgren.

BELOW

Top, 'Young Harry' holding his favourite model of Joe, which he called 'Jennifer'.

Bottom, The test for the famous tug-of-war sequence in *Mighty Joe Young*. We see a number of wrestlers, including Primo Carnero, Man Mountain Dean and the Swedish Angel, competing against Joe with Jill (Terry Moore) standing behind him. The entire foreground is a miniature, including Joe of course, and was shot against a rear-projected image of the wrestlers and Terry Moore.

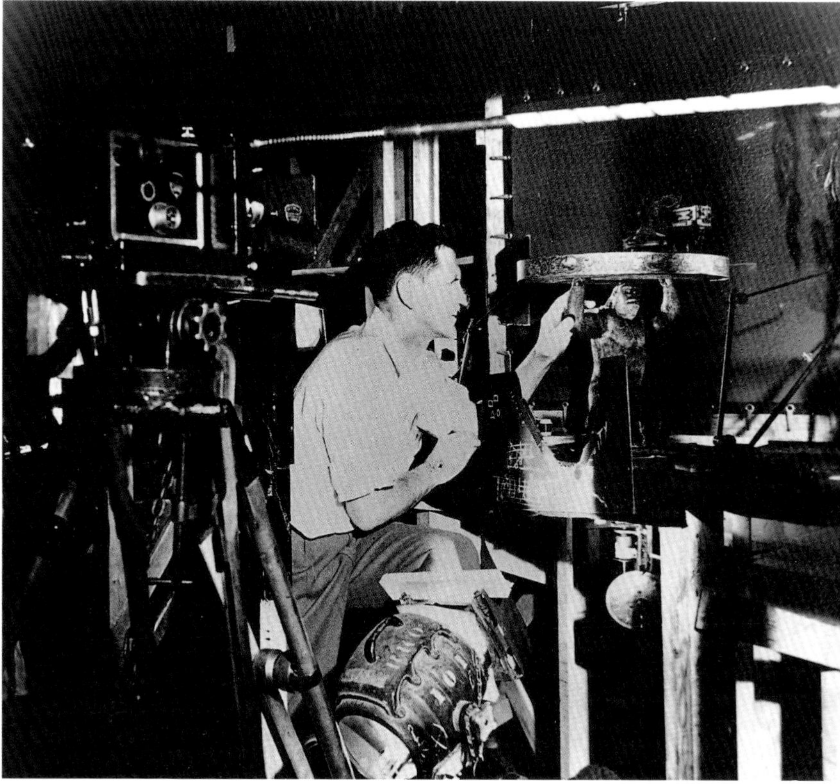

ABOVE LEFT
Pete Peterson works on the animation for the truck sequence.

ABOVE RIGHT
Pete Peterson animates Joe holding the turntable on which Jill is playing the piano. Joe and Jill are models and had to be animated together. Notice how cramped the area is with lights, camera and supports for the animation table. Ray also animated some of this sequence.

RIGHT
Ray animating Joe for the roping sequence in *Mighty Joe Young*. He is using a centre-finder or gauge whilst moving 'Jennifer'.

JY-Pub-A7

TOP FAR LEFT
Filming *Mighty Joe Young* on the Pathe back lot during the live-action roping sequence. From left to right, standing, Ben Johnson and J. Roy Hunt, the cameraman. Seated, Ernest Schoedsack, Merian C. Cooper and Willis O'Brien, who looks worried.

TOP LEFT
A production meeting during *Mighty Joe Young*. Editor Ted Cheesman, Willis O'Brien and Merian C. Cooper.

BOTTOM LEFT
The team watch the rushes. At the rear are the editor, Ted Cheesman, the director, Ernest Schoedsack, Willis O'Brien and, next to him, Ray. In the second row George Lofgren is on the extreme right. The rest are unidentified.

ABOVE
O'Brien circa 1955 holding a triceratops model for *Animal World* (1956).

ABOVE RIGHT
O'Brien proudly holding his Oscar ® that he won for *Mighty Joe Young*.

FOLLOWING SPREAD
Advance industry leaflet for the US west coast area premiere of *Mighty Joe Young*. Note the tag line, 'They Made Him Live!!' and that the team was now preparing *Valley of the Mist* for Jesse L. Lasky Productions which sadly remained unrealized.

reactions to O'Hara whom he doesn't like; and he often displays very ape-like but even more human curiosity, when faced with a caged lion in the jungle, for instance. Cooper was keen that Joe should show these emotions but sadly overstepped the mark when he had Peterson animate the character in the back of a lorry twiddling his fingers and doing a comic routine. This was a step too far in the direction of *Son of Kong* and trivialized not only the character but also the film's narrative and was deplored by Obie and Ray.

The animation and effects were completed in fourteen months and *Mighty Joe Young* was released on 30 July 1949 to generally good reviews. The film would never achieve the status or box-office success of *King Kong* but it did produce healthy returns over a period of time. It was Cooper's insistence on instilling humour, making Joe into an object of fun and derision, that did most to make the film second-rate by preventing the audience from taking the fantasy element seriously. Joe's famous predecessor had been a heroic and ultimately a tragic figure. Joe was just the central character in a rather mundane story.

At the American Academy Awards in 1950 Obie picked up an Oscar for *Mighty Joe Young*. The award was not given to him personally but for Best Special Effects, an honour that should have been delivered to him for *King Kong* seventeen-years before (when *King Kong* was released in 1933 there was no category for special effects). Ray was with him on that evening, both men wearing rented tuxedos. Ray remembers Obie being very nervous, as he had thought that the other nominee, *Tulsa*, (1949) would win the category. It didn't. Obie went up on stage and accepted the award with much emotion and just a few tears. The statue should have been kept by the producer but, realizing the work Obie had put into *Mighty Joe Young* and all their previous pictures, Cooper told Obie that the award should be his and it was always displayed proudly on a side table in his lounge. The sad thing is that Obie would never again make a film that matched the success of *King Kong*, or even *Mighty Joe Young*, and that led, inevitably and understandably, to his disillusionment with Hollywood and its film-makers.

There followed a series of near-miss projects, including, in 1950, *Emilio and Guloso*, or *The Valley of the Mist* as it became known, which Ray also worked on as assistant to Obie. After many months of trying to find finance, or even interest, the project was left to languish. In 1952 Cooper was involved with the widescreen Cinerama process, which involved projecting three overlapping images onto a screen with an aspect ratio of 2.5:1, and asked Obie if he would look into the possibility of remaking *King Kong* in colour using the process. The new film was to be called *The New Adventures of King Kong*. With his usual diligence, Obie produced a huge volume of sketches, storyboards and key drawings but the project was dropped when the technician involved in designing the complex three-projector system required for the animation rear projection, suddenly died of a heart attack. After that Obie worked on a number of projects for television and an idea for an amusement park (a simulated trip-to-the-moon ride), which he submitted to Disney. Neither the television projects nor the moon-ride materialized. He then wrote outline stories for a number of films, including *The Last of the Labyrinthodons*, *The Vines of Ceres*, *Below the Bottom* and *The Devil's Slide* all of which were bought by producers the Nassour Brothers, but again none reached the screen. Then, in 1955, he wrote a story with Darlyne called *The Beast of Hollow Mountain*, which was again bought by the Nassour Brothers. It was eventually made

THE YEAR!
Biggest opening day in years at Grand, Chicago! Now starting West Coast Area Premiere!
IT'S ALIVE!
RKO HILLSTREET DOWNTOWN

IT'S ALIVE!!

"MIGHTY JOE YOUNG"

WILLIS H. O'BRIEN
(of "The Lost World" and "King Kong")

Technical Creator — Supervisor

RAY HARRYHAUSEN
First Technician

They made him live!!

Now Preparing—**"VALLEY OF THE MIST"**—for Jesse L. Lasky Productions

---

Peter Peterson
George Lofgren —*Technical Staff*
Marcel Delgado

Harold Stine—*Photographic Effects*

Linwood Dunn—*Optical Photography*

Who helped make
The
"MIGHTY JOE YOUNG"
Live

"MIGHTY JOE YOUNG"

Released by RKO

NOW PLAYING—PANTAGES • RKO HILLSTREET THEATRES

into a Cinemascope film but without Obie's involvement. This hurt Obie a great deal and the producers' decision not to let him work on the effects resulted in a poor, muddled picture. The models were crudely made (even though they had used Marcel Delgado's *Gwangi* armature) and the animation, was certainly substandard.

The following year he was asked by another producer, Irwin Allen, to design and animate a dinosaur sequence for a wildlife feature to be called *The Animal World* (1956). This time the project did go ahead and he designed the models and miniature backgrounds together with sequences depicting a group of dinosaurs and their struggle to survive. Although Allen did use some of Obie's ideas, the models were designed and built (very badly) by Pasqual Manuelli and Harold Wilson in the Warner Bros studio and, to save time, wire-operated mechanical puppets were used for the close-ups. Obie again asked Ray to carry out the animation. Ray feels that by this time Obie had lost any desire to animate. When he had begun his experiments 42 years earlier, the thrill of animating his creations and seeing them live and breath, had been the joy of his life, now, after so many failures and disappointments, the thrill had faded and Obie was resigned to working as a designer and manager, leaving the actual animation to students such as Ray. It is worth mentioning the painted background landscapes [see page 104] seen in the film's animated sequences. These were executed by Jack Shaw who was a superb artist who had worked on the glass paintings for *Mighty Joe Young* and whose work conveyed a marvellous sense of depth. Sadly, he suffered from severe depression and shortly after completing *Animal World* he committed suicide.

There is some controversy about how Obie's next movie came about. One theory is that the effects had been executed some years before for another unrealized project, but this is untrue. The reality is that in1957 Obie was approached by producers Jack Deitz (who had been one of the producers on Ray's *The Beast From 20,000 Fathoms*) and Frank Melford to deliver the effects for a project to be called *The Black Scorpion*. The screenplay had been written to cash in on the contemporary spate of movies about giant rampaging bugs. This time the idea was that a horde of deadly giant scorpions would emerge from a crevasse, created by a newly erupting Mexican volcano, to wreak havoc on the surrounding villages and, in the finale, Mexico City. Obie had been trying to avoid the low-budget, monster-on-the-rampage movie for many years, but if that was all he was offered, then needs must.

Since *The Lost World* in 1925 Obie's usual method of working was to sandwich animation between sheets of painted glass to create a three-dimensional effect, and to use mattes to composite the actors into the frame. On *The Black Scorpion*, however, the budget was minimal and to achieve the required effects he was forced to turn to a method that had been developed by Ray for *The Beast From 20,000 Fathoms* in 1952. This technique, which Ray called Dynamation (see Chapter 4), involved inserting the animation into the live-action rather than the other way round and building a minimal amount of miniature scenery. It was a quicker, cheaper and more efficient method of delivering the package. Because of the restricted budget Obie also reluctantly opted to shoot the effects at the Tepeac Studio in Mexico City and, as Ray was then working on *Earth Vs the Flying Saucers*, asked Pete Peterson to assist him with the building of the models and miniature sets, and ultimately the animation. Special effects technician Ralph Hammeras, who had previously worked with Obie on *The Lost World* , was also in Mexico at the time, filming Columbia's *The Giant Claw* (1957), and when he was able he unofficially assisted Obie and Peterson. Hammeras remembered,

> *At the studio, O'Brien remodelled a large dressing room, used for extras, for his workshop and animation rooms. While he was completing his*

BELOW
Two sketches by O'Brien for a project that was called *The Vines of Ceres* and which he eventually sold in the 1950s to the Nassour Brothers, where it languished.

TOP RIGHT
A painting (originally in colour) by O'Brien for Irwin Allen's remake of *The Lost World* (1960). It's an exciting and very visual painting showing, amongst others, brontosaurus, triceratops and allosaurus. Allen employed O'Brien but then made the film with live lizards with fins stuck on their backs.

BOTTOM RIGHT
Producer Irwin Allen with O'Brien looking at diagrams and part of an armature for a triceratops for the film *The Animal World*. The diagram above is for a ceratosaurus.

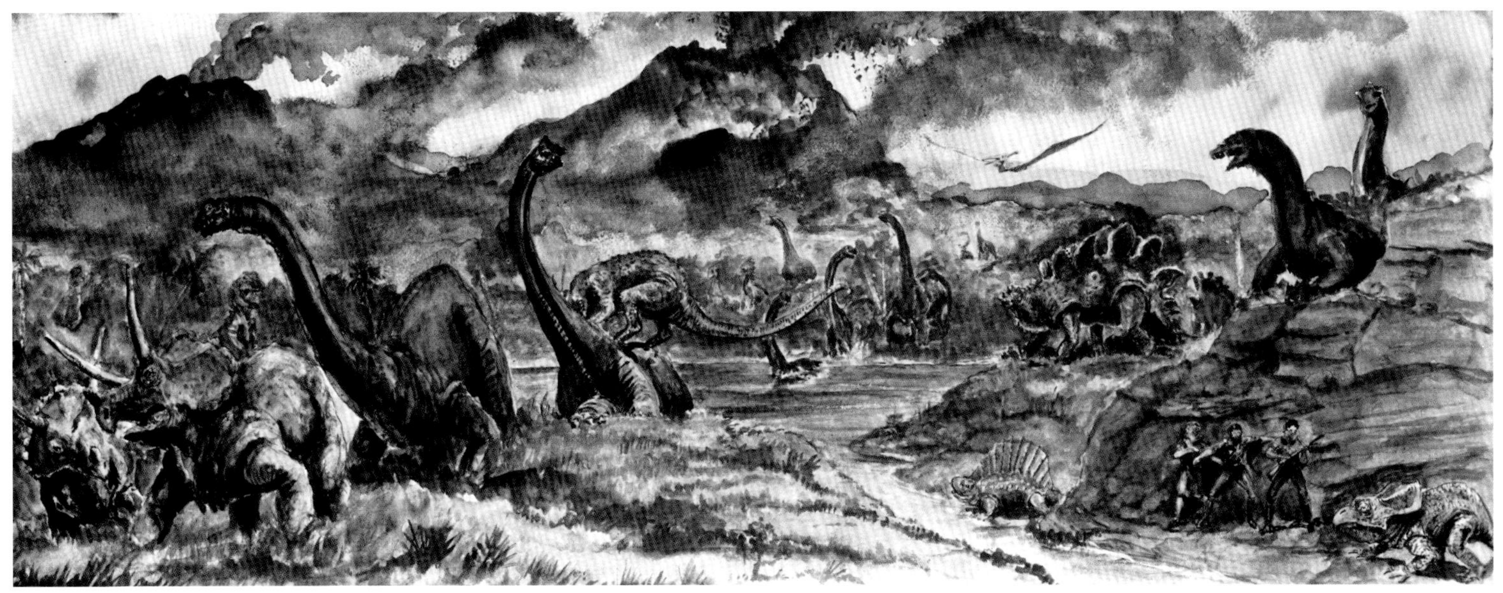

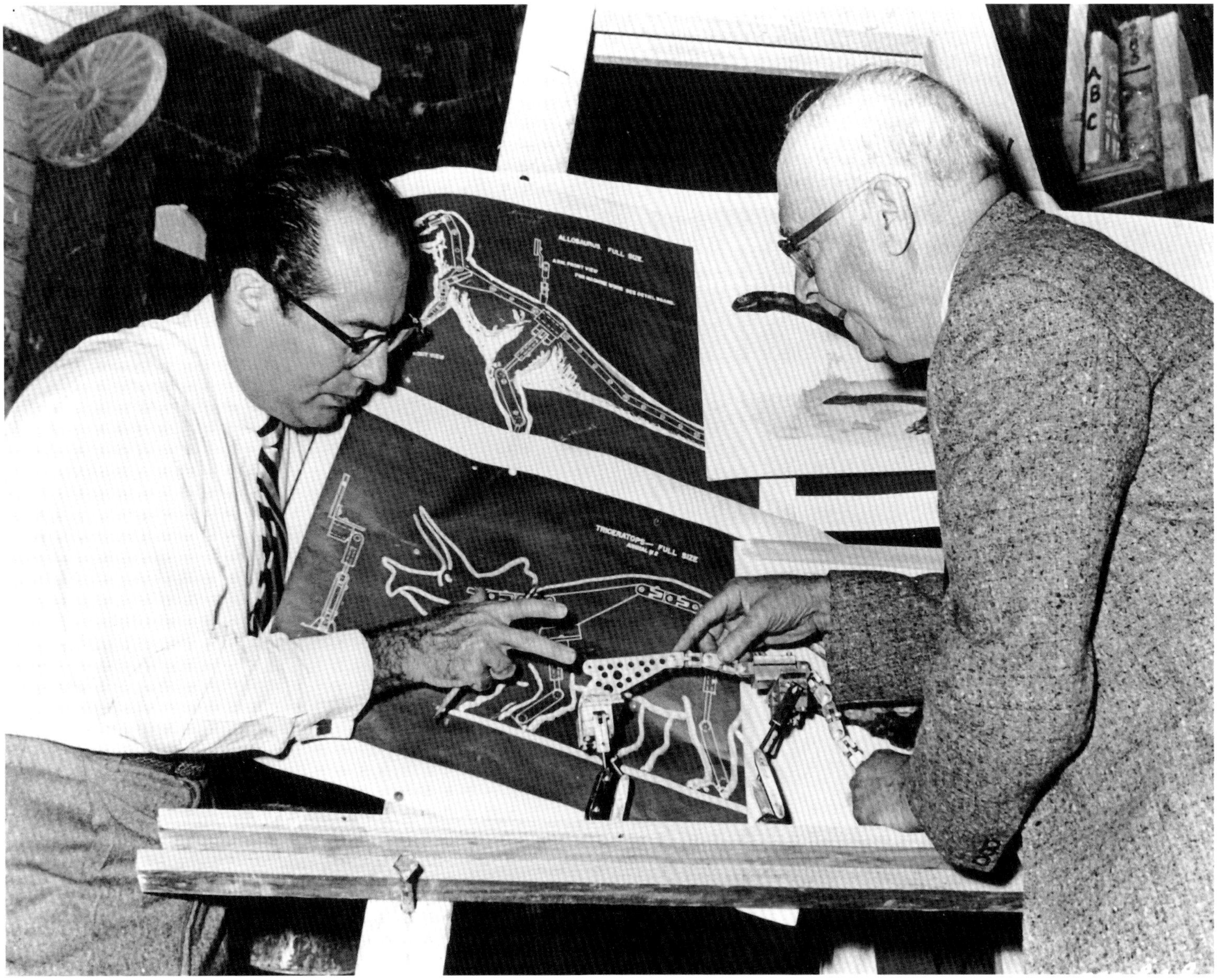
ALLOSAURUS FULL SIZE
TRICERATOPS— FULL SIZE
ABC

LEFT
The creatures are posed for a publicity shot of the eruption which forms the finale of the film.

BELOW
A colourful poster for *The Animal World*; it relies entirely on the dinosaurs to sell what is a feature-length natural history film.

LEFT
Some rare scenes from *The Animal World* shot a week after the animation was completed.

Top row, from left to right. The mechanical head of a brontosaurus; an animation model of the brontosaurus; an unidentified woman holding the model egg case and baby brontosaurus; the baby brontosaurus emerges from its egg; this scene was animated by Ray who also did most of the other animation.

Second row, from left to right. The mechanical head of the triceratops; two ceratosaurus attack and kill a stegosaurus; an allosaurus fights a triceratops; mechanical models of a brontosaurus and an allosaurus.

Third row, from left to right. A mechanical ceratosaurus; a mechanical allosaurus (Note that the shape of the heads of the ceratosaurus and the allosaurus are almost identical except for the horn on the ceratosaurus. This was because both dinosaurs were made from the same mould with the cerotosaurus' horn added later); an allosaurus stalks a brontosaurus in an animation scene; a brontosaurus laying her eggs.

Bottom row, from left to right. A mechanical ceratosaurus attacking a stegosaurus; a mechanical ceratosaurus being attacked by a mechanical allosaurus; an allosaurus squares up against a stegosaurus; all the armatured dinosaur models on display with two unidentified men standing behind.

> *animation puppets, I helped him with miniatures and painted scenes for the backgrounds – gratis. When I say gratis, it was because O'Brien hadn't any extra money in the budget for my services. So I did whatever I could when I wasn't busy on my own film – just helping out a friend.*[24]

After three months of working in dreadful conditions (because of the low budget the studio treated Obie and Pete with disdain and made sure that both technicians were made as uncomfortable as possible), Obie decided to move the animation back to California, not to another studio, but to Peterson's garage in Encino! A return to California was also made necessary because Obie ran out of money in Mexico. According to Darlyne, 'We lived at a hotel rather than an apartment, and we didn't come home with any money at all.' She also reflected, 'He was not a practical person when it came to handling money, he was too creative.'[25]

The model scorpions (there were only three of them although the film was cut to make it appear that there were more) were crudely made, as indeed were the other models, which explains why it was obviously thought best to keep the lighting low-key. Worst of all is the sequence in which the giant scorpion rampages through the streets of Mexico City; because the production had run out of money the effects were achieved by creating a silhouette of one of the models on a travelling matte and superimposing it on the live-action footage of people fleeing. Thus all the audience sees is a black cut-out of the creature. The best sequence takes place in a huge underground cavern from which the creatures first emerge. The two heroes (Richard Denning and Carlos Rivas) are lowered in a cage to the floor of the cavern and for the long shots the cage, the cable and the men were all models. Once in the cavern we see a large undefined bird fly across the blackness, the last appearance of one of Obie's 'trademarks'. In addition to the scorpions the cave also contains a misshapen and crude worm-like creature, which is killed by one of the scorpions, and a little later a giant spider appears. The two actors are integrated into these scenes by standing in front of a full-size rear projection (the animated creatures had been filmed first to enable the actors to react to them in studio), which is extremely poor and seems to be scratched; perhaps it had been damaged during processing? One scene that does succeed to some extent is the derailment of a passenger train by the scorpions. After the train has crashed the creatures gather around the wrecked carriages feeding on the injured occupants. The train was animated, as, of course, were the people grabbed by the scorpion's pincers. The finale takes place in the Mexico City football stadium with the largest and most terrifying of the scorpions being attacked by tanks and a hapless helicopter which ventures too close for its own safety (this is reminiscent of the allosaurus grabbing the pteradactyl in *The Lost World*). The set is obviously a set and is not well matched with the live-action stadium but the death of the beast by electrocution is at least inventive and, to a degree, spectacular. Throughout the film the scorpion animation is continuously interspersed with close-ups of what were supposed to be the faces of the creatures which have drooling mouths and bulging eyes but, regrettably, look nothing like the animation models or, indeed, real scorpions. This cheap attempt to frighten audiences is a hand puppet and it looks like one.

Viewed today, *The Black Scorpion* is most definitely not a classic of model animation; in fact it would be fair to say that it is positively sad. Coming five years after Ray's innovative *The Beast From 20,000 Fathoms*, which also had a miniscule budget, the film is made up of stock footage, bad acting and sub-standard effects. It has all the marks of an attempt to cash in on a cycle that by then had almost run its course. It is also apparent that Obie found it difficult to come to terms with using cheaper effects to achieve spectacle. His 3-D sandwich method of animation had been tried and tested over many years but the problem was that nobody could afford it any longer. Certainly not the sort of producers who made films like *The Black Scorpion*. In 1959 Obie was responsible for the effects on another low budget monster-on-the-rampage picture that was being made in Britain called *Behemoth, the Sea Monster* [aka *The Giant Behemoth*]. Sad to say, this film was again below Obie's standards. The story concerns a fictitious creature called a paleosaurus, a product of radiation poisoning, which

TOP LEFT
Scenes from *The Black Scorpion* (1957) designed by O'Brien and animated by Pete Peterson.

Top left. A scorpion emerging from the crevasse.

Top centre. A giant spider is another predator that lives in the crevasse.

Top right. One of the scorpions attacks the humans as they are lowered into the newly opened crevasse.

Bottom left. The large black scorpion advances down a railway track.

Bottom centre and right. Several scorpions attack the train and kill the passengers.

ABOVE
Top left. Two scorpions attack the explorers who have been winched down into the crevasse.

Top centre. The train comes towards the scorpions. Almost everything that featured animation in the film used miniature sets.

Top right. The biggest scorpion lies in wait for the train.

Bottom left. A worm creature is attacked by a scorpion in the crevasse.

Bottom centre. More train passengers are killed by three scorpions.

Bottom right. The big black scorpion kills one of the smaller ones.

RIGHT
The black scorpion attacks a helicopter in Mexico City.

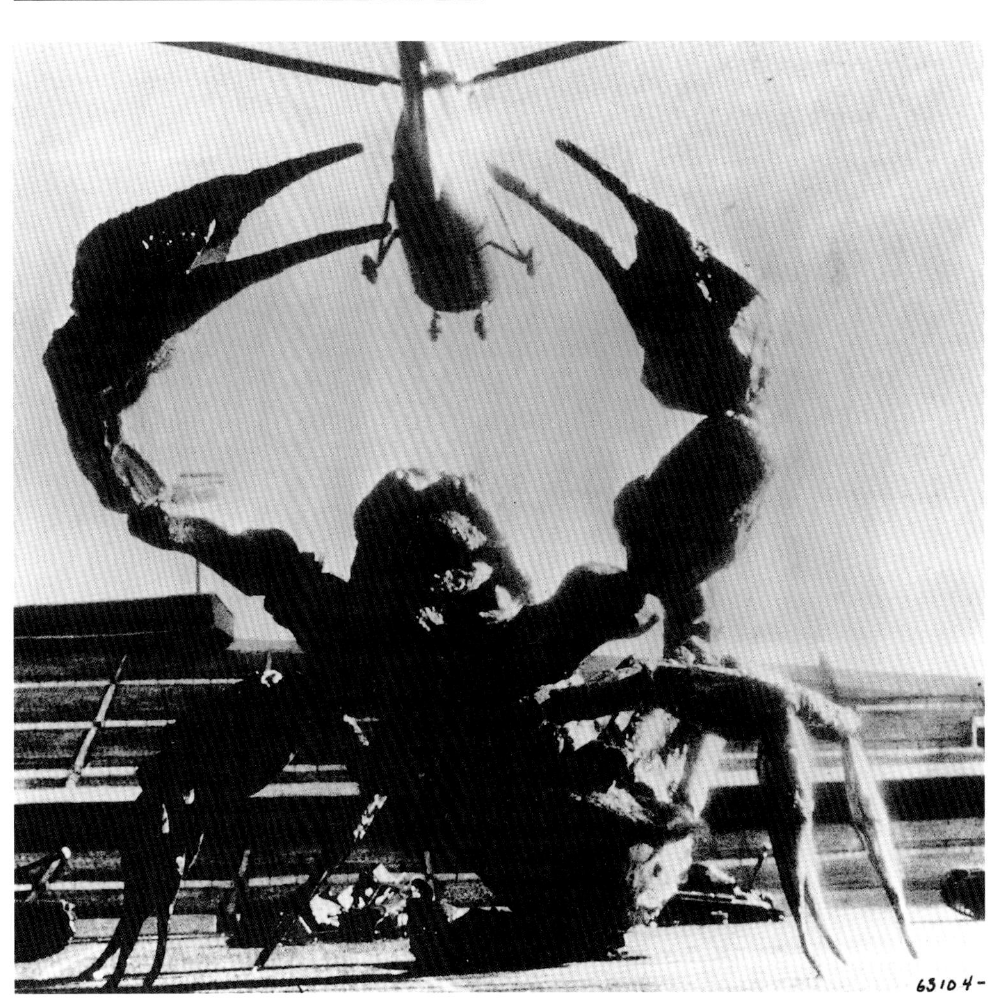

runs amok through London. It was co-directed by Eugene Lourié (the director of Ray's *The Beast From 20,000 Fathoms*) and photographed by Desmond Davis (who was to direct *Clash of the Titans*). The producer, David Diamond, hired Jack Rabin of Studio Film Services, which included Irving Black and Louis DeWitt, to execute all the non-animation work and it was Rabin who hired Obie. The budget was a mere $20,000 for all the effects and Obie only received around $8000 to complete the animation. This was even less than the budget for *The Black Scorpion* and again Obie and Peterson were forced to work in Peterson's garage.

The model of the paleosaur was built by Peterson to Obie's specifications but again, due to the paucity of money, it looked cheap (lumpy and without the usual muscular features associated with Obie's work) although the skin (made from iguana) did look suitably reptilian. It is obvious that not a great deal of time had been allowed for its construction. Ray had taken weeks to design the rhedosaurus for *The Beast From 20,000 Fathoms* but here it is sad to see that Obie had been forced to deliver something way below his usual high standards. To cut costs, the creature is rarely seen in its entirety and some of the animation scenes were used two or three times. There are very few miniatures, aside from the Woolwich ferry, which looks pitiful in its studio tank, the Palace of Westminster and Westminster Abbey. The close-ups of the creature were again taken using a mechanical puppet that was built by Phil Kellison (who had constructed all the miniatures) and, like all mechanical heads, it looks silly and tacky.

Behemoth, the Sea Monster was a sad swan song for Obie. Rather like Orson Welles, he had reached his pinnacle with a masterpiece but was never able to repeat it. That says more about the film-makers and the studio heads of the time than about Obie. He wanted to make first-class fantasy but the producers couldn't, or wouldn't, see that he could make it possible. Even Cooper was limited in his vision.

From 1960 onwards the frustration just got worse for poor Obie. He was hired again by Irwin Allen to work on a proposed remake of *The Lost World* (1960) only to discover, after delivering a mass of drawings and paintings for the project, that Allen had signed him up for his name, not his abilities or his animation expertise. Instead of animating the dinosaurs Allen used live lizards and iguanas with artificial fins stuck on their backs. The result was an insult to Doyle's story and to Obie's earlier version. In Ezra Goodman's book *The Fifty-Year Decline and Fall of Hollywood* Obie comments,

> *The story was completely changed. You wouldn't recognize it. They claim that the live technique looks smoother, that animation is jerky. I don't think so. I'd like to see them use a copy of real dinosaurs with animation. But I guess it's all a matter of taste. They felt it would take too long to animate. It takes quite a crew with these reptiles. With the big screens, you can't carry focus with Cinemascope and you have to be farther than five feet away.*

Of course what he was saying was that it wasn't 'smoother' or less time-consuming, it was just cheaper, a fact that simply frustrated him further in his ongoing quest to promote his style of animation.

In February 1962 Obie's friend and recent animation colleague, Pete Peterson, died in surgery due to kidney cancer (for some ten years he had also been suffering from multiple sclerosis). Peterson's death was yet another blow to a man already suffering from an overdose of bad news; but, typically, Obie carried on against all the odds. What else could he do? He was searching for that final big film to finish on.

With his next project he thought he had found it. He developed a story that contained two characters close to his heart. It was called *King Kong Vs Frankenstein* and he produced a one-page outline which is reproduced here.

> *My original idea of the King Kong-Frankenstein picture is to shoot it in 35mm, color, and not attempt the super-wide film, which would add much to the cost and not much to the entertainment value.*
>
> *As for the story, I still feel the original formula used in this kind of picture still holds up, that is, the excitement of capturing the monster in the wilds and bringing them back to civilization for the big chase, using fresh locations and gaga. I don't feel it necessary to show or explain how or why the Frankenstein creature came to be. Nor do I believe in using electronic devices to control it, only that Frankenstein was experimenting in the wilds of Africa and that his creation went amuck, destroying the professor and his laboratory. The news reaches New York through a montage of TV*

FACING PAGE, LEFT
A close-up of the Behemoth. Note the iguana skin covering.

FACING PAGE, RIGHT
A poster for *Behemoth, The Sea Monster* (1959) under its American title *The Giant Behemoth*.

ABOVE
A recent photograph taken by Dennis Muren of the Behemoth model showing the latex, which is slowly decaying.

BELOW
Two images of the creature stalking its prey through the streets of post-war London.

and newspaper flashes, showing some long shot pictures of the huge beast. Then we go on with my original story of the promoters capturing the Frankenstein monster, also Kong, using San Francisco for the final location, working in the Golden Gate Bridge, the Cable Cars etc.... This will have all the ingredients of King Kong *plus the Frankenstein monster, which will add tremendously to the action, and animation is at its best with fast action.*

I chose Africa for the locations because it will add realism and action, as there must be thousands of feet of good 'stock' footage.

It should not be difficult to add a boy-girl situation into the act without getting too involved.

I was in hope that this picture could get under way and finished while King Kong I is still a favorite.[26]

Obie took the idea to Dan O'Shea, the attorney for RKO who introduced him to another producer with whom Obie worked on the script. Unbeknown to Obie, however, the producer approached a Japanese film company and the project was in part eventually made, without Obie's knowledge or approval, in Japan as *King Kong Vs Godzilla* (1963). The Japanese used a man in a bad ape suit. Obie seriously considered taking out an 'intent to defraud' lawsuit against the producer but because he had saved no money and knew that the lawyers would be the only ones to win, he was very reluctant to take it further. Darlyne said of this time, 'He never learned to protect himself, in spite of the fact that he took up boxing. He was always in too much of a financial spot to risk losing a job and hitting back. The monsters he conjured up were nothing to the monsters he encountered in the human world.'[27]

In 1962 Obie was hired by Film Effects of Hollywood as a consultant and director of animation on Stanley Kramer's production of I*ts a*

ABOVE AND BELOW
Two conceptual drawings by O'Brien showing how he saw the stage production that would reveal King Kong and Frankenstein's monster to the waiting world for his proposed *King Kong Vs Frankenstein*.

Mad, Mad, Mad, Mad World (1963), but as with the remake of *The Lost World* he was employed solely for his name, which seemed to literally break his heart. On 10 November 1962, during the shooting of a short animated scene at the conclusion of the film, he went home feeling unwell. When he arrived home Darlyne recalled, 'He felt as if he had acid on his stomach and thought that was causing a slight pain in his chest.' She went on,

> *He laid down for a while and just had milk toast for dinner and left the table and went into the living room to watch television. I was looking at the television when I heard an odd kind of cough from him and looked toward him. He was falling over on his side. He had evidently died sitting up because when I rushed over to him, his eyes had no expression whatever.*

The ambulance was called but when it arrived he was pronounced dead. He was 76 years of age. 'I am positive the tension of being out of work during the last two years and the frustration of the *King Kong Vs Frankenstein* deal, had a lot to do with the heart attack that took Obie's life,' Darlyne said some time later.[28]

So ended the life of the man who had succeeded in developing the art of model animation to the highest degree and in so doing gave us 'living' dinosaurs and a 'star' called Kong – The Eighth Wonder of the World. According to his wishes, he was cremated and his ashes were interred at the Chapel of the Pines in Los Angeles.

In an interview given by Darlyne O'Brien to film historian Kevin Brownlow, circa 1970, she said of Obie, 'He was a kid right up to the day he died… he was still just a boy and a dreamer. He never seemed to grow up.' Other tributes came from Marcel Delgado who remarked, 'He was a wonderful man, sincere, kind hearted and with a good sense of humour, a lot of fun. No one could ask for a better friend.'[29] Hard-nosed producer Marian C. Cooper also paid tribute to Obie, 'I considered him a genius of the first order and *King Kong* would have been impossible for me to produce and co-direct with Schoedsack without Willis O'Brien's artistry and skill.'[30] In 1997 Obie was posthumously awarded the Windsor McCay Award by Asifa-Hollywood, the United States chapter of the International Animated Film Society, in recognition of a lifetime of contributions to the art of animation.

Without Obie the art of model animation would probably have taken longer to mature and a fourteen-year-old boy called Ray Harryhausen might have become a plumber. Ray may be the father of model animation combined with live action and related effects, but Obie was the grandfather. He was the man who developed and nurtured the art of stop-motion animation and without his foresight and inventiveness the art would have never realized its full potential. Whereas the early pioneers in model animation had used it as a 'gimmick' to make money, Obie had seen the potential of combining models with live actors and making the model the focus of the story rather than a bit-player.

Obie said in 1933, soon after the release of his greatest achievement,

> King Kong *represents the goal of more than twenty years. For that long a time - and that is a long time in motion pictures – I have delved into bygone periods, studied the life of animals long before the descent of man, preparing myself for the day when someone would dare to reproduce on the screen the giant beasts that once ruled the world. Without knowing it, I was waiting for* King Kong.

ABOVE LEFT
Comparison drawing by O'Brien of King Kong with a human.

ABOVE
Comparison drawing by O'Brien showing the comparative sizes of Kong and the monster.

BELOW
Willis O'Brien the star-maker, early 1960s.

CHAPTER FOUR

THE BEGINNING OF DYNAMATION AND CREATIVITY IN MOTION

The stop-motion process provides a unique form of fantasy that is difficult to analyse because it provides an atmosphere of a dream world rather than fake reality. If you make it too real the fantasy can be broken.[1]

There were three major landmarks in the first fifty years of the history of model animation. The first, achieved by Obie, was combining animation with live action in the same frame; the second, devised by Ray, was the set of techniques that he and producer Charles Schneer christened Dynamation, which provided a 'simplified' and more flexible means of combining the two. The third, for which the credit must also go to Ray, was to extend the range of subject matter, so that model animation was no longer limited to films about creatures (usually prehistoric) rampaging through modern cities but now embraced other branches of fantasy such as legends and mythology. This third development opened up new and virtually limitless horizons for the art.

In the first of our two previous books, *An Animated Life*, we described Ray's career and the making of his films, and in the second, *The Art of Ray Harryhausen*, we presented a gallery of his unique artwork. Thus, as much of the story has already been adequately covered, we will devote this chapter to a discussion of two other aspects of the history of model animation in which Ray played a major role. The first is the genesis of Dynamation (this was discussed in the first book but here we attempt to chronicle the full history) and the second is the way in which Ray managed to give each of his creations a distinct personality or character. Had he not had a gift for this his models would have remained just that, models which would have failed to come to life on the screen.

Ray never attended university to study model animation – at the time there were no courses that even remotely encompassed such a specialized subject – though he did study elementary cinematic techniques at night classes at the University of Southern California. Fortunately, he possessed a natural artistic talent, which, once his imagination had been captured by *King Kong* in 1933, he applied to building models and manipulating them in order to bring them to life on-screen. He was clearly no ordinary young man and it is clear, in retrospect, that from the day he saw that giant ape come crashing out of the jungle he knew what his vocation would be, even if at that time he had no idea as to how he would pursue it.

Ray was never exactly an apprentice to Willis O'Brien but rather a young enthusiast who became inspired by Obie's work and subsequently had the good fortune to meet him and then to work with him on several occasions. Like Obie, Ray taught himself through experimentation,

PREVIOUS SPREAD
Left, the Hydra from *Jason and the Argonauts*. The photograph shows just how complex the model was. Ray liked a challenge!
Right, a colour test for the Hydra in its miniature set.

BELOW
A sketch by Ray showing the Dynamation setup.

TOP RIGHT
Two views of Ray animating the Medusa for *Clash of the Titans*. In the left-hand photograph the coloured cellophane disk used to simulate the flicker of flames in her hair is visible at the extreme left. The wooden matte frame is in the foreground.

BOTTOM RIGHT
Almost the entire Dynamation setup captured in one rare photograph. In the background we can see the rear-projection screen showing the live action. On the animation table the Kraken is gripping two rocks as it raises itself from the water. The 'rocks' were in fact wooden blocks on which the model's hand were placed; you can clearly see that they are matted out on the matte glass placed between the table and the Mitchell camera in the foreground. When the film was re-run through the camera they would be replaced by real rocks on the rear-projection screen with everything else matted out.

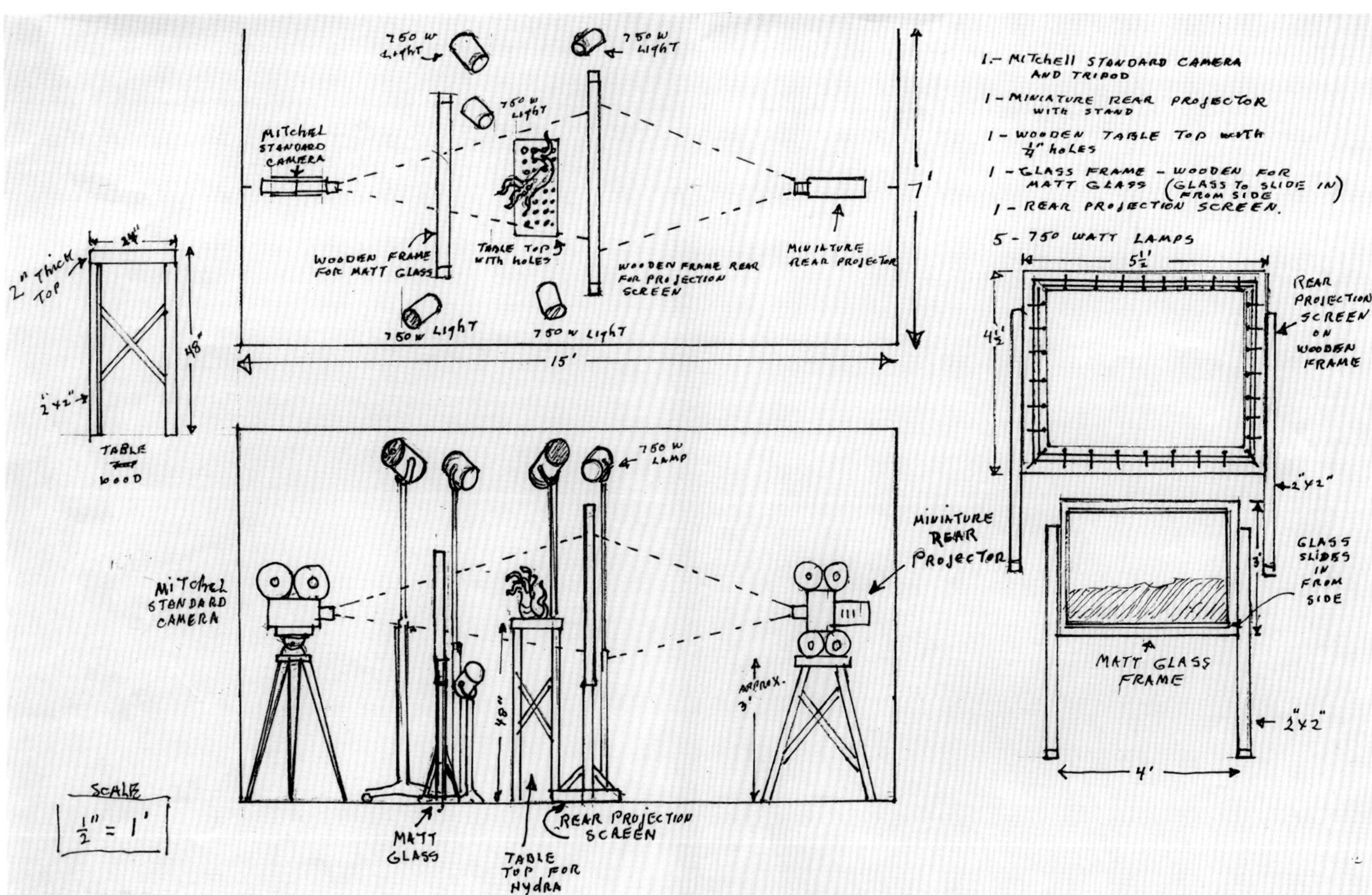

ABOVE
Ray had to begin somewhere. Here we see his cave bear with a tiny model human. This was one of his first experiments in building miniature sets and animating models. This photograph was taken in 1935 outside his parents' house. He soon realized, as the background sheet billowed in the wind and the shadows moved as the sun swept around, that there was still a way to go before he perfected the process.

BELOW
Three frames from a test for *Evolution of the World* (1938-40). In the first we see a model human climbing a palm tree to escape a brontosaurus. In the second the human is plucked from the side of the tree and in the third the man is seen in the brontosaurus' mouth. These images not only illustrate Ray's talent for set construction but also show how strongly he was influenced by *King Kong*, which contains a similar scene in which a sailor is attacked by a brontosaurus.

which in his case involved making a number of short films that he calls his 'teething rings'. It was these films that set him upon the long road of developing his own unique techniques and style, in the end producing feature films that rivalled, and even surpassed his hero's considerable achievements.

After completing *Mighty Joe Young* in 1949 Ray realized that the future of the art could not rely on Obie's tried and tested methods which involved using huge, detailed glass paintings to sandwich his models, so creating an illusion of depth. Although the results were excellent, this process took too long and consequently incurred huge costs. In short, with Hollywood cutting back on production costs and concentrating on making successful low-budget pictures, Obie's techniques were doomed. However, even though the accepted wisdom around the studios was that fantasy films, particularly if they had to utilize model animation, were no longer feasible, Ray believed that they did have a future. Determined not to let his career falter he looked around for other ways of combining animated models with live-action. He knew he had to find a way of making fantasy subjects easier to shoot and therefore more commercially viable. The solution he came up with would become known as Dynamation and would not only provide economy and flexibility but would also enable animators to expand the range of storylines they tackled and ensure that the art survived into the future.

Ray also realized that if he was to succeed in what he wanted to do he would have no choice but to work alone. He knew that, with his type of animation, independence was a necessity. Aside from the prohibitive costs of the huge number of technicians that Obie had had to employ on *Mighty Joe Young*, he also didn't want someone to talk him out of how he knew a scene should look, especially if he knew it was right. To achieve what he felt was right he had to work as a one-man operation and, aside from his final feature *Clash of the Titans*, always managed to achieve this aim although there were several occasions when outside forces tried to bring in other animators 'to try to speed things up'. It is because his films all bear the stamp of his own beliefs and methods that they have a unique cinematic look.

Even though Ray would only assemble all the components of Dynamation after 1949, he had recognized the possibilities of the two main elements of the process before the war. The first of these was the use of a rear-projection plate to create a live-action background against which a model could be animated. In late 1946 and early 1947 he took the first tentative step when he filmed a sequence in which an animated caveman walked in front of a waterfall. This was achieved by using a rear-projected waterfall in front of which the model walked onto the screen, looked around and then ambled off. This was his first use of a rear-projected image. But, although the model was surrounded by a miniature foreground set, the sequence did not create an effect which genuinely combined the animation and the live-action landscape. To fully integrate the two on-screen the model needed to be 'inserted' into the live action.

Although Ray hadn't had any 'professional' experience in combining animation and live-action up to that time, he had experimented with mattes as far back as 1938 by matting images such as water into an animation setup. If *this* was possible then why not 'split' the screen with mattes, to 'insert' a model or models?

The process worked as follows. After the live action had been shot it was rear-projected, frame by frame, on to a screen behind Ray's animation table. Ray's first task was then to establish a matte line that split the screen into two parts, the upper, or background, area and the lower, or foreground, area. A matte and counter-matte would then be produced. Next, with the foreground matted out, Ray would animate the model in front of the rear-projected live action in the background. Once the shot was complete, the film in both the camera and the rear projector would be rewound, the matte replaced by the counter-matte which obscured the background, the model removed and the process repeated. The result was a new version of the original live-action shot into

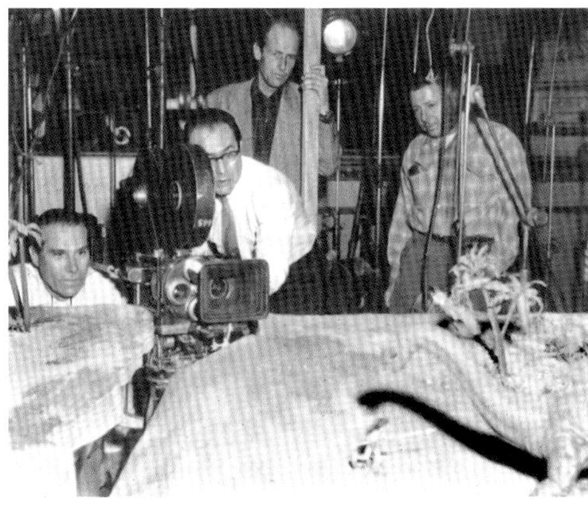

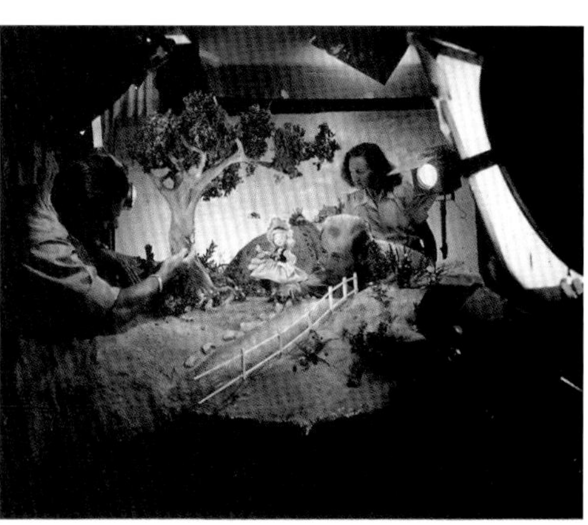

ABOVE TOP
Ray animating cards in October 1942 for George Pal Productions. Ray doesn't recollect that this was for a *Puppetoon* and thinks it was for a separate George Pal project. George occasionally took in other work unrelated to the *Puppetoons*.

ABOVE MIDDLE
Ray (on the left), a painter called Pete Stitch (middle) and Obie (right) during the production of *Mighty Joe Young*. This is one of only a few images Ray has of Obie and himself together.

ABOVE BOTTOM
Working on *Animal World* (1956). Ray is behind a vertical wooden support in the background whilst producer Irwin Allen 'pretends' to be directing the animation of the brontosaurus in its miniature set. This was a publicity setup to show that Allen was a hands-on producer.

ABOVE TOP
The mooncalf featured in *First Men in the Moon* (1964) in its miniature lunar set. The mooncalf was one of the most difficult models to animate as the number of legs necessitated a caterpillar-like motion, which caused Ray a lot of problems.

ABOVE MIDDLE
'Young Harry' animating Joe during the roping sequence for *Mighty Joe Young*.

ABOVE BOTTOM
Ray animating Hansel and Gretel for *The Story of Hansel and Gretel* (1951).

ABOVE TOP
Ray works with Les Bowie, an excellent British special effects technician mostly famous for his work on the Hammer horror films. They are overseeing the construction and photography for part of the interior of the lunar caves.

ABOVE MIDDLE
Ray and effects cameraman Bert Willis during the making of *Mighty Joe Young*. Note the glass painting behind.

ABOVE BOTTOM
Ray animating Little Miss Muffet for his first Fairy Tale, *Mother Goose Stories* (1946).

TOP FAR LEFT

A setup for the unfinished *Evolution of the World* showing the model brontosaurus in a miniature set framed in the foreground by a glass painting, done by Ray, of vegetation. This 'sandwiching' of the model between the background miniature and a foreground painting gave depth to the scene and was a system that Obie had devised for *The Lost World* in 1925.

TOP LEFT

The Giant Ymir being attacked by a dog in *20 Million Miles to Earth* (1957). Because the dog looks so rubbery, and therefore unconvincing, Ray decided that the scene of the fight would take place in shadow, which occurs just after this shot.

BOTTOM LEFT

Ray in his dad's garage photographing the Jupitarian model in a miniature set. Note the miniature picket fence above Ray's head and a swamp drawing above the animation table. He is using a camera loaned to him by a friend which was the forerunner of his Kodak Cine Special.

BELOW

A fun piece. This is a paste-up done by Ray using his model triceratops that featured in *Evolution of the World*. He and his father posed in several different positions which were roughly in proportion to a full-sized triceratops. Ray then cut them out and pasted them into the setup. The figures on the extreme left and on the horn of the creature were his father, whilst Ray is seen running away in the foreground. Ray was always experimenting with new visual techniques to see how useful they might be for his film projects.

which the model had been seamlessly inserted. This was, in essence, the secret of what became known as Dynamation

The first feature film on which Ray used the process was *The Beast From 20,000 Fathoms* (1952), but before beginning the production Ray made various tests to ensure that the process he had devised, which was at this stage largely theoretical, would actually work. He had assured the producers that it would, so he now had had to make sure of all the elements. Using an early non-armatured model for the Beast and stock footage of a river for the rear-projection plate, he photographed a 16mm test reel of the Beast in the river in his home studio (the hobby house). He realized from his earlier experiments that when you re-photograph an old image (in this case the background plate) with a first-generation subject (the model), the first will not be as sharp as the second. To overcome this problem Ray simply photographed the whole thing with the model slightly out of focus, thus ensuring that both rear projection and model seemed as if they had been photographed at the same time. Fortunately all the elements worked and *The Beast From 20,000 Fathoms* became a reality, Ray's first solo feature film and an landmark in model animation and cinema history.

Although using actual locations, whether fantasy or otherwise, rather than miniature sets did create a far greater degree of 'realism' there were two other factors that were fundamental to making Ray's films work convincingly. The first was fluidity of movement, and, more specifically, movement that was appropriate to the physical appearance of each model. This may seem obvious, because without fluidity a model is likely to look like a model in a set rather than a creature in an actual location. Fluidity comes with experience and with experience comes an instinctive feel for how, and how much, a particular model needs to be moved to make its actions look convincing. To take two simple examples, Talos, the huge bronze giant in *Jason and the Argonauts*, had to move slowly because of his apparent size and weight, while the allosaurus Gwangi, which was also large, had to move quickly, like a reptile, but

LEFT
The rhedosaurus featured in *The Beast From 20,000 Fathoms* (1952). It is seen on the animation table and being animated in front of a rear-projected still image of a New York street. The exceptional amount of character that Ray managed to instill into this creature makes it one of the most enduring monsters, aside from Kong, of course, in movie history.

BELOW LEFT
The Beast immortalized in bronze.

BELOW
Trog as he is today. He is a large model, 17" (h) x 9"(w), and was designed and constructed to accommodate close-ups. Because of his human form he was a natural for a primitive human characterization and was a joy to animate.

TOP RIGHT
The achelon from *One Million Years BC*. Like Trog, he spent so much of his time in close up that he needed to be larger than normal, 23" (l) x 14" (w) with a shell made of resin. He was a relatively simply creature to animate as he only possessed four flippers, a neck and head. The hardest part was to animate him pulling himself along on those flippers.

TOP FAR RIGHT
The giant bronze statue Talos standing on the animation table waiting to attack the Argonauts. Again this model was reasonably simple to animate as he had to move in a ponderous and jerky manner to accommodate his height and weight and to reflect the fact that he is supposed to be made of bronze.

not so quickly as to destroy the illusion of size. For Ray, inspiration quite often came when he was looking at the animation table at the beginning of a sequence. He would usually begin with one simple move and then think, 'Where do I go from here, what will be the next move?', something that was usually obvious by then. In other words, one pose would lead to another. Such spur-of-the-moment creativity was a hallmark of both Ray's work and Obie's and contrasted very strongly with the pre-planned sequences of movements used by George Pal for his *Puppetoon* series [see Chapter 5]. Because the *Puppetoon* animation was all planned out before animation was even begun, there was little or no scope for spontaneous creativity. With a fully armatured model sitting on the animation table there were few restrictions as to what it could be made to do, as long as it ultimately corresponded with the live action on the rear-projection screen.

The other factor essential to creating realism was giving each model a distinctive character, or at the very least making it act appropriately. A model that lacks character is likely to be dull and uninspiring. It is obvious that a humanoid model will need to act in a way that is convincingly human-like, but even an inanimate object like a spaceship presents the animator with the chal-

BELOW

Various frames from *Evolution of the World*.

Top row, left to right. The brontosaurus ambling through the jungle, note the foreground painted glass vegetation (the setup can be seen on page 118 top left); the allosaurus leaps over the camera and onto the miniature set, by means of aerial wires, to attack the brontosaurus; an allosaurus attacking a triceratops.

Bottom row, left to right. The allosaurus attacking the horn of a triceratops; the allosaurus snarling, there is an obvious debt to Obie's snarling allosaurus and brontosaurus in *The Lost World*; the allosaurus looks up from a meal and stares at the camera. This last wasn't really for *Evolution of the World* but was done as a joke for one of Ray's friends.

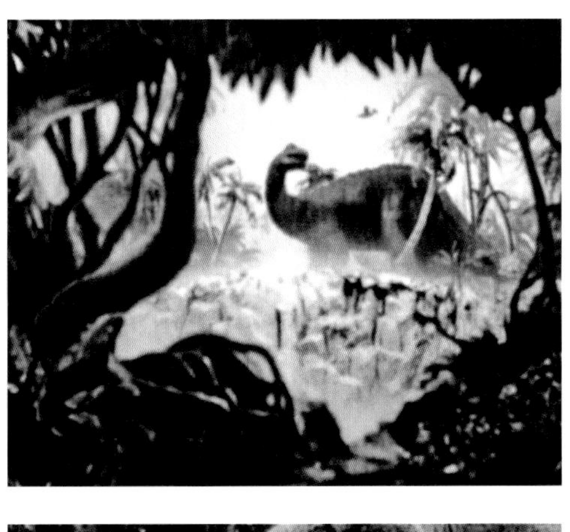

lenge of giving its design and movements a consistent style. Whatever it may represent, the animator must put his soul into a model. The effort involved in establishing and maintaining a consistent character for each model can be exhausting, especially in the case of more complex characters.

Naturally any decisions about a model's character and the way in which it should move must begin with its design. That is why it is essential than the animator should always be involved with the design of a model right from the start. For it is the animator who has to determine what it will do, within the constraints set by the screenplay and the live action that has already been filmed, and how it will move. For example, the design and construction of Medusa was extremely detailed and went through many changes, not only because of the challenge of creating a figure that was both human and snake-like, but also because Ray had to assess what was going to be required of the model in each scene and this meant that both the model's appearance and its internal armature had to be modified to meet the unique demands that would be made of it.

Sometimes models were required to make only very basic movements, for example the archelon from *One Million Years BC*. All that was required of him in the script was to appear at the top of a sand dune and lumber down the slope to the sea, with the occasional threatening roar and sideways glance at the cavemen. The moving elements of the model were the flippers, head, neck, mouth and eyes. When faced with the challenge of animating such a creature the questions the animator has to ask are: what will it do as it moves down to the water? How should it react to humans, which a real archelon would never have encountered? And how can its movements be made to resemble those of a turtle, the archelon's nearest living relative? It was easy to make the creature impressive simply by making it larger in relation to the humans than it would have been in 'reality'; but it also had to be designed in a way that would allow the model to make all the possible permutations of actions that a 'real' archelon would have been able to make. Simple though the archelon appears to be he still had to be a 'living' dinosaur.

Another creature that might have seemed straightforward on paper, but was certainly not so in reality, was the giant crab in *Mysterious Island*. The crab began its acting career when Ray purchased it live in Harrods Food Hall. The crab's next port of call was the Natural History Museum in London, where Ray arranged for it to be humanely killed so that an armature could be made around which the shell, claws and legs could be reassembled. Although Ray knew the rough dimensions (the crab had been chosen for its size) it wasn't until it was dead that Ray could begin to design the armature that would

LEFT, FROM THE TOP

Ray animating the allosaurus Gwangi and the elephant for *The Valley of Gwangi* (1969). The entire arena, or bullring, is a live-action rear-projected image but the floor is an animation table, cut to resemble the floor of the arena and tilted.

Ray animating the Minaton for *Sinbad and the Eye of the Tiger* (1977). The Minaton was another of those creations that didn't lend itself to characterization.

Ray animating the baboon for *Sinbad and the Eye of the Tiger*. Because of its humanoid form, and because it was supposed to have once been a man, the baboon lent itself fairly readily to characterization – though the task was made more complex because it was necessary to show the ape gradually taking over from the human.

Ray getting in on the picture whilst animating the beautifully made tiger for *Sinbad and the Eye of the Tiger*. For this creature Ray studied tigers and other large cats in London Zoo and so was able to achieve a graceful feline walk or stalk.

The wasp featured in *Sinbad and the Eye of the Tiger* on the animation table.

It is unusual to find so many images of Ray animating, but on *Sinbad and the Eye of the Tiger* there were a number of tests that Tony found in the collection and it is from these that the above images were taken.

RIGHT

Top left. A publicity shot of Ray adjusting the dragon in its miniature lair for *The 7th Voyage of Sinbad*.

Top right. Another publicity shot showing Ray looking down at his dragon emerging from the cliff face.

Middle left. Ray animating the large single tentacle pushing up through the road of the Golden Gate Bridge. The tentacle was mounted on a screw device that allowed it to slowly push through the miniature roadway, frame by frame.

Middle right. The large tentacle again, this time pushing through the gate of the miniature Oakland ferry terminal. The pavement, small arch and people on the right-hand side are matted in to the animation set.

Bottom left. One of the Washington DC buildings in the process of crumbling for *Earth Vs the Flying Saucers*. Instead of high-speed photography, which was too expensive, Ray animated the building crumbling by hanging each section on wires.

Bottom right. Ray animating the destruction of another building using the same method.

ENTRANCE
OAKLAND FERRY
SPEED LIMIT
10

allow the creature to come to 'life' again. Because of the weight of the shells, especially the main shell, the armature had to be especially strong but at the same time flexible, as such a creature would be expected to be quite agile, even one that would appear to be twenty feet high. Also, when Ray received the shells back he quickly realized that the shell that made up the crab's underbelly, was going to restrict animation movement so he had to design and fit a more flexible latex substitute. Even though the armature had been designed with the weight in mind, the entire creature had also to be suspended on three, sometimes four, aerial wires. Another problem that arose was that the feet were pointed and could not accommodate threaded holes to fix them to the animation table. Ray was therefore forced to drill tiny holes through the tips so they could be secured by wires threaded through holes in the table. This had the effect of increasing the time it took to animate the creature. As Ray had never tried animating a crab before he purchased several small live crabs to enable him to study their movements before he started to design the crab sequence. Real crabs tend to move sideways but Ray wanted his crab to confront the human actors head-on, so its movements were generally restricted to forwards and backwards and manipulation of the large pincers with which the creature threatens its opponents and appears to interact with the live action – in fact, the man it seizes was a model.

Although the physical actions of a crab are complex because the body has so many limbs, for more intricate movements, such as dance, a model does not necessarily have to be designed with more joints, just the correct joints. Kali, the bronze statue featured in *The Golden Voyage of Sinbad* (1973) had not only to perform an Indian dance to introduce her to the audience, she also had to fight Sinbad and his men with her six arms. Therefore she had to be extremely versatile. When designing the armature, and to accommodate the Indian-influenced movement where we see the head moving from side to side, Ray ensured that the armature would be able to do everything he wanted without any problems. The same applied to the snake woman in *The 7th Voyage of Sinbad* and the Hydra in *Jason and the Argonauts*, although of course the latter wasn't required to dance. It was, however, extremely complex, not just because it had seven heads and a double snake-like tail, but because of how it had to perform with humans.

As these examples make clear, the proper design of a model is essential and this, in turn, depends upon the animator's ability to envisage

ABOVE
The giant crab on the beach in *Mysterious Island* (1961). In the background the actor Michael Craig (who was on the rear-projection plate) is falling off a raised wooden platform which is hidden by the crab's body.

ABOVE RIGHT
Ray with producer Charles Schneer discussing the crab sequence for *Mysterious Island*.

RIGHT
The crab as he looks today. From this angle he is little changed but the latex joints and underbelly have all now deteriorated and the armature, although still complete, has loosened so that he had to be held up whilst this photograph was taken. The dimensions are 16" (w) x 16" (h), whilst the claws are 9" long and 3" wide. As with other living creatures, or those with modern descendants, Ray made a study of crabs to observe how they moved, although in the film he had it move mostly forwards and backwards whilst a real crab tend to move sideways.

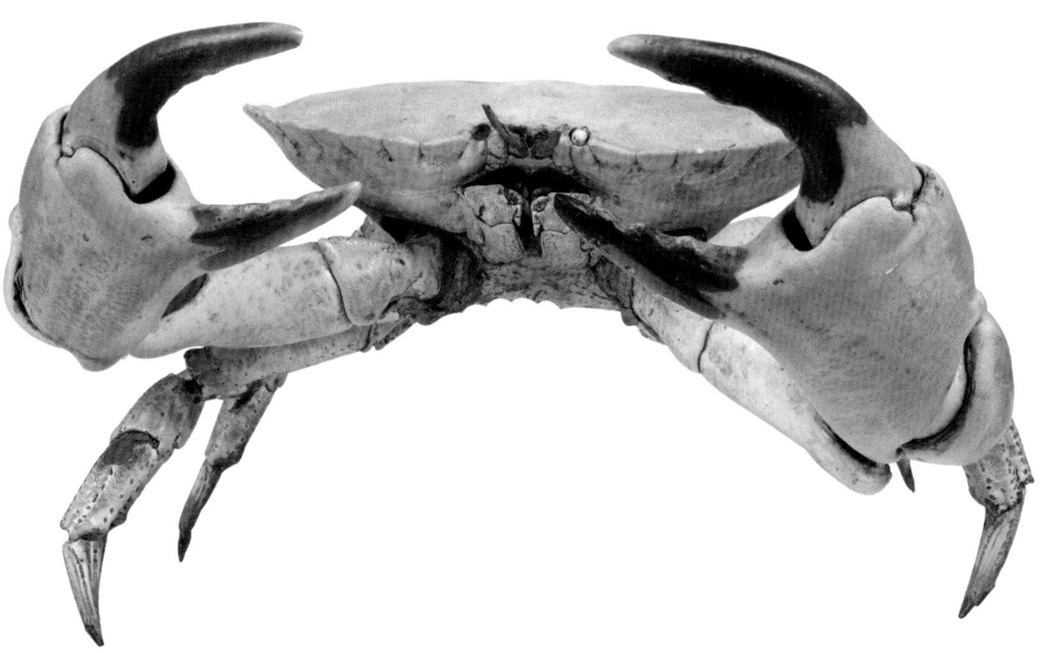

BELOW
Four test stills taken during the animation of Kali for *The Golden Voyage of Sinbad* (1973).

Top left. Kali attacks Sinbad and one of his men.

Top right. A test card on the animation table that obscures the Kali model, and which enabled the laboratory to colour grade the footage.

Bottom left. Kali in action on the animation table in front of the rear-projection screen. Note the screws below the animation table that correspond with Kali's feet. Ray used these to secure the model to the table. In this case they were long to allow quick access in order to move the model, over the years Ray used many different types of fixings.

Bottom right. A scene showing Kali with the animation table removed by the spilt screen.

the model's repertoire of movements well before animation actually begins However, it is only when the model or models are on the animation table that the most creative phase of the animator's work, giving each model a distinctive character, can begin. Of course, animators themselves each have their own taste and personality and so each will perceive aspects of a model's character in a unique way. Ray's creatures often have a 'Harryhausen' signature, a certain way of holding themselves and moving. For example the Cyclops in *The 7th Voyage of Sinbad*, the Cyclopean Centaur in *The Golden Voyage of Sinbad* and the Ymir in *20 Million Miles to Earth*, all share a distinctive stance and way of moving: holding the arms up but bent at the elbow and turning their bodies to compensate for their theoretically considerable weight. These along with other distinctive actions are Ray's way of interpreting movement and have become a trademark.

The simplest of models such as those used in a puppet film will benefit from being given a degree of individuality, though in a Dynamation project, the need to coordinate animated movement with live action often dictated the ways in which a model's character could be expressed. But in every case the trick is for the animator to put himself in his model's position and ask, 'What would I do in this situation?'

Ray's earliest experiments, specifically with dinosaurs, tended to concentrate on rather basic animal behaviour, such as snarling and roaring at other creatures. These and similar reactions were based on creatures he had seen in *The Lost World* and *King Kong*. Even seventy years on these early experiments are still impressive but most of them

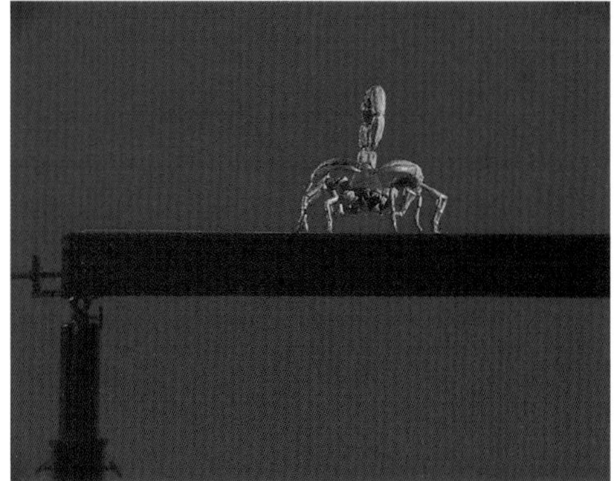

ABOVE
Ray with the first armatured skeleton featured in *The 7th Voyage of Sinbad*. He still has this, although it was reused in *Jason and the Argonauts* and now he can't recall which one it is.

RIGHT, FROM THE TOP

The Cyclops featured in *The 7th Voyage of Sinbad* holding a model human, which he is about to place in the cage. He is standing on an animation table and behind him is the rear-projection screen.

The cyclopean centaur and the Gryphon face each other on the animation table for *The Golden Voyage of Sinbad*. Although the Gryphon didn't have a large part to play in the film it is one of Ray's favourite creatures. The centaur was part-humanoid, part-horse so there were elements of both in his performance.

One of the nasty scorpions form *Clash of the Titans* on the animation table ready to be photographed against a blue screen which will allow it to be composited into the live action. With scorpions there is not too much of an opportunity to instill character.

Poor old Trog from *Sinbad and the Eye of the Tiger*. He is standing on his animation table waiting for the next shot.

seem basic because there is a lack of characterization. Ray still had to learn that character was an essential factor in bringing his creations to life. This changed when he began work on *Evolution of the World* in 1938. During the animation he realized that he needed to give the dinosaurs some element of character if they were to seem 'alive' and so he tried to express that character through the movements of their tails and limbs and over the years these simple ways of bringing out the characters of his models became instinctive and an integral part of Ray's animation.

Observation makes an essential contribution to any animator's art and in order to further improve his characterizations Ray began to study people and animals. A natural observer, Ray would always note people's mannerisms, especially if they were a bit out of the ordinary. Of course, the ways such observations are interpreted in the course of animation are subjective and individualistic, and in Ray's case his observations were translated into what became the 'Harryhausen effect'. For example, although Ray is not generally keen on boxing and wrestling, he did find himself becoming interested in aspects of both sports, particularly the stances adopted by the opposing fighters and the movements they

ABOVE TOP
Ray animating the wasp on its aerial wires for *Sinbad and the Eye of the Tiger*.

ABOVE
Ray photographing the Fountain of Destiny miniature set in Spain for *The Golden Voyage of Sinbad*.

TOP RIGHT
Ray, circa 1958, on the floor of his house in Malibu with four of the creatures that featured in *The 7th Voyage of Sinbad*. On the left at the back is the dragon, on the right at the back is the Cyclops, middle is the baby Roc and in the foreground, the creation that started it all off, the skeleton who looks like he is skating.

RIGHT
Ray apparently struggling to animate the Kraken for *Clash of the Titans*. Because of the thick layer of latex the Kraken was difficult to manipulate.

made as they ducked and dived to avoid each others' attacks. There was to have been a scene in *Mighty Joe Young* in which two gorillas fight on the top of a cable car and Obie wanted them to slug it out like two boxers, while at the same time moving in a gorilla-like fashion. To give Ray food for thought and first-hand experience, Obie took 'young Harry' to his first boxing tournament. Sadly, the scene was dropped from the final script but everything Ray saw there was stored away for use in future projects.

So observation and experience are vital ingredients in achieving a good flow of believable movement on the animation table and to illustrate this we have selected a number of key sequences from Ray's films.

Let's begin with 'flying' creatures, perhaps some of the hardest models into which to instill character. Some of the most basic creatures in this category are the pterosaurs, which include pteranodons and pterodactyls. Ray made two films that featured such flying, carnivorous reptiles. In *One Million Years BC* Raquel Welch is grabbed by one of these creatures and carried off to its nest to provide a meal for its young, while in *The Valley of Gwangi* a boy is plucked from his horse by one. Neither of these brief

BELOW
A variety of flying creatures

Top left. Ray animating the pterodactyl on aerial wires for *One Million Years BC* (1966). It was extremely cold during the filming, hence the coat.

Top centre. HRH Princess Muna al-Hussein, the British wife of King Hussein of Jordan, who visited Elstree Studios in North London where Ray was making *One Million Years BC*. During the visit Ray showed her some of his creatures.

Top right. The pterodactyl in *The Valley of Gwangi* showing the top and bottom edge of the rear-projection screen.

Bottom left. Ray animating the mother Roc seen in *The 7th Voyage of Sinbad*. It was a very heavy creature so needed four wires to support it.

Bottom centre. The mother Roc in detail.

Bottom right. Ray adjusting the baby Roc.

scenarios offers scope for a huge amount of characterization, but in the first Ray did have a scene in which the young reptiles indulged in a feeding frenzy. In order to keep such a scene going Ray had to ask the question, 'What should they be doing?' They wouldn't just sit their chewing and munching. They had to be doing something that was both visually interesting and would seem natural to the species, although it had to be based on what we can observe in nature today. Like modern predatory birds, the creatures did not have hands with which to pick their prey apart and would have had to swallow it whole or in large chunks. It was therefore reasonable to suppose that they would behave like a hawk or heron which, once it has a juicy morsel gripped firmly in its bill, makes a characteristic movement, bringing its head forward and then jerking it sharply back and up, to get the food started on its way down the gullet.

It was equally challenging to find a way to instill any character into the mythological two-headed Roc in *The 7th Voyage of Sinbad*, mainly because of the brief time it appears on the screen. The baby Roc comes and goes relatively quickly and in those scenes Ray simply had it trying in vain to fend off the attacking sailors by thrusting at them with its two beaks. Since it is a newly hatched chick, albeit a very large one, the audience's sympathies lie with the baby Roc and the best way of giving it character was to make it attractively white and fluffy - everyone likes a fluffy chick. However, when the huge mother Roc arrives and reacts by attacking the men, flapping her wings and lurching up and down in an attempt to surprise and kill them, Ray modelled her actions on those of a bird protecting her young from danger.

Much more interesting are the homunculi in *The Golden Voyage of Sinbad*. These creatures were partly humanoid in design and so lent themselves to clear characterization. Ray had long wanted to animate such a creature and so set about designing it in such a way that, however scary its appearance, it could also be seen as an abused victim of its creator's evil, thus ultimately gaining sympathy from the audience. He elicited this sympathy in two key scenes.

The first is set in the Vizier's subterranean vault when the first homunculus is discovered and Sinbad damages one of its wings. Although there were other reasons why the scenes of the creature running around the floor in the foreground were photographed from such a low angle, the primary one was that it helped Ray to make the audience feel compassion towards the creature as it pathetically struggles to avoid Sinbad's clutches. With one wing hanging useless it seems to have lost all its evil character and become simply an injured animal. The scene had been written in the script as 'The homunculus is

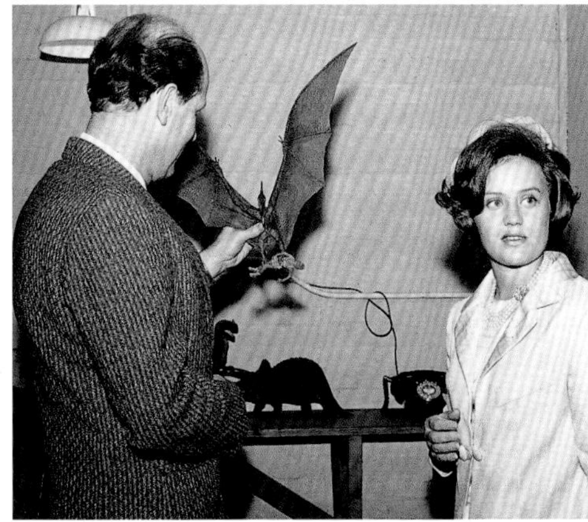

TOP
The pterodactyl featured in *The Valley of Gwangi*.

LEFT
The poor homunculus (he didn't want to die) featured in *The Golden Voyage of Sinbad*. Ray was able to give the creature quite a lot of character, which allowed the audience to have some sympathy for it, even though it was the tool of the evil Koura.

BELOW
The armatured horse Pegasus (24" (h) x 18" (l) x 15" (w)), which was restored in 1997, and the armatured figure of Perseus (12" (h) x 6" (w)) both featured in *Clash of the Titans*.

TOP RIGHT
The models of Pegasus and Perseus in flight, suspended by aerial wires. The problem with a flying horse is knowing what to do with the legs during flight, a problem Ray solved by having it gallop, which was at least cinematic.

BOTTOM RIGHT
The mechanical Bubo, as featured in *Clash of the Titans,* in all his glory. For twenty-six years he had languished in Ray's London garage until he was rediscovered by Tony and photographer Andy Johnson, in a corner, packed up in a case which happened to be the last one left to look at.

BOTTOM FAR RIGHT
Bubo in action. This photograph has also been recently rediscovered and shows the small model of Bubo suspended on an aerial brace in front of the rear-projected image of Perseus reaching up for him. Note the unit that the brace is attached to. This was a screwed device that enabled the animator to move the brace sideways.

wounded and falls to the floor, but manages to limp across the room to hide behind some draperies.' Nothing else. No attempt was made at that stage to detail what the actions of the creature would portray. However, once the model was on the animation table Ray chose to have one of the wings just hanging down, which creates genuine empathy. The vulnerable creature's fear of Sinbad and the Vizier is then highlighted when Sinbad reaches behind a trunk and, because it is unable to fly, the creature backs away. It is all part of the pantomime, to persuade the audience to feel something for the creature.

Then there is the birth of the second homunculus (the first disintegrates when Sinbad captures it). Just as he did with the birth of the Ymir in *20 Million Miles to Earth*, Ray begins the characterization soon after life is given to the homunculus. It stretches, rubs its eyes looks up at the men and slowly, as though trying them out, moves its wings; all of which conveys the mixture of confusion, anxiety and vulnerability that would be felt by any new-born creature. Ray also included two shots that link the animation with the live action. The first is when the creature shies away from Koura (its creator) and the second is the reverse, when Koura backs away from the creature when it flaps its wings. These seemingly small touches help to make the scenes moving and cinematic.

Although human characterization wasn't necessary in the case of Pegasus, the flying horse in *Clash of the Titans*, its actions had to be similar to those of a real horse, so it throws its head back, flicks its tail and lifts a front leg in the way that horses do when they anticipate movement. Ray naturally gave the tiny prehistoric horse, the eohippus, in *The Valley of Gwangi* the same traits but there was also, by chance, one shot taken during the live-action photography that he was able to use to give the tiny creature an extra degree of naturalness. During the shooting one of the real horses happened to be sniffing around at about the right height for an eohippus and the moment was captured on film. Months later, back in the studio, Ray used that footage to create a scene in which the real and the animated horses appear to sniff at each other, as though curious. This was something that could never have been planned. Although it is essential to plan out the basics of a scene in advance because of the limitations of time and budget, leaving room for spontaneity whilst filming live action often helps to create a scene that conveys a strong sense of originality and realism. Going back to Pegasus, there was the thorny problem of how the horse should fly. This may not seem to be a problem until you consider what it should do with its legs while flying. It was

a problem that haunted Ray throughout the design and the live-action photography, right up to the point where the model was standing on the table. The question was, would the legs hang beneath it or should they be given movement? In the end he opted for the action of a gallop, which gave the creature an improbable but cinematic and graceful appearance.

The cyclopean centaur in *The Golden Voyage of Sinbad* is half horse, half human and its actions obviously needed to reflect this. So, when the creature first appears from the mouth of the subterranean cave and sees the heroine, Margiana, it stops and raises its front leg and momentarily holds this horse-like pose which gives us the impression that it is somewhat surprised to see her. (Previously, when Ray animated the triceratops in *One Million Years BC* he made it react in the same way when its grazing was interrupted by a sound; probably this was not something such a dinosaur would have done, but in cinematic terms it works). The human side of the cyclopean centaur is evident in the same scene when Margiana faints and the creature pulls its upper body and arms back as though surprised. It is a marginally melodramatic action but in fantasy, melodrama is often necessary.

It might be assumed that dinosaurs would present a problem when it came to characterization but this is not necessarily true, at least not in the case of Ray's creations. Thanks to the experience Ray gained during his amateur experiments,

TOP LEFT
The tiny eohippus as it appeared in *The Valley of Gwangi* . This little prehistoric horse was given movements similar to those of a modern horse. The lifting of a fore leg is a trait that Ray has used many time with horses, or horse-like creatures, to denote anticipation or to indicate listening.

ABOVE
The eohippus as he is today. His legs are not what they used to be but otherwise he is in reasonably good condition. His dimensions are 18" (l) x 9"(h) x 7"(w).

RIGHT
The original armatured cyclopean centaur from *The Golden Voyage of Sinbad*. He was half-horse and half-human, so Ray gave him some horse traits, for example the raised leg again. Note the way the arms are pulled back at the elbow and the open hands held forward. This is one of Ray's trademarks.

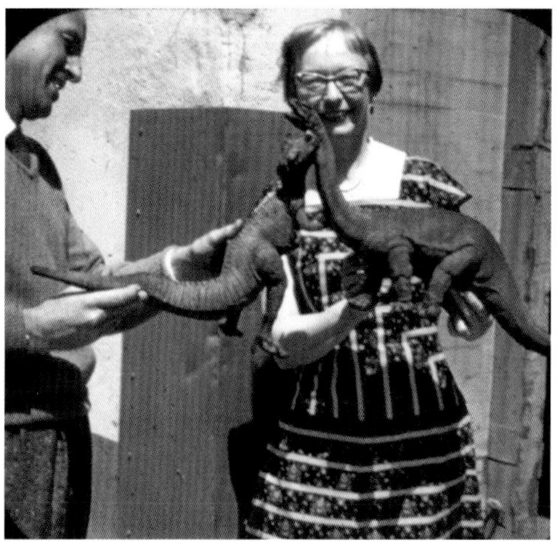

ABOVE LEFT
Ray holding the alligator featured in *The 3 Worlds of Gulliver* (1959). The model he is holding is the original armatured version which no longer exists

ABOVE CENTRE
A rare image of Ray, on the left, holding an armatured ceratosaurus from *Animal World* (1956), while an unidentified woman is holding the armatured brontosaurus also featured in the film. The picture was taken outside the stage where the animation was photographed on the Warner Bros lot.

ABOVE RIGHT
A close-up of the rhedosaurus from *The Beast From 20,000 Fathoms* (1952). As with all Ray's reptilian dinosaurs the tail was the most expressive element of the creature.

LEFT
The ornithomimus which appeared in *The Valley of Gwangi*. This is how he looks today and, as he didn't spend too much time under the lights, his condition is very good.

BELOW
The restored hard rubber stand-in model of the alligator from *The 3 Worlds of Gulliver*. This is now the most complete model of the creature.

all of his four-legged prehistoric creations have a degree of individuality. Amongst the most exciting examples are the rhedosaurus in *The Beast From 20,000 Fathoms*, the allosaurus Gwangi, the ceratosaurus and the young allosaurus in *One Million Years BC* and a modern survivor from prehistoric times, the alligator in *The 3 Worlds of Gulliver*.

With most of Ray's land-based dinosaurs the most expressive part of the model was the tail. Since the turn of the twentieth century, when the artist Charles Knight began visualizing living dinosaurs, it had been generally thought by palaeontologists that most of the animals, including those that walked on two legs, would have stood with their tails on or near the ground and would have only raised them when walking or fighting to balance their bodies. Sometime during the 1970s this view seemed to change and a number of major dinosaurs, such as the large carnivores and even the long-necked browsing species, are now visualized with their tails always raised to counterbalance their huge bodies. The accepted wisdom apparently changed because no evidence had been found of dinosaur tails being dragged along the ground. However, the old view still prevailed throughout Ray's career and Ray finds the new interpretation marginally distasteful because he feels that when depicted with raised tails the creatures look awkward,

ABOVE

At the rear is the armatured allosaurus *Gwangi*, star of *The Valley of Gwangi,* towering over the armatured model of Raquel Welch which featured in *One Million Years BC*. On the right is the head of a hard rubber stand-in for the triceratops, also used in *One Million Years BC*.

RIGHT

A close-up of Ray studying Medusa during the animation for *Clash of the Titans*. This is the scene where Perseus has cut off her head and she is squirming in agony.

cumbersome and as if they are suffering from acute constipation! Nevertheless, it is through the movements of their tails that Ray's dinosaurs express their personalities and emotions, no matter whether they are angry, frustrated or simply showing off. Moreover, using tails in this way had other advantages – it diverted the audience's attention. Ray always felt that if people's attention was focused on the tail they would not criticise other aspects of the animation.

Tails aside, there are a few other distinctive actions that help to make Ray's dinosaurs more 'real'. Just as dogs bark and lions roar, it was reasonable to suppose that flesh-eating dinosaurs would also be able to roar. Indeed they do, but in Ray's films they more often snap at everything that is likely to get in the way. The sound of the gnashing teeth is often more frightening than the roar.

The animation of the young allosaurus in *One Million Years BC* was also the result of thinking about its likely instinctual reactions. The pushing forward of the head and the snapping jaws are simple examples of this, but if you watch carefully you will also see the creature instinctively reach out towards John Richardson with its tiny, ineffectual front legs as though it is trying to catch him.

As in the case of the aerial creatures, nearly all of Ray's carnivorous creations flick their heads back when they are eating to gulp down their prey. Good examples of this in larger creatures are the scene when Gwangi the allosaurus is eating and the scene in *The Beast From 20,000 Fathoms* in which the rhedosaurus swallows an unfortunate policeman. In the latter scene we see the man's kicking legs sticking out of the creature's mouth before the creature throws its head back to swallow him. The swallowing action was something that Ray had noted as a young man when he watched his dogs eating large pieces of food. Incidentally, there is no mention in the script of the policeman meeting this gruesome fate, so when Ray decided, on the animation table, to show the creature with the man in its mouth, he had to make an inch-and-a-half-high figure of the policeman out of copper wire. The purpose of the shot was not only to enhance the realism of the scene but also to horrify and to show how big the creature was in proportion to the humans.

The death of a creature in a Harryhausen movie usually calls for some dramatic final action, call it a last gasp. In *The Beast From 20,000 Fathoms* the rhedosaurus is seen struggling as it dies amid the flames of the burning roller coaster. The director of the film, Eugene Lourie, likened it to the death of an opera tenor. These death throes were usually very important for Ray, not only because there were visually exciting but because so many of the creatures, from King Kong onwards, were meeting their deaths at the hands of human beings through no fault of their own, and Ray always felt that they deserved a melodramatic finale. Moreover, it was not just the death of Kong that had impressed this point on Ray, he had also been influenced by the demise of the stegosaurus in the same film. When that creature was dying, the tail expressed its efforts to hang on to life; it rippled like a wave effect, the

ABOVE

A rare image of the animation for the snake woman featured in *The 7th Voyage of Sinbad*. Behind is the rear-projection screen with the live action, which includes about half the width of the round carpet. In the foreground is the animation table with the other, matching, half of the carpet. The carpet bridges the live action and the animation, completing the depth of the scene. Snakes, like tentacles, were always a favourite of Ray's. The tails and the bodies lent themselves perfectly to model animation.

BELOW

Three scenes with the dragon from *The 7th Voyage of Sinbad*.

LEFT
On the left Ray is animating the models of Trog and the tiger for *Sinbad and the Eye of the Tiger*. On the right is the combined scene with the animation action integrated, via a split screen, with the rear-projection plate.

BELOW
Highlights of the titanic fight between the cerotosaurus and the triceratops in *One Million Years BC*. First they square off each looking for a mistake on their opponent's part which will provide an opening. Then in the bottom middle and right images the triceratops fatally wounds the ceratosaurus, now suspended on aerial wires. with its horns.

BELOW RIGHT
Another fight to the death, this time between the dragon and the Cyclops in *The 7th Voyage of Sinbad*. Notice the stance of the Cyclops in the first image. His arms are pulled back with elbows bent and open hands, in that 'Harryhausen pose'.

tip then rose and vibrated defiantly before finally collapsing The action is effective and cinematically very exciting. Ray used tails in a similar way several times; for the death of the Hydra in *Jason and the Argonauts* and again, although on a smaller scale, for the death of Medusa – in her case the tip of the tail was that of a rattlesnake. Another great dramatic death scene involves the slaying of the gryphon by the cyclopean centaur in *The Golden Voyage of Sinbad*. After the gryphon has been killed the centaur is fatally injured by Sinbad and falls on top of the gryphon's corpse where it melodramatically expires, like a star-crossed lover at the end of an opera.

A fight is a perfect vehicle for expressing emotion and drama, something Ray had learned all those years before when he watched boxing and wrestling matches with Obie. One of the highlights of *One Million Years BC* was the titanic battle between the triceratops and the ceratosaurus. At first the ceratosaurus, the aggressor and larger of the two, seems favourite to win and indeed dominates the battle almost throughout until it makes one final, fatal mistake. The triceratops, although less agile and less well armed with teeth, does have its two horns and when its opponent drops its guard, it fatally wounds the carnivore in the belly. In animating the violent battle Ray managed to give each huge beast small but characteristic traits and movements that, taken together, expressed their individuality. Ray didn't plan any of it. Again, all that the script said was that there was to be a fight and that was it, the details would only come when the models were on the animation table. Only then did Ray consider how the two creatures might behave in such a situation. For example, the triceratops would naturally want to protect itself and would keep its horns pointing towards its opponent, while the ceratosaurus would display the confidence which came from being the more powerful of the two. Ray began the fight by hav-

ing them circle each other like a pair of boxers or wrestlers each looking for an opening in their opponent's guard, and after that one pose led to another. The only limitations were imposed by the need to have the creatures in certain positions when their movements had to be integrated with live-action footage.

Another example of the ways in which Ray's observations helped him to make his creatures' actions more life-like is the fight between the Cyclops and the dragon in *The 7th Voyage of Sinbad*. In one shot the dragon is on the ground and the Cyclops has his arm around its neck. When his hold is broken the Cyclops staggers back along the side of the dragon's body, as though taken by surprise and thrown off balance. Taken in isolation, it is a throw-away action but, when combined with other movements improvised by Ray as the fight progressed, helped to build up a dramatic, complex and believable sequence. One such improvisation comes later in the fight when the Cyclops has the dragon in a half-nelson hold and pulls the dragon's head up, raising one leg as he does so, as though straining with the effort. Until Ray had arrived at that point he had no idea what the Cyclops might do, but again an apparently trivial action helped to give the fight substance. It was an example of spur-of-the-moment creativity being expressed in motion.

The brontosaurus, or as it is now called, the apatosaurus,[2] in *One Million Years BC* was a creature that Ray had looked forward to animating. He had planned a scene in which the dinosaur's long neck would reach into a cave occupied by humans and had also intended the creature to take part in the spectacular finale. But by the end of the live-action photography, the producer, Michael Carreras, had cut these scenes. However, because the model had been built it was decided that the brontosaurus would provide the audience with a brief introduction to the animated action yet to come. All that we see is a brief long shot of it slowly walking across the screen. But although the scene is short Ray still found a way to give it greater realism using one of his tricks. About half way through the shot the brontosaurus turns his long neck and head to look behind it. Ray couldn't just allow it to amble across, it would have been boring, but that simple pause and backward glance gave the scene an interest it would otherwise have lacked and ensured that the audience would realize what an impressive creature this was.

One of Ray's favourite uses of by-play is to make his creatures look down before taking a step, a movement that seems to come perfectly naturally to both large carnivorous dinosaurs and humanoid creatures, though it is primarily a human trait rather than animal one. A good use of this little piece of action occurs in *Mighty Joe Young* when Ray has Joe look down and then up again before he walks forward. Red Riding Hood does the same thing in *The Story of Little Red Riding Hood* (1950) as does Gwangi in *The Valley of Gwangi*. It seems something that any creature might do, but in the case of a creature many feet taller than a human, it helps to emphasise its size and presence.

Another of Joe's actions that is very distinctive is the way that, as he pounds on the roof of a lion cage, he looks around him. This was inspired by the behaviour of a chimpanzee that Ray observed at a zoo; when the ape pounded on a large log it looked around to see if anyone was taking any notice.

An animator does, however, have to be cautious about instilling too much quirky character into his creations otherwise what should be dramatic is likely to turn into comedy. That is what went wrong with *Son of Kong* and indeed with sections of *Mighty Joe Young*. In both films primates did things that real primates wouldn't do. In *Son of Kong* the young gorilla sucked its thumb and scratched the top of its head like Stan Laurel, which was silly and added nothing to the character except to make it look ridiculous. Again, in *Mighty Joe Young* there is a scene, animated by Pete Peterson, that shows the gorilla sitting on the back of a truck and spitting. In both cases these actions were counter-productive because they were far too human-like to work, except as comedy. True, in both films a comic effect was what was intended, but it had the effect of destroying all credibility. Ernest Schoedsack, the director of *King Kong*, *Son of Kong* and *Mighty Joe Young* was largely responsible for these episodes and whilst working on *Mighty Joe Young* Ray would often hear him say, 'If you can't make it

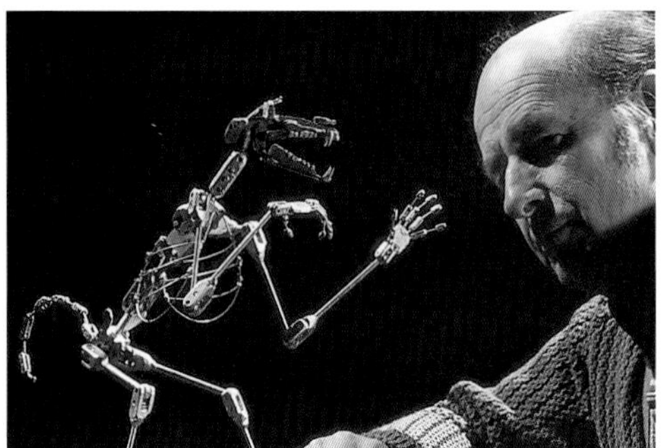

ABOVE
Various animation test shots for *Sinbad and the Eye of the Tiger*.

Top left. Ray smiling at the camera in a test in which the large and the small baboon models can be seen in their respective cages against the rear-projection screen.

Top centre. Ray animating the baboon playing chess on the ship's deck.

Top right. Animating the baboon in Melanthius' cave.

Bottom left. The baboon armature.

Bottom centre. Ray between the rear-projection screen and the model baboon, which is seated on a stool and playing chess with Princess Farah (Jane Seymour). You can just make out Seymour on the screen behind Ray.

Bottom right. Ray with the large model baboon.

LEFT
A close-up of the large model baboon (the armature of which is seen above) holding the chess piece. His dimensions are 16" (l) x 14"(h) x 9"(w).

drama, make it funny'. Schoedsack had obviously missed the point that Kong had been effective because he was always believable, despite his size and the fact he had a crush on a blonde girl.

If attempts at broad comedy are misguided, a lighter touch can still be used with good effect. For example, at the beginning of *Mighty Joe Young* Ray shows Joe eating a banana whole, skin and all, and then near the end of the picture he is seen peeling off the skin before eating another one – a subtle way of saying he had become 'civilized'. This was genuinely and constructively amusing, while at the same time bridging the gap between ape and human. The subtlety may go almost unnoticed but nevertheless helps to build up Joe's unique character.

Continuing on the theme of humanoid creatures, the baboon in *Sinbad and the Eye of the Tiger*, which has been transmogrified from a human form, also required a combination of animal and human actions to point up the fact that he wasn't what he appeared to be. It was also intended to suggest that the human within the baboon was slowly being swamped by animal instincts. It was a very complex balance to strike. Ray realized that it would be fatally easy to allow the creature to become comic because that is usually the effect of an animal mimicking human behaviour. He therefore designed several scenes to ensure that this wouldn't happen. When the baboon is playing chess with Princess Farah (Jane Seymour), on several occasions he scratches himself as an ape would but this is counterbalanced by having the creature hold his hand to his mouth as though shocked by something. Ray used a combination of such 'pantomime' actions to suggest conflicting animal and human instincts. Another example occurs when Melanthius (Patrick Troughton) holds up a mirror to the baboon. When the creature sees its own reflection, it is clear that it realizes that it is looking at its own image because it raises its hand to its mouth, conveying surprise followed by horror. It then weeps, further emphasizing the human element within. Ray had pre-planned this scene carefully, filming the live action with the specific reactions of the creature in mind, but when it came to the animation Ray simply thought about how a human would react to seeing himself in the form of an ape, and an ugly ape at that, and his empathy is evident in the scene.

When faced with the Cyclops in *The 7th Voyage of Sinbad*, Ray was very conscious of the fact that it was humanoid in shape and he didn't want people to think it was a man in a costume. (He confronted the same problem with Calibos in *Clash of the Titans*.) He therefore designed the Cyclops with cloven hooves. That solved the man-in-a-suit problem, but it also meant that Ray had to think about how a huge hooved, biped

ABOVE
The Cyclops in *The 7th Voyage of Sinbad* licking his lips as his meal cooks.

LEFT
The rear-projection screen shows, from left to right, Jane Seymour, Taryn Power, Patrick Troughton and Pat Wayne, whilst in front of the screen the baboon sits in his cage. For the live action Seymour has to pretend the baboon was there and act to it. Whilst animating Ray had to move the model so that it would seem to react to her.

creature would walk. His solution was to make the creature's movements seem rather calculated, almost as though it is unsure of itself. By giving him this slightly laboured stride, Ray was able to accommodate the size and build of the creature. As far as the human aspects of the Cyclops are concerned, they are best illustrated in the scene where he captures several sailors and crouches down, putting his hands on his knees. Again, when the Cyclops has placed the sailors in the wooden cage, instead of closing the door as one might expect, he casually flicks it shut with the back of his hand. These are very human actions, but may not be consciously recognized as such by the audience, which does not mean that they are not effective. The most famous Cyclops scene is the one where the monster licks his lips as he roasts one of the sailors over a fire. The act isn't there necessarily for a laugh; it is there because Ray felt that such a creature *would* be licking its lips.

Perhaps the most humanoid of all Ray's creations are his skeletons in *The 7th Voyage of Sinbad* and *Jason and the Argonauts*. As they are human skeletons it is assumed they will react as a human would. The first action to suggest this occurs when the seven skeleton warriors face Jason and his men and crouch in a menacing fashion, like wrestlers poised to grapple with their opponents at the start of a match. Another Harryhausen touch occurs when a skeleton kills one of Jason's men (Andrew Faulds) and Ray, instead of cutting away to another shot, or having it go around the body, has it jump over Faulds' body. Ray didn't want him to just step over it. That would have been mundane. This seemingly simple action took more time to create because the skeleton had to be suspended on wires to allow it to jump. But the end result seems natural, in as much as it is a living skeleton, and therefore looks as though it was filmed with the live-action.

The ghouls that feature in *Sinbad and the Eye of the Tiger* are less intriguing although their scenes do take place at night, which is what Ray wanted for the skeletons in *Jason*. In one brief shot the ghouls run from right to left across the scene, but Ray didn't want them to just run across the screen so he had the first one come on and then turn around as though to see where the other two were. He never planned the action but when it came to animation he felt that he had to get one of them to do something to make the scene more interesting.

In animation, one pose leads to another and once an initial idea 'happens' the movement develops with apparent inevitability, like a domino effect. Take the coming to life of bronze statue Talos in *Jason and the Argonauts*. Ray didn't know how he would animate it until he was faced with Talos crouched on the animation table. Although he knew that Talos had to get off the plinth, as yet he hadn't worked out how he could accomplish this. Of course, his choices were dictated by what the next scene would require, but the first question was: how to make the statue come alive dramatically? Suddenly Ray remembered a Japanese film he had once seen where a girl had been facing away from the camera but her head rotates almost completely whilst her torso remained stationary. The head turning was the key to the scene and so Ray gradually animated Talos to look down at two of Jason's Argonauts; the torso remained static while the head slowly and menacingly turned to face the camera and then Talos climbed down from the plinth. That opening action dictated the entire sequence and suggested to the audience that this was going to be bad for the Argonauts.

In this chapter we have described only a handful of examples that illustrate Ray's approach to the art of animation. In essence, what you see as animation on the screen is an expression of Ray's personality enhanced by the fruit of his observation of people and animals. This is the animator's way of acting. There are two final rules. Firstly, once that first movement has been initiated the animator has to visualize what will follow as a series of still frames, each of which follows on from the last. Secondly, the animator must always think ahead, carefully planning everything from the design of the models to the live-action photography so that he knows all the parameters within which he must work when the time comes to start the animation.

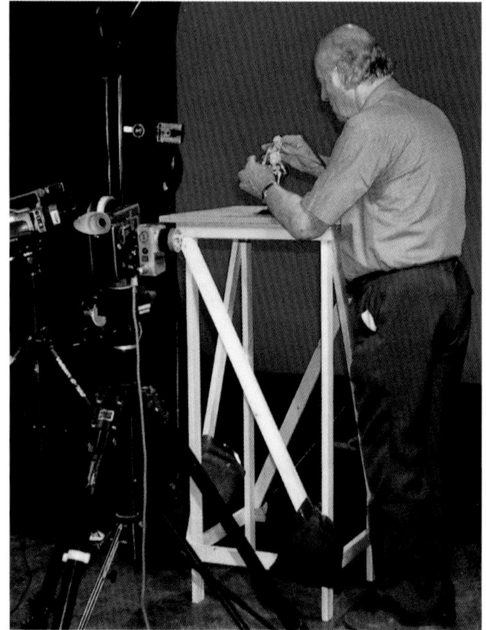

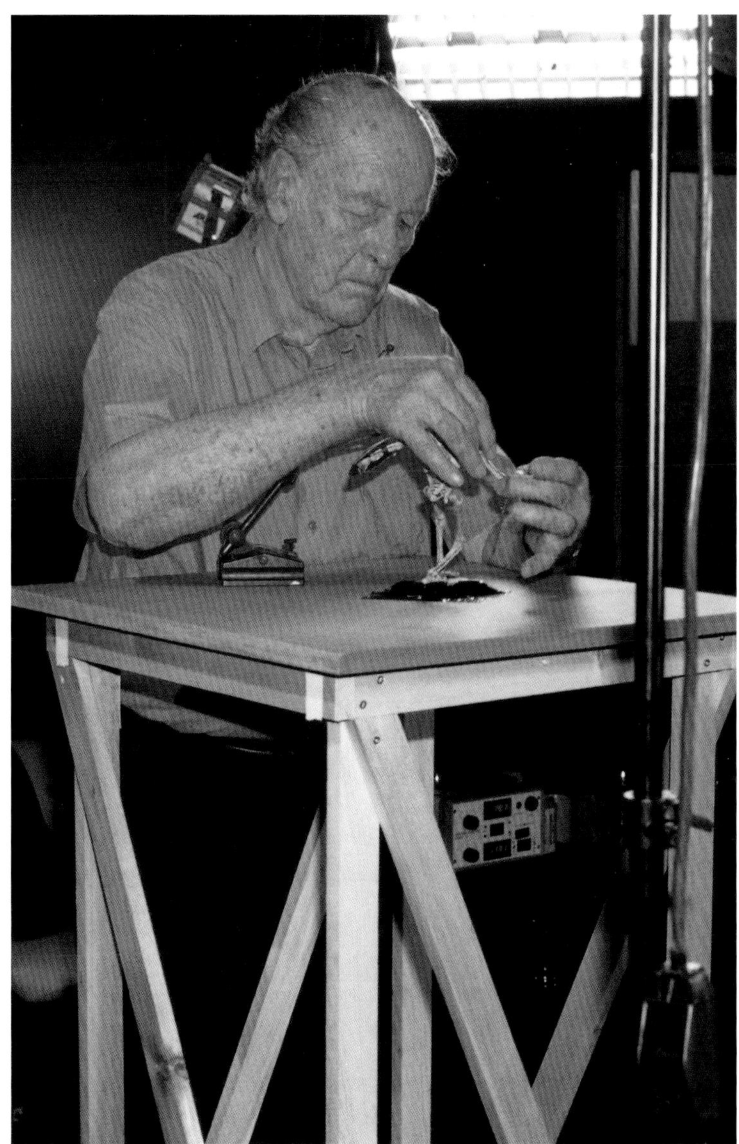

FACING PAGE

Top, Ray circa 1956/57 with his drawing board and the first model skeleton used in *The 7th Voyage of Sinbad*.

Bottom left, Ray at work sketching, again circa 1956/7, with the skeleton 'watching'.

Bottom right, Ray animating in 1999 for *Working with Dinosaurs*. There were in fact two cameras. One was 16mm with a stop-frame facility which recorded the animation of the one skeleton and the other was a video that recorded the entire process throughout the day so that when shown at the proper speed it condensed the animation process into a few minutes.

ABOVE AND LEFT

Three more shots taken by Tony of Ray during the day of animation for *Working with Dinosaurs*. A gauge can be seen in the top left image and the two cameras are both clearly visible in the bottom image.

Ray hasn't animated a feature film since1981. However in 1999 when we were both involved in a British documentary called *Working With Dinosaurs*,[3] it was decided to demonstrate the process of model animation with Ray animating one of his own creations. In a small studio in North London, we set up a 16mm stop-motion camera, an animation table and one of the surviving skeletons to allow Ray to animate the model as it rose from a crouching position to a standing one and then turned to look at its creator. The idea was that the animation would later be combined with live-action footage of Ray so that the skeleton would appear to be as tall as Ray. I was privileged not only to watch the animation but also to act as official stills photographer. I was the only one allowed to be with Ray throughout the animation process, so my excitement at the prospect was intense. It was heaven. However, I was perhaps too excited. As Ray went about the long arduous process of animation I kept asking him why he was doing this or that. Eventually, but very politely, Ray turned to me and said, 'It would be best if you refrained from talking otherwise I am never going to finish this.' I was mortified, not because I had been told to keep quite, but also because my jabbering had interfered with his concentration. After that I was as quiet as a mouse but it was an effort.

It was amazing to watch Ray plan and execute the model's movements. The intervening eighteen years since his last feature hadn't slowed him down. The old magic was still there. Even though he was only animating one model, he was totally involved with the figure and the ultimate outcome. The care and attention to the minutest detail was wonderful to behold and, as far as I am aware, this was the only time Ray has been photographed actually in the process of animating.

Four images of work on *The Story of the Tortoise and the Hare* (2000-2). The film had been started by Ray in 1952 and was completed in 2002, fifty years later. Designed by Ray the film was largely animated by two talented animators, Mark Caballero and Seamus Walsh. In the photograph at bottom left, Mark can be seen on the extreme right of the picture and Seamus on the extreme left. In the image below the final miniature set can be seen with Ray's original Kodak Cine Special on a dolly setup.

CHAPTER FIVE

O'BRIEN AND HARRYHAUSEN CONTEMPORARIES – 1930-1970

During the 1930s, when Obie was working on his greatest creation and Ray was only just beginning his fascination with the art, there were few other individuals taking any interest in model animation, and those that were saw it only as one of a variety of visual effects. Slowly, however, with the advent of the 1950s, interest in the art increased, largely as a result of the contemporary cycle of monsters-on-the-rampage movies. The public's appetite for these fantasy films encouraged a number of individuals to try their hand at model animation and so the 1950s and 1960s would turn out to be a golden age for the art.

Some of this potential new talent had, like Ray, been inspired by *King Kong*, which would continue to weave its spell over subsequent generations, but these potential animators were also being inspired, not just by Ray's films, but by his methods of bringing his creations to life, using cheaper and more easily available methods. They realized that such techniques could help them bring their own dreams to fruition and they would devise their own methods, working in parallel with or along similar lines to Ray's own Dynamation. Eventually the vogue for the monster-on-the-rampage movies which had inspired this renaissance would decline, giving way to more inventive and ambitious science-fiction and mythological projects.

America was still at the heart of this surge in the fashion for films that showed people co-existing – not always very peacefully – with impossible creatures. However, there were also a few outside America who found their own ways of using model animation; some of them would find a market for simple puppet animation but there others who would recognize its versatility when combined with live action.

Alexandr Ptushko was sometimes called 'The Soviet Walt Disney' but it would be more accurate to say that he was a Russian Willis O'Brien. In 1934 Ptushko saw *King Kong*, and it convinced him that the way forward for model animation was to produce films that featured both animated models and live actors in the same frame.

Ptushko was born in Lugansk, now in the Ukraine, in 1900 and began his film career in 1927 when he went to work for the Moscow-based Mosfilm Studio. Initially he constructed puppets for model animated films made by other filmmakers, but because of his enthusiasm and professionalism he soon became a director and designer in his own right, making a series of stop-motion films between 1928 and 1932 that featured a character called Bratishkin. It was during the making of these films that Ptushko managed to refine his animation techniques and even made tests combining puppets with live action. In 1933 he assembled an animation team and began work on his first feature film, a project called *Novyi Gulliver* (*The New Gulliver*). It tells the story of a Russian boy called Petya (played by Vladimir Konstantinovich Konstantinov whose only film this was) who falls asleep during a commune outing and dreams that he is a new Gulliver, washed ashore on Lilliput. He finds that he has been tied up on the beach but is eventually released and becomes the guest of honour at a feast held by the monarch of Lilliput. Being a good Stalinist, he is appalled to discover that Lilliput is a decadent, bourgeois society controlled by capitalist profiteers, and before he wakes up to reality he helps the workers in the King's underground munitions factory overthrow their decadent rulers. All a bit heavy, perhaps, but the joy of this film is not in its blatant propaganda storyline or political aims, but in its conception and execution. It was a remarkable undertaking as Ptushko reputedly utilized some 'three thousand finger-size character models of revolutionists, bloated plutocrats, crooners and burlesque queens' (to quote the publicity of the time). However, it is more likely that there were actually only fifteen hundred models, although that number, if accurate, still represents an incredible achievement. The models were made largely of clay and the key characters possessed detachable heads allowing them a range of expressions. Over sixty sets were used in the film, and a lot of time, effort and resources were spent completing the optical work that combined the models with the one live actor. It is reputed that over fifty technicians, including artists, modellers and animators, worked on the picture for two years. It was halfway through the making of *Gulliver* that Ptushko saw O'Brien's *King Kong* and was amazed and inspired by the film to such an extent that he utilized some of the techniques he had seen.

Released worldwide in 1935/36 *Gulliver* quickly gained international acclaim, more for its cinematic innovations than its Stalinist plotline, although one reviewer for *The New York Times* wrote, 'In addition to the technical finesse, the film has genuine wit in its sly assault on bourgeois institutions.' *The New Gulliver* counted Charlie Chaplin among its great admirers, which led in part to Chaplin's *Modern Times* (1936). Always on the lookout for new animated pictures Ray also saw it in 1936, when he was sixteen, and he too was inspired, although perhaps not as much as by *King Kong*. Ray remembers that his mother took him to see the film, which had just been released in the US, and he was mesmerized by the huge number of tiny animated figures, although the political message contained in the story went right over his head. The film was responsible, to some extent, for inspiring the Czech animators of the 1950s and although largely forgotten over the intervening years, it is now gaining new admirers and Ptushko is being recognized as the genius he was.

Following the success of *The New Gulliver*, Mosfilm allowed Ptushko to form his own stop-motion production department, which became known as

PREVIOUS SPREAD
Left, three of the seven armatured heads (Pan, Lao and Merlin) that were seen sprouting from the body of the Loch Ness monster featured in the climax of *7 Faces of Dr Lao* (1964). These were animated by Jim Danforth and are now, along with two other heads (these can be seen on page 172), in The Deutsche Kinemathek Museum Für Film und Fernsehen in Berlin.
Right, Ray looking at the models of Pegasus and Perseus featured in *Clash of the Titans* (1981) with Jim Danforth. These are the same models featured in close-up on page 130.

TOP
Alexandr Ptushko circa 1930s.

ABOVE
Alexandr Ptushko circa 1960s.

BELOW LEFT
A scene from *The New Gulliver* (1935) showing the live-action actor's legs and feet bestriding the marching and Lilliputian revolutionaries. This one shot shows just how many tiny models Ptushko had to animate.

BELOW CENTRE
One of the 'thousands' of miniature puppets used in the film.

BELOW RIGHT
The Russian poster for *The New Gulliver*.

'The Ptushko Collective'. Between 1936 and 1938, the unit would produce fourteen animated short films, usually based on Russian folktales, that included *Repka* (*The Little Turnip*) (1936), *Volkl i Zhuravl* (*The Wolf and the Crane*) (1936), *Lisa i Vinograd* (*The Fox and the Grapes*) (1936), *Rodina Zovet* (*The Motherland Calls*) (1936), *Vesyolye muzykanty* (*The Merry Musicians*) (1937), *Skazka o rybakel i rybke* (*The Tale of the Fisherman and the Goldfish*) (1937), *Zaveshchaniye* (*The Will*) (1937), *Lisa i Volk* (*The Fox and the Wolf*) (1937), *Malenky-Udalenky* (*The Little Darling One*) (1938) and *Pyos i Kot* (*The Dog and the Cat*) (1938). In most cases Prushko is credited as artistic supervisor of these pictures although he was occasionally responsible for the story and the script, and in some cases directed.

In 1938 Ptushko began work on another animated/live-action feature called *Zolotoy Klyuchik* (*The Golden Key*) an adaptation of Carlo Collodi's novel *The Adventures of Pinocchio.* Although hugely successful in the Soviet Union when it was released in 1939 *The Golden Key* didn't receive a wide distribution elsewhere and it was to be Ptushko's last film featuring model animation. However, after the war he did made a number of fantasy films that included *Sadko* (heavily cut and retitled *the Magic Voyage of Sinbad* for the States) (1953), *Ilya Muromets* (retitled *The Sword and the Dragon*) (1956) and *Sampo* (retitled *The Day the Earth Froze*) (1959). In 1968 Ptushko began work on the feature *Ruslan and Ludmila*, which took a total of four years to complete. Sadly, a few months after the film's release in 1972, Ptushko died. Like O'Brien, his near contemporary, Ptushko will always be remembered in film history for one film, *The New Gulliver*, and though its message has somewhat dated, the film is undoubtedly a classic and a milestone in the history of model animation.

Although brought up in America, Lou Bunin was also Russian. Born in Kiev in 1904, he left Russia at a very early age and received a training in art at the Chicago Art Institute. His ambition was to be an artist and sculptor so he went to France to attend the Academie de la Grande Chaumiere with the sculptor Bourdelle. When he returned to the US in 1930 he held a one-man show of his art in Chicago and the following year he travelled to Mexico to become an assistant to the painter Diego Rivera. While he was in Mexico he developed an interest in marionettes and on his return to Chicago began a marionette theatre. This led him to experiment with animating and filming puppets which, in turn, led to his first animated film, a short subject called *Pete Roleum and his Cousins* (1938), made for the Petroleum Industry stand at the 1938/39 New York World's Fair. It was a thirty-minute colour film that featured an animated bug eating a leaf and when insecticide is sprayed on the leaf the bug rolls over and dies. Although not exactly a classic it did lead to other offers of work in the field of information and industrial propaganda and slowly Bunin began to be noticed.

In 1942 Bunin was invited to work for a number of top Hollywood studios including Warner Bros, Paramount and Universal, filming animated inserts and other optical effects and it was whilst there that he met Michael Myerberg with whom he planned an animated version of Richard Wagner's fourteen-hour opera cycle *The Ring of the Nibelung* which they intended to reduce to four hours. The conductor Leopold Stokowski was also to be involved and together they worked for three years on this extremely ambitious project. However, just when it seemed that Universal Pictures might finance the film, it was dropped because the Hollywood executives realized the close association between Wagner's work and the Nazi regime.

The year he arrived in Hollywood Bunin directed as well as animated *Bury the Axis* (1943), a political propaganda film for the US government, which satirized the leaders of the Axis powers – Hitler, Mussolini and Hirohito. Filmed in colour, the six-minute film lampooned all three figures by using heavily stylized puppets (wonderfully modelled by Bunin) and having them sing derogatory songs. Aside from the three central figures Bunin also animated a stork, a snake (this was an introduction to Hirohito), geese and a tank. It's a wonderful piece of wartime propaganda that is as fresh today as when it was made.

In 1943 Bunin was invited by MGM to work for them on various productions including a prologue for their all-star musical *Ziegfeld Follies* (1946). In one section of this entertaining insert there is a lobby scene for which Bunin animated twenty-five separate models simultaneously. He

BELOW
Nine scenes from the US propaganda film *Bury the Axis* (1943) by Lou Bunin. The three leaders of the Axis – Hitler, Mussolini and Hirohito – are lampooned in this original and still very amusing animated slapstick film. It begins with a stork delivering Adolf, then has Mussolini as Hitler's obedient dog and Hirohito as a 'snake in the grass'.

BELOW
Several images showing Bunin, or at least his hands, at work on a model of a horse or mule. They show the mould, the latex model being extracted and the painting of the model.

BOTTOM
Bunin's greatest achievement, the very ambitious and brilliant *Alice in Wonderland* (1951). Aside from the last image, all the scenes show Alice (Carol Marsh) combined with the models, which were all designed by Bunin.

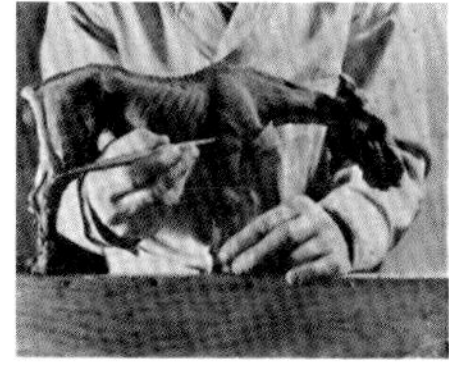
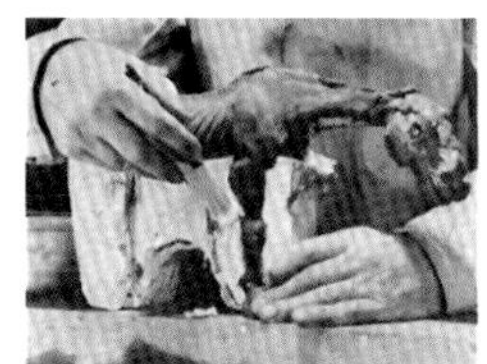
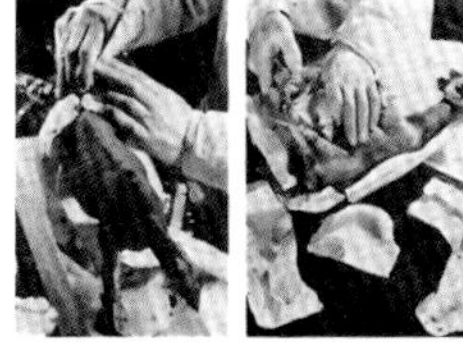
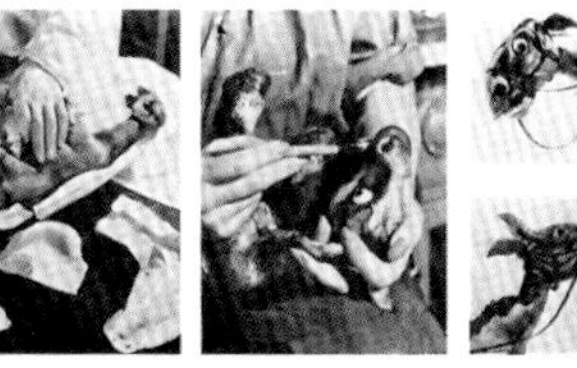

was assisted by twenty-five other technicians, including some from the Disney and Fleisher studios[1], but the models and animation was designed and executed by Bunin. It is a superb piece of work and is perhaps the best section of a lacklustre film. Bunin remained at MGM for a few years working on minor effects sequences, but was fired and blacklisted as a result of McCarthyism.

Bunin cherished an ambition to shoot a feature film of Lewis Carroll's *Alice in Wonderland* using model animation. Unable to raise the money in Hollywood, he travelled to England in 1948 where the J. Arthur Rank Organisation agreed to find some of the production money for the film in which Bunin would combine a live-action Alice with animated models. Following a prologue sequence that takes place at Christ Church College in Oxford where Charles Dodson (Lewis Carroll was his *nom de plume*) was a fellow and in the garden of Alice Liddell, who had inspired the character of Alice, we then see Alice (Carol Marsh) following the animated white rabbit into Wonderland.

The project began production in 1949. It was photographed in Technicolor, cost one million dollars and was filmed in two versions, one English and one French. All the animation was executed in a studio in Nice, France using eighty technicians, several of whom were on loan from MGM, including Irving Block, a matte artist, and Lloyd Knechtel. The complex and surreal story called for many optical effects including multiple rewinds and travelling mattes, and, most remarkable of all, the synchronization of the voices with the models. The characters and costumes for the models were based on the drawings by Sir John Tenniel, the original illustrator of the book. Bunin set himself the task of animating multiple puppet scenes, including the Queen of Hearts' cricket party in which at least twenty puppets appeared at the same time. Although it might seem that a scene with multiple dancing lobsters would require multiple lobster puppets, Bunin used only two. We see the lobsters dance towards a flower, which is slightly off-centre and it was this flower that concealed the camera lens. Bunin cleverly animated the two models between two mirrors facing each other, which had the effect of creating endless rows of lobsters.

At about the same time as Bunin began animation work on the film, in Hollywood Walt Disney was also beginning his two-dimensional adaptation, also to be called *Alice in Wonderland* (1951). The Disney company approached Bunin and Rank to request that they hold up the release of their version for three years, so that Bunin's film didn't piggy-back on the publicity for the Disney's three-million-dollar film. After spending so many years in planning and production Bunin felt that this was unfair and opened his version first, calling it *Lou Bunin's Alice in Wonderland*. Disney immediately took him to court; but the judge dismissed the case on the basis that there had been several previous ver-

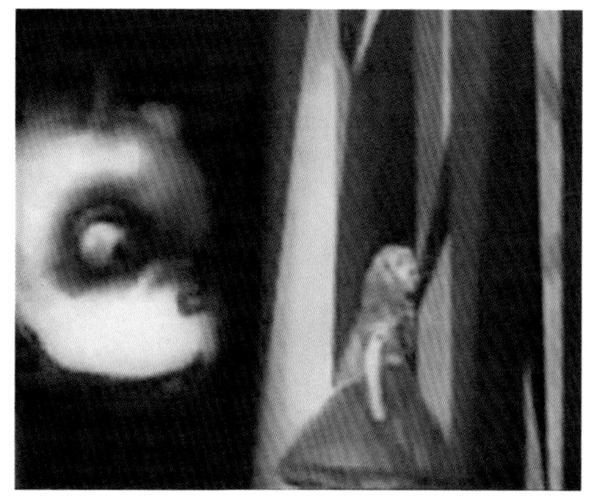
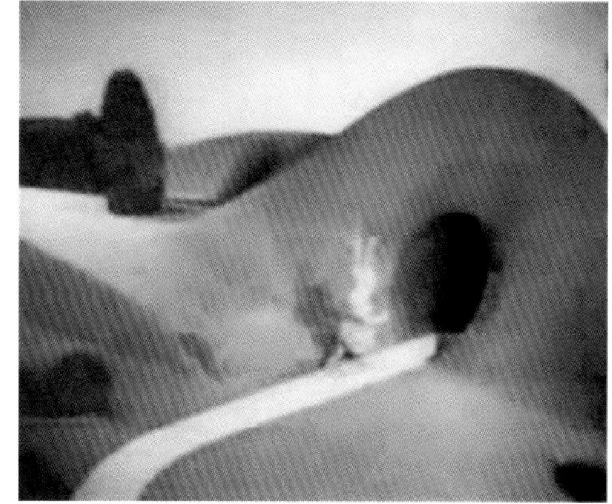

sions of the story and that the novel was by then in the public domain. Sadly, Bunin's adaptation and execution of the novel is mostly forgotten today, although it is far more enjoyable than Disney's sterilized version. Right up to his death in 1994, aged 89, Bunin was still struggling to get the film restored and out to a wider audience.

Following *Alice in Wonderland* Bunin didn't make another animated feature but concentrated, for the remainder of his working career, on animated short subjects, inserts and credits for US television programmes, industrial films and American commercials. Although his body of work was considerable Bunin, like so many other animators, will be remembered for a single film, the technically innovative *Alice*.

Towards the end of the 1930s a project that Obie and Harry O. Hoyt, the director of *The Lost World*, had begun in 1926 at First National reared its head again, although this time without any input by Obie. *Lost Atlantis* was to be about the legendary lost continent of Atlantis on which dinosaurs co-existed with humans. In 1938, Hoyt teamed up with special effects technician Fred Jackman to develop and film this adventure for Columbia Pictures. Twenty-five model dinosaurs were reputedly built (at a cost of $600 each), including a tyrannosaurus rex, a stegosaurus, a ceratosaurus and an allosaurus, all or most of which featured in ten minutes of test footage which was shot at the studio. Sadly, either because of costs or for some other reason, the project was cancelled by the studio head, Harry Cohn. Then in 1940 the same studio again resurrected the project, this time as a Technicolor production, with models designed and constructed by Edward Nassour and Walter Lantz, but once again, after some test footage had been shot, the production was cancelled.

Rather surprisingly, during the war years very little model animation was used in propaganda film-making. Ray had made attempts to show the medium's versatility by making two films, *How to Build a Bridge* (1941) and *Guadalcanal* (1945), but there was little or no interest. However, aside from Bunin's *Bury the Axis* there was another rather odd little film called *Revolution in Toyland* (1942), which we think it is worth a mention because of its bizarre story. The eight-minute black and white film made for Sterling Films tells of a toy-maker who is using toys to smuggle out secrets to the Allies. One day a Gestapo officer comes calling and the toy-maker escapes out of the window. The officer falls over one of the toys and then, in a daze, the nasty Nazi is attacked by the toys. In the end the toys win. The model toys would appear to be made of wood and wire and the animation is somewhat basic. The name of the person or persons responsible for the animation is sadly unknown to us; but the number of animated models in the film is impressive – there is one scene of the toys breaking out of a cupboard in which there appear to be in excess of twenty separate models.

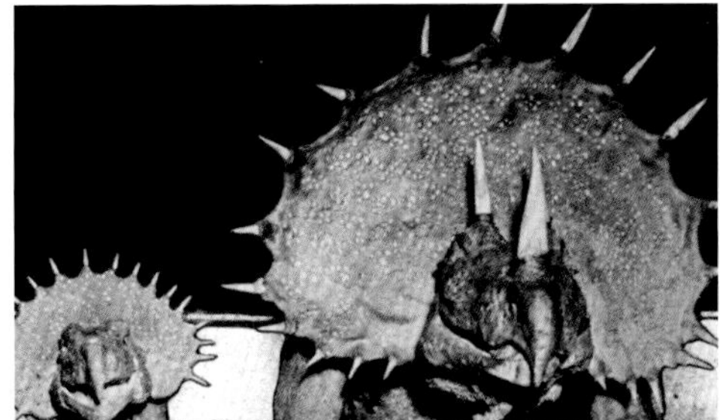

ABOVE
Three images of the unrealized *Lost Atlantis*.

Top left. Two styracosaurus (or possibly arrhinoceratops or anchiceratops).

Bottom left. Two unknown technicians (one could possibly be Fred Jackman) animating and photographing the tyrannosaurus rex in its miniature set. These are the only known photographs showing the effects for the film. According to Stephen Czerkas in his book *Cine-Saurus*, 'Almost twenty minutes of animation were filmed but the movie was never completed and the footage has been lost.'

Above. The same tyrannosaurus rex or allosaurus standing in an ancient gateway.

The 1940s would see the appearance of a number of key figures associated with model animation. The most important of these was animator, director and producer George Pal. Pal was born György Pál Marczinsák in Cegléd, Hungary in 1908, his mother and father were entertainers and his grandparents had been members of the Hungarian National Theatre. It became apparent from an early age that George Jr. also had a leaning towards the arts, in his case architecture, which he studied at the Budapest Academy of Arts. However, whilst there he also studied drawing and carpentry, both of which would be extremely useful to him when he began making films. At the age of twenty, he graduated from the Academy and went to work at Hannia Films in Budapest, designing and making title cards and posters. It was during his time at Hannia that he became fascinated with cartoons, especially American cartoons, and began to research how they were made. Eventually he built his own equipment and started to produce his own two-dimensional shorts.

In 1931 he left Budapest for Berlin where, within only a few months and despite the fact that he could not speak German, he became head of the UFA Studios. Pal was ambitious and in the following year he left UFA and set up his own cartoon studio, which rapidly flourished. It was at this point that he first ventured into model animation when he was commissioned to produce a commercial for a cigarette company. After spending hours and hours drawing cigarettes, Pal had

RIGHT
A rare photograph taken during the early days of *Puppetoons*. George Pal is on the left, reaching over the miniature table, Willis O'Brien is on the right with his arms on the table and Ray is behind him. The cameraman, Paul Sprunk, is behind Pal and someone called Jordan is in the centre, behind the light. The camera assistant between Jordan and Sprunk is unknown.

BELOW
The great George Pal in his office with the Strauss model featured in *Mr. Strauss Takes a Walk* (1943).

BOTTOM LEFT
George Pal looking through a miniature of the Paramount Pictures Studios gateway.

BOTTOM RIGHT
Ray animating the models for *Hoola Boola* (1941). Working on Pal's *Puppetoons* was Ray's first paid job in the world of animation.

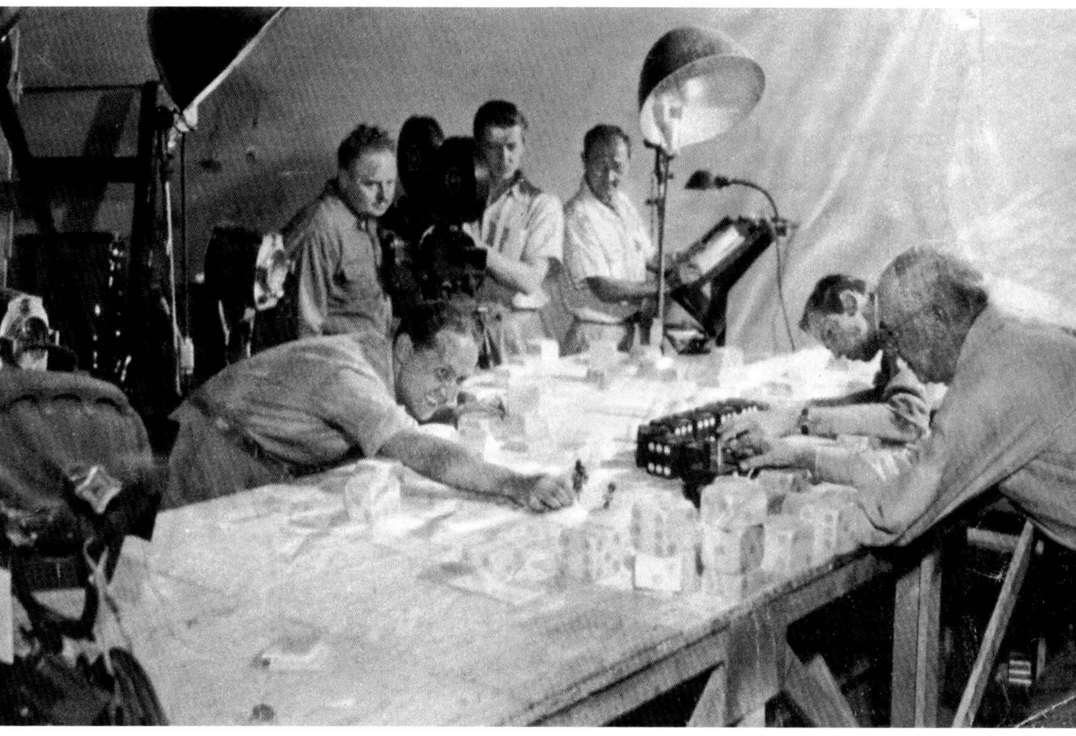

the bright idea of animating real cigarettes and, following tests, he asked the manufacturers if they minded if the commercial featured actual cigarettes rather than drawn ones. Pal was given an instant go-ahead and he spent three weeks animating the cigarettes to music. He recalled, 'They liked it so much that they ordered other films where cigarettes spoke. So we put little mouths on them – no face yet, just mouths. And then we put faces on them, and put hats on them, and put arms and legs on them. I built wire legs with buttons for feet and made a series of legs that way. And that was the birth of *Puppetoons*.'[2]

By 1933 the Nazi party was in power in Germany and, as both he and his wife were Hungarian nationals, Pal found himself being investigated by the Gestapo. With the little money they were able to scrape together they left Germany for Prague where Pal wanted to open an animation studio. He searched Prague trying to buy an animation camera and found that there were none, so he designed and built his own stop-motion camera, which, in those days of uncertainty, was so versatile that it could be packed away in a suitcase. It wasn't long before Pal moved again, this time to Paris where he set up a makeshift studio in his hotel room. Here he filmed model stop-motion films for Philips Radio who were based in Holland. After he had produced a number of these very successful films for them Philips asked if Pal would consider basing himself in Endhoven in Holland, which he did. There, working in a garage, he photographed in colour the short film *The Ship of the Ether* (1934) in which a glass spaceship (made from real glass) is propelled by ether waves. Moving his studio to a marginally more up-market butchers shop, he produced more commercials for Philips, Horlicks, Unilever and the US-based advertising company J. Walter Thompson Amongst the best of these shorts are *Philips Cavalcade* (1934), *The Sleeping Beauty* (1935), *Vier Asse* (1936), *Sinbad* (1936), *What Ho, She Bumps* (1937), *Sky Pirates* (1938), *Radjorør – revolusionen* (1938), *Philips Broadcast of 1938* (1938) and *Love on the Range* (1939). It was during this period that he, along with an American film-maker, Dave Bader, came up with the title *Puppetoons*.

Gaining a visa to visit America in 1939, just before the outbreak of the European war, Pal was asked to be a guest lecturer at Columbia University and to exhibit the shorts he had made in Europe. As luck would have it, whilst he was in New York Barney Balaban, the President of Paramount Pictures, saw *Love on the Range* at a party and was so

excited by it that he made some enquiries about Pal and discovered he was visiting the US. He quickly contacted him to ask if he would consider making puppet films for Paramount, basing himself in Hollywood. It was a dream come true for Pal and he eagerly accepted the offer.

Once established in Hollywood, Pal opened a small studio in a converted garage on West McCadden Place and called his company George Pal Productions. He immediately set about planning a series of *Puppetoons*, which he described as 'Color cartoons in three dimensions'.[3] The production process would begin with a script, usually written by Pal and Jack Miller, the story-sketch artist, following which the music was composed and recorded, along with dialogue and sound effects. Pal and his artists would then produce a series of sketches showing the action in each scene and these would be filmed to ensure that the action would flow. Whilst this was going on a team of technicians, including wood carvers, would make the puppets, each of which would be equipped with a range of heads with different expressions, a range of legs for walking and rubber latex arms and hands with wire cores.

Pal produced one *Puppetoon* every six weeks, beginning with *Western Daze* (1941) followed in the same year by *Dipsy Gypsy*, *Hoola Boola*, *The Gay Knighties* and *Rhythm in the Ranks*. It was at this embryonic stage in the development of Pal Productions that an enthusiastic young animator arrived. His name? Ray Harryhausen. Ray recalls that George was a congenial, kind and generous man who always seemed to be looking out for talented technicians, hence Ray's employment. He was very easy to work with and was a perfectionist, working throughout the night reading the next project for the next day. He would take between ten to twenty-five weeks to plan and make copious sketches of each film. Pal was a thorough person, Ray recalls, his drawings were meticulous and his calculations of timings for music and dialogue were exact to the last second. When the twenty-year-old Ray started at West McCadden Place he and George shared the animation work between them, with Ray animating on one set whilst George worked on another to save time. Ray worked on thirteen of the *Puppetoons*, including the five titles mentioned above as well as *Sleeping Beauty* (1941), *Jasper and the Watermelons* (1942), *The Sky Princess* (1942), *Mr Strauss Takes a Walk* (1942), *Tulips Shall Grow* (1942) (which was nominated for an Oscar ®), *The Little Broadcast* (1942), *Jasper and the Haunted House* (1942) and *Jasper and the Choo-Choo* (1942). Later, other technicians, including the cinematographer John Abbott and animators like Wah Chang, Gene Warren, Phil Kellison and Willis O'Brien (who only stayed a week or so), were employed. By 1945, when Ray left, the team had swollen to forty-five.

Pal received an Academy Award® in 1943 for the 'Development of Animation Techniques' and the *Puppetoon* series continued until 1947 when Pal filmed *Romeow and Julicat*, an insert made for the Paramount feature *Variety Girl*. In all, Pal produced forty-two *Puppetoons*, although this number should be compared to the two hundred shorts he is said to have made in Europe before he emigrated to America.

By the time Paramount called a halt to the production of Pal's innovative but stylized *Puppetoons* he had already decided to try and produce feature films, some of which he hoped would use his animation techniques. He had several projects in mind and when Peter Rathvon, a friend of Pal's, set up his own production company, Eagle-Lion, he signed Pal to a two-picture deal, the first of which would be *The Great Rupert* to be followed by a project that had the working title of *Operation Moon*.

The Great Rupert (1949) is a sentimental black-and-white film about a squirrel called Rupert who has been trained to dance a Scottish reel for a Vaudeville act. With Christmas approaching, a down-and-out family of acrobats, led by the hugely enjoyable Jimmy Durante, rent the apartment formerly occupied by Rupert's trainer and Rupert accidentally helps them by stealing money from the landlord's secret horde. The film was directed by Irving Pichel and, in addition to Durante, it starred Terry Moore (who had appeared in *Mighty Joe Young*), Tom Drake and Queenie Smith. However the 'real' star of the film was the squirrel. Although most people believed it to be real (there were some cutaways of live squirrels), it was in fact an articulated puppet animated by ex-*Puppetoon* animator, Fred Madison[4] assisted by cameraman John S. Abbott. The animation of the model (and some other items such as juggled walnuts) is at times erratic but for the majority of Rupert's brief appearances the creature is believable and amusing. Although the film was popular with family

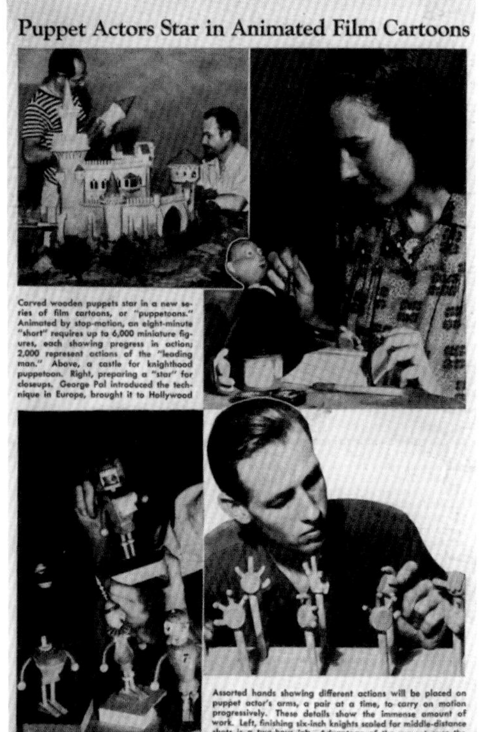

Puppet Actors Star in Animated Film Cartoons

Carved wooden puppets star in a new series of film cartoons, or "puppetoons." Animated by stop-motion, an eight-minute "short" requires up to 6,000 miniature figures, each showing progress in action; 2,000 represent actions of the "leading man." Above, a castle for knighthood puppetoon. Right, preparing a "star" for closeups. George Pal introduced the technique in Europe, brought it to Hollywood

Assorted hands showing different actions will be placed on puppet actor's arms, a pair at a time, to carry on motion progressively. These details show the immense amount of work. Left, finishing six-inch knights scaled for middle-distance shots is a two-hour job. Advantage of the puppet over the

FAR LEFT
A page from *Popular Mechanics* magazine showing Ray and others working on the *Puppetoons*. The photograph at the top left of the page shows two technicians building miniatures for what would become *Gaye Knighties* (1941) and at top right a young lady is painting one of the puppets. At the bottom left are some of the 6-inch knight models and in the bottom, right Ray is looking at assorted replacement sets of hands. The caption claims that 6,000 miniature figures were required for each short film of which 2,000 were for the 'leading man'. Ray never liked to count so we must except that this is correct.

LEFT
Ray reaching over a beautifully constructed miniature set to move the models for *Gaye Knighties* (1941).

ABOVE
The *Puppetoon* production crew outside George Pal Productions Inc on West McCadden Place in 1940. The figure in the centre with his mouth open and hand raised, is George Pal and behind him, just looking over his head, is a youthful Ray.

audiences and is still shown on television at Christmas, it was not a huge success at the time of its release.

However, Pal's next venture would not only break box-office records but also set a new trend in science-fiction films. *Destination Moon* (1950) was written by science-fiction author Robert Heinlein with Alford 'Rip' Van Ronkel and James O'Hanlon. The film contains a lot of special effects but there are only two sequences that feature model animation. The first is a long shot that occurs whilst the crew of the spaceship *Luna* are on their way to the moon in which several animated models of spacemen are seen walking on the outer hull of the spaceship. The second is the long shot of the spacecraft after it has landed upright in the Harpalus crater in which we once again see tiny animated figures, this time climbing down the exterior ladder onto the moon's surface. Both sequences were animated by the same technicians who had worked on *The Great Rupert* but this time John S. Abbott was credited as 'Director of Animation' with Fred Madison as animator. *Destination Moon* went on to earn Pal the 1950 American Academy Award ® for special effects in 1951.

Pal's next two films were also extremely popular at the box office and have become science-fiction cult classics. *When World's Collide* (1951) and *The War of the Worlds* (1953) raised the technical accomplishments of the genre to a new level and made Pal the top fantasy producer, but neither utilized model animation. Nor did his three subsequent pictures, *Houdini* (1953), *Naked Jungle* (1954) and *The Conquest of Space* (1955) – another venture into science fiction, or as Pal saw it science fact. It wasn't until 1958 that he returned, at least in part, to model animation.

For over twenty years Pal had wanted to make *Tom Thumb* and in 1957 he took the project to MGM who readily agreed to back it with a budget of one million dollars on one condition:

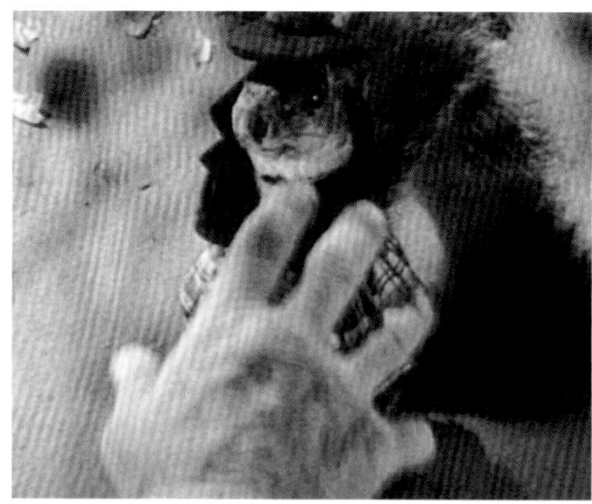

that the picture was made at the MGM Studio at Borehamwood in England. Pal, too, had one stipulation: because the project contained a huge amount of special effects, which he could visualize better than anyone else, he wanted to direct it himself. However his first directorial venture was not to be a smooth ride: the problems began when he arrived in England, as he explained:

> *Then the problem of British labor laws came up, and they wanted to put an English director on the picture. So I reminded them of our tight budget and said, 'If you put another director on it, it will take an awfully long time to get it ready,' It's very difficult for a director who is not well versed in special effects to direct a picture like this. And I had been producing for so long that it was no problem for me. Fortunately the head of the union loved the* Puppetoons, *and when I showed him my presentation, he said, 'We have nobody who can direct this. You are the one to do it.'*[5]

The young American dancer-actor Russ Tamblyn, who had appeared in MGM's hit *Seven Brides For Seven Brothers* (1954) and had been nominated for an Oscar for *Peyton Place* (1957), was cast in the title role, a part that Pal had originally intended to be played by an animated model. Most of the rest of the parts were played by British actors, including June Thorburn, Terry-Thomas, Peter Sellers, Bernard Miles, Jessie Matthews, Ian Wallace, Peter Butterworth and Peter Bull. *Tom Thumb,* based on the Brothers Grimm fairy tale, tells of an elderly couple who wish for a little boy, 'even if he were no bigger than my thumb', and so are sent the miniscule Tom Thumb by the Forest Queen. The remainder of the film relates his exploits with various unscrupulous characters ending, as one would expect, with everyone living happily ever after.

Although he came to realize that his main character had to be a real actor, Pal had always planned that a number of other key characters should be played by models animated in the *Puppetoon* style. When the project was given the green light, he asked Dutchman Joop Geesink[6] to carry out the work, but Geesink's quote was way over Pal's allocated budget. Pal then considered setting up a special studio and leading the work himself, but as he was already both the producer and the director time would not allow for this. He then looked around for some of the animators who had worked alongside him on the *Puppetoon* series, namely Wah Chang and Gene Warren, but the company they had set up when the *Puppetoons* had finished had gone out of business. However, as luck would have it (and as Hollywood legend tells it), just before Pal was to set out for England to begin principle photography he bumped into Gene Warren in the street. Warren told him that, along with Wah Chang and Tim Barr, he had set up another special effects company called Projects Unlimited. On the spot, Pal signed Projects Unlimited to do the animation effects. It was therefore Warren, Chang and fellow-animators, Don Sahlin and Herb Johnson who designed and animated the characters Jack-in-the-Box, Con-Fu-Shon, the Yawning Man, and all the other toys that come to life, a task that took a total of five months to complete. The animation of these wonderfully original characters was superb and the sequences rate as some of the best stylized model animation ever achieved. Pal was both surprised and delighted, as was MGM, when the film was a huge success on its release. In the studio's eyes Pal could do no wrong and they told him that he could make whatever he wanted, so he chose to film H.G. Wells' *The Time Machine.*

The Time Machine (1959) tells the fantastic story of a time-traveller who journeys from the turn of the nineteenth century into the future. On the way he makes three stops: the first in 1917 when the First World War is raging; the second in 1940 when London is suffering the blitz; and the last in 1966 to witness the beginning of a nuclear war that destroys civilization. The machine reaches its final destination in AD 802,701 by which time mankind has divided into two races; mutated humans called the Morlocks, who had originally sought sanctuary below ground after the atomic war, and the Eloi, humans who stayed and thrived above ground. The time-traveller discovers that the first live off the second and helps the Eloi to defeat the Morlocks and then travels back to 1899 to collect some books and return to help mankind begin again. Produced and directed by

LEFT
Scenes showing the animated squirrel in Pal's *The Great Rupert* (1949). Audiences believed the squirrel to be a trained animal but it was in fact animated by Fred Madison.

TOP RIGHT
David Pal, son of George Pal, animating the elves designed and constructed by Wah Chang for 'The Cobblers and the Elves' sequence from *The Wonderful World of the Brothers Grimm* (1962).

TOP FAR RIGHT
Gene Warren animating 'Con-Fu-Shon' for *Tom Thumb* (1958).

BELOW
Don Shalin animating 'Con-Fu-Shon' for *Tom Thumb*. Shalin is holding a second, replacement, head ready to fix on to the main body of the model.

BOTTOM LEFT
Don Shalin animating a section of the dragon featured in *The Wonderful World of the Brothers Grimm* (1962).

BOTTOM RIGHT
Don Shalin animating the singing elves featured in *The Wonderful World of the Brothers Grimm* (1962).

Pal, the film starred unknowns Rod Taylor and Yvette Mimieux with Alan Young playing the time-traveller's friend.

Once again the film contained several model animation sequences, though far fewer than *Tom Thumb*. To render the effects and animation, Pal again approached Projects Unlimited and it was Wah Chang, Gene Warren and Tim Barr, assisted by George Pal's son David Pal, who designed, constructed and executed most of the effects. There are various time-lapse sequences, including flowers opening and closing, a shop mannequin that has its clothes frantically changed as the decades slip by and a candle that melts down as the time-traveller watches it from the time machine. What little animation the film does contain mainly occurs when the traveller is testing his machine in the laboratory. We see a potted plant with its flowers opening (the following shots of flowers are time-lapse), a snail dash across the floor and apple blossom fade and apples grow. Much later in the film, during the final fight with the Morlocks, the time-traveller kills one and it slumps in a corner of the cavern. When the traveller pushes the lever to escape we see the disintegration of the Morlock's body, which includes an eye popping out of its socket. Wah Chang constructed the body of latex and other elements over a full-size skeleton and Dave Pal animated the decay. *The Time Machine* was another huge worldwide success and it won an Academy Award® for its innovative visual effects. As so often happens in the film business, *The Time Machine*, the high point of Pal's career, was followed by a slow and sad decline.

His next picture was *Atlantis, The Lost Continent* (1960), again for MGM. Because there was a writers' strike going on in Hollywood at the time of pre-production, the MGM executives wanted to get the picture under way quickly. Pal tried to argue that the script was nowhere near ready to

put into production and that the miniscule budget proposed would not do justice to the scope of the story, but in the end he was forced to concede. Consequently the film was a disaster. It contained an array of special effects, mostly miniature, all designed and executed by Projects Unlimited. There was to have been a sequence using model animation in which men flew with artificial wings, but these scenes were cut from the final release after unfavourable previews.

Pal's next picture was *The Wonderful World of the Brothers Grimm* (1962), based loosely on the life of the Grimm brothers and their fairy tales. At the time MGM had a deal with the Cinerama Company, which had invented an ultra-wide-screen process using three cameras and projecting the images simultaneously onto three screens.[7] The executives at MGM were looking around for an appropriate subject for which to use the process and, as Pal had been pushing for the project to go ahead for some time, it was chosen to be the first feature to be made in Cinerama. Sadly, the film as a whole is disappointing but it does contain a considerable amount of excellent model animation.

Pal directed the fairy tales and Henry Levin directed the main Grimm brothers story. Again, the Projects Unlimited team took on the special effects, with animator Jim Danforth working on the dragon sequence in 'The Singing Bone' section, the main animation sequence, together with Don Shalin and Dave Pal. The dragon model, designed and constructed by Chang, used a steel ball-and-socket armature covered in latex rubber rather than the usual wooden Pal *Puppetoon* construction. In total, the dragon sequence took four months to execute, as did the other animated model section, the 'Cobbler and the Elves' story. Again Chang designed and constructed the elves, which were approximately twelve to eighteen inches high, but for this section Pal reverted back to his replacement technique with the animation being carried out by Don Shalin and David Pal.

Although *The Wonderful World of the Brothers Grimm* was given a massive amount of publicity and hype by MGM and Cinerama, it was a worldwide box-office failure and, sad to say, it has come to look more and more dated in the years since its release.

In 1963 Pal began work on what would be his last picture of note, *7 Faces of Dr Lao* (1964). Again made for MGM it starred, in a variety of roles, the talented and versatile Tony Randall. The screenplay was based on a novel by Charles G. Finney called *The Circus of Dr Lao* a story set in the 1920s about a Chinese showman, one Dr Lao, who brings his unusual circus to the small mid-western town of Abalone, Arizona. The circus exhibits are Pan, the Greek god of joy, a giant serpent, Medusa, Merlin, Appolonius, the Abominable Snowman (played by Pal's other son Peter) and the Loch Ness monster, all of which play a part in gradually changing the lives of the town's inhabitants. Projects Unlimited were once more employed to design and carry out the effects, the centrepiece of which was the Loch Ness monster sequence, which in itself took three months to animate. In the film the monster grows from a tiny creature into a huge beast and for the sequence showing its growth Jim Danforth constructed and animated twenty separate articulated models, each

BOTTOM LEFT
Wah Chang with his own Kodak Cine Special camera, circa late1930s. The picture was taken by his wife Glen Chang.

BELOW
The animation models featured in the singing elves section of *The Wonderful World of the Brothers Grimm* (1962).

BELOW, BOTTOM
A set of the replacement heads, designed by Wah Chang and used for the Yawning Man sequence in *Tom Thumb* (1958).

RIGHT
Gene Warren and Wah Chang planning an animation sequence for *Tom Thumb* (1958) with the replacement heads for the character Con-Fu-Shon in front of them.

BOTTOM RIGHT
Wah Chang at home with his model of a tyrannosaurus rex constructed for the short film *Dinosaurs, The Terrible Lizards* (1970); it later featured in the television series *Land of the Lost* (1974) as the t. rex affectionately known as 'Grumpy'.

slightly larger than the last. When the monster reverts back to a tiny creature the entire process was reversed and this part of the sequence was executed by fellow animator Pete Kleinow.

Kleinow, nicknamed 'Sneaky' Pete, was born in 1934 in Indiana and had developed an early interest in model animation. His first professional employment was at the Clokey Studios working on various television series, *Gumby*, *Outer Limits* and *Davey and Goliath*, and *The Wonderful World of the Brothers Grimm* was his first feature film. However, his ruling passion was for music and during the late 1960s and early 1970s he worked with The Byrds and Joe Cocker. In 1974 Pete returned to animation and effects working throughout the 1980s and 1990s on features that included *Caveman* (1981), *Star Wars: Episode V - The Empire Strikes Back* (1980), *Gremlins* (1984), *Terminator* (1984), *RoboCop 2* (1990), *Terminator 2: Judgement Day* (1991) and *Army of Darkness* (1992). He died in Petaluma, California in 2007 from complications relating to Alzheimer's disease.

7 Faces of Dr Lao was another film that did poorly at the box office and, although innovative, it is not too hard to see why. In places it is quite surreal. Today it is seen by some as a landmark fantasy film but as far as we are concerned it is the quality of the model animation that makes this film special.

The failure of the film reflected badly on Pal and he was not able to produce another feature for almost four years. *The Power* (1967) was his last for MGM and is fundamentally about human beings with superhuman powers. It starred George Hamilton, Susan Pleshette and Michael Rennie. There are several sequences that incorporate model animation, including some *Puppetoon*-like toy soldiers that threaten Hamilton, and a hallucinatory sequence that includes a skeleton falling into blackness, and the freezing and then the melting of Hamilton's head. The film was an even bigger disaster at the box office than *Dr Lao* and in Britain only made it as the second half of a double bill.

Although George Pal was continually working on other projects, like a sequel to *The Time Machine*, he would make only one more picture, *Doc Savage, The Man of Bronze* (1975). This was also a box-office failure and a sad end to a productive and pioneering career. Without doubt Pal gained a place in the history of cinema with a number of remarkable films which, in turn, gave the art of model animation a huge boost in the 1950s. Pal died in 1980 in Los Angeles of a heart attack and his passing was mourned by a great many people in the industry, including Ray who had remained close friends with him throughout all the years since his work on the *Puppetoons*.

We have made passing mention of Wah Chang and Gene Warren who worked with George Pal and of their company, Projects Unlimited, which did the effects for his later films, we now need to look at their careers in more detail because of their individual contributions to art of model animation.

Wah Ming Chang was born in 1917 in Honolulu, Hawaii. When he was two years old his parents moved to San Francisco to open the HoHo Tea Room, on Sutter Street. Chang recalled that the tearooms were a haven for various artists and at the age of seven he met an artist, Blanding Sloan, who encouraged his passion for sketching. It was also at this time that Chang developed an interest in marionette construction, which eventually led to him performing in a one-man show with his marionettes. Because of his talent, Chang received a scholarship to the Peninsula School of Creative Education in Menlo Park and whilst there continued his marionette performances in company with several other students.

ABOVE
Gene Warren animating the Julicat model for the *Puppetoon* sequence *Romeow and Julicat* seen in the Paramount Pictures feature film *Variety Girl* (1949).

RIGHT
The wonderfully sleepy but funny Yawning Man featured in *Tom Thumb* (1958).

FACING PAGE
Gene Warren animating the Yawning Man for *Tom Thumb* (1958)

In 1937 he made his first animated model film and, although an amateur like Ray, he painstakingly trained himself in art. Two years later, aged twenty-two he joined the Walt Disney Studios as a member of the effects and model department, where his job was to sculpt wooden models of characters to enable the animators to visualize them from all angles in their drawings. Then in the summer of 1939 tragedy struck. He was hospitalized with severe influenza, which was in fact polio. The result was that Chang lost the use or both of his legs and it would be a year before he was able to walk with the aid of leg braces, which he was still wearing when Ray met him on the *Puppetoons*. Although Ray was on the verge of leaving Pal Productions by then, he got to know Chang very well and, even though the two were never close friends, they stayed in touch over the years. Ray remembers Chang as one of the nicest men and most articulate animators he has ever met, who often came over for dinner with his wife Glennalla (Glen) in those early days. The last time Ray saw Chang was when he went up to see George Web, an art director on *Mighty Joe Young*, who lived in Carmel; since Chang lived in the same area they both went to see him. Glen had recently passed away but Chang was still happily drawing and sculpting.

When the *Puppetoons* wound up in 1947 Chang set up his own production company with Glen to make educational films. Sadly, business was slow so he joined Gene Warren to form Centaur, an effects company. Warren, who was born in 1916, had also begun his career as an animator at the George Pal studio working on a number of *Puppetoons*, one of which was *Date with Duke* (1947) featuring the voice of Duke Ellington. He was also largely responsible for the *Romeow and Julicat* sequence that Pal designed for the 1947 film *Variety Girl* about the romance between a cat and a dog, which used typical *Puppetoons* models with wire for armatures and a series of wax replacement heads.

In 1956/57 one of Centaur's first features was the cheap science-fiction production *Kronos* (1957) about a giant alien robot. The Kronos model, which was very crude and completely impractical, was designed and built by Chang and animated by Warren. Warren recalled, 'All the action scenes with Kronos were accomplished with stop-frame photography of the simple, very unsophisticated puppet (about ten inches in height) against process plates with foreground set pieces to allow the puppets to make actual contact with the ground.'[8]

After changing the name of their company to the more descriptive Projects Unlimited, Chang and Warren were joined by Tim Barr who took a largely administrative role. In 1957 things began to pick up, although their first feature *Monster From Green Hell* (1958) was not perhaps

the most auspicious start. Projects Unlimited was commissioned by effects producers Jack Rabin and Louis DeWitt to deliver the stop-motion work for the picture, although neither the company or Chang and Warren received a credit. Perhaps they didn't mind. The film featured scenes of giant wasps and one scene of a fight with a giant snake, but these were poorly designed and crudely animated. The budget didn't allow for proper ball-and-socket models so Chang and Warren were reduced to using wire as an internal skeleton instead.

Projects Unlimited were then commissioned by George Pal to work on *Tom Thumb* (1958), the beginning of an association which, as we have already seen, was to last for many years. Their primary task was to animate a large number of toys in Tom's bedroom, so they employed Don Shalin and Herb Johnson to assist. In the sequence there are a number of shots that show Russ Tamblyn (Tom) dancing with the toys, these effects were accomplished with the aid of split screens and travelling mattes. Chang recalled

> *The two main puppet characters were Con-Fu-Shon and the Yawning Man, which I made. Both of those had [a] series of faces or heads and these were done in wax. In the Yawning Man's case a wax face was made and put on the head with registration pins, so that they were always accurately registered. The average number of heads will be from twenty to thirty dialogue heads, and faces that smile or laugh or yawn.*[9]

Project Unlimited were again asked by Pal to provide all the effects, including all the time-lapse and miniature work, for *The Time Machine* (1960), which understandably won Gene Warren and Tim Barr an Academy Award ® for best special effects. Unfortunately Chang was left out of the awards because of the way the credits for the film were submitted to the Academy. Although upset at the time, Chang was a forgiving man and celebrated the award alongside Warren and Barr.

For Projects Unlimited 1959/60 was a busy time as they were also commissioned to execute the effects for a dinosaur picture called *Dinosaurus!* (1960). The film featured a brontosaurus and a tyrannosaurus rex (both poorly constructed by Marcel and Victor Delgardo) the latter of which had a fight with a mechanical digger in the climax! It was a slight film redeemed only by the animation delivered by Chang and Warren, assisted by Phil Kellison, Dave Pal, Don Sahlin and Tom Holland

Phil Kellison was one of the many backroom boys who never achieved wide acclaim as an animator but he was in fact a good reliable artist, animator and technician. He, too, worked as an

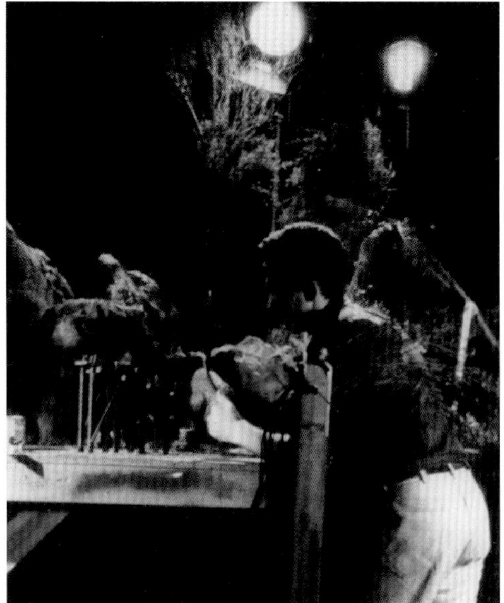

FAR LEFT
Marcel Delgado putting the finishing touches to the tyrannosaurus rex featured in *Dinosaurus!* (1960). After thirty-five years of building models, beginning with *The Lost World* (1925), this was one of the last films Delgado worked on.

LEFT
Don Shalin animating the tyrannosaurus rex for *Dinosaurus!* (1960).

BELOW
The brontosaurus with a boy on its back, featured in *Dinosaurus!* (1960).

BELOW, BOTTOM
The tyrannosaurus rex (seen in the picture at top left with Delgado) fights the mechanical digger.

RIGHT
The hugely respected Phil Kellison posing with two of the creatures featured in *Jack the Giant Killer* (1962). On the left is Galligantua and on the right is the six-tentacled sea monster.

animator on the *Puppetoons*, built some of the miniatures for Obie's *The Giant Behemoth*, supervised the process photography on *Jack the Giant Killer* (1961) and animated many well known US commercials, for example the 'Pillsbury Doughboy' and 'The Jolly Green Giant'.

Don Sahlin made a cameo appearance in *The Time Machine* as the window dresser and would continue to work for Projects Unlimited as a designer and animator until it folded. He subsequently found true fame when he met Jim Henson at a Detroit puppetry convention and became Henson's main designer and puppet-builder in the 1960s and 1970s, specifically for the hugely successful *Sesame Street* and *The Muppet Show* television programmes. He passed away in 1978 and in his honour Henson had a bench dedicated to him and placed on Hampstead Heath in London.

Journey to the Seventh Planet (1961) was produced by American International Pictures (AIP) and Cinemagic, with the live action being shot in Sweden. The story concerns a group of astronauts who travel to Uranus and encounter various awful (really awful!) creatures, including a very silly and badly animated cave monster that truly defies description. Warren, Chang and Jim Danforth were responsible for the animation and received no on-screen credit for their efforts to enhance this truly bad film. In the same year Projects Unlimited worked on George Pal's *Atlantis, the Lost Continent* (1961), which used model animation for the giant crystal weapon and an unused sequence of birdmen.

Next came two major projects, the first of which must have seemed at first glance to be a potential commercial success. Unfortunately, what may look good on paper doesn't always turn out that way when realized on the screen. After the huge box-office returns for Ray's *The 7th Voyage of Sinbad*, producer Edward Small decided to make *Jack the Giant Killer* (1962), which was a blatant attempt to cash-in on the previous film's success. It must have niggled Small that, when the *Sinbad* project had been offered to him some years before, he had declined, pointing out to Ray that costumes films were not popular and completely failing to recognize that the project's originality lay in the effects. To guarantee *Jack the Giant Killer's* success Small commissioned some of the key talent from *The 7th Voyage*, including the director Nathan 'Jerry' Juran, Kerwin Mathews. who had played Sinbad, and Torin Thatcher, who had played the magician Sekoura. What Small failed to realize was that he hadn't employed the one person who really mattered, the person who had dreamed up the initial storyline and conceived the key sequences for *The 7th Voyage* – Ray himself. Jim Danforth, who worked on some of the *Jack the Giant Killer* animation, said of the film,

> *...they tried to copy all the elements which they felt had made* Sinbad *successful. They got the same leading man, the same villain and spent considerably more money on the film than had been spent on* Sinbad*; unfortunately, in my opinion, at least, they were not able to make a good film. They were so unhappy about it, in fact, that Edward Small doesn't want to hear the word 'animation' again, and would never entertain the idea of doing another one.*[10]

There were, not surprisingly, many problems with the film. The major ones are that the storyline appears to have been pieced together as the live-action production progressed and that the effects were woven around the poor storyline rather than the other way round, which is how Ray and Charles always made their films. Another problem, or problems, are the models themselves. The firm of Howard Anderson (a special photographic effects company founded

in 1927 and run by Howard A. Anderson) was commissioned to carry out the special effects and they, in turn, asked Projects Unlimited to deliver the model animation. Wah Chang and Gene Warren designed a great many of the effects and models while the armatures were constructed by Victor Delgado. The featured creatures included a mechanical doll which grows into a Cormoran, a horned giant (remarkably similar to the Cyclops in *The 7th Voyage of Sinbad*), a dragon/gargoyle-like flying creature, a six-tentacled sea monster and another giant called Galligantua, which this time had two heads. In addition there are various human figures and even a dog. Without exception, the models look dreadful, which is surprising considering Chang and Warren were usually such perfectionists. We can't blame the budget either because, as Jim Danforth has pointed out, the production budget was at least healthy. The models seem to possess little or no muscular detail and the skin finishes appear shiny and rubbery, lacking any credibility, even as fantasy creatures. One of the golden rules in animated fantasy is that the creatures must at the very least always look plausible.

The animation was credited to Chang, Warren and Tim Barr, but in reality it was overseen by Phil Kellison with the animation itself executed by Jim Danforth, Tom Holland, Don Sahlin (who did several tests for the animation, though none of his work was used in the final film) and Dave Pal. Before the release Edward Small announced that it had been filmed in a new process called 'Fantascope', 'a revolutionary new system of trick photography';[11] again the reality was rather different, Fantascope was very similar to Dynamation, utilizing split screens and rear-projection plates in exactly the same way.

The key animation scenes begin with the Cormoran mechanical doll, which performs a dance with the Princess throughout most of which the lighting flickers during the animation, which suggests the animators had the same problems as Ray did with his first colour film, *The 7th Voyage of Sinbad*. Next comes the Cormoran growing into a giant and kidnapping the Princess, a sequence which concludes with Jack killing it. Torin Thatcher, who plays the evil Pendragon, then conjures up Galligantua, which appears to be very similar in design to the Cormoran except for his two heads, fair hair and fangs, and this very unconvincing creature then does battle with the awful sea creature that seems to have been designed by a plastic toy-maker on a bad day. Finally, the dragon/gargoyle possessed by Pendragon attacks Jack's boat. Again this creature is very poor in design and resembles something made of Plasticine. Although the animation is not of the best quality, it does have moments of fluidity and occasional glimpses of characterization, especially during the mechanical toy's dance. *Jack the Giant Killer* did have story potential but it seems that Small never realized that the story depended on the animation and visual effects, and although Projects Unlimited and their animators made brave efforts to enhance the overall look of the film, the responsibility for its failure has to lie with the producer.

When 'Jerry' Juran came to visit Ray in London in 2001, a year or so before he died, the three of us talked at length about the films he had directed for Ray and Charles. At one point I asked him about *Jack the Giant Killer*, and he looked at Ray and then me and said that he could never understand why the film wasn't a box-office success. Ray and I had no intention of disillusioning him. Jerry was a wonderful man and an extremely versatile and talented director, ideally suited to fantasy films. When he directed live action he was always able to take full acount of the effects which would be added later.

The next production Projects Unlimited were involved with was another George Pal film, *The Wonderful World of the Brothers Grimm* (1962), which was a prestigious production but would once more prove to be a commercial failure, again not because of poor effects but because of its story construction. The film was shot in Cinerama, which entailed the use of three purpose-made animation cameras, which gave Wah Chang and Projects Unlimited a few headaches. The animation was completed by Jim Danforth, Don Sahlin, Dave Pal, Tom Holland and Peter Von Elk who were all uncredited. Although inconceivable today, it was quite normal before the 1970s for technicians to be uncredited, even when their input was not just crucial to the success of the film but its real 'stars'. *The Wonderful World of the Brothers Grimm* consisted of three Grimm fairy tales, beginning with 'The Dancing Princess' which contains only one animation sequence of a flower that curls its petals into a face and yawns. The next is 'The Cobbler's Tale' which features a group of elves that look much like characters from the *Puppetoons* and even re-used the heads of 'The Yawning Man' from *Tom Thumb*. The models for this sequence were again built by Chang and the animation was executed by Dave Pal, Don Shalin and Jim Danforth with good detail in the characterization of each model. The third and final segment is 'The Singing Bone' which featured a jewel-encrusted, fire-breathing dragon designed by Chang and animated by Danforth. It is this delightful character that is the overall 'star' of the film in terms of both animation and characterization. In an early scene the creature seizes and gulps down a spear thrown by actor Buddy Hackett. When the dragon swallows the spear we see a bulge caused by the spear's progress down its throat. Another lovely touch is the dragon licking its lips as it waits to eat Terry-Thomas. Although the film as a whole doesn't flow, there are moments when the animation brings it to life and at least enables the fairy tale sections of the film to be moderately entertaining.

The next project was *7 Faces of Dr Lao* (1964) which also had its problems. The company were again asked by Pal to execute the effects, with Chang, Danforth, Warren and Pete Kleinow (the last two uncredited) working on the animation. There are a number of animated sequences but it is the finale, showing the appearance and growth of the Loch Ness Monster, as animated by Jim Danforth, Wah Chang and Pete Kleinow, that is by far and away the most exciting and enjoyable. The monster begins as a tiny little fish-like creature and grows to dinosaur proportions. At one point, when the creature is threatening two humans, it sprouts six heads on long monster-like necks, which are those of the other Dr Lao characters, the purpose of this development is unclear to the audience but it is, nevertheless, an extremely good piece of animation. Overall, the animation in this sequence is superb and the monster's flicking tail and ungainly walk are perfect.

One of the last major projects Chang worked on would be their last for George Pal. *The Power* (1967) was a present-day science-fiction thriller for which Projects Unlimited executed several animation sequences, although all are part of the running storyline rather than being key sequences. They depict, amongst other things, a malevolent battalion of toy soldiers (animated by Dave Pal); the head of the actor George Hamilton freezing and disintegrating followed by his facial skin burning away to reveal his skull (animated by Warren): and finally a skeleton falling into blackness (animated by Pete Kleinow). Warren explained that 'All the scenes involving George Hamilton's head were accomplished [by] stop-frame on a wax model of Hamilton taken from a life mask.'[12] Although all the brief animation sequences were inventively designed and animated they could not save the film from box-office obscurity.

Soon after *The Power*, Projects Unlimited was wound up and Chang went back to freelancing. However, in 1969 Chang and Warren formed another company called Excelsior! AMP (the AMP stood for Animated Motion Pictures), but in the following year Chang and his wife moved to a house he had designed in Carmel Valley. There Chang decided to use his feature skills to produce educational films, amongst them *Dinosaurs... The Terrible Lizards* (1970) an eleven-minute documentary about dinosaurs, which he made with Douglas Beswick. Chang would continue to work in films and for television, mostly designing props and creatures rather than animation (he had been responsible for designing various prop equipment for the original series of *Star Trek*), but his first loves were painting and sculpting.

Wah Chang passed away on 22nd December 2003. Warren went on to work on a number of television series, which included *Land of the Lost* (1974) for which he was the stop-motion director, and *The Man from Atlantis* (1977) for which he worked on the photographic effects. He continued working in the field of effects until 1996 and died the following year. Excelsior! had closed its doors in 1980 but Warren's son, Gene Warren Jr, took over from his father with his own company Fantasy II, and won an Academy Award® for *Terminator 2: Judgement Day* (1991).

One key animator who had a huge influence on the art and other animators, but whose work did not combine model animation with live-action, was Jiri Trnka. His work is some of the most respected and innovative in the art. Born on 24th February 1912 in Pilsen, in what was then Czechoslovakia, Trnka had a natural leaning towards the arts, especially models, which was perhaps enhanced by his grandmother's talent for making dolls and toy animals. Aged twelve he participated as a designer in the Holiday Camp Theatre, which was a marionette group run by Josef Skupa, a schoolteacher who later became one of Czechoslovakia's most famous marionette players. Skupa taught Trnka the process of making marionettes, how to operate them and, most importantly, how to instil character into them. Between 1929 and 1936 Trnka went on to study at the Prague School of Arts and Crafts and after graduating he established a marionette theatre of his own in Prague, called The Contemporary Theatre of Puppets, which was extremely successful. However, his passion for puppets was soon leading him to experiment with stop-motion animation and articulated puppets and in 1937 he created two characters, Spejbl and Hurvinek, who were to achieve wide acclaim in Czechoslovakia.

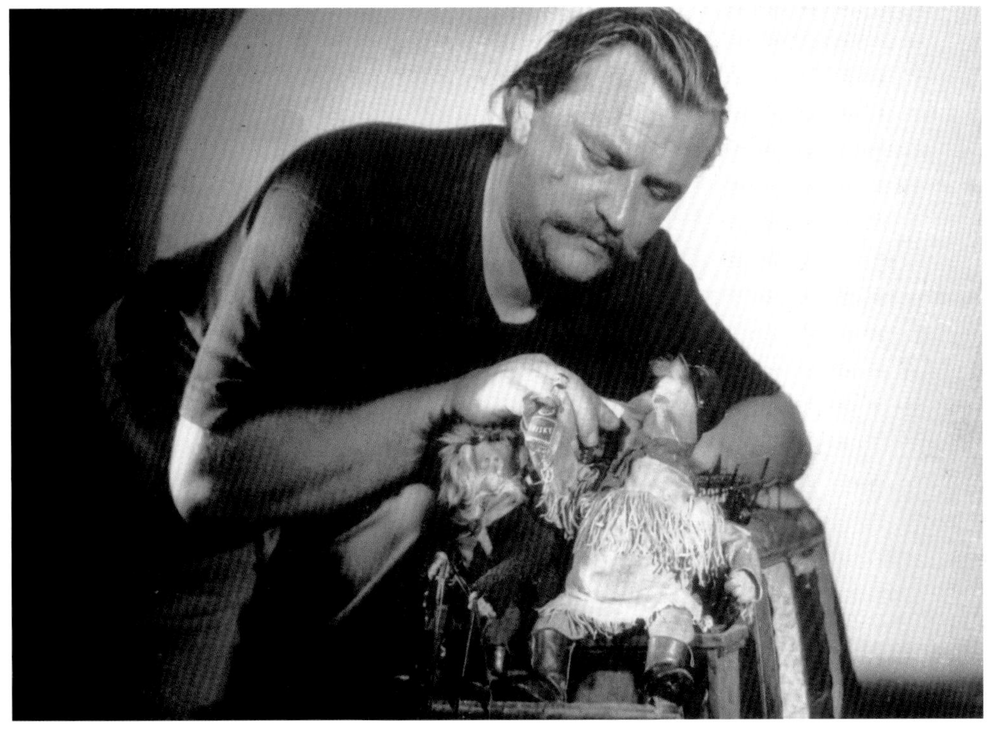

The war closed down his theatre and his film production, so for the duration Trnka concentrated on designing theatrical sets and illustrating children's books. At the end of the war in 1945 the Czech film industry was nationalized; so instead of reopening his marionette theatre, Trnka, along with other friends and colleagues, began an animation unit which was called 'Trick Brothers', at the Prague Film Studio. Trnka specialized in model animation because of his fascination with puppets – he once said that they have, 'more presence' than drawings. He liked their slowness of movement (compared with graphic images), their 'solidity and stillness'. His early short films usually drew for their subject matter on Czech traditions and folk tales, which would continue to inspire his work throughout his career. Some of his films from this period were *Grandpa Planted a Beet* (1945), *The Gift* (1946), *The Animals and the Brigands* (1946) and *The Czech Year* (1947). The last (the Czech title is *Spalicek*) was reputedly his favourite and was his first feature film, made in six parts. It was based on the book by Alois Jirásek which illustrated traditional Czech folk customs throughout the year. The success of these films meant that in 1947 Trnka was allocated the complete upper story of an old villa near the city centre where he opened the Prague Puppet Film Studio (today called The Studio of Jiri Trnka). In the same year he also won an award at the Cannes Film Festival.

After the Communist coup d'etat in 1948 the new government subsidized all Trnka's work in the belief that animated puppet films could not contain anti-Communist messages, but of course they did, albeit in a subtle manner that presumably escaped the notice of the politicians. The Prague Puppet Film Studio produced at least one puppet film a year; amongst some of the most famous are *The Emperor's Nightingale* (*Císaruv slavík*) (1948), *Song of the Prairie* (1949), *Prince Bayaya* (1950), *The Golden Fish* (1951), *Old Czech Legends* (1953) and *The Good Soldier Schweik* (1954), based on three episodes from the novel by Jaroslav Hasek in which Trnka experimented with commentary and dialogue. In 1959 he made *A Midsummer Night's Dream*, which captured the spirit of Shakespeare's play and which

BOTTOM LEFT

The great Czech animator Jiri Trnka working on one of his stylized models.

BELOW

Top row, Two frames from *Ruka [The Hand]* (1965).

Middle row, from left to right. One of the wonderful models featured in *Císaruv slavík* [*The Emperor's Nightingale*] (1948); Jiri Trnka animating his uniquely styled models; Tnka's epic folk tale in six parts *Spalicek* [*The Czech Year*] (1947), possibly his favourite film.

Bottom row, from left to right. Another of the models from *Císaruv slavík* ; Jiri Trnka animating; another still from *Spalicek* [*The Czech Year*] (1947). Note the ghostly driver, resembling a character from Tim Burton's *The Nightmare Before Christmas* (1993).

debuted at the Cannes Film Festival in 1960 when Trnka was hailed as 'The Walt Disney of the East' (journalists often invoked Disney's name because he was best known for animation, even if it was not the same kind of animation), a title he hated as his work bore little comparison to that of his American contemporary. Other films followed. *Obsession* (1961), *Cybernetic Grandma* (1962) a futuristic allegory, *The Archangel Gabriel* (1965) based on tales from *The Decameron*, *Mrs Goose* (1965) and, perhaps his best known film, *The Hand* (1965), a parable of an artist working under oppression.

At a reception to celebrate the screening of *The Emperor's Nightingale* in Paris, the model of the emperor was shown to the famous French director Jean Cocteau. He remarked,

> *I witnessed a strange thing. Friends were struck with awe. They were almost afraid of touching the mysterious and miraculous little creature, who was no longer an actor, nor an emperor, nor a puppet, but Trnka's soul which has assumed the appearance of the emperor. You can no doubt imagine how awful it is to touch a soul and pass it on as if it were an ordinary object of art.*

A very moving and true assessment, not only of Trnka but of all animators, many of whom would agree with Cocteau that they gave their very souls and beings to their models or puppets. In 1966 *Newsday* also paid tribute to Trnka and his unique work by describing him as, 'second only to Chaplin as a film artist because his work inaugurated a new stage in a medium long dominated by Disney'. Trnka died in 1969 in Prague where he had worked all his life. His work has been called 'active dreaming', combining great imagination and poetry with ingenuity, invention, realism and creative vitality.

It would have been interesting to know what Trnka thought of Walt Disney Studios' early foray into the art of model animation, the 1959 short film *Noah's Ark*, which was nominated for an Academy Award that same year. It used Pal-like surreal stick models, which were animated by Bill Justice who, as a two-dimensional animator, had worked on some of Disney's most famous titles. Even though it was a relative success, Disney declined any further excursions into the model field, presumably because he preferred the tried and tested two-dimensional animation. It wasn't until the 1990s that Disney would again produce a model animated film with Tim Burton's *The Nightmare Before Christmas*.

In the 1950s, films that utilized model animation combined with live action were on the increase, to the point where independent low-budget film-makers began jumping on the bandwagon. One such opportunist was Robert Lippert who produced *Lost Continent* (1951). Made twenty-six years after *The Lost World* and eighteen years after *King Kong*, this was a poor man's version of the same theme, a lost island/plateau that contained dinosaurs. The story, which has a contemporary setting, tells of a military and scientific team who are sent by the US government to locate a missing experimental rocket in the Pacific. They trace it to an island, or more precisely to a plateau (on the top of a very unconvincing mountain), which is, of course, inhabited by a variety of dinosaurs, including a triceratops, a brontosaurus and a pterodactyl. The animation, which is poor, is credited to Augie Lohman, a highly respected special effects technician whose work on this film was not one of the his finest moments. The models are basic and the animation is certainly very jerky or, at the very least, intermittently erratic. After various encounters with dinosaurs the group find the lost rocket but are confronted by an aggressive brontosaurus and triceratops, which seem to be just standing around looking for trouble. One of the more exciting animation scenes shows one of the men being gored by a triceratops although the actual killing takes place behind a tree, probably because it would have cost too much to animate the triceratops and a model human.

Little better is *The Beast of Hollow Mountain* (1956). The storyline, about a Mexican town terrorized by a living allosaurus, was based on a concept by Willis O'Brien, although the final product was certainly not designed or animated by him. The models had originally been built by Marcel Delgardo for O'Brien's abandoned *Gwangi* project and the animation of the allosaurus was executed by Jack Rabin and Louis DeWitt, who used both a replacement technique and the more conventional and versatile articulated model animation. The replacement technique used on this film was similar to that used for Pal's *Puppetoons*, movement being achieved by replacing one model with another in a slightly different pose or position. The ads screamed that the film was photographed in 'Regiscope' (based on an uninspired combination of the words 'register' and 'scope') which would have meant little to most people and was basically just another gimmick to get the punters into the cinemas. As Obie once remarked, 'All these name tags for animation, I think I'll call mine "Origimation"'![13]

Rabin and DeWitt had many problems with both the colour (there are many scenes that show severe image grain and fluctuation between the rear-projected image and the lit model) and the fact that producer Edward Nassour had decided to film in 'scope'. Any form of anamorphic lens (commonly known as 'scope' after Cinemascope) tends to accentuate what is known as the 'hot spot', which is an excessively bright point that

FAR LEFT

A poster for Robert Lippert's *Lost Continent* (1951), probably one of the most disappointing animated films because of the soulless models and the lack of imaginative animation.

LEFT

A paste-up image that shows two of the dinosaurs featured in the film. Although the animals are called triceratops, they more resemble arrhinoceratops.

BELOW LEFT

The really dreadful allosaurus featured in *The Beast of Hollow Mountain* (1956) with an unfortunate local in his its claws. Although the story was originally conceived by Willis O'Brien, he didn't work on the final film, a fact which becomes obvious when you look at this model.

BELOW RIGHT

The poster for *The Beast of Hollow Mountain* (1956).

appears at the centre of the projection screen.[14] Obtaining the correct colour balance and at the same time overcoming the hot spot would have presumably entailed a great deal of testing. Overall, the animation for *The Beast of Hollow Mountain* was crude, awkward, jerky and lacked fluidity. No attempt seems to have been made to instill any form of character into either the model (it is so unconvincing, primarily because of its limp-wristed arms) or the animation of the allosaurus (the tail hardly ever seems to move but just lies on the ground). The film is a good example of how not to film model animation and, together with *The Lost Continent*, illustrates how independent producers, while eager to use the technique, were not ready to allocate a decent budget and get the right people for the job.

Another major animator (and another Czech) who was working in the 1950s and 60s and who is, surprisingly, almost forgotten today was Karel Zeman. He designed, directed and animated a number of key fantasy films that combined model animation with live action. Although never mainstream, because of the language problem, his major films with their surreal designs did have a wonderfully exciting and innovative sense of adventure. Zeman was born in 1910 in Moravia in Czechoslovakia, and his interest in marionettes began whilst attending business school, although at this early stage of his life he had no thought of making it his life's work. After business school he had a short stint as a shop window dresser after which he travelled to France to study at the Art School of Advertising. Following graduation he secured a job in an advertising studio in Marseilles designing posters and it was here that he had his first taste of film-making when he was involved with an animated soup commercial. On completion of the film he realized that this is what he wanted to do and when he returned to Prague he continued making animated commercials using puppets. In 1943 he showed some of his films to Elmar Klos, another film-maker, who instantly offered Zeman a job working in the Bata Film Studios in Zlín. There he met animator Hermína Tyrová with whom he made the puppet animated film *Vánocní sen* [*The Christmas Dream*], which won an award at the 1946 Cannes Film Festival for Best Animation. The two would collaborate on two other short films, *Podkova pro stestí* (1946) and *Krecek* (1946), before Zeman moved on to his first solo creation.

In 1947 he began what would turn out to be an extremely successful series of short films featuring a character called *Mr Prokouk*, the first of which was *Pan Prokouk v pokuseni* (1947). Zeman was always experimenting with new ways of animation and in 1949 he made the unique *Inspirace* [*Inspiration*] in which all the characters or figurines were made of glass and were animated by heating them after each frame was shot to allow them to be moved. It is impossible to imagine how much time and effort must have gone into such a process, one that, to our knowledge, he never used again. In 1950 Zeman made *Král Lávra* [*King Lavra*], which won a National Award the same year, and in 1953 he produced his first

feature film *Poklad Ptacího ostrova* [*The Treasure of Bird Island*]. This was followed by *Pan Prokouk, prítel zvírátek* (1955) the last of the *Mr Prokouk* films, and in the same year Zeman discovered his forte with his first pure fantasy feature film, *Cesta do praveku* [*Journey to Prehistory* aka *Journey to the Beginning of Time*], which would make his name internationally. The film, like so many of Zeman's subsequent features, was partially inspired by the imagination of Jules Verne and tells of four boys who journey in a rowboat into a mysterious cave in Manhattan's Central Park and in doing so travel back in time through various ages to witness the prehistoric period and, finally, to the primordial ocean where life began.

The film was shot in Agfacolor (Technicolor was too expensive), and had the distinction of being the first feature film made in Europe in which stop-motion dinosaurs played a major role. Zeman incorporated a variety of stop-motion model animals and dinosaurs, around fifty in total[15], including woolly mammoths, rhinoceros, giraffes, a phororhacos, a deinotherium, a sabre-toothed tiger, brontosaurus, stegosaurus, a phororhacos, styracosaurus, ceratosaurus and pteranodons, some of which he incorporated with live action by using split screens and mattes. Antonin Horák, who worked with Zeman on this film and subsequently on *Vynález zkázy*, recollected that, 'the rubber models were fairly small, about 50cm. Everything was photographed on the original negative with mattes and counter mattes.' First the live-action children who appeared in the bottom section of the frame were photographed by a cameraman from Prague with Horák as stand-by. Later, back in Zlin, the dinosaurs where inserted into the upper part of the frame. Horák goes on, 'For each scene about 10 metres of test footage was shot to determine the matte line for the counter matte and special filters to match the live-action and lighting animation.'[16]

Although some of the shots are rudimentary, the inventiveness of many of the scenes, for example the boys being attacked by pteranodons, are exciting and occasionally spectacular, especially when one considers that the film is shot in colour. There are some mechanical props employed, but the bulk of the creatures are animated and most are animated with fluidity, style and originality. The models themselves are good, although not as detailed as either Delgado's fine work or Ray's. The success of *Cesta do praveku* permitted Zeman to indulge his passion for fantasy and allowed certain of his subsequent features to find favour and even bigger success with audiences abroad.

In the same year as *Cesta do praveku* was released, Zeman had already begun work on another fantasy film, this time almost entirely based on the fictional adventures of Zeman's hero, Jules Verne. *Vynález zkázy* [*The Invention of Destruction, The Fabulous World of Jules Verne, The Diabolic Invention, Weapons of Destruction, The Deadly Invention*] (1958), is an extraordinary achievement and is perhaps Zeman's most accomplished feature. The story tells of a professor and his assistant who are kidnapped by

TOP LEFT
The remarkably talented and inventive Karel Zeman animating glass figures for the film *Inspirace* [*Inspiration*] (1949). The amount of painstaking work involved in heating up each figure so that it could be moved for the next frame, was simply extraordinary.

TOP CENTRE
The charming short film *Vánocní sen* [*The Christmas Dream*] (1946), which was animated and directed by Karel Zeman.

TOP RIGHT
A mammoth watching the children row along the river of time in *Ceste do proveku* or *Journey to the Beginning of Time* (1954).

ABOVE CENTRE
Karel Zeman, left, directing a sequence of the boys in the boat for *Journey to the Beginning of Time* (1955).

ABOVE
This rare still shows what is possibly a cerotosaurus facing up to a stegosaurus in *Journey to the Beginning of Time* (1955).

RIGHT
Karel Zeman, left, directing actor Milos Kopecky who plays Baron Munchausen, in *Baron Prasil* [*Baron Munchausen*] (1961).

pirates and held captive in a laboratory beneath a volcano so that the pirates can extract details of the professor's wonderful inventions. The film is stunning; the backgrounds are made up of Doré-like drawings and engravings which serve as the settings for both the live action and the model animation. The combination creates a totally unique fantasy world, although one which is not, it has to be said, to everyone's taste. The German film historian Dr Rolf Geisen, who has studied Zeman's work, calls *Vynález zkázy* 'the first truly synthetic movie', which seems an excellent way of summarizing such fantastic backgrounds and animation. Although Zeman designed all the effects it was Antonin Horák, his cameraman, who worked out and realized all the optical effects; because the film was even more complex than *Cesta do praveku* they composited all the images in-camera. Another problem was that there was no Mitchell camera available so Horák was forced to use Slechta cameras, which were far inferior.[17] For some in-camera, bi-pack composites, consisting of five or six different elements, a week or more was required to complete the live-action, miniatures, cut-out animation and stop-motion. Sadly after completing all the difficult trick shots in-camera Horák was released by Zeman because he thought Horák too slow!

When the picture was released in America[18] the posters heralded it as 'The first Motion Picture Produced in the Magic-Image Miracle of Mystimation', a phrase which perhaps takes the prize for the silliest-ever coinage to describe the combination of animation and live action. However, Zeman's animation for the film is on the whole superb and features several birds, humans, fish, various machines such as airships, an eccentric submarine, and finally a giant octopus that emerges from a dark underwater ravine and attacks a group of divers. This last is perhaps the most spectacular and Zeman's animation for this scene and all of the other incidental animation is fluid and consistently ground-breaking.

For many years Ray had entertained the idea of making an animated version of Gottried Bÿrger's classic stories *The Adventures of Baron Munchausen* but the project never came to fruition. However, in 1961 Zeman did realize an animated version of the stories called, not surprisingly, *Baron Prásil* [*Baron Munchausen*] in which a modern-day astronaut lands on the moon where he meets a number of literary space pioneers, including Cyrano de Bergerac, Captain Nichols, Barbican and Baron Munchausen. The Baron realizes that the astronaut needs to experience what a real adventure is like, so takes him on a journey back to his own time, the eighteenth century. There, amongst other adventures, they visit the Ottoman court, rescue a noblewoman, encounter the Turkish fleet, are swallowed by a gigantic fish, visit the bottom of the sea and go to the North Pole. Zeman once again utilized Gothic Doré-style backgrounds and, to add another element to the fantasy, photographed the film in black and white but with colour tinted scenes. Animation scenes include a sailing ship pulled by seven flying horses, a sea serpent, a dragon, a giant spider, a flying fish, a huge whale, a huge carnivorous bird and a sea horse on which the Baron rides. The whole film is a tour de force of fantasy adventure and model animation, with Zeman again achieving an effortless fluidity.

In 1964 Zeman made his fourth feature film, *Bláznova kronika* [*The Jester's Tale*], which is one of his most surreal and rarely seen films. The story tells of a cowardly peasant, a mercenary and a female jester and their attempts to survive the Thirty Years' War and the stupid generals who perpetuate it. Although he uses the same innovative visual backgrounds of Gothic-styled drawings there is only a small amount of animation, confined to two-dimensional cut-outs and tiny humans seen in the distance.

Urradená vzducholod [*The Stolen Dirigible, The Stolen Airship; The Two Year Holiday, The Two Year's Vacation*] (1967) saw Zeman returning to Verne's Victorian fantasy. Five boys steal an airship from the Prague Centenary Exhibition of 1891 and fly it to the Pacific where it crash lands on an island and they meet the legendary Captain Nemo. The animation of airships, a car propelled by horses' legs and a shark is smooth and seamlessly flows with the live action.

Zeman's next film was based on Verne's novel *Hector Servadac* and was called *Na komete* (*On the Comet*) (1970), an unusual adventure that has an underlying moral suggesting the futility of war and how humans seem to revel in fighting each other. It is set in 1888 and tells of a group of French, Spanish and English soldiers who are swept off on a comet, which has skimmed the Earth. When they realize they cannot escape and that the comet is inhabited by a variety of dinosaurs, they agree to a truce and help each other but when the comet eventually returns them to Earth they resume their fighting. Sadly, the film does show a lethargy which suggests that Zeman felt that he had been here before, although this may be due to an obvious lack of production finance. Once again he places his characters into Gothic settings which provide the adventure with a suitable surreal quality. The first animated sequence features a group of dinosaurs, which include sauropods and a tyrannosaurus rex, attacking a makeshift fort, which has been erected by the soldiers to protect themselves from such monsters. Sadly, although there are

a large number of models, none interact with the live action. Other creatures encountered are a sea serpent, pterodactyls, a dimetrodon and styracosaurus.

Karel Zeman went on to make more highly original and inventive feature films amongst which were *Pohádky tisíce a jedné noci* [*Tales of a Thousand and One Nights*] (1974) which consisted of seven stories about Sinbad, *Krabat, carodejuv ucen* [*The Sorcerer's Apprentice*] (1975)

and the Grimm Brothers' fairy tale *O Honzíkovi a Marence* [*Hansel and Gretel*] (1980). However, they didn't surpass or indeed equal any of his Jules Verne-influenced fantasy classics. By 1970 he had completed and delivered his best. Zeman's last film was made in 1979/80 and he died in Prague in April 1989 before he was able to witness the advent of the Velvet Revolution. His unique styles of visualization, storytelling and animation have survived him and, although not in the same league as O'Brien and similar animators, his work is now highly respected and has, gratifyingly, found a new audience with today's fantasy-loving public.

It is quite extraordinary how many model animators were born in Czechoslovakia. Perhaps it was the Czech tradition of puppetry that inspired them to experiment with puppets and cinema or perhaps it was the Czech love of storytelling. Whatever the reasons, there are far too many Czech animators to mention them all, but we feel that we have to give credit to one final example. Bretislav Pojar was closely associated with Jiri Trnka and is famous for his two- and three-dimensional short films but his forte seems to have been the latter. Born on 7 October 1923 in Susice, he studied architecture at the Academy of Fine Arts but when the Nazis closed the universities he went to work in the AFIT Studio, a pivotal point in his life. Following the end of the war, Pojar, along with Trnka and other animators such as Jan Karpas, Bohuslav Šrámek and Stanislav Látal, became part of a new animation department at the Prague Film Studio, which was affectionately called 'Trick Brothers'.

TOP LEFT
The wonderfully eccentric submarine featured in *Vynález Zkázy* [*The Fabulous World of Jules Verne*] (1958).

ABOVE, TOP PICTURE
Karel Zeman animating the submarine for *The Fabulous World of Jules Verne*.

ABOVE, MIDDLE PICTURE
A giant octopus rears up from a deep abyss to attack divers in *The Fabulous World of Jules Verne*.

ABOVE, BOTTOM PICTURE
The interior of the submarine that shows the gothic or Doré style of the backgrounds against which Zeman set all his characters and models.

LEFT
An American poster for *The Fabulous World of Jules Verne*.

His first films of note were as puppeteer assistant to his mentor Jiri Trnka and these included *Román s basou* [*The Story of the Bass Cello*] (1949) and *Cisaruv slavik* [*The Emperor's Nightingale*] (1949). In 1951 he made his directing debut with *Perníková chaloupka* (1951) and, although he continued assisting Trnka, he also produced his own films which included *Lev si zaridit byt* [*The Lion and the Song*] (1959), which won the Grand Prix at the first annual Annecy Festival in 1960.[19] The following year Pojar left Czechoslovakia for Canada where he began a long association with the National Film Board of Canada and it was during his time there that he produced some of his best-known work. Pojar was, and still is, an animator who loved breaking boundaries and experimenting with new techniques to enhance the art of animation, whether it was two- or three-dimensional. After the fall of Communism in Czechoslovakia he moved back to what is now the Czech Republic and his last film to date is *Filmfám 2* made in 2006.

To complete this chapter we have kept one of the most respected and underrated model animators till last. Although mentioned earlier, Jim Danforth is perhaps not a name that would

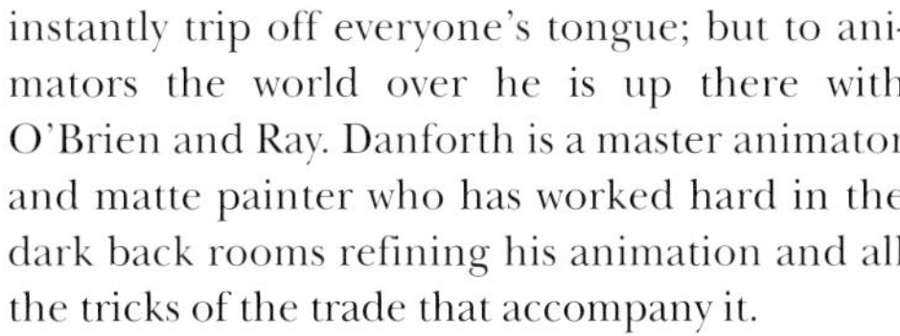

instantly trip off everyone's tongue; but to animators the world over he is up there with O'Brien and Ray. Danforth is a master animator and matte painter who has worked hard in the dark back rooms refining his animation and all the tricks of the trade that accompany it.

Danforth was born in 1948 in Ohio and grew up near Chicago, Illinois. At the age of twelve his parents moved to California which is where he first saw *King Kong* and *The Thief of Bagdad* (1940) and, like Ray, became fascinated and obsessed with the fantastic images in both films. Intrigued by how Kong moved, he began experimenting with ventriloquism and then marionettes, giving puppet shows to the local kids. It wasn't until three years later, aged fifteen, that he found out about stop-motion animation via some Kodak publications. Although he had no idea about armatures and latex, he began tentative experiments using his father's 8mm Keystone camera that didn't have any stop-motion facility; only when he had saved up enough money could he progress to a more professional 16mm Bolex. Like Obie and Ray before him, the course of Danforth's life was determined by his early experiments and the wonder of seeing inanimate objects come to 'life'.

ABOVE TOP
A young Bretislav Pojar in the process of animating circa 1950s.

ABOVE LEFT
Pojar's *Velryba-Abyrlev* [*Elahw the Whale*] (1977).

ABOVE CENTRE
More wonderful Pojar puppets featured in *O te Velké Mlze* [*Thick Fog*] (1975).

ABOVE RIGHT
Bretislav Pojar back in Czechoslovakia working on a project, circa 1990s.

RIGHT
The versatile and extremely talented Jim Danforth working on *When Dinosaurs Ruled the Earth* (1971). A giant crab is seen on the animation table in the foreground.

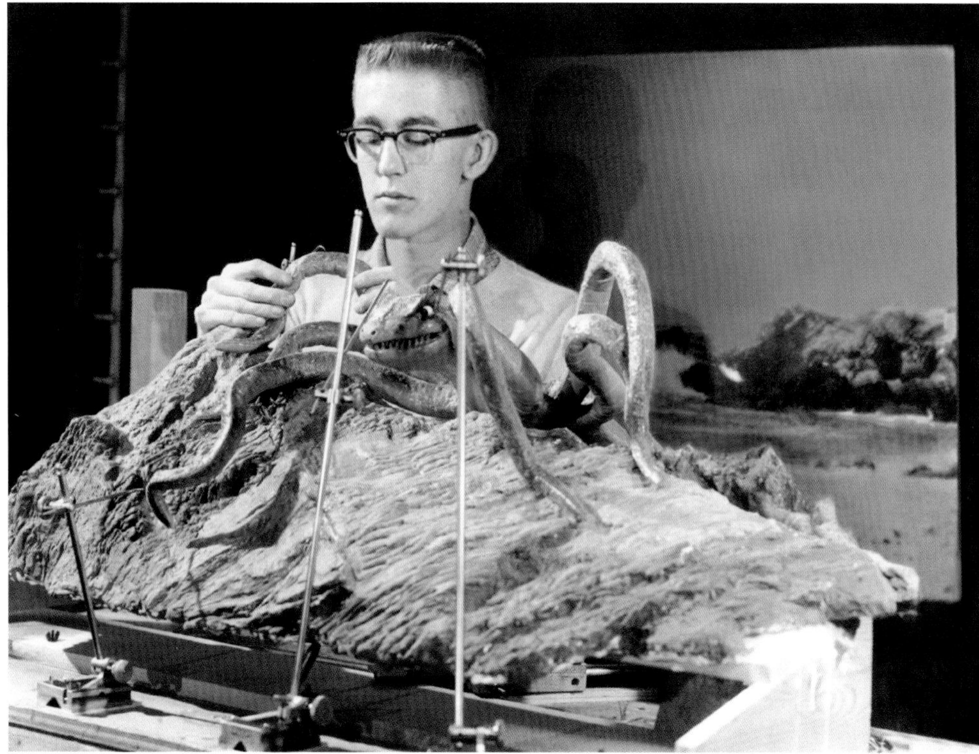

When he finished high school, aged eighteen, he looked around for a job in the animation field and found one with a small company called Clokey Productions (run by Art Clokey) working on *The Dinah Shore Show* television series, including a sequence for an Easter special in which Dinah 'danced with an animated rabbit that appeared to be about five feet tall'.[20] This was followed by six months of work on a number of fourteen-minute films for the Lutheran Church called *Davey & Goliath*. Making full use of what little spare time he had, Danforth got to know Wah Chang and Gene Warren at Projects Unlimited and helped out as an uncredited assistant animator on George Pal's *The Time Machine*. This led to him being offered a job working for the company full time. Two years before, Danforth had begun working on a personal project called *The Princess of Mars* for which he had produced a range of drawings and paintings. George Pal had presumably thought these visualizations good as he helped Danforth to 'stage a presentation at MGM for Hulbert Burroughs and ERB Inc, Attorneys'.[21] Sadly, despite Pal's enthusiasm, this intriguing project remained unrealized.

His first film as animator at Projects Unlimited was *La Vendetta di Ercole* (*Goliath and the Dragon* or *Hercules' Revenge* or *Vengeance of Hercules*) (1960) followed by the disappointing science-fiction adventure *Journey to the Seventh Planet* (1961). However, his first big break came in 1961when he worked on much of the animation undertaken by Projects Unlimited for the fantasy adventure *Jack the Giant Killer* (1962). Ironically, at an earlier date Danforth had independently quoted $3000 to Howard Anderson[22] for the construction of the models for the film but it wasn't accepted. The models were designed and made by Wah Chang and Danforth has remarked that 'I didn't like the puppets. It's quite difficult to animate a puppet when you don't find it aesthetically pleasing. Especially when you have to look at it with intense concentration, day after day.'[23] Almost the climax of the movie (and perhaps the best sequence) is the fight between Galligantua (the two-headed giant) and the sea monster. Danforth recalled how the sequence came about: "The battle between the two-headed giant and the sea monster was shot once by two other animators and [Edward] Small didn't buy it. So it was re-shot. I didn't do all the second fight; we used a couple of shots from the first and the other animators [working on the project] re-did a few shots. But I did most of the second fight myself.' Like Ray, Danforth prefers working on his own. 'It's much easier that way, especially when they're [the models] are all tangled up as they were with the tentacled sea monster. It's hard to co-ordinate it with two people and you find you're tripping over each other.'[24]

The effects took nearly ten months to complete and the production was Danforth's first experience animating with professional rear projection, a process he had witnessed when he had

TOP LEFT
Jim Danforth animating the complex sea monster sequence for *Jack the Giant Killer* (1962). The rear-projection screen can be seen behind him whilst the model sits on a miniature rock that will exactly match the one on the rear-projection plate.

FAR LEFT
The dragon/gargoyle creature featured in *Jack the Giant Killer* animated on wires to react to the rear-projected image of the escaping boat.

LEFT
Jim Danforth at work animating the jewelled dragon featured in *The Wonderful World of the Brothers Grimm* (1962).

ABOVE
Another shot of Jim Danforth animating the dragon from *The Wonderful World of the Brothers Grimm*. In this and in the previous image the all-important surface gauge can be seen.

ABOVE RIGHT
The jewelled dragon as it appears in the film with actor/comedian Buddy Hackett.

visited Ray during the final stages of production of *The 7th Voyage of Sinbad*. 'I suggested that they use the system of split screens in conjunction with process projection – a system which I freely admit was "stolen" from Ray Harryhausen, who devised it. No one there knew about that system, and there really had never been any intention of using it in the film.'[25] Ray remembers Danforth visiting when he was animating the dragon and Cyclops fight. Danforth was a very intense and knowledgeable young person who arrived carrying a notebook and throughout the time he was there showed an interest in absolutely everything and made copious notes.

In 1962 Projects Unlimited worked with Pal again, on the effects for *The Wonderful World of the Brothers Grimm* on which Danforth, along with the other animators, was forced to struggle with the three-camera Cinerama process. There were two cameras constructed specially for the film 'which shot the frames in succession'; Danforth recalled the frighteningly time-consuming method of shooting the animation. 'A panel was exposed then the camera was moved to a click stop. B panel was shot. The camera was moved into a third position and C panel was shot. Then it was all racked back to the beginning again. In some cases we were shooting six exposures for one frame on the screen.'[26] Danforth helped Dave Pal with a few of the elf scenes for 'The Cobbler's Tale' and also a scene in 'The Dancing Princess' that showed a flower going to sleep. However, the key sequence to which he contributed was the one featuring the dragon in 'The Singing Bone' story.

In preparation for the task he studied animal movement at the local zoo where he would sit for hours watching the exhibits in their cages. Along with George Pal and Gene Warren, he worked out the dragon's human-like character that allowed the creature to be the most entertaining element of the movie. It seems extraordinary that Danforth didn't receive a screen credit for his extensive work on the picture, an omission that he admits made him extremely angry.

In the summer of 1962 Danforth went to work for another company, called Film Effects of Hollywood, on a short animation sequence for Stanley Kramer's *It's a Mad, Mad, Mad, Mad World* (1963). He was employed to construct some mechanical miniatures and to shoot some high-speed miniatures and seventeen animation shots, of which only a few were used in the final cut. He recalls: 'I did that [the film] because I had hoped to work with Willis O'Brien who was working on the film. However, between the time that I made the arrangements and the time I actually started working, Obie had died.'[27] Danforth had first met Obie at Projects Unlimited when the pioneer had come in for a visit, and subsequently when he had his interview at Film Effects.

Danforth returned to Projects Unlimited in early 1963 to work on the pre-production for *7 Faces of Dr Lao* designing and then on the animation of the Loch Ness monster, which began in the late summer of 1963.[28] In total, the sequence took three months to shoot and required the exposure of some 12,900 frames for the nine minutes the creature appears on the screen. Danforth recalled,

The fish [the first tiny model] was a little clay thing that we just flopped around. Then six solid clay models were substituted in series to grow into the first wire-armatured Loch Ness monster. That was positioned and animated for a second or two. Then the next six series were used for it to change into its second intermediary stage, which was a wire-armatured puppet animated for another second or two. Then finally it was the full-grown puppet, which had a ball-and-socket armature. The camera was tracking in to make it grow also. Then the monster was matted in over the live action. The shrinking of the beast was shot just the reverse. That was animated by Pete Kleinow.[29]

Although Danforth was not pleased with the final design of the model, the sequence remains the best and most complete model animation sequence in the film for which Danforth was nominated for an American Academy Award ® but lost out to *Mary Poppins*.

Between 1964 and 1969 Danforth worked on various projects, all uncredited, building the miniatures on *Father Goose* (1964), as an animator on *I'd Rather be Rich* (1964), as a model-maker on *Strange Bedfellows* (1965), as a matte artist and animator on *That Funny Feeling* (1965) and designing and constructing miniatures for *The War Lord* (1965). He returned to Projects Unlimited to work on several episodes of the television series *Outer Limits*, a credit sequence for *Hallmark Hall of Fame* for designer Saul Bass, a few commercials and educational films and then, finally, the last film Projects Unlimited made, *Around the World Under the Sea* (1966) for which he designed and built several miniatures.

The day Projects Unlimited closed down he went over to Cascade Pictures to design and animate the 'Pillsbury Dough Boy' and 'Nestles Man' commercials and an animated sequence for a television episode of *Here's Lucy* (1968). In all, Danforth was at Cascade for about three years. In between the projects at Cascade he worked on an amateur project called *Equinox* (1967) with Dave Allen and Dennis Muren[30] and *Raiders of the Stone Ring* (1968/69), an uncompleted feature that was resurrected in 1978-84 as *The Primevals*. The story was to begin with an adventurer relating his trip into a lost world inhabited by Vikings and dinosaurs which included a giant lizard and a giant ground sloth, with the climax showing a flock of pterodactyls attacking a Zeppelin.

In March 1968 Danforth heard about a project to be made in England by Hammer Films, a follow-on rather than a sequel to *One Million Years BC* (1966) called *When Dinosaurs Ruled the Earth* (1971). However, it wasn't until later that year that he was contacted by the distributor Warner Bros to see if he was available to animate the creatures for it. Of course he said yes, but wanted to get his other commitments for Cascade out of the way first. He travelled to England in August to talk with Hammer and then returned again in September for the live-action photography in the Canary Islands and at Shepperton Studios. It wasn't until January 1969 that he began animation and effects, which took him a total of seventeen months, ending on 17 June 1970.

When Ray was working on *One Million Years BC*, he demanded and was given involvement with the screenplay. But the script for *When Dinosaurs Ruled the Earth* had already been written by Val Guest and J. G. Ballard and had

BELOW LEFT
Two more armatured heads (Appolinius and Medusa) out of the seven seen sprouting from the body of the Loch Ness monster in *7 Faces of Dr Lao* (1964).

BELOW RIGHT
Two frames showing the Loch Ness monster on the rampage in *7 Faces of Dr Lao* (1964). In the top image he has a victim in his mouth. This was one of the finest and smoothest animated sequences to appear in any of the Pal productions.

RIGHT
Images from *When Dinosaurs Ruled the Earth* (1971).

Top left. A beautifully designed and sculptured, but unnamed, dinosaur protecting its young from cave girl Victoria Vetri.

Top centre. A baby dinosaur just hatched. This was one of the best sequences in the film.

Top right. The dinosaur with its back to the camera threatening cavemen on the rear-projection screen. In this shot the realistic wrinkles and folds of skin can be seen on the back and neck.

Second row left. The beach cavemen try to capture the rampaging plesiosaur. Although in black and white this is an excellent example of the use of split screen. The foreground cavemen and hut are part of the bottom section matte while the cavemen in the background are part of the rear matte.

Second row centre. Jim Danforth animating the plesiosaur.

Second row right. Another shot of the plesiosaur lumbering along the beach towards the cavemen.

Third row. Three frames showing the giant crabs (designed and animated by Jim Danforth and built by David Allen) attacking the beach village.

Fourth row. The model rhamphorhynchus (a pterosaur), designed and animated by Jim Danforth. The rhamphorhynchus aerial scenes were some of the best in the film because Danforth tried to avoid a strobing effect. In Neil Pettigrew's book *The Stop-Motion Filmography* he states, 'In most of the flying shots, he [Danforth] tapped the puppet's wings, causing them to swing slightly on the wires during the long camera exposure, thereby suggesting a blur and eliminating much of the offensive strobing that had marred similar sequences.'

received final approval. The creatures, too, had already been selected[31] although Danforth did get to design and construct them and was allowed some leeway when sequences required experience and creativity.

> *The original death of the plesiosaur was to have been achieved by having several men stand on each other's shoulders in a human pyramid to pour fat on the back of the monster and try to ignite it. When that didn't work out they tried their second plan, which was to grab a dead tree, which is lying on the beach. They all run forward towards the plesiosaur, which obligingly sticks its neck down and opens its mouth so that they can shove it down its throat. I just couldn't see that on the screen. Besides, a plesiosaur thrashing around with a tree sticking out of its mouth seemed a bit ludicrous so I talked them into a fire death.*[32]

Creatures featured in the film included a pterodactyl, a chasmasaur (a horned dinosaur, part of the triceratops and styracosaurus family), a plesiosaur, huge man-eating crabs and an unnamed dinosaur and its newly hatched baby. There were to have been other sequences including a dimetrodon, a triceratops, sea monsters (that one would have included the monsters being swept up by a tornado) and giant ants but these were all cut before the final script. The screenplay was way too ambitious in terms of both the budget and the time constraints set out in the schedule. Even with scene cuts, Danforth was forced to bring over another animator, David Allen, whilst he concentrated on producing glass shots and matte paintings (needed because Hammer had cut back on sets). Allen executed approximately 80% of the chasmasaur sequence and several of the baby dinosaur shots.

Just after the film was completed, Danforth commented on the animal motion.

> *It depends on the animal. If it's a realistic animal – something specific – then it would have to move in a specific way. Of course no one has ever seen a dinosaur, but we do know the proportions of the limbs and, roughly, how they were articulated. So you try to conform to that and you go to the nearest living animals that might be similar and these won't always be reptiles. You might look at an elephant. For the chasmasaur sequence we spent a lot of time studying films of baboons because it's one of the few animals in which the legs are jointed in the same way.*

He went on, 'It tends to inhibit your style if you just copy the action. There might be time when you would want to do that, like if you were duplicating a human figure. But usually it's better to understand the action thoroughly and then do it.'[33]

Although the animation work on the picture by Danforth and David Allen is exemplary, the picture is, as already suggested, ultimately let down by a less than competent script and the use of general stock footage, including lizards made up to look like dinosaurs (from the 1960 version of *The Lost World*). Costing far more than its predecessor, the film didn't achieve the success of the *One Million Years BC*; although the effects were nominated for an American Academy Award® Danforth was again unsuccessful, losing out to yet another Disney film, *Bedknobs and Broomsticks* (1971).

Although there had been constraints, Danforth had now had, to a degree, the opportunity of designing and animating his own feature film, which provided him with an international profile. Regrettably, neither the film nor the Oscar nomination led to another such offer and he spent the next few years working on a series of mediocre features as a matte artist. Although a feature of sorts, *Flesh Gordon* (1974) is one that Danforth is allegedly not pleased to own up to, which perhaps accounts for his name being spelt on the credits as Mij Htrofnad (Jim Danforth backwards). This soft porn film was a spoof of the old 1930s Buster Crabbe *Flash Gordon* serials, complete with wires, shaky miniatures and ill-proportioned smoke effects; but the list of those involved is also a Who's Who of future effects and animation artists, including David Allen, Dennis Muren, Doug Beswick, James Aupperle, Stephen Czerkas and Laine Liska (see Chapter 6).

The film includes three key animation sequences. The first features a seven-foot creature called a penisaurus, a cross between a snake-like cyclops and a triceratops, which was animated by Bill Hedge. The second involves a creature called a BeetleMan,[34] a robotic creation made of metal and constructed by Rick Baker (who would become famous as a makeup artist), which was animated by Danforth. The conclusion of this sequence shows Flesh fighting the

creature on a stone staircase, which is reminiscent of the stone spiral staircase in *The 7th Voyage of Sinbad*. The final creature is the Great God Porno or Nesuahyrrah (Harryhausen spelt backwards and Ray has never been too sure whether this was a compliment or otherwise) who climbs to the top of a tower with the girl much like Kong did before him. The excellent animation for this model was mostly done by Robert Maine, with James Aupperle and David Allen animating several scenes. Also involved on this sequence were Dennis Muren and Danforth who worked on the lighting set-ups for some shots.[35] Aside from executing the animation for the Beetle-Man sequence, Jim also did the superb matte paintings seen in the film. There was a sequel made in 1990 called *Flesh Gordon 2 – Flesh Gordon Meets the Cosmic Cheerleaders* but Jim didn't work on that. The first had obviously been enough.

In 1974/75 Danforth was working again at Cascade Pictures. In addition to that he was offered more work as a matte artist on *The True Story of Eskimo Nell* (1975) and *The Reincarnation of Peter Proud* (1975). Although Danforth possessed a reputation as a multi-talented artist who could turn his hand to painting, model and miniature construction and animation, the animation jobs seem to have been few and far between. In 1976 he was offered a small amount of work, although uncredited again, on *The Crater Lake Monster* (1977) a rural version of the 1950s monster-on-the-rampage craze but this time with a plesiosaur. David Allen was credited as the Stop-motion Supervisor with Danforth, Randy Cook, Phil Tippett and Jon Berg (more future names) all uncredited. Allen did almost half the animation but brought in Randy Cook and Phil Tippett to help, with Danforth being involved with only a few shots. There was only one model (fifteen inches long and designed by Allen and Tippett with an armature designed and built by Jon Berg) so using multiple set-ups was not a possibility; they had to shoot the model scenes one by one.

In 1980 Danforth was asked to help Ray on *Clash of the Titans* (1981) alongside Steve Archer when Ray began to get badly behind schedule after problems with the animation film stock.[36] Based at Pinewood Studios in England Danforth executed a large amount of the animation of the flying horse Pegasus and most of that featuring the two-headed guardian Dioskilos, with Archer assisting when necessary. Ray had set ideas about how the characters should react and so what you see on the screen is how Ray storyboarded the sequences but Danforth's animation is, as always, fluid and realistic.

Immediately after *Clash* Danforth returned to the US to work on *Caveman* (1981) as a visual effect supervisor although he was once again uncredited, allegedly because he left the project two-thirds of the way through production.[37]

The film was a silly comedy that never rose above zany schoolboy humour and it seems a pity that so much good design and animation was wasted on such a poor storyline. Danforth's contribution was to design and construct various models, including the horned lizard and a superb tyrannosaurus rex which was mostly animated by Randy. *Caveman* was followed thirteen years later by *Dragonworld* (1994) about a dragon discovered and captured in the Scottish Highlands and put on exhibition in a theme park called Dragonworld. The armatures were constructed by Jeff Taylor and most of the animation was executed by Danforth, Paul Jessel, Joel Fletcher and Harry Walton and shot at the David Allen Studios with Chris Endicott supervising. The cartoon design of the dragon sadly lets the film down but the animation does achieve charm.

Although Jim Danforth's talents far surpassed those of many contemporary artists, the opportunities to work with his first love, model animation, were coming to an end. Danforth's last picture to date was *The Prophecy* (1995) for which he worked as a matte artist and executed the matte photography. He once commented that 'Animators and trick film-makers were considered by Hollywood to be technicians rather than performers, or artists, or film-makers,'[38] a sentiment that would be echoed by Ray and, we suspect, most other animators. However, there were other animators working and waiting in the wings, animators who had every intention of changing the face of model animation and the way in which it was perceived by producers.

FACING PAGE, TOP
This is an advertisement that Cascade Pictures put together circa 1975 to show the creative talent pool at Stage 6. Stage 6 was the home of the animation and visual effects division of Cascade Pictures of California. Standing to the right is Jim Danforth; lying down in front is Dennis Muren; sitting in the middle row are, from left to right, Bill Hedge, Laine Liska and Mike Minor; in the back row, from left to right, are David Allen, Ken Ralston, Tom Scherman, Harry Walton and David Stipes.

FACING PAGE, BOTTOM LEFT
Jim Danforth executing one of his superb matte paintings for the finale of *Planet of Dinosaurs* (1978).

FACING PAGE, BOTTOM RIGHT
Jim Danforth, Ray and an unknown technician posing during the production of *Clash of the Titans* (1981).

ABOVE
Jim Danforth, one of the industry's most respected animators posing with a key drawing he executed for an unrealized project called *Dark Continent* (1994) (subtitled *A Sherlock Holmes Adventure*) in which the detective was to have stumbled into a prehistoric arsinotherium in darkest Africa. In the foreground is the maquette of the creature.

CHAPTER SIX

THE CHILDREN OF OBIE AND RAY

'Stop-motion can be such a magical art; capable of expressing personal creativity in a way that, for me, I have yet to experience even with the best CG. Perhaps it's the intrinsically surrealistic nature of the process. CG seems so often obsessed with being "real", but stop-motion can be better than real, it can be awe inspiring.'

JON BERG – ANIMATOR

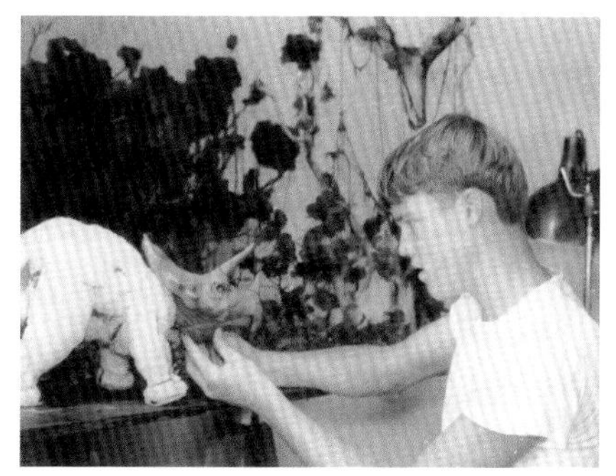

Since the early 1970s a new generation of innovators have extended the frontiers of model animation. Most were inspired primarily by Obie and Ray's work and several acknowledge that seeing *The 7th Voyage of Sinbad* was the catalyst that shaped their careers. As we have already seen, if someone has dreamed of making their own fantasies a reality it takes just one original movie to motivate them to do something about it. It is more than likely that the *Lord of the Rings* trilogy has set a few young dreamers on the path to an effects career.

Ray was fortunate to have been able to work almost entirely on his own, but his was a unique set of circumstances. The next generation would not be so lucky, or perhaps it never occurred to them that such an arrangement was possible. Many of them had begun their careers working at places such as Cascade Pictures and Clokey Studios, where they became accustomed to working in groups. In the 1970s and 80s, decades which were rich in fantasy projects, they gradually fanned out across the industry. Previously, only Ray and a handful of other animators were able to persuade producers that model animation could be big at the box office; but these children of Obie and Ray found it far easier to convince contemporary producers that they held the keys to a box-office goldmine.

This renaissance of model animation began with groups of determined individuals, sharing the same dreams and often planning projects that, like Ray's *Evolution of the World*, were perhaps somewhat over-ambitious. Most of them were also very low-budget but they gave some great animators and technicians an opportunity to test the water and launch their careers.

One such a project was *Equinox*, the brainchild of the now-famous special-effects creator Dennis Muren who raised the princely sum of $6,500 in 1965 and, with a group of young friends and some inexperienced actors, set about filming a supernatural fantasy story that he had written with Mark McGee. Shooting with a 16mm Bolex camera they photographed the live action in California while the animation was carried out in the pool house behind Muren's home. Muren edited the film on his 16mm projector and tape-splicer. When filming and effects were completed in 1967 the film ran for a total of 70 minutes. Muren then set about finding a theatrical distributor. Eventually Jack H. Harris (the producer of *The Blob* (1958) and *Dinosaurus!* (1960)) agreed to buy the film on condition that he could blow the original 16mm stock up to 35mm and extend it by eleven minutes for commercial release. Muren readily agreed and Harris brought in Jack Woods to shoot new scenes with the original cast, but it wasn't until 1970 that Woods' revised version was released. The plot centres on four young people who find a cave in which they encounter an old man (Louis Clayton, Dennis Muren's grandfather and a major contributor to the movie's budget) who gives them a mysterious book that, when opened, releases a number of Satanic creatures.

In retrospect, the film's technical credits read like a roll-call of great effects personnel. Muren was co-writer, co-director, producer and effects photographer. David Allen, a close friend of Muren's, helped him to execute the animation and Jim Danforth rendered the mattes and cel animation. Although Danforth had been in the business for some years (see Chapter 5), both Muren and Allen were novices, eager to use every visual trick in the book, including matte paintings, miniatures and forced perspective as well as model animation, not only because the story demanded it but also because they wanted to experiment.

The concept of the film and the storyline were primarily determined by the fact that Dave Allen had already been experimenting with three stop-motion models that he had constructed. The first was an ape-like monster, which he called Taurus,[1] the second was a lanky skeleton based on Ray's skeleton in *The 7th Voyage of Sinbad* and the third was a green cephalopod inspired by the nautiloid cephalopod in *Mysterious Island*. The other creature that appears, a flying demon, was specially designed and constructed for the film. The ape-monster and the flying demon are the most original creatures in the film. Although somewhat jerky (possibly due to the blowing up from 16mm to 35mm) the ape-creature[2] displays a degree of individuality, especially as it struggles to survive what proves to be a fatal wound. This sequence also includes a very adventurous front-

PREVIOUS SPREAD
Left, David Allen animating the Achilles puppet in 1987 for *Robot Jox* (1989). A massive project for David Allen Productions, it involved not only fighting stop-motion robots but also extensive high-speed photography of larger versions of the robots filmed out in the desert. Right, a young Phil Tippett, aged fourteen, sculpting a triceratops, which was unused, for Bill Stromberg's 16mm short film of Ray Bradbury's *Sound of Thunder* in 1965.

ABOVE
Forry Ackerman visits David Allen at his work desk at Cascade Pictures in the late 1960s. Cascade's Stage 6 and the workspace above the stage was a second home for Allen and many of his own projects were developed here out of hours.

BOTTOM LEFT
Allen working on *Happy Easter*, a *Davey and Goliath* special (1967). Allen balked at following the Clokey Studio's policy of shooting the animation in 2's (12 positions per second) and shot in 1's (24 positions for every second) instead.

BOTTOM RIGHT
Allen animated the entire baseball sequence for the *Davey and Goliath* special, *Happy Easter*. He only worked at Clokey's for a few months in 1967 and regretted not staying longer.

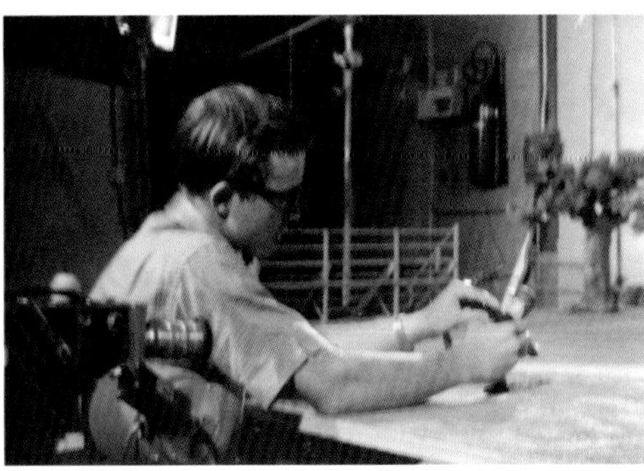

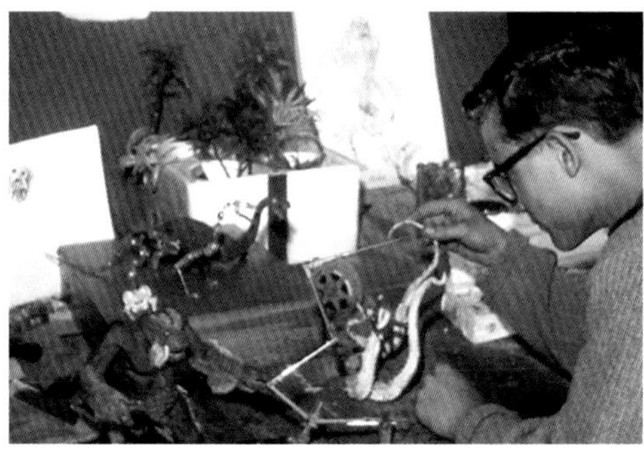

projected image of Barbara Hewitt running in front of the creature, never an easy thing to achieve in pre-CG days and something that Ray avoided because of time constraints.

The flying demon is also extremely original although, it has to be said, not the best of models. Its design is effective but the 'skin' is simply too rubbery. Throughout the demon sequence the animation is on the whole smooth and Muren and Allen allowed the monster to swoop towards the camera (much like Ray had the harpies do in *Jason and the Argonauts*) and in one shot it picks up one of the boys. Although perhaps not a classic, there is no doubt that *Equinox* is a fascinating landmark film which not only contains animation footage of a high standard but also makes an inventive attempt to create a new subject for model animation.

David Allen was a naturally talented animator and has become one of the most respected in the business. He was born on 22 October 1944 and, like so many other animators before and after, was endowed with artistic talents which he channelled into model animation after seeing a re-release of *King Kong* when he was six years old. He graduated from high school in 1960 and in December of that year he wrote a letter to Ray in England asking questions about animation and was delighted when Ray replied in detail to his enquiries. He was fifteen when he constructed his first armatured model, a skeleton that was inspired by Ray's *The 7th Voyage of Sinbad*, and in 1978 he said, 'I'm sure the long shadow of Ray Harryhausen will leave its mark on my entire career.'[13] In May 1962 Allen put an ad in an issue of *Famous Monsters of Filmland* magazine which said, 'Kalling all you *King Kong* lovers. David Allen wants to correspond with you.' Mark McGee, a friend of Muren's, was the first to respond and soon the three were viewing and analysing 16mm prints of science-fiction, horror and fantasy films. In July of 1962 Allen began his first stop-motion tests and in the November he also met Jim Danforth (who would become a close friend) for the first time at Forry Ackerman's home.

In 1964, aged twenty, Allen continued his animation tests while attending college and in 1965 he built an unused astronaut model for *The Wizard of Mars* (1965) and worked on the miniature sets for *Women of the Prehistoric Planet* (1966). After college he joined the Clokey Studios working on the *Gumby* television series and performed his first professional animation for the *Davey and Goliath* special called *Happy Easter* in 1967. In the same year he moved to Cascade Pictures, where he would spend ten years animating iconic commercial characters such as Hans for Nestles Crunch chocolate, the Pillsbury Doughboy, the Planter's Peanuts mascot, Swiss Miss instant coffee and Mrs Butterworth. It was

TOP LEFT
An early rear-screen process setup of Allen's Taurus creature on display at the old Los Angeles Zoo. As part of an unfinished amateur film, the creature breaks out and terrorizes the neighbourhood. The model was reused for *Equinox* (1971).

CENTRE LEFT
A young David Allen with some of his early stop-motion puppets and artwork. On the left is the Taurus puppet. Allen is positioning a tentacled creature using a homemade surface gauge – both models were eventually used in the film *Equinox*. On the wall is an armature skull drawing by his hero Willis O'Brien.

BOTTOM LEFT
This photo of the Taurus model was taken years before *Equinox* was shot but was later used as a publicity still for the film. Allen's parents' home is seen at the lower right.

BELOW LEFT
Allen at work on the Volkswagen 'King Kong' commercial (1972). The camera is animated to tilt down as stop-motion planes on wires fly overhead.

BOTTOM LEFT
Allen animating the Swiss Miss character for a commercial in the 70s.

BELOW
Allen at Cascade Studio in the late 60s posing with the Pillsbury Doughboy, an extremely popular advertising character which he animated in over a dozen commercials.

also at Cascade that he created the legendary 'King Kong' Volkswagen commercial in 1972, which recreated the end of the 1933 picture.

Equinox, for which he animated the octopus-like creature and the ape-monster amongst others, was his first feature. He took a break from his work at Cascade to help Jim Danforth, who was working in England on *When Dinosaurs Ruled the Earth* (1970) for which he animated most of the chasmosaurus sequence. On his return to California he worked on another outside project, *Flesh Gordon* (1974) after which he left Cascade to form his own company, David Allen Productions, taking on a number of projects that included *The Crater Lake Monster* (1977). This is another film that has gained a cult following and offered a golden opportunity for other budding animators to make their mark. Although only Allen's name appears on the screen, Randall (Randy) Cook, Phil Tippett, Jon Berg and Jim Danforth also worked on the animation. Filmed in 'Fantamation' (another silly synonym for Dynamation) this rural monster-on-the-rampage movie is ponderous and dull although redeemed to some extent by the all-too-brief appearances of a plesiosaurus. What animation there is is smooth and believable, only the humans are unbelievable. After a few extremely brief appearances of the creature's head and neck the finale of the film sees the local sheriff slaying the monster with a bulldozer. All somewhat reminiscent of the end of *Dinosaurus!*, but much less dramatic. The animators were allowed little screen time to develop any characterization in the creature although the neck and tail are visually exciting as they swipe and slash at the humans. Allen was responsible for approximately half of the animation with other animators contributing the rest. The one model of the plesiosaurus was approximately fifteen inches high and was designed by Allen and Tippett with the armature designed and built by Berg.

Allen next collaborated with Randy Cook on animating the aliens in producer Charles Band's *Laserblast* (1978). Allen's relationship with Band, which would last for over twenty years, was similar to that between Ray and Charles Schneer, although Band's films were usually in the horror or splatter category. Perhaps the one exception is *The Day Time Ended* (1979), which, despite a respectable cast (Jim Davis, Chris Mitchum and Dorothy Malone), was a strange and confused attempt to cash in on the success of *Close Encounters of the Third Kind* (1977) but failed to deliver in any way, except in the case of the generally superb animation filmed at the David Allen Studios with Paul W. Gentry as Director of Special Visual Effects. Randy Cook was responsible for most of the animation with Allen contributing a sequence with Tom St Amand, who designed and built the armatures for the four key models. The end matte painting of the 'City of Light' was executed by Jim Danforth. The four models include a tiny pixie-like alien that flits around rooms to no apparent purpose (animated by Allen), two stunning anthropoid creatures (a Troll Lady and the Wolf Lizard) that fight each other to the death and a mechanical craft with two arms that fires a destructive beam. The best animation sequence is the fight between the two alien creatures. The models are well designed and finished and Randy Cook's animation of the fight is creative and fluid. No part of the models' anatomy is left static, all appendages seem to be constantly in action.

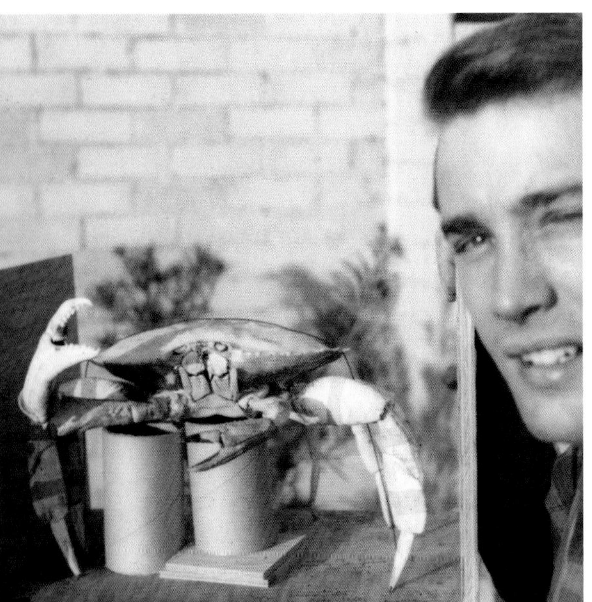

ABOVE LEFT
The animation model plesiosaur featured in *The Crater Lake Monster* (1977) just after it was painted. The head was sculpted by Allen, while the body was by Phil Tippett.

ABOVE
A posed photograph of David Allen animating the model plesiosaur for *The Crater Lake Monster* on a makeshift set after the filming was completed.

FAR LEFT
While production was underway in England on *When Dinosaurs Ruled the Earth* (1970), Jim Danforth asked David Allen in the States to construct a crab model for the film and then send it to him. As Ray did before him (on *Mysterious Island*) Allen used an actual crab shell as the basis of the model. The puppet underwent cosmetic modifications after it arrived in England to give it the distinctive look it has in the film.

LEFT
Two shots of the chasmosaurus featured in *When Dinosaurs Ruled the Earth*, which Allen animated for the film after Jim Danforth had invited him to England to help with the animation.

BELOW
Allen carried out about 25% of the animation of the Great God Porno (Nesuahyrrah) puppet for *Flesh Gordon* (1974).

BOTTOM
In 1978, Allen animated a sequence involving an alien pixie creature for *The Day Time Ended* (1979). Here the creature is standing on a rig that allows it to 'skate' through the frame.

BELOW CENTRE
Animating the pteranodon for *Caveman* (1981) outdoors! For a quick shot of the creature coming at the camera, David used the actual sky outside the studio as the backdrop.

BELOW RIGHT (TOP)
Models of Atouk (Ringo Starr) and the horned lizard dinosaur are prepared for their next animation session in the film *Caveman*. The shots involving the Atuk puppet astride the lizard were animated by Pete Kleinow and Randy Cook.

BELOW RIGHT (BOTTOM)
Allen animating one of the tyrannosaurus models in front of a photo blow-up for *Caveman*.

As Visual Effects Supervisor on *Caveman* (1981), a misguided attempt to make dinosaurs a subject for childish humour, Allen took over from Jim Danforth (who had left the production about two-thirds of the way through, citing problems with the producers). Other animators included Pete Kleinow and Randy Cook, with James Aupperle, Spencer Gill, David Stipes, Laine Liska and Ernest Farino (uncredited) also on the effects crew. Again, the models and animation transcend lamentable acting and script. The models were beautifully constructed by Danforth and include various dinosaurs, the best of which is a plump tyrannosaurus rex which Neil Pettigrew in his *Stop-Motion Filmography* calls 'one of the finest models ever to grace an animation table, up there with *Son of Kong*'s styracosaurus, Gwangi and the Cyclops'.

Q–The Winged Serpent (1982) [aka *Q*] was an ingenious little low-budget feature that leaves a deep impression because of the excellent animation. It sometimes resorts to schlock horror, but overall it is an innovative and humorous addition to the monster-in-New York genre. The 'winged serpent' is the Aztec god Quetzalcoatl, which is causing mysterious deaths and disappearances while nesting in the top of the Chrysler Building. *Q* was produced, written and directed in amateurish style by Larry Cohen with the effects executed by Dave Allen, Randy Cook, Peter Kuran and Lost Arts. Reputedly, the creature sequences were added at a later date as Cohen had originally wanted the monster to remain unseen but relented when he saw Allen and Cook's proposed model and commissioned them to execute the design and animation. It was a wise decision as the creature is the highlight of the film. 'They were working with a very low budget and shaky background plates of New York that had been shot from a helicopter without any thought to future composite effects. Allen and Cook worked wonders in view of the situation...'[4]. For most of the time it is on the screen the creature is in flight and to avoid strobing (a jerky effect), Allen and Cook had the model glide for many of the shots and, when wing movement was necessary, 'each frame of film would be rewound and re-exposed with the wings in a slightly different position, creating the illusion of a blur'.[5]

There are three key scenes in the film. The first is a very effective and atmospheric use of the shadow that the creature casts onto the various skyscrapers as it flies around searching for prey. This was done by Peter Kuran and achieved by cel animation (the shadow, or moving elements, were drawn on a series of transparent sheets of cellulose acetate, a form of two-dimensional animation, which were superimposed on the live action). The second is the battle to kill the creature as it flies around the Chrysler Building in which we see several people snatched from the top and falling to their deaths. The finale of the battle sees the third and perhaps best shot of the creature as it lands, badly wounded, on a pyramid-shaped roof that was matted-in in front of a rear-projected image of a building. This is our first real look at the entire creature, which has a long tail, a long neck crowned by a beaked, gar-

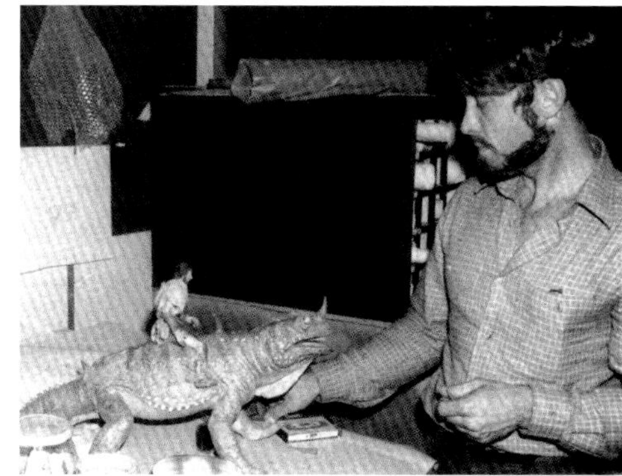

goyle-like head and ragged wings, a cross between a dragon and a pterodactyl, all beautifully designed by Cook. The armature was constructed by Allen from models he had used in *The Howling* (1981) and *Caveman* 'and even a pair of wings originally machined by Marcel Delgado for a dimorphodon in the unfinished *Creation*'.[6]

Between features, Allen, like other animators, often worked on commercials to enable him to pay the bills. But in 1986 he also worked on what is probably one of the best films of his career, **batteries not included* (1987). This film demonstrates how a great animator can give even inanimate objects a sense of purpose and pathos. Remarkably, Allen makes us believe that the 'stars' of the film, tiny flying saucers, are living beings with genuine emotions. Directed by Matthew Robbins and starring the husband-and-wife team of veteran actors Hume Cronyn and Jessica Tandy, the simple story concerns the occupants of a New York tenement block who refuse to leave despite the fact that it is due for demolition. In the best traditions of fairy tales, help arrives in the form of two saucers, which not only help the tenants but, with the aid of their 'offspring' and other saucers, restore the decaying building to its former glory. Aside from the wire rigs and radio-controlled on-set usage (the mechanically operated models), Tom St Amand executed the Go-Motion animation (Go-Motion is an electronic system that coordinates the movements of camera and models to ensure that each frame of animated action is very slightly blurred, as is the case with live action) and Allen carried out excellent rod puppetry as well as traditional model animation. Surprisingly, all of these various methods gel in a natural and believable way, thanks, no doubt, to the careful pre-planning of the all the effects well in advance of live-action photography.

There are several animated shots worth mentioning, although the various different effects interlock so smoothly that it is difficult to distinguish which shots are achieved by means of animation. During the 'birth' of the 'offspring' there is a shot of the 'father' saucer cutting up a Pepsi can and feeding it to his mate to keep her strength up. It is a simple throwaway scene that evokes feelings of great tenderness. Another, touchingly funny scene shows one of the 'offspring' emerging from a toilet bowl for which Allen cleverly matted the model and the seat into live footage. There are other notable shots but the best by far is when the 'parents' are teaching the three 'children' to fly from the tenement staircase. One of them hangs by its robotic arms and the 'mother' cuts away the wood so that it drops. This is both sensitive and funny. The entire film is a feel-good fairy tale that is a joy and, although sentimental, does not overdo the melodrama. Allen's work is superb, both technically and in his characterization of the metallic beings.

Following **batteries not included* came *Willow* (1988), which was a disappointment – though not because of Allen's excellent work. He then

ABOVE LEFT
A shot from *Q–The Winged Serpent* (1982) in which the creature lands on a miniature roof split into a live-action plate.

ABOVE TOP
For a distant shot of the gremlin flying away in *Twilight Zone – The Movie* (1983), Allen animates the creature spinning in place, whilst the camera was animated to create the bigger moves.

ABOVE
Allen animating the puppet of Anty, an ant that the miniaturized kids befriend in the film *Honey, I Shrunk the Kids* (1989). After dismissing the way ants actually move as too erratic, Allen based Anty's walk on that of a beetle for a more dramatic look, which better matched the on-set prop ant.

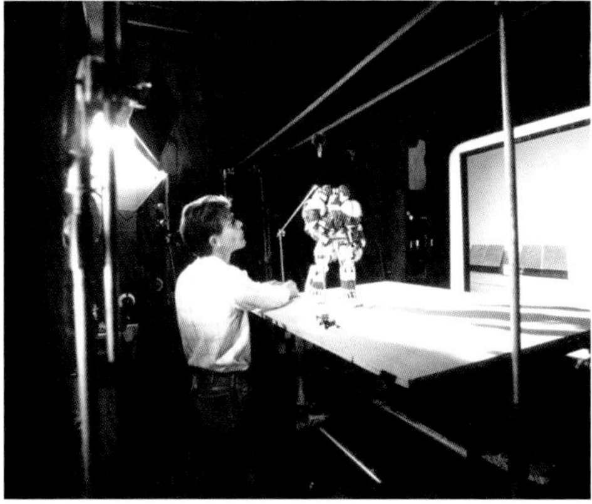

ABOVE
In a stairway set for **batteries not included* (1987), Allen animates the 'mother' saucer helping a 'baby' saucer to fly. The 'baby' is supported by tungsten wires attached to a rig above the handrail.

ABOVE CENTRE (TOP)
The robot puppets for *Robot Jox* were so heavy that they often needed to be supported by tungsten wire sliding along overhead rails while walking.

ABOVE CENTRE (BOTTOM)
One of the associates of David Allen Productions, Chris Endicott, animates the miniature t-rex called 'Elvis' for *Prehysteria!* (1993).

ABOVE RIGHT
Allen animates the killer puppet, Blade, as it runs and jumps off a bed in an exciting shot from *Puppetmaster II* (1991),which Allen also directed.

worked on the very successful Disney film *Honey, I Shrunk the Kids* (1989), where he was responsible for a complex sequence in which live miniaturized children were seen riding on the back of an animated ant.

Over a period of years Allen was not only involved with major film productions but with low-budget ones as well. He gained a reputation for making economical effects look expensive which was exemplified by *Robot Jox* (1989) in which immense gladiatorial robots transform into an array of vehicles and weapons. Next came *Puppet Master* (1989) which would become a successful series, the last of which was made in 1994 (the second was directed by Allen himself). In 1993 Allen and his crew produced diminutive dinosaurs for *Prehysteria!*, on which he was assisted by Chris Endicott.

In 1986 Allen was nominated for an Oscar® for *Young Sherlock Holmes* (1985) but, in a cruel twist of fate, the nomination wasn't for animation but for his work using rod-control (a method he had used first in **batteries no included*) to manipulate cakes and pastries. One of Allen's last jobs was working on the animation for *Special Effects: Anything Can Happen* (1996) a film made in the Imax format for which he again recreated King Kong, but this time in San Francisco.

As far back as 1968 Allen had been planning a project that has undergone an amazing Odyssey, possibly unmatched in the history of motion pictures. To begin with the film was to be called *Raiders of the Stone Ring*, a fantasy adventure featuring the crew of a Zeppelin who find themselves flying over the crater of a vast dormant volcano which is occupied by prehistoric creatures and evil lizard-men. Subsequently, it became a stop-start project that went through a series of metamorphoses. By 1974, when it got a new title, *The Primevals*, the story had changed to that of a group of scientist/explorers who go in search of the mythical Yeti in the Himalayas where they discover a strange tropical land and a mysterious race of alien lizard-men living in an ancient city. The film was to be directed by Allen from a script by Allen and Randy Cook with Allen having overall control of the visual effects, which would naturally include a great deal of model animation. In the project's earliest phase, in the late 60s, people like Jim Danforth, Dennis Muren and Bill Hedge made up the enthusiastic crew. In 1978, Randy Cook, Tom St Amand,(who fabricated armatures for the models), Ken Ralston (who sculpted several of the lizard aliens) and Phil Tippett were all involved to one degree or another, although all of the models were designed and constructed under Allen's supervision and in some cases made by Allen himself. Although Allen's involvement was considerable, he always saw the project as a collaborative one. His associate Chris Endicott remarked that, 'It was never his wish to do all or even most of the animation himself. He would joke about the "army of animators" that would be coming any day for him to conduct.'

In 1970 Hammer Films in England became interested for a while and produced a poster but the parties could not come to terms.[7] The project then languished, only to be revived again in 1975 when the storyline was registered by Allen and Cook. In 1978 producer Charles Band refinanced the project for a brief period during which Dave Carson and Jon Berg worked alongside Allen. Allen was determined that this was to be a project that would feature model animation at its very best but through the 1980s and well into the 90s it was again put on hold because of the rising costs and the production company's financial difficulties. At various times, it was planned to include a variety of creatures, amongst which were a giant spider, a prehistoric ground sloth and alien-controlled robots, but three creatures were intended to be the 'stars', the lizard-men, the Yeti and the 'river lizard', a mysterious, hybrid beast resembling a cross between a rhinoceros and a dinosaur.

Finally, in June 1994, principal photography, with Juliet Mills as the main star, began in Romania and the Italian Alps under Allen's direction. Photography was completed in September but the film's problems were not over. Returning to the States to begin the animation effects Allen was advised that Full Moon, his principle backers, had severe problems and all production was halted. In February 1995 Allen animated a six-shot sequence on his own time and in 1996 Charles Band was able to raise more finance and it was planned that all the animation should be executed by Allen and Chris Endicott, with occasional help from friends. According to Chris, 'given the lack of funding for a properly scheduled post-production period, Allen simply arranged to do those shots that most interested him first' and was able to complete over 90 of the total of approximately 200 stop-motion shots. Animator Kent Burton was later brought in to help out and eventually did a great deal of the work. Endicott estimates that, 'high-speed miniature effects, matte paintings and 100 animation shots remain to be completed. The film now exists in a polished rough-cut with temporary sound effects and temporary score.'

The reason that work on the film finally came to a standstill was that David Allen died on 16 August 1999 before he was able to complete it. Chris Endicott recalls that,

> *From 1995 until his passing in 1999, he devoted most of his time to the post-production stop-motion and visual effects. Shortly before he was diagnosed with cancer, he described* The Primevals *as the culmination of his entire career, and he considered the effects for it the best he had ever done. Once he became sick, the ever-resilient Allen continued working on shots until shortly before he died.*

Endicott goes on to say,

> *Interestingly, the film finally went into production under the shadow of* Jurassic Park *and the looming presence of the growing CGI movement and David saw the project as a voice for the continued validity of dimensional animation in films of this type. [Over the years] Dave saw that what the film represented had changed from a reaction to other films using stop-motion effects during the 1970s into a declaration of the continuing viability of this technique in the late 1990s.*
>
> *He honestly respected the possibilities of today's digital wonders, but he took umbrage at the assertion that the one technique replaced the other.* The Primevals *was going to show that stop-motion still had something to say.*

Ray met with Allen regularly when he was in LA and their last meeting was only a short while before his death. David Allen was one of that special breed of animators who was able to animate with realistic fluidity and who, unlike Ray, always liked to analyze everything, which is apparent in his work. Like many who knew him, Chris Endicott will always be grateful to Allen, 'Knowing David Allen, working with him, learning from him, represents what will undoubtedly be the best experience of my life.' '*King Kong* was everywhere in his life', recalls friend and effects artist Bill Hedge. 'You couldn't have a five-minute conversation about any subject without David somehow turning it towards *King Kong* and making a corollary or some sort of reference that was just always spot-on.' He lived and breathed *Kong* and the art of animation.

Dennis Muren is one of only two special-effects artists to have their name on the Hollywood Walk of Stars, the other is Ray Harryhausen. But whereas Ray has won only one special Oscar ® for 'a lifetime of technical excellence', Muren has been awarded no less than eight Oscars ® for Best Visual Effects, which were all richly deserved. Dennis Elmer Muren was born on 1 November 1946 in Glendale, California and as a youngster became fascinated with both special effects and film-making. His parents gave him a $10 Keystone 8mm camera and he experimented in making effects movies with his various friends and neighbours, including Rick Baker.[8] But, 'It was just a hobby. I never thought it would be a career.' He did a lot of animation using models made out of wire and foam rubber and trying to reproduce scenes from *The 7th Voyage of Sinbad* as well as his own imaginary creatures. He experimented with split screens, volcanoes blowing up and whatever else seemed spectacular to him – and all in his backyard. To assist his understanding of special effects he would study stills in Forry Ackerman's *Famous Monsters of Filmland* magazine and also shoot stills and 8mm of films such as *The Invisible Man*

RIGHT, FIRST TWO ROWS
Images from *The Primevals*.

Top left. In 1968, Allen and Dennis Muren, photographed the live-action sections of a promotional film for *Raiders of the Stone Rings*, a project that would become Allen's beloved film, *The Primevals*

Top centre. In a fully miniature shot, the Yeti chases two lizard-men though the scaffolding of a strange arena. The Yeti then hit the scaffolding and the pieces came falling down towards camera the shot got more and more complex.

Top right. A rod, hidden from the view of the film camera, supports the Yeti puppet as it runs on all fours through a miniature setup. Allen thought this shot one of the best in the film.

Second down, left. Chris Endicott animates a lizard-man gunner reacting. Although David performed the vast majority of the stop motion in this yet unfinished work, animator Kent Burton and others, also contributed.

Middle row, centre. Allen animates a lizard-man operating the controls of a mind-control gun in 1996. The puppet and prop were originally filmed in 1978 as part of an aborted earlier version of the film.

Middle row, right. Allen animates a lizard-man puppet. This one puppet was originally built in the 60s using the armature from a Pete Peterson Beetleman puppet.

RIGHT
Top picture. In 1995, Allen once again got a chance to design and animate a recreation of the original 1933 *King Kong* puppet for *Special Effects: Anything Could Happen* (1996).

Bottom picture. For *Special Effects: Anything Could Happen* Allen performed all the Kong animation from the top of a ten-foot ladder in a smoke-filled stage, with some shots taking almost 24 hours of continuous animation.

Far right. Award winners David Allen and Ray, with Chris Endicott, at the Omega Awards ceremony on 23rd July 1999. Allen sadly died a few weeks later.

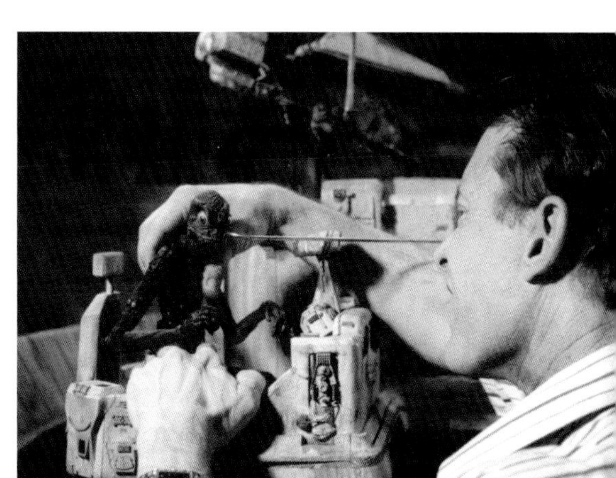

SONY

movies, *The Wizard of Oz* (1939 and *The Dam Busters* (1954) straight off the television screen in order to study them in detail later.

In the early 1960s, when Muren was a teenager, he visited Ray at his US home in Malibu, California. Ray recalls that he was too young to drive so his mother brought him over. It didn't take Ray too long to discover that young Muren was a fan of both his work up to that point, especially *The 7th Voyage of Sinbad*, but also of Obie's work, with the emphasis on *King Kong*, and Ray remembers him as a very impressive young man. About the same time, around 1961, Muren met animator Phil Kellison who was working on *Jack the Giant Killer* and asked Muren if he would like to visit the effects studio. Muren unhesitatingly said 'Yes'. His mother again drove him down to Hollywood and that's where he became acquainted with Jim Danforth and the rest of the team at Projects Unlimited.

He studied business and took an A.A. degree, minoring in advertising 'so at least I could do special effects for commercials. I crammed my classes into Tuesdays and Thursdays so I could make movies Mondays, Wednesdays and Fridays.'[9] Whilst still at college he approached his family to try to raise finance to produce his first film. His grandfather had put aside some money for his education and, with the family's approval, along with his friends David Allen and Mark McGee, he started to put together what would become *Equinox*. The movie was a tour de force of effects but it also illustrated at that very early stage in his budding career the passion for new and improved techniques would be the basis of his career. 'I learned more doing that film than I would have during four years at film school.'[10]

Between 1969 and 1975 Muren was employed by Cascade Pictures of California as a freelance effects cameraman working on commercials such as Pillsbury and the Green Giant. In 1972 he worked for Charles Cahill & Associates Educational Films on the effects photography for *The Solar System: Islands in Space*. During this time he was also involved as an effects technician with another cult landmark animated movie *Flesh Gordon* (1974) for which he worked on the miniatures and rear projection as well as carrying out the lighting set-ups for a number of shots in the Nesuahyrrah/Great God Porno sequence with Jim Danforth.

Now came a crossroads in his life.

> *Most of the movies being made with special effects back then were union movies, and I didn't care to work on them because they were too structured. But at some point I thought I should at least work on one and see what it was like. I picked* Star Wars *because I figured that if I was going to do a Hollywood movie, I might as well do it with a director I liked, and I really liked George Lucas. I didn't know him, but knew John Dykstra, so I contacted him. I pushed for an interview, got it, and I told them how much money I wanted. They said they couldn't afford to pay me.*

Faced with such a dilemma he had to make a choice, 'Did I want to do *Star Wars* for less money than I made doing commercials?'[11] He chose *Star Wars* and Industrial Light and Magic (ILM) and never looked back.

Star Wars [*Star Wars: Episode IV - A New Hope*] (1977) was a landmark film that employed a whole gamut of effects techniques. Muren was employed primarily as second cameraman on the special photographic effects for the film under Dykstra. However, he did supervise the animators for the one animation sequence in the film, the miniature alien chesspieces, which were animated by Jon Berg and Phil Tippett. Berg and Tippett made ten very original alien models (only eight were used) for the sequence which stands out, amongst all the spacecraft and aliens, as one of the most striking and amusing. ILM started out as a company that would produce the effects for *Star Wars* but when the film became a worldwide hit ILM's services were required by everyone who wanted to make a movie with high-class effects.

Next came *Close Encounters of the Third Kind* (1977) on which Muren carried out the photography for the mothership effects and then *Battlestar Galactica* (1978) as Visual Effects Director of Photography.

George Lucas then began planning a sequel to the first *Star Wars* (he had reportedly conceived of nine possible episodes), this time to be called *Star Wars: Episode V - The Empire Strikes Back* (1980) and Muren was now Effects Director of Photography, responsible for all the animation, which it was planned should play a much bigger part in this film's storyline. Phil Tippett, Jon Berg and Doug Beswick were the animators, with Ken Ralston, Tom St Amand and Dave Carson also involved. A motion-control rig was devised that allowed far more control of the camera and the models, and which also delivered a naturalistic blur to the animation. There are various animated scenes in the movie, mostly in the first half. Aside from an Empire droid, the first animated creation is the alien Taun-taun which Luke Skywalker and later Hans Solo use to travel over the snowbound terrain of the rebel planet. It looks like a cross between a dinosaur and a very hairy camel. Also animated were the Imperial Walkers (also called AT-AT – All Terrain Armoured Transport), lumbering, 120-foot-high animal-shaped machines as well as a smaller and impossible mechanical Scout Walker (nicknamed the 'chicken-walker' by the crew) all of which the rebels attack and in part destroy. The sequences in which they are used are superb, not only because they are exciting, but also because the standard of animation is so high (although Ray had animated only one mechanical being – the Minaton – the technique of stop-motion animation did lend itself very favourably to mechanical creations), helped considerably by the motion-control. Muren is reported to have said that this film was the hardest he ever had to work on, and one of the most rewarding.

Muren and his team took the next step in advancing animation technology with the conception of Go-Motion[12] for the film *Dragonslayer* (1982). This was a development of the experimental motion-control rig used on *The Empire Strikes Back* which delivered near-perfect animation. Muren was again Supervisor of Special Visual Effects with Phil Tippett, and Ken Ralston being credited as Dragon Supervisors and Tom St Amand, Stuart Ziff and Gary Leo as Dragon Movers. Sadly, *Dragonslayer* is a dull and uninspired film, aside from the effects (how many times have we said that?), mainly due to a poor screenplay and direction by Matthew Robbins. The dragon (Verminthrax Perjorative), though, is a wonder to behold. Beautifully designed by David Burnett and lovingly animated by means of the Go-Motion system, the model attains such believable and fluid movement that when we first saw it, back in 1982, it was almost impossible to believe that it had been achieved by animation. It was Muren who was largely responsible for these innovations and, along with Stuart Ziff, he received a Technical Achievement Citation from the American Academy ® for his work on the Go-Motion system.

Whilst Muren was shooting *Dragonslayer* at Pinewood Studios in England, Ray (who was making *Clash of the Titans*) visited him and was

FACING PAGE, FAR LEFT
Dennis Muren working on the flying demon model for *Equinox* circa 1966. The model was built by David Allen and Muren constructed the set.

FACING PAGE BOTTOM
Dennis Murem, at bottom right, as cameraman on *Equinox* (1967) with David Allen (behind Muren) animating the Taurus creature. It is a miniature set in front of a painting in acrylics by Allen.

ABOVE
Muren working on the miniatures for *E.T. The Extra-Terrestrial* (1982). Muren is positioning the tiny ET puppet, which operated from below by a rod. The action took place in a miniature set with a painted night-time background and was shot slightly high-speed.

extremely impressed with what he saw. Indeed, it was that visit, together with the completed film, which helped to convince Ray that his traditional type of animation had had its day. The computer had arrived. It wasn't just *Dragonslayer*, but the cumulative effect of Muren's last four films that would begin the transition from traditional effects (optical and stop-motion) to what would become CGI.

Muren and ILM went from strength to strength. He won an American Academy Award ® for Best Visual Effects (with Carlo Rambaldi and Kenneth F. Smith) for *E.T. – The Extra-Terrestial* (1982) although there is little model animation in the film. Director Steven Spielberg opted for the more tactile mechanical alien designed by Carlo Rambaldi. Most of the scenes that utilized animation were the flying sequences, which were again achieved with Go-Motion shot against a blue-screen (which allowed any background to be optically inserted, in this case a forest and the full moon). Tom St Amand and Mike Fulmer constructed the armatured models and miniature bikes, whilst Muren was responsible for the animation.

Next came the third instalment of the *Star Wars* saga, *Star Wars: Episode VI - Return of the Jedi* (1983). This film marked a turning point in the fortunes of *Star Wars* and the beginning of the end of what, in the first two films, had seemed to be a new phase in effects development and a trend towards original, entertaining and spectacular storylines. *Return of the Jedi* is a disappointing film that partially parallels the first film, right down to the destruction of another Death Star. Apart from some cut-away shots, model animation is only evident in the rebels' battle with the two-legged, twenty-foot-high Scout Walkers. Muren supervised the entire sequence, with Go-Motion creating very realistic effects of the Walkers striding through the forest trees, which were in fact painted on glass. 'The puppets were animated by Phil Tippett and Tom St Amand, with Go-Motion rods attached to the legs and rotating chassis'[13] of the models. Once again Muren won the Best Visual Effects award from the American Academy ® and his first Best Visual Effects from the British Academy.

In 1984 Muren worked as Post Production Effects Supervisor on the disappointing television film *The Ewok Adventure*, although it did contain some superb animation by Phil Tippett and Jon Berg. In the same year came *Indiana Jones and the Temple of Doom* (1984) for which Muren returned to model animation, adapting a 35mm still camera to take shots of the model carriages and humans for a runaway mining train which was animated by Tom St Amand. Again, Muren won Best Visual Effects from both the American and British Academies. There followed

Young Sherlock Holmes (1986) for which Muren supervised the scenes in which a character is attacked by flying gargoyle-like harpies (designed by Tom St Amand and animated by Harry Walton) operated with the Go-Motion system.

Innerspace (1987) was another *Fantastic Voyage* (1966) but with a sense of humour. Dennis Quaid takes an ill-timed trip through Martin Short's body. All the effects were supervised by Muren, for which he won yet another Best Visual Effects award from the American Academy ®, but there is only one sequence that contains any animation, which is the final battle between Quaid's submersible pod and the villain's pod, beautifully animated by Harry Walton.

Techniques for the computer manipulation of digitally stored images (either scanned or computer-generated) were further refined on *Willow* (1988), a below-average sword-and-sorcery epic directed by Ron Howard and produced by George Lucas. Muren designed the effects and the best animation sequence is the two-headed dragon. The model was designed and constructed by Phil Tippett and animated by Harry Walton and Tom St Amand.

By the end of the 1980s special visual effects had, according to Muren, 'hit a dead end'. The boundaries had been pushed as far as was possible in optical effects and miniatures. Where to go from here? The answer, of course, lay with more sophisticated computerized effects.

> *The digital stuff did come in, all that kind of research on computers had been done with Apple [Macintosh] figuring out how to mass produce products and PC's, and Adobe, and the Knoll brothers with Photoshop, the Solitaire film recorder doing slides for business presentations for major corporations that actually could turn out a digital image on a piece of film that looked like a photograph. And that was unheard of [up to that time], but all the work had already been done, and what we did was we put those things together, and the result was* T2 [Terminator 2: Judgement Day] *(1991).*[14]

It was in this film that Muren spearheaded the move from traditional models and miniatures to CG.

The last film for which model animation, albeit in modified form, was used in conjunction with live action, was *Jurassic Park* (1993) in which, along with Steve Williams and Mark Dippe, Muren ushered in a new era of computer-generated imagery. Spielberg had originally intended to utilize Go-Motion for the creatures but quickly changed his mind when shown a test of a CG t. rex shot against a live background. However, a number of the shots were based on a variation of traditional stop-motion, called video animatics. This directly used animation to model the movements of CG images. Also used were Dinosaur Input Devices (DIDs), complex armatures, which although not directly photographed, were animated like a conventional stop-motion model. Encoders were attached to points on these armatures representing a dinosaur's joints and other parts of its anatomy and when the armature was moved by the animator the encoders recorded the changed positions so that the movements could be reproduced by the computer-generated creature. Thus conventional model animation was used to determine how the final CG image moved.

Muren continues to work for ILM as Senior Visual Effects Supervisor and also consults for Pixar. He is actively involved in the evolution of the company, as well as the design and development of new techniques and equipment. His last project was *War of the Worlds* (2005), on which he led a team that created a series of complex effects within an amazingly short period of three months.

Muren began his career by working on model animation and it was his fascination with the work that led him first to pioneer improvements to the tried and tested techniques and then to take the effects business to new heights with Go-Motion and then computer graphics. 'I like to see it and I like to do it. I like the audience to see them. There is nothing like sitting in a theatre with hundreds of people around you screaming at something you've done.'[15] Perhaps he feels on occasions that things have gone too far: 'I got into this because special effects were just that: special. They were unique and different. They're not special anymore. You see them everywhere.'[16] He has also been quoted as saying,

> *At the moment it [CG] is still fairly impersonal, when you look at it you can't relate to what you're seeing, if there's an artefact or something, to anything really that you understand, except like a video game. With stop-motion in the olden days you could understand that King Kong's got this fur that is moving around funny, but you recognize it as fur. Now it is hard to do that with CG fur. It is hard to connect to the stuff because it is all so synthetic. I very much miss the feel of the stop-motion shop, or the wood shop or the machine shop, the smell and sound of it, the camaraderie, you don't get that anymore.*[17]

An incredible amount of talent worked on the first *Star Wars* franchise and a tremendous number of artists were discovered because of it. One of them

FAR LEFT
Rigging a high-speed miniature shoot of the falling Walker for *Star Wars: Episode V: The Empire Strikes Back* (1980)

LEFT
At ILM in 1980, the dragon featured in *Dragonslayer* (1981). This is a composited publicity photo. The puppet was sculpted by Phil Tippett and the armature designed and constructed by Tom St Amand.

ABOVE
Innerspace (1987). Photographed at ILM in 1986, this is the model miniature pod shot against blue screen and composited over a miniature background.

ABOVE RIGHT
Dennis Muren (in light shirt) and Steven Spielberg (right) looking at a computer previsualization of an upcoming shot on the set of *War of the Worlds* (2005). Also in the shot are Dan Gregorie (left), the previz artist and Adam Somner (blue shirt, centre) the First Assistant Director.

RIGHT
This impressive scene from *Jurassic Park* (1993) was entirely CG. The apatosaurus was composited over a background shot in Hawaii. This was perhaps the most important sequence in the film. Muren and his team had to sell the dinosaurs as 100% real in order for the film to work. The challenges included shots of long duration, unforgiving daylight, dinosaurs behind the trees and actors to give it scale.

was Ken Ralston. Although he began his association with *Star Wars* on the first in the epic series as assistant cameraman in the optical and effects unit, it wasn't until he worked on *Star Wars: Episode V–The Empire Strikes Back* that he began executing model animation. He was responsible for a number of shots in the film, including the thrilling shot of a model Luke Skywalker swinging on a rope and pulling himself up under one of the huge Imperial Walkers and a long shot of Skywalker clinging to a mast below the cloud city, Bespin.

Ralston joined Tippett for *Dragonslayer* as one of the Dragon Supervisors and animated the picture's spectacular flying dragon sequences with Tom St Amand but was uncredited for his animation of a toy Hulk flying around the room on a toy horse in *Poltergeist* (1982). He was one of three Visual Effects Supervisors on *Star Wars: Episode VI–Return of the Jedi* (the others were Richard Edlund and Dennis Muren) and worked with St Amand again, animating shots of the hovering barges during the Sarlacc monster sequence at the beginning of the picture. The film won him an American Academy Award ® for effects, an honour he shared with Edlund, Muren and Tippett. He was Visual Effects Supervisor on *The Golden Child* (1986), *Who Framed Roger Rabbit* (1988) and *The Rocketeer* (1991).

Planet of Dinosaurs (1978) is another of those films that kick-started the careers of a group of effects artists, namely, James Aupperle, Stephen Czerkas and Douglas Beswick. Although undoubtedly flawed, the film is a minor masterpiece of model animation. The story of a motley group of space-wrecked travellers who crash land on a planet inhabited by dinosaurs, was conceived by Aupperle, written by Ralph Lucas and produced and directed by James K. Shea. The film is low-budget science fiction, an updated combination of *The Lost World* and *Swiss Family Robinson*, and although poorly acted and directed is worth watching for the animation and the excellently constructed creatures. The project came about when Czerkas met Shea through mutual friends. According to Czerkas, 'Shea wanted to produce motion pictures' and was 'very enthusiastic about what could be achieved with stop-motion. Jim Aupperle and I were already friends and had been experimenting together with stop-motion for a couple of years or so, and we joined forces with Shea. It took quite a while to get everything going as raising money was very difficult. Eventually Shea was successful in pulling it all together to the point that we all decided to just do it.'

Live-action photography for the project began on 19 June 1976 in the Vasquez Rocks area of the California desert which had been much used by many productions, including the original series of *Star Trek*. The special effects, specifically the animation, were begun in the summer of 1976 and completed late in 1977. The first sequence to be shot by Aupperle and Czerkas was the struthiomimus one, filmed on a small stage at Scott Sound in Hollywood, but then the effects were relocated to a storefront in Glendale, on the San Fernando Road, which were converted into an animation stage. Czerkas recalls that, 'It was a really neat building that was long and narrow... well suited for rear projection... and big enough that we had room left over to have miniature sets as well as a front-projection set up at the same time.' Aupperle also remembers that, 'We generally kept three [animation] setups going, a rear-projection unit: a front-projection unit and a unit for miniatures.' The first animation they carried out in their new studio was of the horned dinosaur. Aupperle did the animation for that sequence and the backgrounds were all rear-projected.[18]

At that point Aupperle and Czerkas hired Douglas (Doug) Beswick to join them and from then on Beswick carried out most of the animation. Aupperle pays tribute to him: 'Doug is a fine animator and greatly enhanced the quality of our effects.' When necessary, Aupperle and Czerkas assisted and Jim Danforth supplied the film's four fantasy paintings.[19] The models, all beautifully and realistically designed and constructed by Czerkas, include an outstanding tyrannosaurus rex and a fictitious rhedosaurus, a tribute to Ray and his creature featured in *The Beast From 20,000 Fathoms*. This tribute may have been inspired by a visit by Ray paid to the Glendale studio during filming but Jim Aupperle has told us that, 'Stephen and I both place the rhedosaurus among our top favourite of Ray's myriad monsters. We felt that by giving the great Beast a cameo in our film we were acknowledging the immense debt we both feel to Ray. We had to make the rhedosaurus more of a baby size because one as large as the original would have made a meal of our tyrannosaurus instead of the other way around.'

Although the producers may have skimped on everything else, they didn't hold back on the dinosaurs. Sadly, we have been forced to select only three out of the many dinosaur sequences that, for us, stand out as primary examples of smooth animation and good composites with the live action. The first is a fight between a stegosaurus and the tyrannosaurus rex, which is beautifully animated by Doug Beswick and displays an understanding of animal and human behaviour. The human element is in the circling of both huge creatures as they look for the all-important weaknesses in their opponent. The bodies of both creatures are moving all the time and these movements, especially those of their tails, are the outward expressions of their emotions. In the end the tyrannosaurs wins by biting the stegosaurus' head and then taking a bite of its flesh and flicking its head backwards to allow the meat to go down its gullet.

The second sequence features the ceratopian dinosaur. This creature was a combination of elements from various ceratopian species and resembles a styracosaurus with its spiked fan (which covered the vulnerable neck area of these creatures) and vicious single horn. Because Czerkas had built the model it was dubbed the Czerkasaurus during animation. Harvey, played by Harvey Shain, discovers a nest of large dinosaur eggs, which is defended by the mother. Chasing Harvey to the edge of a cliff, the creature lowers its head, paws the ground with its front leg like a bull and charges the defenceless man, piercing him with its horn. This is shown in close-up and was achieved by taking a section of the horn away with each frame to make it seem as though it was penetrating the live actor. The next long shot shows the creature with the screaming man impaled on its horn (both were of course models) at the cliff edge and the man falls to his death, which was achieved by animating the model of the man on aerial wires. Although the first sequence is superb, this one far surpasses it with in terms of originality and skilful animation techniques.

The final sequence we have selected is the one in which the humans bravely try to lure the massive tyrannosaurus out of its cave. All the models are very good but this one is the most

RIGHT
Classic animation moments from *Planet of Dinosaurs* (1978).

Top row, from left to right. 1. The brontosaurus, beautifully designed and constructed (as indeed are all the models) which appears at the beginning of the film. Stephen Czerkas animated this scene. 2. The magnificent tyrannosaurus rex, animated by Doug Beswick, makes its appearance. 3. The tyrannosaurus rex squares off against a stegosaurus. 4. The t. rex gets the better of the poor stegosaurus which only has its tail with which to defend itself.

Second row, from left to right. 1. The ceratopian or horned dinosaur, nicknamed the Czerkasaurus, skewers one of the humans on its horn. 2. A giant black spider runs up the leg of one of the women survivors. 3. An allosaurus attacks a group of the humans. 4. One of the men throws a spear into the back of the allosaurus.

Third row, from left to right. 1. One of the men tries to hold off the allosaurus. 2. The tyrannosaurus rex reaches down, in a startling sequence, to grab the head of the allosaurus. 3. The two struthiomimus watched by a human survivor. 4. The gigantic tyrannosaurus rex takes a human carcass back to its cave.

Bottom row, from left to right. 1. The rhedosaurus (a tribute to Ray and his creature seen in *The Beast From 20,000 Fathoms*) looks down on an unfortunate human. 2. The tyrannosaurus rex challenges the rhedosaurus. 3. The t. rex catches and kills the rhedosaurus. 4. The t. rex gets his just deserts on a wooden spike rigged up by the human survivors.

detailed and best proportioned with well-defined muscles and a superbly realistic scaly skin. The sequence begins with the dinosaur emerging from the darkness of the cave into the light, moving towards the camera, which is both frightening and cinematically effective. One of the humans throws a spear which the creature pulls out of its neck. It then pursues the humans and impales itself on a stake they have set up, which recalls Ray's young allosaurus meeting the same fate in *One Million Years BC*, with the difference that this time the stake is not held by the humans but fixed in the ground. The animation of the creature's momentum as it hits the stake is realistically achieved for a creature of its size and the lifting of its head and the subsequent roar of pain followed by its final demise is perfectly acceptable. Beswick's animation for the sequence is faultless.

Regrettably, the film took several years to find a theatrical release but, gratifyingly, went on to win a Saturn Award in 1980, presented by the Academy of Science Fiction, Fantasy & Horror Films, in the Best Film Produced for Under $1,000,000 category, which made specific note of its stop-motion effects.

Doug Beswick is known for both his animation and also for mechanical effects (mechanically operated creatures). He was born in Jamestown, New York in 1947 and in 1951 his family relocated to San Fernando. As a teenager he had little interest in movies until he saw *King Kong* and *The 7th Voyage of Sinbad*, both of which captured his imagination. For months he puzzled over how the effects were achieved and recalls, 'We didn't have all the magazines and books back then that people have today. The main source of my research was a magazine called *Famous Monsters of Filmland*.' It was in this cult magazine that Beswick read about Ray and a technique called Dynamation. Of course, he had to try it out and, using the family 8mm standard camera and clay models, shot experimental films in his backyard. Learning as he went along, he progressed to making more elaborate models, using latex over wire armatures, and filming his version of *7th Voyage*, which he called *Phantom Island*. The results weren't perhaps exactly up to Ray's standards, but he was happy with the film and when he left high school in 1966 he was determined to find a job as an apprentice model animator.

His first interview was with Jim Danforth, who was then working at Cascade Pictures. Disappointingly, he didn't get the job, although Danforth did recommend him to Art Clokey at Clokey Studios who was making a television show called *The Adventures of Gumby*. Again, he failed to

get the job and reluctantly worked as a box boy in a supermarket while continuing to search for a way into the world of model animation. Three months later he was offered a job at the Clokey Studios building props on an animated television show called *The Adventures of Davey and Goliath*. There he worked with animators Ray Peck and Peter Klieno and two years later became a fully fledged animator, filming various television episodes, including *The Adventures of Davey and Goliath*, *Davey and Goliath Holiday Specials* and *The Adventures of Gumby* and *Gumby* Specials.

In 1970 Beswick knew he had to branch out into the visual effects industry, which led him to a number of projects. His first assignment was to assist the legendary Wah Chang with model construction and animation on the educational film *Dinosaurs, The Terrible Lizards* and two years later he worked on his first feature film, *Beware the Blob* (1972) for which he animated the 'Blob' freezing effect in the climatic ice rink sequence. This was followed by a job as Effects Technician on *Flesh Gordon* (1974), and he then did the armature construction for the models in television's *Land of the Lost* (1974) and was the animator, again for Wah Chang, on the latter's educational film *Alphabet Roll Call* (1975).

In 1977 he was invited by Aupperle and Czerkas to be the chief stop-motion animator on *Planet of Dinosaurs*. This was a pivotal stage in his career during which he perfected his personal style of fluid animation. He sculptured the famous 'Cantina Band Members' for *Star Wars: Episode IV - A New Hope*, assisted Jon Berg and Phil Tippett in animating the Imperial Walkers sequence, and helped Tom St Amand with the armature construction for the taun-taun creature in *The Empire Strikes Back*.

Beswick was by now much sought-after as a designer and builder of models and also for his exceptional animation skills and he opened his own studio, Doug Beswick Productions, in 1984. He constructed the two 'Terror Dog' armatures for *Ghostbusters* (1984) and handled the model construction for the hugely successful *The Terminator* (1984). For *The Evil Dead 2: Dead by Dawn* (1987) he not only animated the 'Linda Corpse' dance sequence but also designed the models. More horror films followed with *A Nightmare on Elm Street 3: Dream Warriors* (1987) for which he supervised the model construction and animated the 'Freddy Skeleton', the 'Freddy Marionettes' and the 'Freddy Skeleton' in the junkyard sequence.

In 1988 Beswick supervised the model construction for the animation sequences in the innovative *Beetlejuice*, as well as animating the Sandworm, Fireplace and Sculptures sequences for that film. In the following year he animated the skeleton chopping through the door for *After Midnight* (1989) and designed and constructed, as well as animating, the diving board and the comic book sequences for *A Nightmare on Elm Street: The Dream Child* (1989). He then went on to animate the Bat Gremlin and the Spider Gremlin sequences for *Gremlins 2: The New Batch* (1990), to construct and animate models for *Harley Davidson and the Marlboro Man* (1991) and the Fred model for *Drop Dead Fred* (1991) as well as animating the 'Thing' hopping across the pond lily pads in *The Addams Family* (1991). Returning to familiar territory, he designed and constructed the model tyrannosaurs rex and mastodon for *Doctor Morbid* (1992) as well as animating the huge 'ticks' in *Ticks* (1993) and supervising the model construction and animation for the Iceberg Monster and the Chockie sequence for *Cabin Boy* (1994).

In 1994 Beswick's life changed when he received an offer from the special effects company VCE to design and construct the models for a

ABOVE LEFT
Doug Beswick animating the allosaurus attacking the girl for *Planet of Dinosaurs*.

ABOVE
Beswick again, animating the death of the tyrannosaurus rex on the wooden stake.

RIGHT
Doug Beswick animating the Freddie skeleton featured in *A Nightmare on Elm Street. Part 3: Dream Warriors* (1987). The armature and construction was by Yancy Calzada and the Visual Effects Director of Photography was Jim Aupperle.

FAR RIGHT
Beswick animating the Bat Gremlin for *Gremlins 2: The New Batch* (1990). Again, the Visual Effects Director of Photography was Jim Aupperle, whilst the armature was designed by Yancy Calzada and Hal Miles and the sculptor was James Kagle.

BOTTOM RIGHT
The 'Linda Dance' or 'Dancing Corpse' sequence from *Evil Dead 2: Dead by Dawn* (1987). This sequence was beautifully animated by Beswick entirely on a miniature set using a number of surface gauges. The fog was added later as an optical composite by David Snipes. The sculptor was Steve Wong, the armature was by Yancy Calzada and the photography was handled by Jim Aupperle.

BOTTOM FAR RIGHT
Beswick (left) and Yancy Calzada (right) during the animation of a sequence for *Beetlejuice* (1988). Again the armatures and modeling were by Yancy Calzada and the photography was by Jim Aupperle.

television movie of *Hercules*. It was whilst he was working on this project that Kevin O'Neill encouraged him to try his hand at learning the new animation technique called CGI. He was intrigued and used the new system while working as 3D animator on the first season of *Hercules: The Legendary Journeys*. He was then asked to join fellow animators Kevin O'Neill and Kevin Kutchaver in a new effects company to be called Flat Earth Productions. There he worked on more episodes of *Hercules* and also other television series *Zena: Warrior Princess* and *Young Hercules* and on the movies *Mortal Kombat 2: Annilation* (1997), *Blade* (1998) and *Dungeons and Dragons: The Movie* (2000). In 2000 Beswick formed Cantina Pictures to provide visual effects for a number of feature films including *Scary Movie 2* (2001) and *Frailty* (2001). But his lasting legacy has to be his superb animation on *Planet of Dinosaurs* which is truly a key film in the history of model animation.

Of the three animators who worked on *Planet of Dinosaurs* Stephen Czerkas has perhaps done the least in the way of animation, but his work as a designer and builder of articulated models on that film and several subsequent ones was superb, even better than that done by Marcel Delgado. Stephen was born in 1951 in Los Angeles. He inherited his artistic abilities from his father who was a title artist in the film and television industry, [20] but his main interest was painting and sketching. Stephen watched his father and became a self-taught sculptor, a skill which he channelled into model- and film-making. His influences as a child were O'Brien and Ray's work and also the paintings of Charles R. Knight. 'If it were not for them, I would not have developed the interest I have in stop-motion and in dinosaurs,' he says. When he was about six he saw *20 Million Miles to Earth* and *The 7th Voyage of Sinbad* on the big screen and they kick-started his enthusiasm for fantasy. He experimented with making his own articulated models of dinosaurs, dragons and monsters from his imagination and used them in short films, which he filmed on 8mm. This fascination led, as with so many other kids with imagination, to the film business.

His first job was working on *Flesh Gordon* for which he made a three-inch model of the Great God Porno. This was followed by *Planet of Dinosaurs*, for which he designed and constructed all the dinosaurs. He fondly remembers the sacrifices the project required of those involved:

> Planet of Dinosaurs *was done on such a very limited budget that it might deserve a new category of distinction, if not an award, for how far the limited funding was stretched and for what was achieved with it. What was lacking in finances was made up for by a lot of hard work and dedication by everyone involved. Early on, I even took on a night job which allowed me to sculpt some of the models at night… balancing them on the handlebars of my bicycle as I pedalled home… and then get back to work on the film. Somewhere in there, I found time to sleep. But life and working on* Planet *was like that. It did not come easy, but it was a wonderful time in my life.*

After *Planet of Dinosaurs* he worked on the Satur-

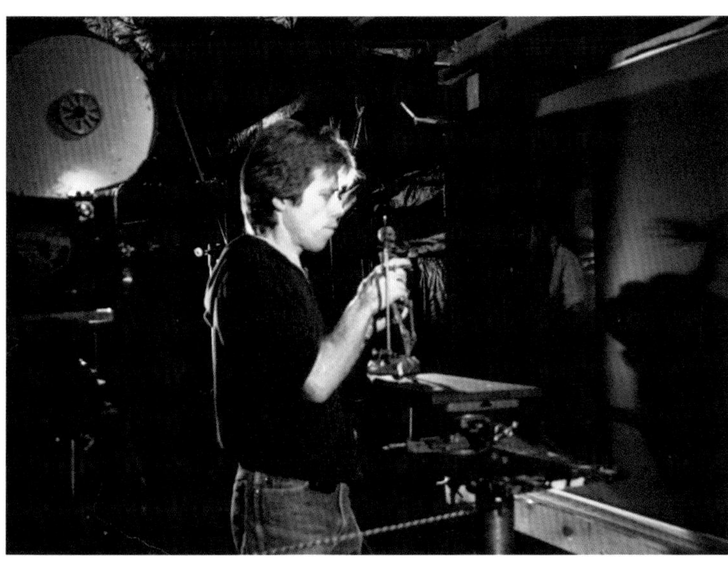

day morning children's television series *Jason of Star Command* (1978-81), again with Jim Aupperle.

Next came *Caveman* for which he designed and built the 'pop-eyed' dinosaur and in 1984 he worked on his last feature film, *Dreamscape* (1984) for which he constructed the Snakeman and Dennis Quaid models, which Aupperle animated.

In 1982 Czerkas had begun a career transition to palaeontology, working for the Academy of Natural Sciences in Philadelphia casting the fossils of Jack Horner's Maiasaura nestling duck-bill dinosaur and reconstructing its skeleton. After making *Dreamscape* he saw that his future was in real dinosaurs and so left the industry to create life-size models of dinosaurs. He and his wife Sylvia co-founded The Dinosaur Museum in Blanding, Utah and have been directors since 1992. Looking back, he reflects, 'Unlike so many others like myself who were similarly inspired to go into either special effects in motion pictures, or the field of palaeontology, I have perhaps been the most fortunate of all in that I have been able to have a career in both professions.'

The third artist who worked on *Planet of Dinosaurs* was James (Jim) R. Aupperle, a remarkable and inspired animator. Aupperle was born in Pasadena, California in 1952 and from a very early age had a vivid imagination (name us an animator who didn't?) which was stimulated when he happened to catch a showing of *King Kong* on television. From that day on he sought out cinemas showing fantasy films and saw, sometimes more than once, *The 7th Voyage of Sinbad, Mysterious Island, Dinosaurus!* and *Jack the Giant Killer*. As with all young budding animators he asked, 'How was it done' and the answers came in 1963 when he discovered a copy of Forry Ackerman's *Famous Monsters of Filmland* #24 on his local news stand. 'That issue had the first of a four-part series on *King Kong* and was the first time I ever saw an explanation of stop-motion, puppets, rear projection and armatures. I was hooked from that moment.' Subsequently he managed to find back issues devoted to Ray, which he 'studied over and over'.

Whilst at high school he happened to meet and befriend Rob Maine and Fred Niblock, the first people he had met who shared his passion for model animation. 'Rob was much more advanced in his animation and I learned so much from him about building puppets and armatures.' Rob would go on to do a great deal of the animation for the Great God Porno in *Flesh Gordon*. Together with Maine and Niblock, Aupperle shot a short film on Super 8mm called *When Nightmares Walk* and had a mention and several photographs published in *Famous Monsters of Filmland* #69 around 1970. Later they made another short film called *The Great American Dinosaur*, which they photographed with a 16mm Bolex camera. On that film Aupperle began experimenting with front projection to composite their actor (Fred Niblock) into shots of the stop-motion dinosaur.

He was still a high school student when he saw an article in the *Pasadena Star-News* about some local young people who had created their

LEFT TOP
Stephen Czerkas sculpting detail on a clay model of a ceratosaurus. The model was intended for use in *Planet of Dinosaurs* (1978) but was not used in the film.

LEFT MIDDLE
Czerkas with his clay brontosaurus maquette along with the drawing he created as a guide. The brontosaurus was one of the last models to be constructed for *Planet of Dinosaurs*.

LEFT BOTTOM
Czerkas looks back at some of the models that appeared in *Planet of Dinosaurs*.

BELOW
Czerkas animating the brontosaurus for *Planet of Dinosaurs*, working between the miniature foliage and the enlarged photo that was used for the background. The absence of a shirt was due to the extreme heat and the confined space.

RIGHT
Left to right, Jim Aupperle, Stephen Czerkas and Doug Beswick pose for a photo after the completion of *Planet of Dinosaurs*. Beswick is holding one of the two t. rex models that were used in the film. Note the allosaur model in front of the Mitchell camera, and, directly above Czerkas' head, a large head and neck model of the t. rex used for close-ups.

very own feature-length monster movie called *Equinox*. Because they lived in the same area Aupperle managed to find Dennis Muren and Mark McGee in the phone book [21] and he contacted them. 'In conversations with Dennis I learned about front projection and many other camera and lighting techniques and so redoubled my efforts and tests to learn all I possibly could. Dennis was an incredible help and source of knowledge and inspiration in those early years'. In 1970 Aupperle was invited to meet Ray at Forry Ackerman's 'Ackermansion' for a stop-motion day. There he also met another young and very local enthusiast, Stephen Czerkas, and they have been friends ever since. 'My aptitude was towards photographic work and Stephen was, and still is, an incredibly talented sculptor. We found we could work together with our talents and temperaments complementing each other perfectly.'

Aupperle's first professional job was to work on *Flesh Gordon* where he assisted Rob Maine with lighting and camera work and carried out the animation on the finale sequence. For several years after that he didn't find any professional film work but took a job as a night security guard, which allowed him to have his days free to continue tests using his 16mm Bolex in his parents' garage.[22] During this period he also wrote story treatments and produced storyboards for a number of projects, none of which were realized but were 'useful in learning how to attend meetings and make presentations'.

In 1975 Aupperle was introduced to James K. Shea who wanted to produce and direct a feature fantasy film, which eventually became *Planet of Dinosaurs*. Although only in their mid-twenties, Czerkas and Aupperle were put in charge of creating all the visual effects for the film and later they persuaded Doug Beswick to join the team. Beswick carried out most of the animation, while Czerkas concentrated on designing and building the sets and models and Aupperle took care of the miniature lighting and camera effects with the occasional foray into animation.

After completing *Planet of Dinosaurs* Aupperle and Czerkas heard that the Filmation Studio was planning to produce a live-action science-fiction series called *Jason of Star Command*. They made an appointment to see producer Lou Scheimer and showed him a reel of their effects from *Planet of Dinosaurs*. He was extremely impressed and both artists were hired on the spot and split the animation work 50/50 throughout the series. After the series finished Aupperle did mostly freelance effects camera work, contributing to *Caveman*, where he worked with Jim Danforth, and working for Randy Cook on *The Thing* (1982), *Ghostbusters* (1984), *The Gate* (1987) and *I, Madman* (1989). He also worked for David Stipes carrying out matte camera work on the series *Creepshow* (1982) and *"V"* (1984).

For *Dreamscape* (1984) Aupperle was able to do the animation as well as effects camera work for the Snakeman scenes and then did animation as well as constructing the models (tentacle-like plants) for John Carl Buechler's *Troll* (1986). James Belohovek, who had built many of the miniatures on *Dreamscape*, also worked with Aupperle on *Troll* and a number of subsequent productions. Doug Beswick asked Aupperle to do the effects camera and lighting on a series of feature films that included *A Nightmare on Elm Street 3: Dream Warriors* (1987), *Evil Dead 2: Dead by Dawn* (1987), *Beetlejuice* (1988), *A Nightmare on Elm Street: The Dream Child* (1989) (on which he also worked directly for New Line at another rented stage photographing miniatures and effects inserts), *After Midnight* (1989), *Gremlins 2: The New Batch* (1990) and *Cabin Boy* (1994).

In 1990 Aupperle moved to Berkeley to work on miniature camera and lighting effects for Phil Tippett on *RoboCop 2*, after which he returned to the San Francisco Bay Area to work

ABOVE LEFT
Jim Aupperle taking a light reading in a front-projection setup for *Planet of Dinosaurs* (1978). The model was created by Stephen Czerkas and the animation was executed by Doug Beswick.

ABOVE, TOP
Aupperle with one of the Terror Dogs models featured in *Ghostbusters* (1984). Aupperle photographed the sequence in 65mm whilst Randy Cook sculpted and animated the models at Boss Films.

ABOVE
This sequence for *Beetlejuice* (1988) was shot at Doug Beswick Productions and Aupperle was responsible for the lighting.

for twelve months (again on miniature camera and lighting effects) on the innovative *The Nightmare Before Christmas* (1993). Like so many animation artists, Aupperle found that the effects industry was changing and stop-motion work had started to dry up as CGI burst upon the scene. Aupperle knew he had to change and started with Photoshop on an Apple Mac making the transition to computer effects in 1996 on Disney's *Dinosaur* (2000). He has continued carrying out CG lighting for such films as *Hellboy* (2004), *Charlotte's Web* (2006), *Meet the Robinsons* (2007) and *The Spiderwick Chronicles* (2008). He reflects that 'The tools may have changed but many of the skills I learned doing stop-motion and miniature photographic effects continue to be important parts of my work.'

We mentioned *The Crater Lake Monster* when discussing David Allen. Another fine artist who cut his teeth on that film was Jon Berg who was born in 1946 in Los Angeles. One of his earliest and most vivid memories is of sitting in the dark, 'watching through fingers clenched over his eyes, as a giant ape pitched boulders at a cowboy against a cliff wall.' He was just three years old and, as Ray always says of his own first encounter with *Kong*, he has 'never been the same since'. Berg recalls that 'the image and the name, *Mighty Joe Young*, became a compelling, but dream-like element to my preschool years. It wasn't till years later that I found out my half sister, Dorothy, had taken me to see a picture she thought would be something like a Lassie movie.' When *Joe* was re-released, Berg caught a trailer for it on the family's brand new TV and, though he had no idea how it was done, he had proof that that 'big monkey' was no dream.

When his parents took him to see a re-release of *Snow White and the Seven Dwarfs* (1939) Berg realized that the film had obviously been achieved by means of drawings which were somehow made to move, and through Walt Disney's then-new TV show, *Disneyland*, and other sources, the basic concept of stop-motion animation became clear. It led to him making little flip books in grade school and selling them to his classmates. Around the same time *King Kong* was shown on television, and Berg was hooked!

> *While* Kong *didn't look 'real' he somehow looked* better *than real. 'How did they do that?' The answers came slowly, given the dearth of available information at that time, through laborious experimentation in a workroom my parents allowed me to commandeer. It was a wonderful experience of discovery; and however crude the early results may have been, the gratification of seeing something I had made appear to move on its own, was indescribable.*

Through a mutual friend, David Allen, and others, Berg eventually shared his own experiments and this subsequently led to a job at Cascade Pictures working as an animator on commercials including the Pillsbury Doughboy. This was a happy time for Berg, 'Under the wonderful tutelage of the head of the effects department, Phil Kellison, I had the privilege of working with, and forming lifelong friendships with, Phil Tippett, Dennis Muren, Ken Ralston, Jim Danforth and

TOP FAR LEFT
Jim Aupperle animating the Great God Porno or Nesuahyrrah in 1972 for *Flesh Gordon* (1974). The miniature rear projection and lighting is by Jim Danforth.

TOP LEFT
Jim Aupperle with the Great God Porno featured in *Flesh Gordon*. Aupperle is in the process of setting up the shot but it looks like the model had other ideas. Most of the animation for this sequence was by Rob Maine (Aupperle assisted on this shot), whilst David Allen executed some shots and Aupperle about five shots.

FAR LEFT
The photography for this sequence for *The Thing* (1982) was by Jim Aupperle (using a 35mm Panavision lens) whilst the animation was by Randy Cook. The miniature set was constructed by Sue Turner and James Belohovek. The animation shots with the Blair monster were not used in the final cut although three tentacle animation shots were kept.

LEFT
Aupperle with the 35mm Mitchell camera with the Panavision anamorphic lens ready to photograph the animation for *The Thing*.

BELOW
One of the animated monsters featured in the television series *Jason of Star Command* (1978-81). Jim Aupperle and Stephen Czerkas carried out all the animation whilst another crew did all the spaceship effects. The effects were filmed on 35mm and Aupperle used front projection to do all the composites with the live action. In this photograph two surface gauges are being used to register the movements of the creature.

others.' At Cascade he learned that he was far from the only one of his generation to be set on the stop-motion path. 'All of us, each in our own way, had been compelled to explore our common inspiration; the sense of wonder and awe at watching something that just *couldn't be, be*'.

Berg's first job at Cascade was to work on the science-fiction spoof of 1940s Republic serials, *The Further Adventures of Major Mars* (1976). He didn't do very much on the production, 'Most of the Cascade guys were involved. I think I may have shown up a few times and held a gobo or something.' None was credited and Berg was again uncredited for his work constructing the armature for the one model plesiosaur and miniatures in *The Crater Lake Monster*.

Through Muren, Ralston and Tippett he became involved in work on *Star Wars: Episode IV–A New Hope* working with Tippett, first of all on designing alien costumes for the Cantina sequence and then building and animating the creatures seen in the holographic chess game. Berg is very grateful for the chance to work on the picture. 'The success of the film opened up opportunities for us all to participate in the creation of images that have become inspirational to a whole new generation.' In 1978 he and his friend David Allen designed the lizard-men aliens for *Laserblast* (1978) for which he constructed the models, and he went on to take charge of overall effects on *Piranha* (1978).

He returned to ILM for *Star Wars: Episode V - The Empire Strikes Back* as part of the animation team. He designed and co-animated, with Tippett and Doug Beswick, the impressive Imperial Walkers (he also constructed, with Tom St Amand, the smaller Scout Walkers). He was credited as 'Dragon Consultant' on *Dragonslayer* and then worked on his third *Star Wars* adventure, *The Return of the Jedi*, as a Creature Consultant with Chris Walas. The following year he was a Creature Consultant with Phil Tippett on *The Ewok Adventure*.

By this stage he was much in demand and worked on a number of pictures, including *Gremlins* (1984), *2010* (1984) and *The Fly* (1986), in various capacities and as a model-maker on *RoboCop 2*. Just on the cusp of the digital revolution Berg was the mould-maker and wire armature builder for *The Nightmare Before Christmas* (1993).

In recent years, Berg has focused his attention on creative writing. 'As I have matured, I realized that a robust story is the framework upon which compelling imagery is dependent. Implicit in my affection for the works of Willis O'Brien and Ray Harryhausen is the love of a great adventure story.' Berg is a multi-talented artist and technician who has enjoyed his life working with fantasy. 'Because of the good fortune to have been exposed at such an early age to what Merian C. Cooper called his "amazing adventure in the unusual", I ignored the advice of my father to get a job at Sears and Roebuck, and follow a dream, and live what has so far been another "amazing adventure in the unusual".'

The last but by no means the least of the four great animators who participated in *The Crater Lake Monster* was Randall (Randy) William Cook, now famous as the digital animation designer and supervisor for *The Lord of the Rings* trilogy. However, like most of the new boys, he began his film career as a model animator.

Cook was born in 1951 in West Palm Beach, Florida but in 1954 moved with his mother and sister to live with his grandparents in California. His earliest influences were art (mainly the artists Mort Drucker and Jack Davis, whose caricatures appeared in *Mad* magazine), television (*The Adventures of Superman* premiered the year he was born and he was a fan of stars such as Dick Van Dyke, Jonathan Winters [23] and Ernie Kovacs) and, of course, movies. Cook recollects that his first experience of films was when he was eighteen months old, when his mother took him to see *Lili* (1953) which starred Leslie Caron singing accompanied by some marionettes. Today he is still in love with Caron and the marionettes possibly had a subconscious influence on his future. The first stop-motion picture that he saw was *The Lost Continent* (1951), not one of the true classics, but when he asked his mother about the unusual creatures in it, she told him they were dinosaurs. When he was seven his grandfather took him to see *The 7th Voyage of Sinbad* at a cinema in Livermore. This was much against his mother's better judgement, as she had been taken, also by Cook's grandfather, to see *King Kong* and had been terrified. The young Cook found *7th Voyage* to be compelling, in fact 'a revelation', and he sat through it three more times over the next week. His special favourite was the Cyclops, especially when he first appears on the beach chasing Sokurah.

Cook was eleven when he first began animating with clay, moulding 'little blobs of it to move and transform shape'. He also obtained a poseable, foot-high artist's mannequin, which was 'covered in tea-stained rags and given a clay face to become a mummy: a GIANT mummy, in fact'. These experiments were more about the joy of making things move than about trying to tell a story. 'Throughout high school I kept making little experimental trick films, but was just interested in drawing cartoons and writing for the school paper, as well as acting in school plays: usually in the most elaborate character make-ups the teacher would let me get away with.'

He graduated from Castro Valley High School in the class of 1969. While a student there he had taken an interest in art but dreamed of being an actor or movie-maker, specifically comedies and fantasies (his dream was to direct a twelve-hour version of *Lord of the Rings*). He went to UCLA where he studied motion picture production. Glenn Erickson, a fellow student, recalled:

> *The first day at the dorms I connected with another dormie, an incredibly talented artist and fellow* Valley of Gwangi *addict, Randy Cook. Randy was serious about stop-motion and was already making elaborate gag films and the like; his fame at the UCLA film school would later be assured with the production of his single-8 Project 1, a wicked satire of the (we thought) pompous, politically-correct film school faculty.*

According to Glenn,'The film professors were so dumbfounded at the screening they didn't know how to react.'[24] Randy will never forget the screening of the film, 'Just before my film went on, the student audience was engaged in a heated argument over whether a previous entry had been "heavy" or "beautiful"... they were in need of some comedy.' Cook graduated from UCLA in 1975 and at the suggestion of the animation director Bob Clampett, who had been responsible for the *Looney Tunes* cartoons,[25] he applied for a position at the Animation Training Program at Walt Disney Studios where he studied animation under Eric Larson as well being involved, as a gag-man and a storyboard artist, on the live-action *Herbie Goes to Monte Carlo* (1977).

He had already met David Allen while he was still at college and while he was working at Disney they collaborated on the first drafts of *The Primevals* in 1975/76.

> *I was only interested in writing and directing: the initial plan was for David to produce, write and animate, with me directing and co-writer – until Dave thought the directing job too good to pass up, so we agreed to co-direct as well. Whilst writing with Dave I watched him animating his lizard-man puppets and, as I'd never worked with a 'professional' puppet before, asked if I could take a crack at animating a test shot. It wasn't much good, but showed just enough promise so that Dave got me a job at Cascade Pictures when I left Disney.*

Cook's first professional animating job at Cascade (with David Snipes) involved a tennis ball for a television commercial. The task was basic

LEFT
The alien lizard-men featured in *Laserblast* (1978). The models were sculpted by Jon Berg who also made the armatures, whilst the animation was carried out by David Allen and Randy Cook, who was uncredited.

ABOVE
Randy Cook (left) looks on as David Allen works on a freshly cast troll-creature puppet (sculpted by Lyle Conway) for *The Day Time Ended* (1979). Cook animated the shots of it and the wolf-lizard fighting in the film.

ABOVE RIGHT, TOP
Cook working on *I, Madman* (1989). He has just finished animating a struggle between Jackal Boy and Malcolm Brand (utilizing a puppet of himself, as he played the villain). The projected image on the right is of Cook in makeup.

ABOVE RIGHT, MIDDLE
Cook posing with the finished sculpture of the BlairBug monster for *The Thing* (1982). He is smiling out of relief after completing a difficult phase.

ABOVE RIGHT, BOTTOM
Cook animating the Demon Lord picking up the Glen character seen in *The Gate* (1987). It was extremely difficult to animate let alone use surface gauges in such an inconveniently confined miniature set.

and Cook recalls that there was 'not much opportunity to employ many of the Disney character animation principles there'. He met other artists at Cascade, including the two-dimensional animator Tex Avery, who was famous for creating many classic cartoon characters. While still working full-time job at Cascade, Cook also worked on some of the animation for *The Crater Lake Monster* (Allen animated at night and Cook during the day). Cook received no screen credit but as assistant animator he did get to work closely not only with Allen but also with Phil Tippett, Jon Berg and Jim Danforth. Next he worked on *The Day Time Ended* at David Allen's studio, and Cook and Allen's animated models were the 'stars' of the picture. The animation was supervised by Paul Gentry, the models sculpted by Lyle Conway with Allen carrying out some animation (the tiny alien character) and Cook executing the remainder, which was always fluid and inventive.

Still working at the David Allen Studio, Cook's next project was *Laserblast* (1979) a cheap Charles Band-produced science-fiction movie that featured biped lizard aliens. The models were designed by Allen and Jon Berg and built by Berg with most of the animation being executed by Cook. Next, Cook worked on the comic book *Caveman* for which he constructed some of the models, including the pterodactyl which was based on a wing armature used by Willis O'Brien in his tests for *Creation*. 'I just cleaned the rust off and put it in.'[26] He also carried out some of the animation, including the flying pterodactyl, a drugged tyrannosaurus rex, a triceratops and a brachiosaurus; the latter two were sadly dropped from the final film. Cook has referred to the film as an 'opportunity to get into the farcical behaviour of the dinosaurs. These creatures are played as clowns, so we got to tinker with more anthropomorphic behaviour.'[26]

For the low-budget *Q–The Winged Serpent* Cook designed the model of the flying creature, operated the hand puppet for the baby creature and carried out the excellent animation alongside Allen, including the innovative and thrilling finale battle. His next assignment was on John Carpenter's *The Thing* (1982), a remake of the 1951 Christian Nyby classic. His credit in the film reads, 'Dimensional Animation Effects Created by Randall Cook' and although he produced five cuts of the alien monster for the production only two brief shots survive as they

were 'dropped by Carpenter because he felt they did not cut in well with the mechanical version of the monster'.[28]

Again credited for 'Dimensional Animation' on *Ghostbusters* (1984), Cook animated the Terror Dogs, which are hounds from Hell, horned creatures with piercing red eyes (Cook sculpted the creatures and Doug Beswick made the armatures). Cook's animation is, as always, smooth but he also gave the creatures a half dog-like, half frog-like gait, enhancing the sense that they really come from another world. In the same year he animated a few shots of a space probe and a group of astronauts space-walking for *2010* (1984). His next film was far more rewarding for an animator. For *The Gate* (1987) Cook designed and supervised the special visual effects, which included the use of forced perspective, blue screen, rotoscope and model animation. The 'star' of the film is the Demon Lord. Designed and sculptured by Cook, it is a creature with a huge, long, tapering body, the head of a lizard, six arms and two tentacles. It was an animator's dream. Cook also worked as Supervisor on the animation for the sequel, *Gate II* (1990) in which, along with Steve Archer, he animated various human models and another demon.

By now Cook was gaining a deserved reputation for delivering high-class effects for low-budget productions. *Hardcover* (1989) [aka *I, Madman*] was not exactly a classic fantasy/horror film but Cook designed and sculptured the model of the Jackal Boy (he also played the villain, designing four different make-ups which he applied himself). For *Puppetmaster* he was back at the David Allen Studios helping Allen with 'a scene or two' which included a shot (cut into two shots) of the six-armed gunslinger character twirling and throwing a lasso. Cook followed that up in 1993 with *Puppetmaster IV*, animating, along with Allen, the evil aliens called Totems. But as Cook remembers it,

> *the best thing I did with Dave in those days was the title animation on* Oscar *(1991), a John Landis picture. Dave, Justin Kohn and myself did the animation [a tubby, moustachioed Italian character singing 'Largo al Factotum'] of which I did just under half of it. It was very satisfying and I got to 'act' an opera number. I can't sing, so I LOVED doing that…finally got to 'perform' FIGARO. I think some of the performance was pretty successful.*

It was in the mid-80s when Cook was visiting the Disney studio that he first became fascinated with the possibilities of digital effects. There he met with Glen Keane, who showed Cook a test he'd made with John Lasseter. Cook remembers:

> *It was very exciting, because it used computer-generated backgrounds to create the sort of moving-camera, one-take shots which were only practical in live action. Until then, 'moving camera' in an animated cartoon meant pans or zooms or multi-plane shots.*[29] *Now the animation camera was free to roam around a 'drawn' set just as a live camera could, and, as Orson Welles was a God to me and* Touch of Evil *(1958) was my visual Bible [the film has one of the longest moving-camera shots ever filmed], I naturally saw this as an astonishing breakthrough. But I didn't realize how this advance would apply to the world of live-action movie-making, because nothing photorealistic was on display.*

Over subsequent years Cook watched the advances in computer animation with a detached interest, as cartoons weren't his focus. Sometime in the late 80s, though, he saw some examples of computer animation, which included a very simple animation of a triceratops. He recalls, 'It was more like a model than a cartoon and piqued my interest: were its shortcomings the fault of the computer, or the fault of the modelling and animation? I wasn't a computer programmer, though, and wasn't quite ready to stick my head into the Krell Brain-Boost machine [a reference to the machine in *Forbidden Planet* (1956)].' However, in 1990 special effects expert Peter Kuran excitedly showed Cook something that was obviously revolutionary,

> *a digital blue-screen composite, made on a Macintosh. It had blurs and glass and smoke and hair… and it was flawless! I immediately bought the most powerful Mac I could and started to learn. I got some animation software and found that you could animate key poses just as my 'cartoon' brethren did (something I'd always envied them for). The animation could be blurred, as well, and you didn't have to deal with tie downs and wires.*

With the advent of *Jurassic Park* Cook could see the end of the line for traditional model animation,

> *I was amazed: not just with the exemplary dinosaurs, but with Spielberg's moving camera. Even though I'd seen John and Glen's moving camera test years before, I just did not see this coming and was hugely enthusiastic. This new tool freed us up to create the kind of cinematic spatial movement that I had always dreamed of when doing stop-motion, as well as flawless compositing (with limitless dupes), and with a huge degree of control over detail which I had always despaired of attaining as an animator and sculptor. I naturally embraced the new technology in a death grip!*

Cook was fortunate that he was able to do some on-the-job training with David Allen and Charlie Band at Full Moon on some very low-budget pictures. The work was very uneven in quality, but he was able to try things out on a very modest scale. He even directed a micro-budget film, *Demon in a Bottle* (1995) (shot in three weeks for under a half-million dollars) for which he created a CG comic villain,

FACING PAGE LEFT
Cook animating one of the Terror Dog's (which he also sculpted) for *Ghostbusters* (1984). The glasses on the table were to protect his eyes from the light of the fluorescent-blue screen.

FACING PAGE RIGHT
Cook again with both of the Terror Dogs featured in *Ghostbusters*. The blue screen which was used to composite the live-action footage is in the background. Most days it was very hot on the set, hence the beachwear.

LEFT
Cook animating for *The Thing*. Again this was a very hot, very confined set.

BELOW LEFT
Detail of the Demon Lord featured in *The Gate*, which was designed, constructed and animated by Cook.

BELOW TOP
Cook posing with the Demon Lord upon completion of the special effects photography

BELOW BOTTOM
Cook again working in confined close-quarters on *The Gate*. The camera was inconveniently close to the model, allowing for the use of a wide-angle lens.

> *an enchanted bottle-stopper who menaces and annoys the heroes. He was just an ornamental bronze head which seals a genie bottle, who comes to life and runs around on the hasps which sealed him to the bottle's mouth, while shrieking curses and delivering exposition. It was an early bit of CG character animation and I was quite excited to be doing it, even though* Toy Story *(1995) came out just a few months before we finished. Still, I did personally animate a hundred and twenty-three character animation cuts in as many days, about three-quarters of them being lip sync. His performance is a little crude at times, but at his best he's effective and pretty damn funny. I never could have done that in stop-motion, of course, certainly not in anything close to that time, if at all!*

Many of the traditional animators are today heavily involved with digital animation. One of these is Randal (Randy) M. Dutra who, although he is conscious and deeply respectful of classical model animation, is also immensely proud of his work on *Jurassic Park* (1993) and *The Lost World: Jurassic Park* (1997). Born in 1968 in Castro Valley, California, from the earliest of ages Dutra was always using his hands to draw or sculpt in clay. Dinosaurs and films also figured prominently, particularly the classic Universal horrors such as *The Creature From the Black Lagoon* (1954), the Wolf Man, Frankenstein and Dracula films along with *King Kong* and *Mighty Joe Young*. Dutra recalls his first encounter with one of Ray's films,

> *At the age of eight I saw* The 7th Voyage of Sinbad *for the first time at a friend's birthday party. His parents had rented a 16mm projector and a print of the film, which I had never heard of. It was my introduction to Ray's work. It's not a stretch to say it was an epiphany. I sat transfixed on my folding chair and when the Cyclops emerged from the mouth of the cave in full stride and roaring, it was as if I had been suddenly struck by lightning. I knew it wasn't a man in a suit, but this creature had its own unique* character … *it wasn't reality, but a* mystery *that was far better. Those creatures spoke to me on a very deep level.*

When the film finished the young Dutra wanted it to go on and on so when the other kids had left he asked if he could see the picture again and sat alone to watch it. Again, when it had finished he had 'a sense of loss coupled with exhilaration'. When he finally returned home he acted out all the creatures' parts, 'complete with my arms bent at the elbows when it came to the Cyclops'. When it came to the fencing scene

with the skeleton he leapt about on the furniture with a yardstick in hand trying to emulate Sinbad. 'My parents weren't quite sure what had happened between noon and four, but whatever it was, it was powerful. In their wisdom, they sat me down and in between excited breaths I answered their questions about what I had seen and experienced.' Dutra has had the intervening years to think about why the film was so inspirational to him and so many other people in the business. 'What enthrals us about Ray's work and legacy is two worlds seemingly living together in an impossible, yet believable way. There is an inherent and unique dramatic tension of wonder that holds us firmly in its grasp. And we are ready and willing participants in this artful deception.'

The young Dutra was smitten and concentrated on learning all he could about model animation, and specifically Dynamation. By chance, his mother was at a bridge party where she met a lady called Helen Ramos, who lived across the street and whose son was Randy Cook. 'Randy was then a junior in high school and was steeped in all things Harryhausen. For the year and a half that he [Randy] was home before heading off to UCLA, Randy took me under his wing and was very generous in sharing what he knew about Dynamation.' Even then there were very few books on effects. Ray was still being very protective of his 'tricks'. What information Dutra did discover suggested that they went well beyond what he could achieve, but that didn't stop him. At the age of nine he made his own clay models and miniature sets and began experimenting with his grandmother's wind-up Bell & Howell 8mm camera fixed to a tripod and using his parents' dining room table as an animation platform.

While his fascination for animation developed Dutra continued his interest in painting and sculpting and also the natural world. 'Over the next nine years I would study and observe animals and their behaviours first-hand at a game farm in British Columbia in Canada.' This helped him not only to picture the creatures but to understand how they moved. On graduating in 1977, Dutra enrolled at the Art Students League in Manhattan to study figure drawing and sculpture and when he returned home he worked for three years in a bronze foundry, learning the trade and casting his own sculptures.

In mid-1981 Dutra was approached by an acquaintance who was head of the mould department in the Creature Workshop at ILM. He was hired to begin work on *Return of the Jedi* to make moulds, fabricate and sculpt creatures. One of his first sculpture jobs was the Rancor Pit Monster, based on a design by Phil Tippett. The film-making bug had bitten. After working as the key sculptor and creature fabricator on *Gremlins* (1984), his next two projects were back with ILM on two television films – *The Ewok Adventure* [*Caravan of Courage-An Ewok Adventure*] (1984) for which he was the master sculptor and puppeteer, and then *Ewoks: The Battle of Endor* (1985) on which he was the key creature designer of the dragon and master creature sculptor for the 'Tadpoles'. The second Ewok film also allowed him his first opportunity at feature animation, which were a few shots of the 'Tadpole' creatures and of the dragon; medium close-ups of the creature's head snapping and bearing down on the Ewok who kept him at bay with a spear. 'I was using the Go-Motion system. The camera would expose while the animator-programmed stepper motors moved rods attached to the joints of the puppets – thus a blur would be achieved on film.'

Dutra increased his animation skills working for the Tippett Company on *House II: The Second Story* (1988) for which he animated a fish-monster, a baby pterodactyl which falls headlong into a kitchen sink and finally a zombie-horse. The pterodactyl was in fact his favourite scene, 'It was a tricky action, with a bird-like recovery at the end consisting of shifting weight, head and shoulders.' Following that he was back at ILM working on the creature sculpture for the Dark Overlord that featured in *Howard the Duck* [*Howard – A New Breed of Hero*] (1987) and as the designer, sculptor and fabricator of the demon Sardo Numpsa in the Eddie Murphy vehicle *The Golden Child* (1986).

Back in the realm of animation, Dutra was the key animator of the villainous droid ED-209 in *RoboCop* (1987) for the Tippett Company. The two twelve-inch high model armatures were designed by Tom St Amand and constructed by Blair Clark. The three ED-209 sequences were designed by Phil Tippett and both are full of originality and mechanical/human/animal character, which was ingeniously rendered by Dutra. The droid's first appearance is in the boardroom when it is introduced as 'The future of law enforcement' but when it is given its first command it goes berserk and kills one of the executives. It is a violent but impressive introduction to what is a threatening and malevolent half-mechanical, half-animal creation with its whirling and hydraulic appendages and three-toed feet. Dutra recalls,

> *Of course the fun and the challenge of ED-209 was that he was a faceless robot: a large bumper-like grill for a head, stubby arms that ended in guns, jointed bent legs that could assume strange positions, and heavy feet with three stabilizing toes. I had to design my choreography to exploit what I could of ED-209's character. He was like a big kid, a bully. Not too bright but with a mission. It was this juxtaposition of a child-like awkwardness coupled with lethal abilities that made him interesting.*

It is the droid's second appearance, when it fights RoboCop, that is the highlight of the film and is full of tiny, almost insignificant, touches that make this one of the most powerful and innovative pieces of animation. The characterization begins with RoboCop tearing off the droid's left arm and the droid shudders as though with distress. The next sequence is where the machine is challenged by what humans take for granted – stairs – much as the

LEFT
Randal Dutra (left) and Phil Tippett (right) animating the two hadrosaurs for the Emmy award-winning television documentary *Dinosaur!* (1985). For this production whole sets and special environments were constructed for the dinosaur models to inhabit. It was a project that laid the groundwork for future involvement in *Jurassic Park*.

TOP
Dutra animating the ED-209 droid for *RoboCop* (1988). Dutra remembers the challenge of animating the faceless robot who had to project character and emotion. 'He was like a big kid, a bully. Not too bright, but on a mission. It was this juxaposition of a child-like awkwardness coupled with his lethal abilities that made him interesting.'

ABOVE
Dutra again posing the ED-209 model for *RoboCop*. The articulated model was about eleven inches high. The advantage with that scale is that it is easier for the animator to get his hands solidly around it when animating. The disadvantage is that the parameters of the stop-motion frame-to-frame posing becomes much tighter, and therefore extremely critical.

RIGHT
Randal Dutra posing with the models, designed, sculpted and fabricated by him (over armatures by Tom St Amand) for the Demon Sardo Numpsa featured in *The Golden Child* (1986). This was a major character in the film so two differently scaled models had to be built: a full-body model and one for close-ups.

Daleks used to be in *Dr Who*. Because it had never been programmed or indeed built to tackle stairs, there is an amusing hesitation at the top, followed by the machine testing the first step with its huge mechanical foot, as though testing the water in a bath. It decides to risk it and falls down to the first landing where it writhes and screams like an animal trying to regain its legs and dignity but is unable to do so. It is an ingenious sequence that doesn't necessarily add to the story but most certainly adds to the individuality of the model. Dutra says of the stair sequence:

> *His confusion is palpable, and his tentativeness was amusing – especially after having just blown to smithereens everything in his path in the shots before. He tests with his toes, falls, and then proceeds to throw a tantrum like a baby at the bottom of the stairs. It is recognizing these moments of opportunity that make animating no different from acting.*

The final sequence is almost a throwaway. RoboCop (Peter Weller) returns to the executive building and encounters the same droid (or it could be another?) which tells him he cannot park. RoboCop just blasts away at the machine and we see a wide shot of him striding into the building and from the left side of the screen the leg of the droid appears, followed by the rest of it, or at least what is left of it. The entire top section of the machine has been blown off and it staggers and wobbles before pitching over onto its back. Never before has a mechanical creation been given so much character.

Dutra next worked on the sculpture of Eborsisk, the two-headed dragon in *Willow* (1988) for ILM followed by *Honey, I Shrunk the Kids* for which he animated some of the garden creatures with Phil Tippett. He was a sculptor again on *Ghostbusters II* (1989) for the Tippett Company and then for Chris Walas International on *Naked Lunch* (1990) as the Key Creature Sculptor.

In 1990 he was back with Tippett to animate the final battle sequence with the evil Cain robot in *RoboCop 2*. Although lacking the personality of the droid in the first film, the Cain robot and Robocop models are beautifully designed and constructed and animated by Dutra with style and fluidity. His favourite series of shots were of the Cain robot performing a full forward roll with RoboCop holding on. 'The roll ends with Cain righting himself and backing smack into a brick wall, smashing and grinding RoboCop into the brick and mortar. All of this was done with blurs, moving the puppet manually on a lathe bed during exposures [a cheaper, manual Go-Motion]. It was complicated action but that's what made it all worth while.'

The years 1992 and 1993 were busy ones for Dutra and most other professional animators. First came Tim Burton's full-length animated feature *The Nightmare Before Christmas* (1993) on which Dutra was the key character sculptor of fourteen of the major characters and was also instrumental in designing, developing and sculpting the interchangeable replacement heads of Jack Skellington, which were used for dialogue and expression changes. Finally, he was the key animator on the research and development phase of pre-production.

Next came *Coneheads* (1993) for the Tippett Studio, on which he was co-animator with Phil Tippett of the Garthok creature and its battle with Dan Ackroyd in a four-minute sequence. Finally came *Jurassic Park* (1993), which saw the demise of traditional model animation. Dutra was senior animator for the Tippett Studio throughout the entire production and established character and movement considerations of the tyrannosaurus rex and velociraptors. He was also the sole animator of pre-production research and animation tests – i.e. walking, running, stalking, leaping and extended character shots. These tests were the very first of their kind in this production and were the 'Movement Bible' for all subsequent live-action and production animation discussions. Lastly, Dutra was the senior animator on the entire 'Animatic' phase of the production[30] with specific emphasis on both raptor and t. rex shots – the raptor 'kitchen' and t. rex 'main road' sequences and was responsible for the choreography/blocking and pantomime of the shots.

With *Jurassic Park* the world of special effects had changed. Dutra went on to work on *101 Dalmatians* (1996) as advisor on movement, and *The Lost World: Jurassic Park* (1997) and finally the remake of *War of the Worlds* (2005). He has now returned to the 'real world' and his other love, painting.

Another animator who would be closely associated with *Jurassic Park* is Tom St Amand who has had a long and distinguished career as both a model animator and a computer graphics character animator. Born in Los Angeles in 1951, St Amand claims, like most of the new breed of animators, that his early influences were O'Brien and Ray. He remembers seeing *King Kong* for the first time on television when a group of local kids gathered at a house across the street to watch it. St Amand was mesmerized and overwhelmed and, of course, wondered how it was done. A couple of years later he also saw *Mighty Joe Young*, again on television, and although he realized it was accomplished by the same method he still didn't know exactly how. When he was seven his father took him to see *The 7th Voyage of Sinbad* on the day it was released and took him back several times to see it again. 'It was one of the greatest films of my childhood, and I loved everything about it: the creatures especially, but also the story, the acting, the colour. It was one of those magical movies that took you someplace you could not go in the real world.'

Over the subsequent years St Amand saw more of Ray's pictures and, through the magazine *Famous Monsters of Filmland*, learned that a man called Ray Harryhausen had created the special effects. He began to follow Ray's work, by not only seeing the pictures but by also reading and collecting articles. Because he realized that what Ray used in the films were models or puppets, he became interested in puppets and puppetry and went on to construct his own hand puppets and marionettes, which he exhibited in puppet shows that he devised for the local kids. As he grew older this led to experiments in his dad's garage, sculpting, mould-making and finally building his own crude articulated models, 'My first armature was made of wood, and had ball-and-socket joints.' All this was passionately done in the hope that eventually he would become an animator.

In college he took classes in sculpting and two-dimensional animation, along with drawing, film history and art history. He graduated from UCLA with a film degree in 1974 and immediately began working in television commercials. He took samples of his sculptures to Cascade Pictures and was hired by Bill Hedge to work as an assistant prop maker. 'It was here that I met a number of other people whose stop-motion work had also inspired me, namely Jim Danforth and David Allen. For the first time I had a chance to directly learn techniques from people who had been doing the work for years, and it was the best education I could have gotten.' From these people he learned the business of model animation and quickly gained a reputation as a model-maker, sculptor, prop-builder, machinist and model-animator on a variety of commercials. In 1977 he finally arrived in the feature world when he worked on the armatures for *The Day Time Ended*.

In December of 1978 St Amand was hired by Jon Berg and Phil Tippett to work at ILM on *The Empire Strikes Back*. Under Berg's supervision he built the legs for the AT-AT Walker machines and worked with Doug Beswick on the armatures for the Taun-taun creatures and the animation for the Probot and the Scout Walker. Still at ILM, St Amand animated a miniature car and two passengers in the famous vehicle chase sequence in *Raiders of the Lost Ark* (1981). Following that he built the dragon armatures for two large walking models, two flying dragons and several four-inch human armatures for *Dragonslayer* and then, with Ken Ralston, animated the two small model dragons in the flying sequences. On *E.T. - The Extraterrestrial* he worked on building the models and animating the Go-Motion figures for the bicycle sequence, which was supervised by Dennis Muren.

Now firmly part of the team at ILM, St Amand went on to build the speed-bikes and co-animate (with Tippett) the two-legged Scout Walkers in the forest battle for *Return of the Jedi*. Under Muren's supervision he animated shots for the mine train rollercoaster ride in *Indiana Jones and the Temple of Doom*, 'All of which were done in miniature sets forty feet long, and in smoke.' He also animated a single shot of a Klingon falling into a lake of lava in *Star Trek III: The Search for Spock* (1984). When Tippett formed his own company, St Amand provided armature designs and carried out some animation for the television project *Dinosaur*.

FACING PAGE LEFT
For *Jurassic Park* Dutra animated and developed extensive pre-production character and motion tests of the raptors and the t. rex. Here he animates the t. rex head-butting the Explorer for the t. rex main road animatic.

FACING PAGE RIGHT
Dutra animating the t. rex DID, or Dinosaur Input Device, for *Jurassic Park*. The DID consisted of a traditional stop-motion armature equipped with motion encoders at the joints. The information about the joint movements was then fed into a computer and transferred to a digital model. This allowed traditional stop-motion artists to produce digital results.

LEFT
Two raptor model designed, sculpted and fabricated by Dutra for *Dinosaur!* (1985). The models measured about 7" (h) x 18" (l). Dutra found the shape and character of these animals to be perfectly suited to their function as fast carnivores

BELOW LEFT
Dutra animates a raptor for the kitchen animatic scene in *Jurassic Park*. He was later to create the final animation for the suspenseful sequence using the DID. The posed figures on hands and knees were retro-fitted, store-bought dolls with simple aluminum wire articulated joints.

BELOW
The raptors stalking the children in the kitchen scene in *Jurassic Park*.

One feature seemed to quickly follow another, with St Amand working on the stop-motion team for *Cocoon* (1985) and then *Ewoks: The Battle for Endor*, working with Randal Dutra animating the 'Tadpoles'. He then did the Go-Motion animation for the dancing Pepsi can sequence and co-animated, with Harry Walton and Phil Tippett, the 'Sardo' demon sequence for *The Golden Child* (1986). Next came George Lucas' *Howard the Duck* (1986) for which St Amand carried out the excellent animation for the Darklord under the supervision of Tippett and Walton and this was followed by uncredited work as the model armature builder for *Young Sherlock Holmes*.

During these years St Amand also worked occasionally as a sculptor, mould-maker and fabricator, all important aspects of model animation. 'I believe it is important for anyone interested in this work to have at least some kind of understanding of all the disciplines that go into it, including camera.'

St Amand was next credited with the Go-Motion animation on the extremely original and clever **batteries not included* alongside David Allen, and then designed the armatures for *RoboCop* and a brief animation shot for the flattened villain, Christopher Lloyd, in *Who Framed Roger Rabbit* (1988). St Amand had a little more to do in *Willow* for which he co-animated, with Harry Walton, the two-headed dragon that was designed by Tippett; with Tippett and Walton again, he participated in the animation for the outstanding scorpion/ant battle in *Honey, I Shrunk the Kids*. He was one of the animation team and the builder of the armature for the Cain robot, which consisted of an incredible '700 parts',[31] for *RoboCop 2* and

sole animator on *The Rocketeer* (1991) for which he also built an eighteen-inch model of the Rocketeer.

Again for the Tippett Studio, St Amand worked on *Jurassic Park*. His main task was to engineer and build, with Craig Hayes, the DID (Dinosaur Input Device). He and Hayes also built the armatures for two velociraptors, the tyrannosaurus rex and other carnivorous creatures, and animated the animatic sequences for the film with Randal Dutra. Looking back at *Jurassic Park* Amand recalls that,

> *For us at that time, this was our transition into computer graphics; we still animated a frame at a time, but could see the computer model move correspondingly, and didn't have to worry about surface gauges being accidentally left in shot; we could also, for the first time, go back and edit what we had done and fix props, etc. These were larger armatures than we generally built, and were comprised exclusively of hinge and swivel joints.*

After *Jurassic Park* he worked with Henry Selick on several MTV shorts, including a Clio award-winning one in which one of his ape armatures gives a sleeping guy a haircut. This led to him being hired as an armature supervisor and animator on *The Nightmare Before Christmas* and *James and the Giant Peach* (1996). The latter was the last film on which he officially worked as a stop-motion animator.

In 1997 St Amand made a more formal transition to computer graphics, learning new software and working on features that included a new version of *Mighty Joe Young* (1998), *Wild, Wild West* (1999), *Galaxy Quest* (1999) and *Jurassic Park III* (2001).

Like most traditionally trained animators, St Amand has some regrets about the old ways dying out.

> *I worked in stop-motion for twenty years and put in a fair amount of time before that learning how to build and animate puppets. There are a number of things I miss about the old days, amongst them the spontaneity of the work and the craft of making objects in the real world. My goal was not just to animate creatures; I wanted to learn to build them too.*

Another exceptional animator, already mentioned, is Harry Walton. Born in 1948 in New York, he moved to California in 1958. Not surprisingly, his movie influences were *King Kong, Mighty Joe Young* and *The 7th Voyage of Sinbad*. 'Around the time that *Sinbad* was released I picked up the first issue of *Famous Monsters of Filmland* and soon found out who worked on these movies and got a general idea of how things were done.' He went to high school in Southern California between 1962 and 1966 and during that time, over the weekends, he recruited his brother and neighbourhood friends as actors and crew to help him make a variety of animated and effects-related home movies. These amateur films allowed him to develop early skills. Leaving high school he attended Pasadena City College between 1966 and 1968 where he majored in sign art, a skill that would later become very helpful when he tackled matte painting.

In the early summer of 1968 he landed his first professional job at Clokey Productions after he had shown Ruth Clokey some of those home movies. When he arrived at Clokey, Doug Beswick and Pete Kleinow were already there and were soon followed by Rick Baker. Walton worked as an animator and miniature builder on various shows including *Reader's Digest Special, Davey and Goliath* and *Gumby*. However, the major turning point for Walton was when he was hired by Gene Warren, who was then running his Excelsior! AMP company and who became his mentor from 1970 until 1977. 'I learned a lot from Gene about stop-motion animation and related visual effects. For two years within this time frame Gene had an arrangement with Cascade which meant that I was loaned out to Cascade where I did stop-motion for them and also got to work for Tex Avery.' During his time he worked with Warren on various commercials: a short called *The Tool* Box, a George Pal Puppetoon, and a curious little movie produced by B-movie impresario Jack H. Harris which was called *The Legend of Hillbilly John* (1973) about a boy who meets the Devil. There are apparently two brief scenes that utilized animation, both of which featured a giant vulture. The model of the creature was built by Walton and mostly animated by him although the special effects director, Gene Warren, did execute some of the animation. In Neil Pettigrew's book *The Stop-Motion Filmography*, Walton described the vulture model as 'a wire-armatured puppet, suspended on a fairly sophisticated stop-frame wire rig from which all the necessary scenes were accomplished'. After that he worked on many other television commercials and productions, including *Octaman* (1971) as make-up assistant to Rick Baker, *Land of the Lost* (1974) and *The Man From Atlantis* (1977). He also worked on John Carpenter's feature *Dark Star* (1974) and John Frankenheimer's *Black Sunday* (1977) for which he animated a dirigible in an American football stadium at the climax of the film.

He then returned to David Allen Productions as an animator on *Laserblast* (1978) and although he would continue to work for Allen he also worked for various other effects companies on a mixture of television shows, commercials and features between 1979 and 1985. He then went to ILM and worked on *Ewoks: The Battle for Endor*, as a stop-motion

RIGHT

Top row, left. Harry Walton animating some tools for a sequence called *The Tool Box* for the television special *Curiosity Shop* (1971). This was shot at Excelsior. where Gene Warren supervised the animation. and was produced and directed by George Pal and advertised as his last *Puppetoon*.

Top row, centre. Walton animating the Demon Man for *The Legend of Hillbilly John* (1973). Walton is seen here in a front-projected composite with the Ugly Bird model, which he designed and built. He also worked on about 85% of the animation. The film was his first feature, again made with his mentor, Gene Warren.

Top row, right. Walton animates a scene for a new *Gumby* television series in 1987 at the Art Clokey Studio in Salsalito.

Second row. Left. Walton (left) and Pete Kleinow working on *Davey and Goliath* at Clokey Productions in Glendora circa 1969.

Second row, centre. Walton working on the famous Stage 6 at Cascade animating the *MD Twins* for the 'Forest Friends' television commercial in 1978.

Second row, right. Walton animating his first commercial, *Hamburger Hand,* at Excelsior! AMP circa 1977. Walton not only animated the model but also designed and built it.

Third row. left. Walton working at David Allen's Studio animating the two aliens inside a spaceship for *Laserblast* (1978).

Third row centre. Walton animating the Pillsbury Dough Boy in 1984 at Coast Efx.

Third row, right. Working at the Full Moon Productions effects stage set up by David Allen, Walton is seen here animating shots of the drunken dragon for *Dragonworld* (1994).

Fourth row, left. Walton making repairs to the Sardo model used in *The Golden Child* (1986). This work took place on the ILM stop-motion stage and the model is hooked up to one of the Go-Motion movers.

Fourth row, centre. Sardo being animated by Harry Walton at ILM's stop-motion department for *The Golden Child*. Note the two stepper motors just to the left of the model, which were used to blur the movement of the creature's wings.

Fourth row, right. Walton animates the scorpion at the Phil Tippett Studio for Disney's *Honey, I Shrunk the Kids* (1989). his 'Dynamation' set utilized high quality VistaVision masked projection plates that Walton made with his optical printer. Walton was in charge of the in-camera composites as well as setting up and animating some shots.

Bottom row, left. Walton working at the Phil Tippett Studio in 1987 setting up a 'Dynamation' shot for *RoboCop* (1988). In the VistaVision projection plate can be seen the full size ED-209 which will be replaced by the stop-motion model.

Bottom row, centre. Walton animating the Cain robot for *RoboCop 2* (1990), again at the Phil Tippett Studio. Walton produced all the VistaVision projection plates as well as animating and setting up his own shots.

Bottom row, right. The ILM stop-motion gang in 1986. Left to right, Bob Hill, Terry Chostnert, Kim Marks, the lady in red is unknown, Pat McArdle, Phil Tippett, Tom St Amand and Harry Walton. Not pictured is Randal Dutra.

photographer, on *The Golden Child*, as a Go-Motion supervisor, on *Howard the Duck*, as a stop-motion supervisor alongside Phil Tippett, and again as Go-Motion animator on *Young Sherlock Holmes* and then as the animator of the finale fight between two pods in Joe Dante's *Innerspace* (1987).

Over the coming years he would work for ILM as well as the Phil Tippett Studio. He was a stop-motion animator and composite supervisor on *RoboCop*, the Go-Motion animator and composite supervisor on *Willow* and the stop-motion cameraman for *Who Framed Roger Rabbit*. He was an animator, along with Tom St Amand, on *Honey, I Shrunk the KIds*. He was back at ILM again working as the effects and matte cameraman on *Ghostbusters II*, *Indiana Jones and the Last Crusade* (1989) and *The Abyss* (1990). He was part of the animation team on *RoboCop 2* and an optical effects supervisor on *Terminator 2 – Judgement Day* (1991), *The Nightmare Before Christmas* (on which he was also an animator) and *RoboCop 3* and an animator on *Drogonworld* (1994). In his spare time he worked, as most of the prominent animators did, on David Allen's *The Primevals* in around 1994/5 and his last involvement with traditional animation was on Tim Burton's *James and the Giant Peach*, for which he was the first character animation supervisor and also developed the Character Animation Department.

Walton has been in the business for thirty-seven years and now, in these days of CGI, specializes in character animation, although he is also known for his professional expertise as an artist, technician and supervisor in many areas of special effects.

A name closely associated with Doug Beswick is that of Yancy Calzada, who was born in 1959 and brought up in Pacoima, California. His life was changed, like many before him, when as an eight- or nine-year-old he saw one of Ray's films, this time *One Million Years BC*. He was 'drawn to the sculptures, the motion and the drama of the animation', and knew immediately that this was his future. As a fourteen-year-old Calzada acquired an 8mm camera and began experimenting with clay figures. Of course, his main interests were dinosaurs and monsters. As for other budding animators, information was hard to find and one of Calzada's sources was inevitably *Famous Monsters of Filmland* but he also found information in *Cinemagic* magazine. He recalls, 'The most elusive thing for me was the stop-motion armature. I kept animating with clay and wire armatures, from those early tests through to college.' He graduated from the California Institute of the Arts in 1981 and by then he had put a reel together to try and find some help.

He was lucky enough to contact a film-maker called John Matthews to whom he showed his test reel in 1984. Matthews put him in touch with Rick Garside who was just about to direct a children's film called *Hoomania* (1985). Rick was looking for animators and he gave Calzada his first professional opportunity to work on the film alongside other animators, including Justin John, Kim Blanchette and Bruce Lau. In all, Calzada executed 'about four shots of the main character, a small boy lost in a board game'. He also rendered two paintings for the film that were used as establishing shots. Following that he continued to develop his skills and eventually landed a job at Doug Beswick Productions. 'Working with Doug allowed me to try my hand at all of the essential steps involved in animated effects: sculpting, mould-making, armature construction, and finally the animation itself.' Calzada's first job was to design and construct the armature for the dancing headless corpse featured in *Evil Dead 2: Dead by Dawn* (1987). Next came *A Nightmare on Elm Street 3: Dream Warriors* (1987) for which he first made a series of replacement heads that transform from a shapeless blob into a clay likeness of Freddy Kruger, the villain of the *A Nightmare on Elm Street* series. 'I had to sculpt thirty or so heads, starting with a final likeness and gradually deforming each head. We would later shoot them in reverse order to achieve a "morphing" effect.' Jim Aupperle was Beswick's effects cameraman and it was his job to keep careful track of the animation as they replaced each head, moved the neck joint, and then, to facilitate an in-camera dissolve between heads, shot double exposures of each transition. This was done to help take the edge off of the double exposures of each transition. 'I then did a close up of Freddy's clay hand forming with tiny knife blades extending from each finger. This was also a combination of replacement and straightforward animation. Finally I did a shot of the puppet cutting his strings and dropping down. Doug did the shot of Freddy actually landing on the floor and walking out of frame to complete the sequence.'

The film's most complex sequence sees Freddy Kruger resurrected as a skeleton. Although Beswick carried out all the animation, Calzada created the rotted and grotesque skeleton model.

> *I began by building the armature using mostly aluminium and brass ball joints. Doug stepped in to machine a couple of the trickier items, the steel hinge feet and the steel swivel hip joints. When the armature was complete I then sculpted the bone shapes directly onto the armature using polymer clay, or 'Sculpy', which was baked and glued with cyanoacrylate to ensure adhesion. I then used latex sheeting and tissue to give it some rotting flesh. This was followed with latex, acrylic, and a prosthetic adhesive paint to seal it.*

On *Beetlejuice* (1988) Calzada was finally allowed to do some animation although sadly his shots of the Sand Worm were cut from the final film (Beswick carried out the main body of the animation). However his main task on the movie was to build the armature and the skull for the inner head, which was then sculpted and fabricated by Mark Wilson. Calzada also participated on the other animation sequence that features

BELOW LEFT
Yancy Calzada animating a couple of characters for the Christian children's film *Hoomania* (1985).

TOP RIGHT
A set of thirty-plus replacement Freddy heads, cast in Plasticine and sculpted by Yancy Calzada for *A Nightmare on Elm Street Part 3: Dream Warriors* (1987). They were changed in progressive stages to create the illusion of a transformation from a shapeless blob of clay into a likeness of Freddy Kruger by means of replacement animation.

TOP FAR RIGHT
Calzada prepping the miniature Freddy head which he also sculpted for moulding.

RIGHT
Calzada holds up the stop-motion Freddy skeleton used in *A Nightmare on Elm Street Part 3: Dream Warriors*. The armature is a work in progress and is seen here without the skull which was a slightly modified styrene part from a model kit. It is also still awaiting legs and wire fingers.

FAR RIGHT
Calzada fabricating the Freddy skeleton over the armature. Later the model was finished using tissue and latex build-up to give it a burned and rotted appearance.

two abstract art statues coming to life, for which he sculpted, moulded and helped to build the armatures with Beswick. In the film the sculptures were to grab and hold Jeffery Jones and Catherine O'Hara as witnesses for Beetlejuice's wedding.

> *The grabbing was done 'live' with full-size props created by Bob Short. The shots of the statues coming to life and walking out to grab the two witnesses were achieved with stop-motion. Jim Aupperle lit the miniature set, built by Jim Belohovek. I animated the first three shots of the statues coming to life and exiting the set. Doug and I both animated the last shot, which was a composite shot using a front-light, back-light technique.*[32] *The final composite was put together at Pete Kuran's VCE [company].*

Still with Doug Beswick, Calzada next worked as an animator at Dream Quest Images on the James Cameron undersea science-fiction adventure *The Abyss* (1989). One of his tasks was to animate the robot arm of the one-man submersible that is attempting to pull a retaining pin from a cable during a storm on the surface. 'The sub was a miniature that was mounted to a motion-control pylon. The sub had a self-contained miniature rear-screen process projector that provided a live-action image of the sub's pilot.'

Back at Doug Beswick Productions in 1989, Calzada constructed the model of the skeleton featured in *After Midnight* (1989) and worked on *Gremlins 2 – The New Batch* (1990). He built, along with Hal Miles,[33] armatures for two bat gremlins and a spider gremlin. Beswick carried out the major animation of both creatures with Calzada animating the bat gremlin wing unfolding, which was photographed, 'against a blue screen with a motion-control camera moving gradually to create the illusion of growth, which was then combined with a live-action puppet element shot earlier.' He also animated a shot of the bat gremlin flying and landing after it had been covered with quick drying cement. It lands on top of a church steeple (a miniature built by Jim Belohovek) where the cement dries which leaves it posed alongside the church's stone gargoyles.

In 1991 Calzada began working at David Allen Productions and his first job was to work as a puppeteer on Allen's first directorial effort, *Puppet Master II*. 'David also kindly allowed me to do some stop-motion. I did a couple of shots of a green-headed genie tugging at its chain.' Following that he also designed and built the armature for *Robot Wars* (1993) under the supervision of Mark Rappaport. In 1992 Calzada went back to work for Doug Beswick on *Ticks* (1993),[34] a low-budget monster movie about a group of campers attacked by large ticks in the woods. It had been conceived by Doug Beswick and his company handled not only the animation but also the make-up effects and live-action creature effects. Calzada carried out most of the animation of the tick models, which had been sculpted by Dan Platt. Calzada recalls that the budget

> *wouldn't allow for a fully articulated armature so we resorted to using aluminium armature wire. Doug and I worked together doing a series of shots where we would position the legs of the bug and then pull it forward during exposure with monofilament wire. We would also co-ordinate the wire pull with a pre-plotted camera move that resulted in some very kinetic animation and camera motion.*

After a year of so working as a puppeteer and animatronic designer and machinist at Kevin Yeager Productions on *Child's Play 3* (1991) and *Bill and Ted's Bogus Journey* (1991) he returned to work with Beswick on *Cabin Boy* (1994), an unsuccessful attempt at spoofing Ray's Sinbad movies. There were a number of characters and creatures that Calzada animated, including a shark-man called Chocki and a few shots of the giant snowman (Beswick did most of the animation).

With the demise of traditional animation Calzada decided to change his career. 'I moved into more animatronics and puppeteer work on movies like *Jumanji* (1995) and *Starship Troopers* (1997) before transitioning again into CGI.' Now he works as a digital animator. He is however adamant that he misses traditional animation a great deal. 'If I had to choose between CGI and stop-motion animation, my preference would be influenced by the process as much as the result. Though the design and planning stages are similar, CGI is not as intuitive to me.' He goes on to point out that CGI 'feels too remote from the hands-on process that first attracted me to animation. With CGI those

results may be smoother than any stop-motion I've ever done but in the end I don't get the same personal satisfaction.' He concludes by saying, 'Although I've done much more CGI than stop-motion, nothing in the digital world means as much to me as those few stop-motion movies I have been lucky enough to work on.'

Sadly, we are unable to mention all the names associated with the art of model animation, so we conclude with perhaps another of the most respected, Phil Tippett, who in recent years has gained a reputation for his CG feature films, has also won two American Academy Awards ® and two Emmys ®. However, before that part of his life began he was an esteemed artist in the world of model animation and live-action. Tippett was born in 1951 in Berkeley, California and grew up with a love of the arts, especially cinema. 'I hid out in art class, avoided physical education and sculpted and drew when I was supposed to be doing other things.' As most boys are, he was drawn to dinosaurs and from there to palaeontology. He has commented that, 'Little boys diverge into two groups: one goes into trucks and the other goes into dinosaurs. I went into dinosaurs.'[35] However, at the age of seven his life changed, when he made a trip to the (Berkeley) Oaks Theater to see *The 7th Voyage of Sinbad* in the first week of its release. Unbeknownst to Ray, he was changing lives and spawning many fantasy fans and, in there somewhere, animators. The scene that inspired Tippett the most was the fight with the Cyclops on the beach near the opening of the film. He recalls that, 'From that point on I gradually found ways of appeasing my needs to see this kind of stuff by making it myself.' He had also seen *King Kong* on television in the mid-1950s. It naturally inspired him and he wanted to see it time and again to find out how it was done. He recalls that 'as we didn't have the media available today. You saw the pictures once and they had to resonate in one's own imagination. I did not have any idea what the process was that created the prehistoric beasts and Kong but it was magic that was like a bolt of lightning searing my young brain.' His favourite genres were science fiction and horror and he would catch all of Ray's new films on opening day.

Of course he had to make his own films to try and emulate the fantasy he had seen on the screen and had to find his way through the technical labyrinth; making it up from scratch by imagining what must have gone into the process. To help pay for it he did odd jobs, for example mowing lawns, in order to buy a 8mm camera with a single-frame function to shoot his films, first of all using clay models and then progressing to wire armatures and rubber models. 'I shot hundreds of feet of film and eventually graduated to 16mm.'

When Tippett was fourteen he met independent film-maker William (Bill) Stromberg and assisted him on the weekends and summers until he was seventeen. Tippett helped with live-action photography, painting sets and props and drawing storyboards. Amongst several projects he helped Stromberg put together was an adaptation of Ray Bradbury's *A Sound of Thunder* [36] for which he sculpted the tyrannosaurus rex, constructed the stop-motion model of it and helped Stromberg with setups and even did some animation shots with the creature.

Graduating with a bachelor's degree in art from the University of California, Irvine, at age seventeen, he was invited by Jim Danforth to work as an animator at Cascade Pictures in Los Angeles and remembers that, 'It was the only place in the world, other than Ray, that was doing that kind of stuff – stop-mo and visual effects.' He was there with 'the ten other geeks who were interested in this stuff'.[37] They included David Allen, Dennis Muren, Ken Ralston, Jon Berg and Tom St Amand. On the insert stage, Stage 6, he worked on various animated commercials, including the 'Jolly Green Giant' and 'Brawny paper towels' fine tuning his knowledge and skills. 'It was run by this wonderful fellow Phil Kellison who really encouraged us – it was really the most wonderful place and time and the greatest opportunity to wear a lot of hats.' Tippett was there on and off as a freelancer between 1970 and 1975.

In 1969, aged eighteen, Tippett worked on his first feature film, *Some Kind of a Nut* (1969), a Dick Van Dyke vehicle in which his character revolts against the company where he works because of their stringent rules. It was a low-grade movie for which Projects Unlimited (the company run by Wah Chang and Gene Warren) were hired to carry out some effects. Tippett, who was paid for the first time, animated a model car in front of a rear-projection setup that contained an image of a map of the USA, which was part of a travelling-across-the-country montage.

Between 1975 and 1976 Tippett helped, like everyone else in the stop-motion world, with David Allen's *The Primevals*. 'A number of us assisted Dave on his promotional material for *The Primevals* [as] no one then was really making the kind of pictures that we were good for.' In 1976 Bill Stromberg hired Tippett to work on *The Crater Lake Monster*, although his efforts were uncredited, along with Randy Cook, Jim Danforth and Jon Berg. Primarily, Tippett worked with Allen sculpting and painting the creature as well as 'animating a few shots'. He then joined Jim Danforth on the unrealized *Timegate*.

Also in 1976, Tippett was recruited by George Lucas to work on his new picture to be called *Star Wars* (later retitled *Star Wars: Episode IV–A New Hope*). His appointment came about by a convoluted route,

FAR LEFT
Yancy Calzada sculpting the Snow Man stop-motion model used in *Cabin Boy* over an armature built by Scott Oshita at the Doug Beswick Studios. The model was cast in foam latex, painted white and coated with a layer of baking soda to give it a powered snow finish. The stop-motion shots were animated primarily by Doug Beswick with Calzada assisting with a few close-ups.

LEFT
Calzada animating the model ticks for the film *Ticks* (1993). The set was built by George Wong (who also assisted with the animation) with a miniature rear-projection screen in the window in which part of actress Rosalind Allen can be seen.

RIGHT
Phil Tippett circa 1970, with a light meter.

BELOW
A young Phil Tippett meeting Ray for the first time at Forry Ackerman's house and museum in 1967. According to Phil they are doing the 'two-fingered tyrannosaurus hand shake'!

BELOW RIGHT
Tippett on location in 1968 for David Allen's *The Primevals*.

A guy I knew when I was an art student at UC Irvine was a Navy buddy with Richard Edlund [who was the first cameraman on the film's miniature and effects unit and later a cinematographer]. He knew I was into visual effects and gave me Richard's number as he was crewing up for some big sci-fi show. I spoke with Richard who was looking for camera people, which I was not, and I gave him Dennis Muren's telephone number. Dennis got hired on Star Wars *and he hired Ken Ralston as his AC. They were shooting on the night crew and I'd go out to ILM and visit – then when George needed to shoot inserts for the Cantina [sequence] Dennis put him in touch with Rick Baker and Rick put together a creature shop with a bunch of us out of work stop-motion animators.*

Tippett also recalls what Lucas said, 'When we first got hired to move up from Los Angeles and go to ILM, George said, "Well, we're going to make a few pictures, and then people will probably get tired of us, and then we'll move back to Los Angeles," it didn't happen.'[38] Initially Tippett was hired to help design a number of alien creatures that were to be seen in the Cantina bar. Stuart Freebourn, the British makeup artist, had fallen ill, and Lucas wanted to flesh out the sequence so the unit came up with as many designs as possible within a six-week period. 'We based some material on Ron Cobb designs and Rick [Baker] threw in a bunch of his masks that we built over. Then we shot for two days on a little insert stage in Hollywood. We got to play the characters that we'd made.'

Whilst in production for the Cantina creatures Lucas would occasionally visit and this is where Tippett's life changed. 'He saw some stop-mo puppets that I'd made, sitting on a shelf and he asked if we were animators. He called Jon Berg and me in, about a week later, and said that he was going to do the chess scene with actors in masks but thought it would be more fun if they were animated. So Jon built up some wire armatured things from scratch and I threw in one of my articulated creatures.' The scene, which is played between R2-D2 and Cheewbacca, appears in the background of a sequence that primarily shows Luke Skywalker learning to use the Force to sense his opponent.

On a table in front of Chewbacca and R2-D2 are a number of holographic alien figures, some standing and some fighting. It is beautifully animated and although it is almost a throwaway sequence of shots it gives substance to an otherwise dull scene.

Tippett's next feature had been inspired by the success of *Jaws* (1975) but was basically a traditional monster movie, albeit the monsters were small. *Piranha* (1978) was directed by Joe Dante and concerned mutated versions of the fish that are accidentally released into a local river by a mad scientist. Jon Berg was in charge of the special effects but Tippett was in charge of the creature design and the all-too brief animation, which involved, not piranhas but another experimental horror, a mutant newt!

Back at ILM, Tippett became the head of the Creature Workshop and began work on the next instalment of the *Star Wars* saga – *Episode V–The Empire Strikes Back*, probably the best of the entire series. As mentioned elsewhere, there are a number of superb sequences that are enhanced by Tippett's animation. The first is the Taun-taun creature, a furry, two-legged, horned dinosaur-like animal, ridden by Skywalker, and, later in another shot, by Hans Solo, across an arctic terrain. The armature was designed by Doug Beswick and Tom St Amand but the model was designed and animated by Tippett. There are several long shots of the creature (the close-ups were full-scale) trotting across the snow in long, realistic, measured strides. These creatures follow in the footsteps of previous creations brought to life by traditional animation, but the Imperial Walkers were completely unlike anything previously seen in the history of model animation. A perfect subject for the art, they are colossal, impossibly ponderous machines that walk on four dinosaur-like legs with an array of cannon and guns mounted on the front. There is one specific scene that stands out above the others in this sequence, not only for its effectiveness but also because the animation is flawless. The scene sees one of the Walkers brought down by a rebel speeder craft, which attaches a cable to the machine and then circles it until it can no longer move its legs (the cable was done with cel animation by Peter Kuran). As the cable begins to get taut the machine seems to hesitate and then clumsily crashes to the ground. It is a remarkable visualization of Tippett's thought process in determining how this machine will slowly come to a halt and fall.

It was during the making of *Empire Strikes Back* that Tippett co-developed the new animation technique called Go-Motion.

> *Stop-mo animators had been trying for a while to devise ways of getting the static still frames of the process to integrate better by introducing a blur, the artefact of the shutter in a motion picture camera. All of these were elaborate and time-consuming and didn't look so hot anyway. Ken Ralston and I did some tests very early on in pre-production on* The Empire Strikes Back *with a creature I made for* Piranha *and hooking it up to a motion-control rig. The results looked pretty good. Then Dennis [Muren] and I figured out a way of setting up some full miniature Taun-taun setups with motion control. Only the forward major axis was getting the blur but it really helped the overall look. Then on* Dragonslayer *we were able to invest in a more complete rig that moved more limbs. It was a collaboration between me, Dennis, Jon [Berg], Stuart Ziff (who engineered it) and Gary Leo who*

ABOVE LEFT
The alien chess scene from the first *Star Wars* [*Star Wars: Episode IV–A New Hope*].

ABOVE
Tippett animating the alien chess pieces for *Star Wars* (1977).

RIGHT
Top row, left. Tom St Amand, Doug Beswick, Jon Berg and Tippett posing with the stop-motion Walker models for *Star Wars: Episode V – The Empire Strikes Back*.

Top row, centre. Tippett testing Jon Berg's Walker prototype armature For *The Empire Strikes Back*.

Top row, right. Tippett animating the Walker on the miniature set for *The Empire Strikes Back*.

Bottom row, left. Tippett animating the Taun-taun model on a running rig in a full miniature set for *The Empire Strikes Back*.

Bottom row, centre. Tippett animating the Taun-taun in a blue screen shot.

Bottom row, right. Tippett helping puppeteer the model Probot for *The Empire Strikes Back*.

BELOW RIGHT
Tippett animating the Walker on the miniature set in front of a background painting of the icy landscape by Michael Pangrazio for *The Empire Strikes Back*.

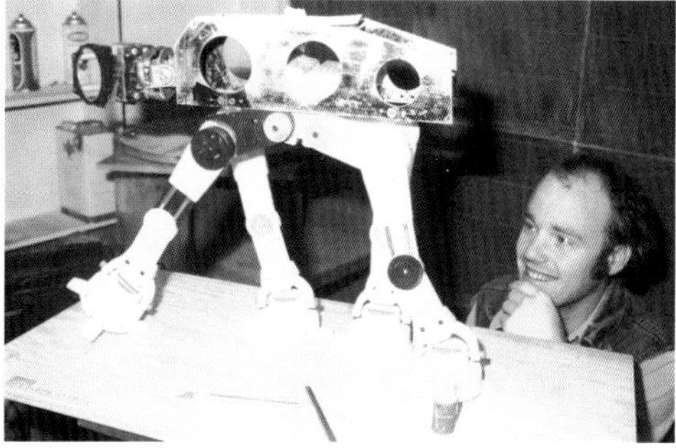

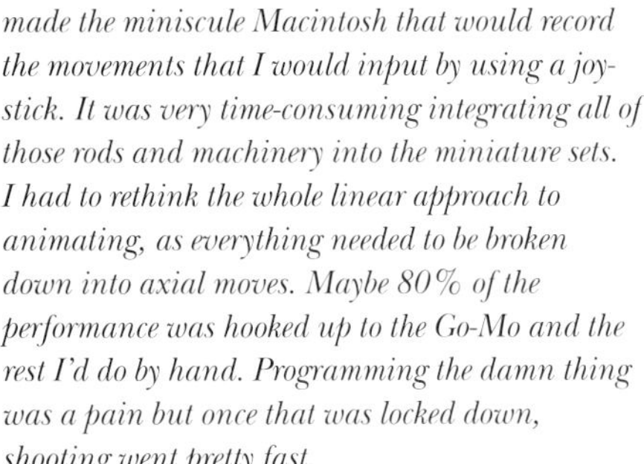

made the miniscule Macintosh that would record the movements that I would input by using a joystick. It was very time-consuming integrating all of those rods and machinery into the miniature sets. I had to rethink the whole linear approach to animating, as everything needed to be broken down into axial moves. Maybe 80% of the performance was hooked up to the Go-Mo and the rest I'd do by hand. Programming the damn thing was a pain but once that was locked down, shooting went pretty fast.

Tippett quite understandably earned his first American Academy Award ® nomination for *Dragonslayer*.

Tippett's last film, whilst still at ILM, was *Star Wars: Episode VI–Return of the Jedi*. He was credited for the makeup and the design, alongside Stuart Freeborn, of such creatures as the Rancor monster (a rod-operated model). He was responsible for the excellent Go-Motion animation (with Tom St Amand) that is seen during the forest of Endor chase, in which we are treated to a number of Imperial two-legged Scout Walkers (smaller versions of the Imperial Walkers seen in *The Empire Strikes Back*) with the pumping gun action on the machines achieved through traditional animation. One of the most impressive shots in the entire sequence is when we see one of the Walkers toppled by logs that have been sent down a slope by Ewoks. It is reminiscent of the Walker brought down in *The Empire Strikes Back*, but here the machine seems to be a living entity as it attempts to sidestep the logs only to eventually succumb to the inevitable and fall. Tippett was awarded an Oscar ® for the film, which was certainly well deserved.

Tippett left ILM in 1983 and his first project was to make a ten-minute experimental film called *Prehistoric Beast* (1983) that featured a tyrannosaurus rex and a herd of horned ceratopian dinosaurs called monoclonius. The models are of the highest quality, right down to the wrinkles, warts and folds of skin and the

ABOVE LEFT
The impressive Verminthrax Perjorative dragon featured in *Dragonslayer*

ABOVE
Tippett fabricating the walking cave dragon for *Dragonslayer* in his workshop at ILM.

BELOW LEFT
Tippett fabricating the Rancor model in his workshop for *Star Wars: Episode VI – The Return of the Jedi*).

BELOW CENTRE
Tippett checking the armature for the Rancor creature, built by Tom St Amand, against the designs.

BELOW
Tippett using Go-Motion to animate the Scout Walker, or Chicken Walker, against a blue screen for *The Return of the Jedi*.

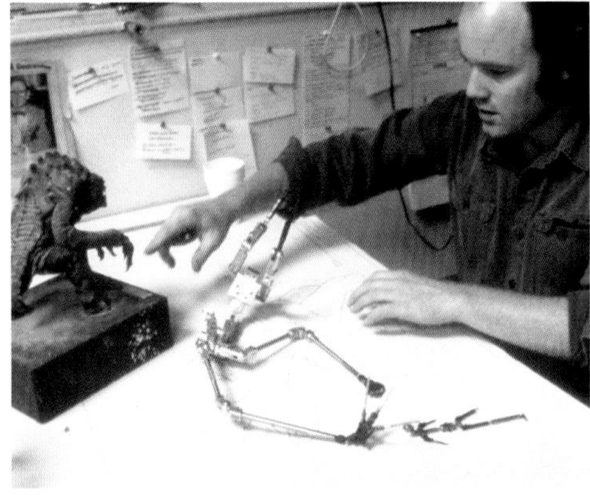

ABOVE
Tippett puppeteering the Leia biker model against a blue screen for *The Return of the Jedi*.

ABOVE RIGHT
Tippett (right) puppeteering a Storm Trooper for the forest bike chase sequence for *The Return of the Jedi*.

animation is outstanding with much time and effort put into the way the creatures move, react and fight. Tippett took about nine months off feature work to make the film, 'I had wanted to make a dinosaur feature for quite a while, and this was going to be like an episode from it, then I culled it down from there for production reasons.'[39]

In 1984 he formed Tippett Studios and the company's first project was the CBS television documentary *Dinosaur* (1985), which won an Emmy Award ® for the special visual effects. However, Tippett continued to work on projects for ILM through his new company. He was the Effects Creative Consultant on *Indiana Jones and the Temple of Doom*, also constructing a number of human articulated models for the film with Tom St Amand, and then worked as Stop-Motion Supervisor on *Ewoks-The Battle For Endor*. This was a poor, second-attempt television spin-off from the *Star Wars* franchise, which is only redeemed by Tippett's undeniably top-of-the-line animation. Among the creatures that appear in the film are the Ewok equivalent of beasts of burden nicknamed 'Tadpoles', which were based on a earlier but unused design by Tippett for the Taun-tauns. They are bipeds with short forearms, much like carnivorous dinosaurs, but with the added feature of a fish-like head with rows of vicious teeth. The next creature featured is a giant bird-like creation with a dinosaur head which attacks the hero whilst he is flying a crude glider. With this film, as well as with *Empire Strikes Back* and *Dragonslayer*, Tippett had taken model animation to another level with the new technique of Go-Motion. Just as Ray did before him, he looked at what was being done in traditional animation and enhanced it with new technology. This was a new era but one that wouldn't last for long.

The 'star' of *The Golden Child*, a disappointing Eddie Murphy production, was undoubtably the demon. Tippett, credited as the Demon Supervisor, was joined by Tom St Amand and Harry Walton for the execution of the animation. Both conventional model animation and the Go-Motion process were used. Next, Tippett worked on the primarily live-action film *Howard the Duck*, which is almost redeemed, but not quite, by the animation finale which sees the villain Jeffrey Jones transformed into an alien, a huge very original scorpion-like creature. The model was designed by Tippett and built by a team that included Randal Dutra. The animation was supervised by Tippett and Walton, with the animation itself carried out by St Amand. There is a sense of pure evil and rage emanating from the animated creature, which is actually terrifying, but this sense of menace is lost when we are reminded that its opponent is a large duck. Tippett was also the supervisor for the model-makers and animators for the flying lizard and the dead cowboy riding the skeleton horse for *House II: The Second Story* (1988) as well as constructing a cat-fish-faced monster and animating it in a few shots.

In 1986 Tippett, along with his colleague and co-founder of Tippett Studios, Craig Hayes, was responsible for the design of the ED-209 droid sequences in *RoboCop*, which were animated very effectively, largely by Randal Dutra.[40] Tippett remembers the design for the droid as being deliberately quirky. 'There was

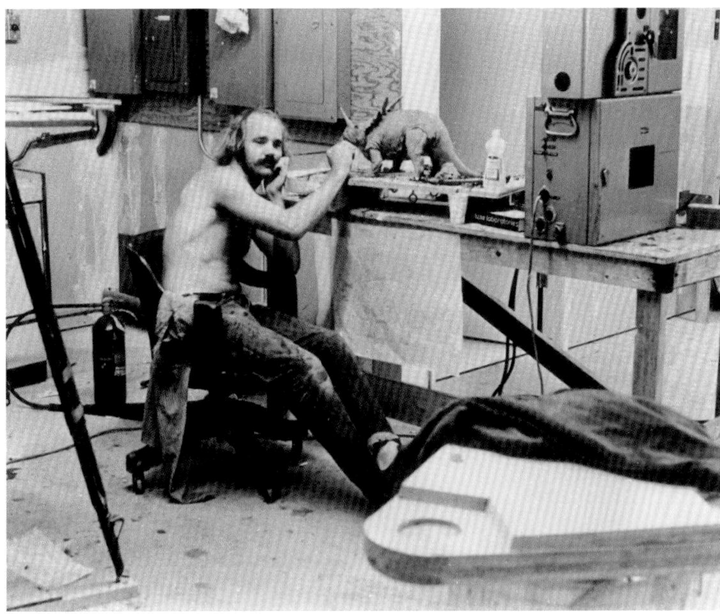

always a somewhat over/under design aspect to ED-209 that was both lethal and silly at the same time, which we all knew had to be played. Craig engineered him as a lethal lumbering buffoon from a similar mind set that had also designed the SUX-9000 – an American auto industry aesthetic that had gone awry – very much like the Detroit auto industry.' The SUX-9000 was in fact a car that is seen in a commercial in the film and was animated by the Chiodo brothers. Always looking for new and improved techniques, Tippett used a VistaVision camera[41] for the rear-projection plates, which had the effect of reducing graininess. The effects had to be produced both quickly and cheaply. Tippett recalls,

> *Overall, there were approximately 55 shots with ED-209 that we had to have in the can in three months. And they were some of the most complicated shots I've ever been involved with. Most of them were action shots with a great deal of camera movement designed very carefully so it would appear that we really had a giant robot walking around. We didn't want the shots to be limited by the fact that we were using animation.*[42]

The director, Paul Verhoeven, was very specific about what he wanted on the picture. For example, he would ask for the droid to walk directly towards the camera and on occasions appear to step over it. These angles were extremely difficult to animate and to get them Tippett had on occasions to remove sections of the model to enable it to get closer.

For *Willow*, produced by George Lucas and directed by Ron Howard, Tippett was the Visual Effects Supervisor along with Dennis Muren and Mike McAllister. He designed, sculpted, fabricated and supervised the two-headed dragon Eborsisk sequence, with animation carried out by Tom St Amand and Harry Walton. One articulated model was constructed for the animation with another, larger, one of just the heads and necks for the close-ups. He worked with engineers on the design of a new, 'more animation-friendly', Go-Motion system. 'Go-Motion rods were used for the most significant parts of the puppet moves (the heads and necks) with the rest (the mouths, eyes, and puppet humans) being moved by conventional stop-motion techniques.'[43] He also executed some last-minute insert shots with some pre-Eborsisk egg hatching. Tippett received his second Oscar ® nomination for his work on the picture.

Tippett's next project was to design and construct, along with Randal Dutra, the ghost-monster that manifests in Washington Square for *Ghostbusters II*. The model was animated by Harry Walton again but this was the only animated shot or scene in the entire film. A number of animators were responsible for the effects on *Honey, I Shrunk the Kids*, including Tippett who supervised and animated, along with Harry Walton and Tom St Amand, the scorpion sequence, which has to be one of the most impressive in the film. The action in the sequence is beautifully planned by Tippett, especially when the scorpion attacks its opponent.

As with all good sequels, the producers of *RoboCop 2* had to try and outdo the ED-209 droid that appeared in the original film. Tippett assembled a team that included Randal Dutra, Jim Aupperle, Pete Kleinow, Harry Walton and Tom St Amand to design, plan and animate the evil Cain robot that was the new adversary for RoboCop. The budget for the picture was not sufficient,

ABOVE LEFT
Tippett sculpting a triceratops in 1976 for the unrealized Jim Danforth project *Timegate*.

ABOVE
Tippett animating a monocolonius on a miniature set with front projection for his short film *Prehistoric Beast* (1983).

RIGHT TOP
Tippett fabricating a sacrificial victim for the lava pit sequence in *Indiana Jones and the Temple of Doom* (1984).

FAR RIGHT TOP
Dennis Muren (left) and Phil Tippett go over the storyboards for the lava pit scene in *Indiana Jones and the Temple of Doom*.

RIGHT BOTTOM
Tippett animating the droid ED-209 against a rear-projection screen for *RoboCop* (1988).

FAR RIGHT BOTTOM
Tippett animating the ED-209 again for *RoboCop*.

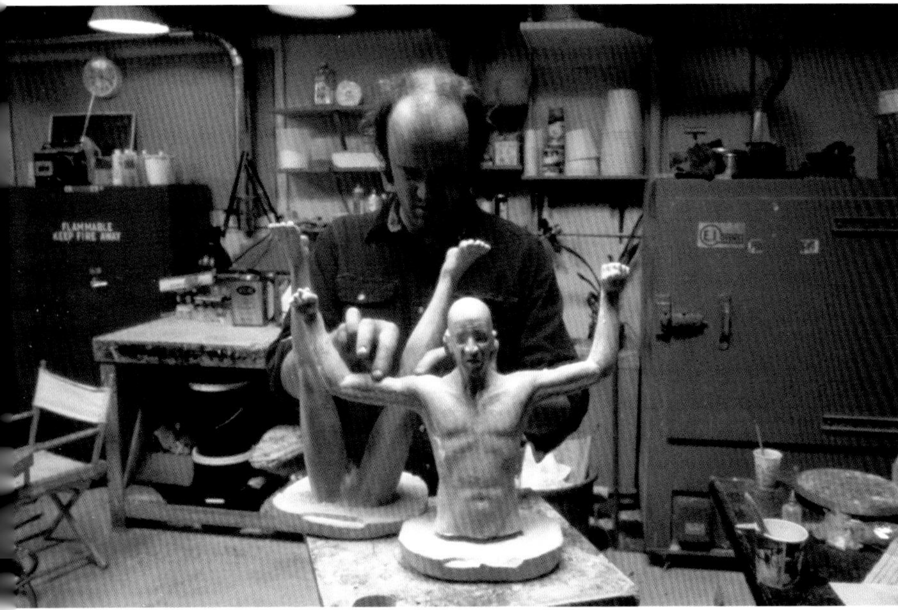

As with RoboCop, *and* Honey, I Shrunk the Kids, *I did not have access to, nor the budget to afford, the complex Go-Mo equipment that we had designed for ILM. Cameraman Pete Kozicheck and I came up with a simplified 3—axis motion-control setup for some shots but most were conventional stop-motion rear-projection setups in the tradition of Ray Harryhausen. I would add blur when possible by shaking the puppets during exposure through various means. The Go-Mo really operated best in a blue-screen setup – it was impossible to hide all those rods when shooting rear projection.*

The Tippett Studios' next venture was *Coneheads* a science-fiction comedy that featured a fantastically grotesque monster called Garthok, a reptilian, dinosaur-like creature that has claws and two enormous inverted tusks. The sequence in which it appears is approximately four minutes long, with the smooth and inventive animation carried out by Tippett and Dutra. Although not exactly a classic film the sequence is certainly one of the highlights in the history of model animation. Finance for the stop-motion was very limited again and Tippett recalls that 'Dan Ackroyd really wanted to fight a stop-motion monster and the producer wasn't too thrilled about paying for it.'

When Steven Spielberg announced that he was to make a film of Michael Crichton's very successful book *Jurassic Park* about genetically produced dinosaurs, it was naturally assumed that the various creatures would be animated models, their reality enhanced by the use of the Go-Motion technique and full scale animatronics. To a some degree the animatronics stayed, but the animation was largely dropped in favour of CGI, although traditional animation would play a crucial part in the film's production. Tippett's involvement began in 1991 when Spielberg, knowing of his expertise in dinosaur movement and behaviour, asked him to supervise the dinosaur animation for the film. It was this project that was responsible for Tippett Studios' transition from traditional animation to computer-generated animation and which led to Tippett being awarded his second Oscar ®.

The team that Spielberg assembled to produce the complicated effects consisted of Stan Winston, who was responsible for the live action dinosaurs, Dennis Muren, whose responsibility was the full-motion dinosaurs, Michael Lantieri, who was to carry out the special dinosaur

LEFT
Tippett directs Adam Valdez animating the CG tyrannosaurus rex for *Jurassic Park* (1993). In front of the computer monitor is a model of the dinosaur and the truck. This image really marks the crossover from traditional stop-motion model animation to the computer generated image. Tippett was largely responsible for the accuracy and character of the creatures in the film.

BELOW
Tippett (left) and sculptor/designer Pete Konig with the finished Draco dragon design maquettes for *Dragonheart* (1996)

effects, and of course Tippett. Producer Kathleen Kennedy said at the time, 'It's a dream come true to be able to land them all on one movie.' Tippett remembers how it all began 'Dennis Muren started approaching VFX (visual effects) conventionally, breaking it down between the full-scale props and the VSX side with Go-Motion, high-speed photography and some computer graphics for the distant herd stuff [the stampeding herd of gallimimus dinosaurs]. But as the guys at ILM pushed the CG camera in closer the creatures really held up.' Tippett goes on,

> *Dennis Muren and I have been friends for years. I was aware of all the breakthroughs going on at ILM at the time and Dennis kept me in the loop. It was clear that they had reached the point where, technically speaking, somewhat photo-real images could be put on the screen. That said, when the edict came down from Steven that all dinos would be CG it took the wind out of my sails.*

The shock of digital animation taking over as the effect of the future was almost too much for Tippett. 'It was really hard for me because I thought it was all over with completely. I got pneumonia. I had people building big, giant motion-control rigs and had hundreds of thousands of dollars floating around. I had to pull the plug on it, and I could see everything going down the toilet.'[44] In *The Making of Jurassic Park* by Don Shay and Jody Duncan, Steven Spielberg remembers, 'At the showing [of the t. rex sequence], Phil groaned and pretty much declared himself extinct.'

But not all was lost.

> *I really did think for a few weeks that the rug had been pulled out, but everyone was very supportive and encouraged me to find a place in the brave new world of computer graphics. At the time most CG animators had been schooled in the so-called classic animation style of Disney – which was more conceptually based in two-dimensional animation. It's another kettle of fish doing animation that needs to be integrated into a photographic background with actors, so Dennis realized and championed the evolution of the Dinosaur Input Device (DID) that was the product of the work of Craig Hayes, Rick Sayer and Brian Knepp that allowed stop-motion animators at Tippett Studio to enter the CG world and that helped melt the glacial divide between conventional stop-mo and conventional CG animation that was being done at ILM.*

After it was decided to go with computer-generated images, Spielberg kept Tippett on to supervise the animation of fifty dinosaur shots for the film on which he acted as Dinosaur Supervisor, producing the dinosaur movements and supplying stop-motion footage on which the computer-generated imagery was based.

RIGHT
Phil Tippett with one of his most popular creations, the Taun-taun featured in *The Empire Strikes Back*.

Tippett recalls,

> *As I'd done a great deal of research re dinos, I was kind of the dino guy as we were mounting the show. Some of the critters needed to be swapped from what was in the book for dramatic and dynamic reasons so I was there for that. Dennis and I worked very closely with Steven designing the dino sequences, went on location for the backgrounds and made sure eye-lines and timings were going to work.*

After live- action photography Tippett returned to work with the animators at Tippett Studio and ILM to ensure that the dinosaurs' performances were accurate and at the same time cinematic. 'It all came back to all that knowledge being transferable from one set of tools to another, although in many ways I still find stop-mo more compelling to look at even if it isn't applicable for today's audience.'

For a while it was difficult to keep the studio afloat but he managed to by investing in new equipment and adapting to the new era.

For the third and disappointing outing of *RoboCop*, with the unoriginal title of *RoboCop 3* (1993), the credits on the film *and* the poster read 'Stop-Motion Animation Sequences Created by Phil Tippett'. After *Jurassic Park* Tippett's name was beginning to mean something to the publicists and the public. The film featured a number of animated models, including a welcome reappearance of the droid ED-209 (this time he is benevolent rather than malevolent), and a flying RoboCop. As with all Tippett's animation it is fluid, inventive and beautifully composited to give the illusion of reality.

Although *Dragonheart* (1996) was primarily a CG effects film Tippett designed the creature (along with Doug Henderson and Peter Konig) and Tippett Studios produced the dragon video animatics for the digital effects. In recent years Tippett has worked as a visual effects supervisor on such films as *Starship Troopers* (1997), *My Favorite Martian* (1999), *The Haunting* (1999), *Evolution* (2001) and *The Spiderwick Chronicles* (2008) even directing and co-producing *Starship Troopers 2: Hero of the Federation* (2004). He says:

> *I find that, depending on the show, I spend most of my time now in preparation and on the set, working with the production team devising a plan then executing it so that the shots will come together in a dynamic yet efficient way. On* Spiderwick *I focused more on the Creature characters design and approach. Tippett Studios and ILM split up the work so when it came to shooting the backgrounds on location in Montreal I would concentrate mostly on the creature coordination with various departments and Pablo Helman on the VFX aspects.*

No matter what the future holds, Phil Tippett's name will always stand out in the history of model animation as one of the great innovators: for his superior designs, for his attention to detail and for his versatile style of animation. Tippett obviously regrets the passing of what he sees as the traditional art of stop-motion animation.

> *As a viewer I find stop-motion more mysterious and compelling aesthetically. I think that part of it may have something to do with the focus and intensity of the performance – more like being on stage and having to get it right for the first time, rather than being able to continually rework a performance, or cutting around various performances editorially. That's because the stop-mo animator is generally more an author of the pantomime. CGI, at the scale used today, generally gets (whether deserved, informed, or not) input and changes from a lot of folk and with the current use of motion capture today many aspects of a performance cross the paths of many different performance craftsmen. There has been some terrific CG animation that could not have been executed with stop-mo but I find the strange combination of meditation and concentration required by stop-mo more amazingly simple as a thing to behold.*

CGI had arrived big time. The heyday of traditional model animation composited with live-action had passed. The pioneers, including Willis O'Brien had taken the mechanics of model stop-motion animation and developed it as far as the technical limits of the day allowed. Ray then took over the concept and developed it further by using a different approach and by steering the technique into new fields of entertainment. Then artists such as David Allen, Doug Beswick, Randy Scott, Dennis Muren and Phil Tippett took over from Ray and developed what he had started as far as they were able; then in the early 1990s, reluctantly (in some cases), discarded the old tried and tested methods of model animation in favour of computer-based techniques. Ray will say the computer is another tool in the animator's toolbox but there are those that truly feel that the soul of fantasy is no more since the demise of model animation.

ACHTUNG
HALT

CHAPTER SEVEN

AARDMAN ANIMATIONS, TIM BURTON AND OTHERS

'Something wicked this way hops.'[1]

'Stop-frame is like live music, played on traditional instruments, compared to a studio recording using the finest instruments in the world, all the latest technology and some electronic instruments. The latter is more polished, more perfect, bigger, better, showier – but maybe lacks humanity. Stop-frame is much less perfect, much less polished, unrepeatable, inaccurate – in a word, human. It all depends on whether the audience care or not about humanity.'

PETER LORD, AARDMAN ANIMATIONS

Model animation is most definitely not dead; on the contrary the art has come full circle, back to its origins, on both professional and amateur levels, with the use of puppets and miniature sets. With the advent of home digital video and computers it is now possible for anyone to experiment with both two- and three-dimensional animation, though the latter seems to be favoured by most amateurs, especially on the Internet. Clay figures and 'brick films' (animation with Lego mini-figures) seem the most popular at this particular point in time and we suspect that a whole new generation of animators are out there, experimenting and inventing, waiting for their chance to play a part in the art's amazing history. Most gratifyingly, in the commercial world, there are a large number of creative individuals, producers and companies who are using stop-motion animation to make critically acceptable and commercial shorts and feature films and it is the work of a selection of these artists, who have led the hundred-year-old technique into a new and wonderfully stylized world, that we intend to discuss, at least in part, in this final chapter.

As we saw in the previous chapter, the producer Tim Burton has championed the art by using it in several hugely successful films. He has remarked that,

> *There is an energy with stop-motion that you can't describe. It's got to do with giving things life, and I guess that's why I wanted to get into animation originally. To give life to something that doesn't have it is cool, and even more so in three dimensions, because, at least for me, it feels even more real. With the large Marge thing or dinosaur – any time we could throw in some stop-motion, the better. We could have had a lot more if they'd let us.*[2]

Burton was born in 1958 in Burbank, California and his reference to '[getting] into animation', refers back to his employment by Disney. In 1976, after leaving high school, Burton attended the California Institute of Arts, which had been founded by Disney as a 'breeding ground' for potential animators. Burton's talents lay in painting, drawing and his influences were, of course, movies (he particularly liked Hammer horror films, the Godzilla series and Ray's work). He decided to enter the Disney animation programme in his second year. In 1979 he joined the Disney staff, apparently because they were keen to have him on board, even though they didn't have a specific job for him. Eventually they made him a conceptual artist and he worked on films such as *The Fox and the Hound* (1981) and *The Black Cauldron* (1985). Recognizing a rare talent, Disney allowed him some leeway to develop his own projects and he came up with a poem and artwork for a project called *The Nightmare Before Christmas*, which was not made, and a stop-motion animated short called *Vincent* (1982). This was a tribute to Vincent Price and used clay characters; Burton recalled, 'On *Vincent* we weren't trying to push the boundaries of great animation. What we were trying to do with it, in a very simple way, was to be more specific with the design. To me, in claymation the design elements get lost. So what we wanted to do was what you do in a drawing, but just spring it to a third dimension.'[3] *Vincent* was followed by *Frankenweenie* (1984) about a boy who tries to bring his dog back to life.

Burton found that stop-motion animation was a wonderful tool that helped him to visualize his innovative, very personal and often dark dreams of bizarre and eccentric characters. In 1984 Burton made his first feature film, *Pee Wee's Big Adventure* (1985) in which Stephen Chiodo animated a character that transforms into a ghoul and also an intentionally bad, red tyrannosaurus rex that picks up Pee Wee's bicycle. The film was a surprise success and was followed by the hugely popular *Beetlejuice* (1988) in which Burton created a world of zany characters and creatures that included animated sandworms, a giant rattlesnake and two metal statues.

In 1991 Burton began production of his $18-million-dollar *The Nightmare Before Christmas* (1993), which was the first full-length film using model animation to be produced by Disney. Directed by Henry Selick, it is a flawed film but is nevertheless ground-breaking in its use of stop-motion to create the surreal worlds of Halloween and Christmas and the characters that occupy them. Burton was, of course, returning to that poem he had written all those years before and this time successfully, bringing to life the grotesque and outlandish atmosphere created by the inhabitants of Halloweenland where most of the story takes place. The graceful animation, always fluid and well conceived, was executed by a team of artists working in San Francisco, including Doug Beswick, Jim Aupperle, Erick Leighton, Rick Hendricks, Harry Walton and Justin Kohn. The film took nearly three years to make and 'contains 74 puppet characters, represented by nearly 300 puppets. One hundred and forty of these were fully armatured with the remainder being either wire-armatured or wire/ball-and-socket combinations.'[4] One hundred and fifty interchangeable heads were used to obtain the range of facial expression required. Burton recalled, 'The characters that were designed for *Nightmare* had the added burden of not having any eyeballs. The first rule of animation is "Eyes for Expression". But a lot of the characters either didn't have any eyes, or their eyes are sewn shut. I thought if we could give life to these characters that have no eyes, it would be great.'[5] The film was nominated for the American Academy ®Visual Effects award but stood little chance when up against *Jurassic Park*.

PREVIOUS SPREAD
Left, Nick Park (on left) and Peter Lord discuss the animation for *Chicken Run* (2000).
Right, Shakespeare as he appeared in Barry Purves' funny and innovative *Next* (1989).

ABOVE
Director and producer Tim Burton poses with the 'Bride' from *Corpse Bride* (2005).

RIGHT
Tim Burton again with some of the other characters from *Corpse Bride*.

Burton followed *Nightmare* with *James and the Giant Peach* (1996), a charming rather than surreal part-live-action, part-animation project based on the Roald Dahl story of an orphaned boy who lives with his two wicked aunts and discovers a giant peach which grows in the garden that leads him to a magical world occupied by talking bugs. It is a beautiful and extremely original film, though at the box office it proved a little too much for audiences. Henry Selick again directed with animation expertly executed by an even larger team of artists.

Burton's last animated film to date is perhaps the best of the three and has parallels with *The Nightmare Before Christmas* in as much the characters are ghoulish but strangely poignant and the 'hero' has to make a journey into the land of the dead. *Corpse Bride* (2005) is a strange title (I remember both of us wondering what on earth a film with such a title would be like) but the film is a superb tribute to the art of model animation and to Burton's particular strain of fantasy. Based on a nineteenth-century Russian-Jewish folktale, it tells the moving story of a romantic triangle formed by the nervous Victor, the downtrodden Victoria and Emily, the Corpse Bride. Again Burton and director Mike Johnson (who had worked as an animator on *The Nightmare Before Christmas*) assembled a huge team of animators and filmed the tale at 3 Mills Studios in London, where Ray visited during production. *Corpse Bride* has the distinction of being the first movie to be shot with still cameras, although the technique had been used before for stop-motion inserts in earlier movies. Stop-motion movies (such as Aardman Animations' *Chicken Run* (2000)) were shot on modified Mitchell film cameras, the same old cameras used to shoot *King Kong*. As confirmed by *American Cinematographer* (October 2005), the camera chosen for the production of *Corpse Bride* was the Canon EOS-1D Mark II, a digital single-lens reflex camera, which also makes it the first stop-motion feature to be shot in digital. *Corpse Bride* was also the first stop-motion film to use Apple's Final Cut Pro. To make the film look as if it had been shot on traditional film stock, each image was processed with a colour profile based on a type of film used for feature-length movies.

The models were made in Altrincham, near Manchester, England, by the leading puppet manufacturers Mackinnon and Saunders and the film was the first stop-motion animated movie to use the new 'gear and paddle' technique for the maquettes' heads. This involved building a complex gear system within the heads of the main characters to which 'paddles' were attached. A soft, skin-like cladding, mainly made of silicone and foam, was placed over the paddles to create the head and then painted. When the gears are operated by inserting an Allen key into small holes in the head or inside the ears, the paddles move, adjusting the facial expression of the character. This made possible much smoother changes of expression and improved lip-sync when compared with the use of replaceable heads. The soft 'skin' also gave the characters a much more natural look.

The film was nominated for a Best Animated Feature Oscar ® but lost again, this time to Aardman's *Wallace & Gromit: The Curse of the Were-Rabbit* (2006). In 2005 Burton was quoted as saying:

> *One of the reasons why I held out on both* Nightmare *and* Corpse Bride *to do it in this medium [stop-motion] is that it felt right for these particular stories. There's something very emotional about the process when it's hand made.*

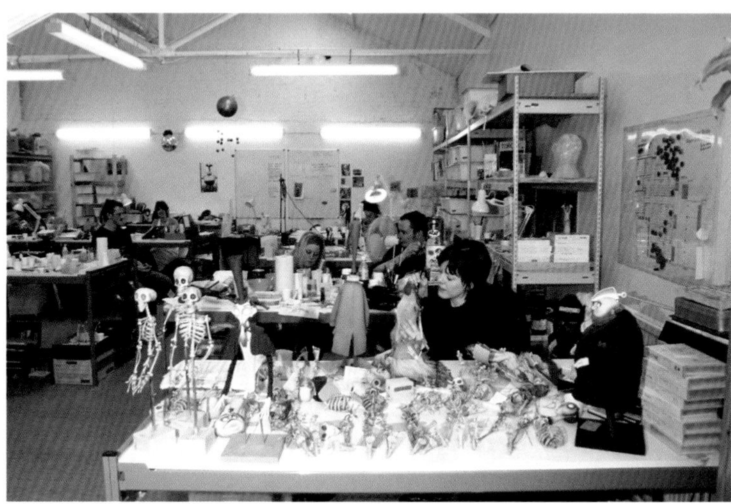

ABOVE
Various scenes of animation and model construction for *Corpse Bride*.

You can see these puppets and the artistry and the beauty for which they're made. The sets and all, you try to marry the medium and the project.

He went on to say, 'We even experimented with people who did computers and they said, "Oh we'd love to do *Corpse Bride*, we'd love to do a test." They did a test and it was very nice looking but it didn't have that raw, primal thing that stop-motion has.'[6]

Burton's passion for traditional stop-motion does not seem to show any signs of abating as he now planning an update of his 1984 short *Frankenweenie* using model animation.

One of the most prominent contemporary independent animators, and there are lots out there, is Barry Purves. His forte is the short film, although he has been involved with a number of features, including Burton's *Mars Attacks!* (1996) as the original Animation Director, and *King Kong* (2005) as the Previz Animation Director in New Zealand. Since 1986, Purves has also directed and animated some seventy commercials, title sequences, animation inserts for films and pop promos, through Aardman Animations, Redwing, overseas agencies, the BBC and his own company, Bare Boards.

Born in Woodridge in Suffolk, England in 1955 Barry J.C. Purves had no formal training in animation but studied drama at the University of Manchester, hoping to become an actor. He now says, 'It was immediately clear that there were better actors than me, but I still had the performance urge, and as animators, we are all performers.' As an animator he now realizes that he has been able to perform 'a much wider range of characters and genres than I would have had if I had made it as a successful actor'.

His primary influences come from the theatre rather than film. 'Theatre is freer because it asks so much of the audience's imagination, to use lighting, design, movement and all those elements to be part of the narrative.' His film influences range from *Mary Poppins* (1964) to *The Birds* (1963). And his favourite animated moment? 'Well that is still Ray's Talos from *Jason and the Argonauts* for so many sublime reasons.' His opportunity to enter the world of animation came when Mark Hall, of Cosgrove Hall Films[7] was visiting the theatre where Purves was working. Cosgrove Hall was filming *Cholton and the Wheelies* (1976) (an animated television series) at the time, and 'after some very enthusiastic correspondence

TOP LEFT
A scene from Barry Purves' *Gilbert & Sullivan: The Very Models* (1998).

TOP RIGHT
Barry Purves with the model of Shakespeare in a glitzy sunburst, appearing as the god Juno at the end of his play *Cymbeline*, as seen in the film *Next* (1989). In actual fact it was a 1950s clock that Purves had found in a skip.

ABOVE LEFT
Purves animating the two central characters featured in the unique and very special *Achilles* (1995).

ABOVE RIGHT
Achilles holding the dead Patroclus in *Achilles*.

from me, Mark gave me a chance to work for the studios'. At Cosgrove Hall he was involved with a number of television projects, including *The Pied Piper of Hamelin* (1981) and the *Wind in the Willows* (1984). He then went to Aardman Animations and made *Next* (1989) along with a number of commercials and television pilots. *Next* was a landmark in Purves' career. It was commissioned by the UK television company Channel 4 as part of the *Lip-Synch* series (alongside Nick Park's *Creature Comforts*) and is a tribute to the performing arts. It shows a struggling actor called Will (William Shakespeare) auditioning for a theatre director called Peter, who is obviously based on Sir Peter Hall. It is a delightfully funny, though respectful, tribute to the theatre and acting; Purves not only animated the superbly designed models but also wrote the screenplay.

When he left Aardman Purves formed his own company – Bare Boards – to write, direct and animate *Screen Play* (1992) for Channel 4, *Rigoletto* (1993) for the Welsh National Opera/S4C/BBC2 and, for Channel 4 again, *Achilles* (1995), perhaps his most innovative and original film to date. This remarkable film, set during the Trojan War, tells of the Greek warrior Achilles, his friendship with Patroclus and his revenge on Hector when Patroclus is killed. Set in a starkly lit arena surrounded by total darkness the models are beautifully and stylishly made, like Greek statues, and the fluid animation along with the concentrated lighting provides the powerful story with a great deal of atmosphere. Purves also considers the film his best work:

> *I tried to give puppets a certain gravitas, dealing with adult themes without raising laughter. Thanks to the beautiful puppets of Mackinnon Saunders, the dramatic lighting of Paul Smith, and design work from Liz Scrine and Barbara Biddulph it is a very rich looking film. Hopefully it tells its story differently from any other film, and is decently animated and directed. A shame those characters are dead as I would have liked to explore their psyche in more detail. Certainly I would love to return to the Greeks again one day.*

Other distinguished projects for which Purves has been responsible are a sixteen-minute film for Channel 4 called *Gilbert & Sullivan: The Very Models* (1998) and *Hamilton Mattress* (2001), a thirty-minute Christmas special for the BBC about

Sludger, an aardvark. Occasionally he has returned to Cosgrove Hall to work on projects such as *Rupert and Friends*, a fifty-two part animated series and in 2007 he wrote a book on animation called *Stop-Motion (and other strange habits)*. He retains a passionate enthusiasm for stop-motion:

> *Stop-motion is a gloriously selfish medium. The audience don't need to know the pleasure we receive from animating in a studio, enjoying the characters come to life in our hands, but that is definitely part of the reason we enjoy it. Stop-motion is also the most intimate form of animation – for all the discussion and storyboards, when it comes down to it, just one pair of hands control a particular puppet, and that directness has to be beneficial for the performance. Well, it gives it a spontaneity and quirkiness that the other techniques don't have. Stop-motion allows for some little unexpected moments that make the character live. Any CG performance is usually the result of a team effort and, without a really on-the-ball director, things can get lost. Stop-motion will never look real, and I'm not sure it needs to these days. We have seen how perfect and fluidly CG reproduces the illusion of real life. Stop-motion enjoys being different. Of course CG is so good at fine tuning and correcting, and duplicating, but I wonder if a CG animator gets the same pleasure that we do from sweating away under hot lights, breaking our backs as we contort ourselves into odd positions around the cameras to move small puppets. I don't think CG and stop-motion will cancel each other out as we can now see what each technique is best at.*

Aardman Animations Ltd, or Aardman Studios, is a phenomenon. They have without doubt done more than any other production company to make international movie audiences aware of model animation. Their films, like those of Burton and Purves, are pure animation and on the whole involve no live action; but the originality, comic characterizations and sheer inventiveness of each of their films, whether shorts or features, is truly sensational.

Aardman was formed in 1972 by Peter Lord and David Sproxton (the name came from a character they had created for the BBC cartoon series *Vision On* (1965-1976)). Peter Lord was born in 1953 in Bristol, England and met Sproxton (who was born in 1954) at school in the early 1970s, when both discovered a fascination for all forms of animation and began experimenting. They were lucky to be able to use a professional camera, a 16mm Bolex, because Sproxton's father was an amateur photographer and a BBC producer. Lord recalls that, 'His dad had all the gear. A clockwork 16mm Bolex, a developing stand (later a tripod) and a couple of photographic lights.' He goes on,

> *We shot cut-outs and used chalk drawings, more as a way of whiling away wet Sundays than with any real intention. We didn't really have a plan but we did enjoy seeing our stuff coming to life on the screen. This all took place at my house where we had more room that Pete (spare room, attic etc) and a garage full of junk rather than cars. I also recall playing with back projection, using a 16mm projector, footage from Jodrell Bank*[8] *and toy soldiers set up in front of a small screen, all in my bedroom (yes, it was cramped).*

Lord remembers that they tried all forms of animation, including two- and three-dimensional work. 'Our first films were 2-D. We experimented with any technique that was more or less easy, low-tech and fast. So that included animated chalk drawings, cut-outs and object animation. We also had some classic teenage fun with pixilation[9] – getting our friends to "fly" around in a field.' They began their professional animation careers while still in their teens when Patrick Dowling, a BBC children's television producer, offered them the opportunity to make short animated films for his programme *Vision On*.

Vision On, a series that had a devoted family following, had begun in 1965 and was a wonderful opportunity for both young men. Working on the last four series (1972-1976) they carried out a number of tasks, including thirteen two-dimensional drawn sequences featuring the Aardman character for one series. Lord takes up the story:

> *Our first broadcast work was of course the very first cartoon (2-D) featuring Aardman himself. Our last experiments in the schoolboy years were with traditional cel animation. We did a cel sequence where Aardman – our superhero character – falls down an invisible hole. It lasted twenty seconds and it was a pretty good idea. So we thought we had a career here, and we made over the next year maybe ten more drawn animated films of Aardman.*

The films were basic and very straightforward, but it was 'hard work and not terribly rewarding'. That was their first year with *Vision On*. Then they hit on the idea of making model-animated films. Lord goes on,

> *Then we hit on the idea of doing 3-D work. We used Plasticine because it was cheap, low-tech and available (we had no idea how to make an armatured puppet – not for years). Suddenly we found that instead of being small fish in a worldwide pond of 2-D animation we were – well, the only fish in an entirely new pond – the clay animation world'.*

Sproxton recalls,

> *We started using Plasticine in a bas-relief sort of way, then we made little figures and shot two or three little model sequences featuring a pair of incompetent burglars. Following that we came up with the Gleebies for* Why Don't You Switch Off Your Television Set and Do Something More Interesting Instead *(1976) (shortened to* Why Don't You....*), which was the sister show of* Vision On. *The Gleebies were simple, long-snouted creatures who went around in a mob causing mayhem and which led eventually to Morph.*

BOTTOM LEFT
David Sproxton posing with the model of Morph featured in the television series *Take Hart* circa 1980.

BELOW, TOP PICTURE
David Sproxton (on left) and Peter Lord animating a man in a dustbin for a sequence to be featured in the BBC series *Vision On* circa 1972.

BELOW, BOTTOM PICTURE
David Sproxton (on left) and Peter Lord with the puppets featured in their film *Babylon* (1986) at an Aardman retrospective at *Le Festival du Dessin Animé* in the Palais des Congrès in Brussels on 11 February 1986.

BELOW CENTRE
Confessions of a Foyer Girl (1978)

BELOW RIGHT, TOP PICTURE
Down & Out (1977).

BELOW RIGHT, BOTTOM PICTURE
Peter Lord with his lead character who features in *Adam* (1991)

Having registered the Aardman name and received their first pay cheques for their work on *Vision On* they both went off to university (Lord to York in North Yorkshire and Sproxton to Durham in North East England) and in the summer breaks they filmed further batches of shorts for *Vision On*.

When they both graduated in 1976, Aardman moved to a permanent home in Bristol, initially to continue their work on *Vision On*, but when the BBC cancelled the show they produced shorts, trailers and commercials. Then came *Take Hart* (1977), another children's series for the BBC, and it was for that programme that the two came up with characters that included the TinPots and Morph, a Plasticine character that really set the seal on the future of the company by becoming a huge hit. It was towards the end of their work on *Take Hart* that Sproxton gave up hands-on animation to concentrate on production and camera work. As the company got bigger he directed and photographed (mostly on commercials etc) whilst Lord directed and animated.

Lord and Sproxton then expanded into adult animation, making two short films, *Down and Out* (1977) and *Confessions of a Foyer Girl* (1978), which they co-directed for the BBC series *Animated Conversations* and which uniquely combined real-life conversational soundtracks with model animation. In 1980 Aardman made the twenty-six part television series *The Amazing Adventures of Morph*, which was again a huge BBC children's success. In 1984 another British television network company, Channel 4, transmitted five more sophisticated shorts for their series, called *Conversation Pieces*, which were *On Probation* (1981), *Sales Pitch* (1983), *Palmy Days* (1983), *Early Bird* (1983) and *Late Edition* (1983) which were shot on 16mm, co-directed by Lord and Sproxton and again combined real-life audio with animation.

Aardman was by now gaining a reputation for originality and quality and when the singer Peter Gabriel approached Lord and Sproxton to make a music video, to be called *Sledgehammer* (1986), they readily agreed and it became another ground-breaking experience. Peter Lord, who animated almost everything at Aardman for many years, including Morph, *Animated Conversations*, *Conversation Pieces*, *Lip-Sync* films and TV commercials, continued to produce shorts that included *Adam* (1991) a six-minute claymation film which he directed and produced. The film was nominated for an American Academy Award ® and British Academy Award but didn't win – 'It was exciting while it lasted.' Lord recalls its conception and production.

> Adam *was made on spec – those were the days. We were a small, very successful studio – there were probably twelve of us. We made a lot of commercials, but it was getting harder to make a series like* Lip-Synch. *So I had animated and directed commercials for three or four years, and I fancied a break. One summer holiday I roughed out a storyboard, then worked it up over the next few months and made the film that winter. Part of my thinking was this: Morph had been enormously successful, and I thought – and think still – that it had some of the most sophisticated animation and cleverest ideas of its day in children's TV. But, very annoyingly to me, it was never taken 'seriously' at animation festivals because it was 'for kids'. Its whole style and*

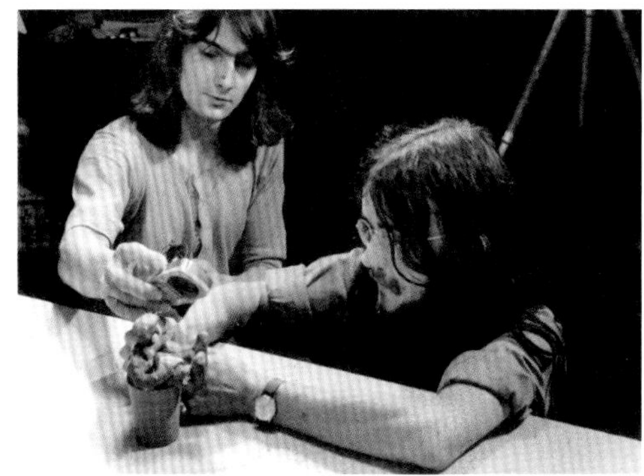

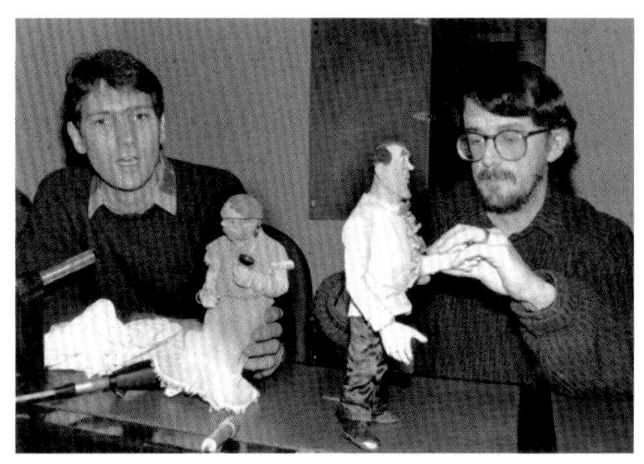

appearance and Tony Hart's voiceover somehow made it impossible for adults to enjoy.

So basically my plan was to do an elaborate Morph sequence but set in a context – with a visual language, which would make it acceptable to an adult audience. Adam's relationship with God was a more colourful and passionate version of Morph and Tony Hart! It was an opportunity to play with all the things I love – notably an English style of full-body performance at once exaggerated and understated if that makes any sense. Adam wasn't Morph – but he did share many of Morph's character traits. The shoot was a pleasure because there were very few different set-ups. Most of the film is set in exactly the same place, so to change shots all I could do was zoom in or out, refocus, and then I was off animating. Animators love to animate, and we love to concentrate. It's a lovely feeling when you've got a good scene ahead of you, you know pretty clearly what you're going to do, you have no distractions and all day just to do it (pausing only to drink tea and, on certain very happy occasions, listen to test match cricket on the radio). Bliss. As I say it was made on spec – because we could afford to – and bought and shown by the BBC.

Lord went on to produce and animate *Wat's Pig* (1996), based loosely on the story of The Prince and the Pauper, which was a more formal commission from Channel 4. Lord goes on,

In a similar way, a few years had passed without me directing anything, so Wat's Pig *was like a creative adventure holiday. The original idea was that it should all be the parallel stories of two twins – but rapidly I accepted that this idea was just folly – because it would have involved twice as much animation. Again, the idea came to me on holiday. My regret is that because of the timing of the production the split-screen was achieved in a very old-fashioned way – by film optical. I mean that the technology existed to edit and composite the film digitally, but that technology was relatively new and relatively super-expensive. It would have been about two hundred times easier to have done it today, digitally, because then I could have effected the edit so much more precisely. As it was, it was one of those projects where you only see your film finally edited, when it's all over and too late to change. Editing the split-screen was a real leap in the dark. Still, I love the look. Maybe I should go back and do a Director's Cut?*

It was around 1985 that Lord and Sproxton decided to hire more animators. Three of the newcomers made their directorial debut at Aardman with Channel 4's *Lip-Synch* (1989) series, all shot on 35mm 'as we had grown up by then'. Two of the shorts were directed and animated by Peter Lord (*Going Equipped* and *War Story*), one by Barry Purves (*Next*), one by Richard Goleszowski (*Ident*) and one by Nick Park (*Creature Comforts*). The entire series was seen as a pioneering event, but it was *Creature Comforts* that seemed to strike a chord with the public. Park's stylized models were animals who talked about their life in a zoo and he won the 1990 Best Animated Short Subject Oscar ® for the film. The film would also lead to a series of similar commercials called 'Heat Electric' for the British Electricity Association and Chevron.

Nicholas Wulstan Park was born in Preston, Lancashire, England in 1958 and his fascination with animation started early. 'I was born and grew up in Lancashire, England where my parents and teachers recognized an ability to draw. Their encouragement gave me a sense of pride and spurred me on to continue drawing. Combined with my love of art, I used to enjoy writing stories in English lessons, especially ones with a strong comedy theme. Basically, I just wanted to make people laugh.' His father, who was a photographer, was able to answer some of the his son's question about animation and, borrowing his mother's standard 8mm camera, which luckily had a single-frame button, he began filming amateur cartoon films at age thirteen in his parents' attic, beginning with a character called Walter the Rat. Sadly the film was lost at the laboratories, but nothing daunted, he went on to make a two-minute film with felt cut-outs called *Rat and the Beanstalk*. After experimenting with all types of animation he entered the BBC's Young Animator's Film Competition which he didn't win, and as a result, at age fifteen he feared that he had reached the end of the road and that, 'someone like me could never get into the film industry'. Plasticine became his preferred medium for animation.

Plasticine was available when I was a teenager and started doing animation. I wanted to be like Disney, trying to film with plastic cels, but it was all too expensive. I didn't have enough money to buy cels, at least not enough to make more that four-and-half seconds of animation. But Plasticine was around, user-friendly and available to the masses. It was great because all you needed was a camera, an Anglepoise lamp and a table. And you would make whatever you like come out of a blob of Plasticine'

Aged seventeen he produced his first animated short called *Archie's Concrete Nightmare* (1975).[10] He studied Communication Arts at the Sheffield City Polytechnic (now the Sheffield Hallam University) where he opted to specialize in animation for the last two years. Using a 16mm camera for the first time, he made two model-animated films and one film using chalk on a blackboard called *Jack and the Beanstalk*, which won a student prize. He was then accepted at the National Film and Television School (NFTS) at Beaconsfield near London; it was there that he met Lord and Sproxton when he invited them to speak to the students. Lord and Sproxton were impressed with Park and after graduating he was invited to work at the studio.

Park's first job was to work on David Hopkins' anti-war film *Babylon* (1986), he also had a part in animating the television series *Pee-wee's Playhouse* (1986) and contributed a dancing chicken sequence to the music video *Sledgehammer*. With the success of *Creature Comforts* he next wanted to complete a film he had begun at the NFTS, which he had called *A Grand Day Out* (1991). When Park moved to Aardman he agreed with the NFTS that they would continue to fund the completion of the film whilst he used Aardman's facilities between 'official' projects. Written and directed by Park, *A Grand Day Out* introduces us to Wallace, an eccentric Lancastrian inventor (based on his father) and his long-suffering dog, Gromit. Wallace has a passion for cheese and when they discover their supply has run out he builds a spaceship to take them to the moon because 'everyone knows it's made of cheese'. The characters were all made of Plasticine and possessed little round eyes, big noses and long narrow mouths (Park's trademark) and Wallace was voiced by British actor Peter Sallis whilst Gromit remained silent. In total, the film took six years to make and had the distinction of winning a British Academy of Film & Television Arts (Bafta) award. The following year the film was nominated for an Oscar ® at the same time as Park's *Creature Comforts*. The latter won. Park's ability to instil distinctive comic personality and

LEFT TOP
Wat's Pig (1996)

LEFT BOTTOM
War Story (1989)

TOP RIGHT
Replacement mouths for Wallace.

TOP FAR RIGHT
One of the model-makers painting a Jacobs Cream Cracker package for one of the Wallace and Gromit films.

RIGHT
Animation in progress for *Creature Comforts* (1989).

FAR RIGHT
Creature Comforts (1989)

BELOW
Wallace and Gromit in *A Grand Day Out* (1989).

BELOW RIGHT
Wallace struggling with his mechanical trousers in *The Wrong Trousers* (1993), and Nick Park animating a scene from the same film.

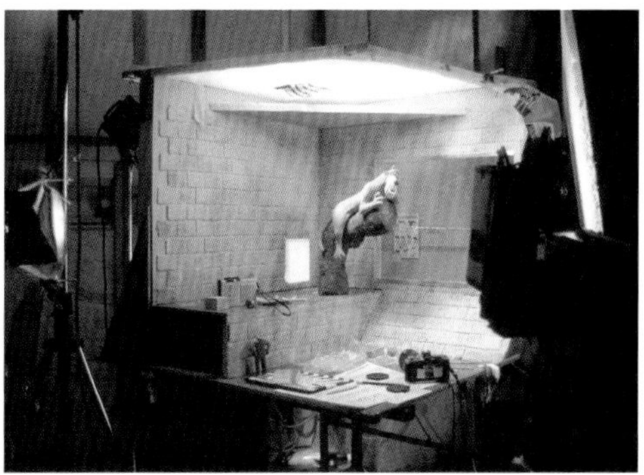

quirky British touches into his animation adds another dimension to his creations, which is undoubtedly why his work is so popular.

The success of the film led the BBC to commission two more Wallace and Gromit exploits. *The Wrong Trousers* (1993) was executive-produced by Lord and it introduced animator Steve Box to the team. It is a wonderfully evocative homage to *film noir* and other iconic movie genres. The two main characters take in a mysterious lodger, a penguin, who uses Wallace's invention of mechanical 'techno-trousers' to carry out a diamond heist. Writing with Bob Baker, Park allowed his characters to achieve an even higher degree of eccentricity and, even more importantly, created a self-contained world based on his North of England background. The film's influences are most prominent during the final chase sequence set on the top of train, reminiscent of so many train chases including Herbert Ross's *The*

ABOVE
A Close Shave (1995)

ABOVE RIGHT
Two scenes of Nick Park at work. Top, filming a sequence for *Chicken Run* (2000) and, below, with Andy Symanowski (on left) looking at some of their animation during the filming of *Wallace & Gromit: The Curse of the Were-Rabbit* (2005).

FACING PAGE, TOP
The three Aardman greats in 2005. From left to right, Peter Lord, David Sproxton and Nick Park.

FACING PAGE, BOTTOM
Nick Park at work on *Wallace & Gromit: The Curse of the Were-Rabbit* (2005). Behind him are, from left to right, Loyd Price, Tom Barnes and David Alex Riddett.

Seven Per Cent Solution (1976) and Michael Crichton's *The First Great Train Robbery* (1978). The film won Park and Aardman their second American Academy Award ® and another Bafta award.

Park's second film in the BBC package, again co-written with Bob Baker, was *A Close Shave* (1995). It again featured Wallace and Gromit – the public couldn't get enough of them and by now the two characters had become a British institution. The film introduced another worthy addition to the Aardman menagerie, Shaun the Sheep, who looks like a poodle-trimmed lamb. Shaun would get his own television series in 2007. This time Park conceded that he could not complete the film for the BBC within the scheduled eighteen months working by himself so he had the assistance of some twenty-five staff, including animators and model-makers, although he had overall control. He personally re-enacted scenes, recorded on video, of how the characters would play out their scenes which the other animators could follow, so keeping a smooth and fluid formula throughout production. Park himself animated the key sequences. This time influences from other films such as *Brief Encounter* (1945) and various science-fiction adventures, for example *The Terminator* (1984), are also evident and the film is again a slick and very funny piece of homage to movie classics. Park also added a further touch of character when Wallace falls for Wendolene, a female doppelganger of himself.

Aardman signed a picture deal with Steven Spielberg's company DreamWorks in 1999 to produce five feature films. The first off the drawing board was *Chicken Run* (2001), which was perhaps a throwback to Park's employment as a teenager in a chicken-packing factory. Co-directed by Lord and Park, the film is a send-up of *The Great Escape* (1963), with the humans replaced by humanized fowl. It is set in a large chicken coop, specifically Coop 17 (again a reference to Billy Wilder's *Stalag 17* (1953)), where a group of chickens, led by newcomer Rocky, formulate a plot to escape the knife of Mrs Tweedy before they end up as chicken pies. The model designs are wonderfully stylized with the usual mouths (in this case beaks) broad and flat and with individualized crests to distinguish the characters. A great deal of effort clearly went into giving each bird a real character and the animation is, as always, smooth and believably fluid, even though there are occasionally some twenty or more models in a single scene. Gratifyingly, the film was an unqualified critical and commercial success.

Aardman initially announced that the second film in the DreamWorks deal would be *Tortoise Vs Hare*, an adaptation of the Aesop fable that was earmarked to be directed by Richard Goleszowski. After eighteen months of pre-production the decision was taken to postpone the project, citing 'script problems and an over-accelerated pre-production schedule'.[11] Ray talked with Nick Park about the project when we launched our first book at the National Film Theatre in London and Park watched Ray's version of the fable after the on-stage chat.[12]

Instead, Aardman decided to make another Wallace and Gromit adventure but this time as a feature-length project, *Wallace & Gromit: The Curse of the Were-Rabbit* (2005). Co-directed by Park and Steve Box and co-written by Park and Bob Baker the film is light hearted but a very respectful tribute to the horror genre. Wallace has invented an 'Anti-Pesto' machine, a contraption that humanely captures and disposes of rabbits. As the Giant Vegetable Competition approaches the creatures are becoming a real pest so Wallace and Gromit are called in. Suddenly, an enormous beast attacks the town's vegetable patches and local aristocrat Lady Tottington employs the dynamic duo to save the day. Each of the film's characters required a number of heads to allow the animator to cover the wide rang of emotions. For example, there were 43 versions of Gromit, 35 of Wallace, 15 of Lady Tottington and 16 of Lady Tottington's suitor, Victor Quartermaines, and in addition there were 20 shaped mouths to cover the dialogue. It was reported that the entire production required 2.8 tons of Plasticine and that there were thirty miniature sets, some of which Ray and Tony visited during the production. Each set was beautifully detailed, especially Lady Tottington's house, her conservatory and the church. Two hundred and fifty technicians worked on the production for nearly five years to produce an average of five seconds of footage a day. *Wallace and Gromit: The Curse of the Were-Rabbit* is a wonderful romp in the world of English gardening eccentricity and outrageous characterization.

In 2007 the BBC commissioned another Wallace and Gromit tale which became *A Matter of Loaf and Death*.

Aardman Animations is without doubt the most original and most commercial animation studio in the world. Its output is extremely British though, perhaps surprisingly, this has not prevented the films it has produced from being commercial successes worldwide. Although their most famous characters are without doubt Wallace and Gromit, each film is unique. Park, Lord and Sproxton, stand now as icons for a new generation. Park has remarked that 'My animation has developed over the years but my fascination for the magic of animation which began at thirteen has remained unchanged.'

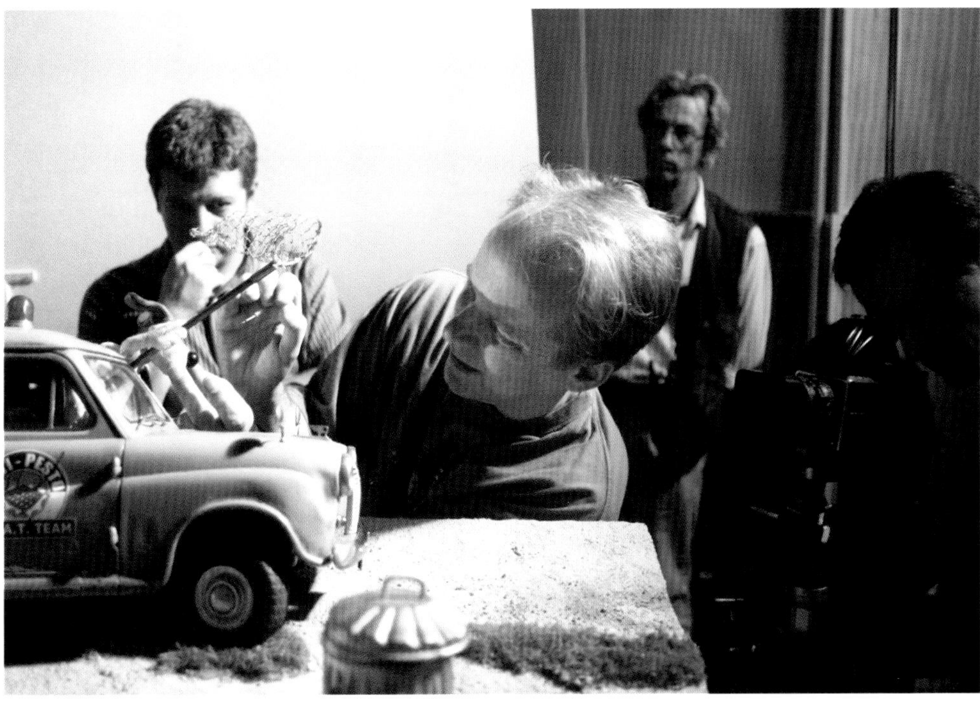

EPILOGUE

When model animation began with films like *The 'Teddy' Bears* back in 1907, it was thought that the technique would never find much use beyond the animation of toys for children's films or family subjects. Today, we can see that, although it has now come full circle, back to puppet characters, albeit very sophisticated puppets, it has also left a rich and enduring legacy that embraces a range of subjects far wider than the pioneers would have believed possible. The world would not have been the same if King Kong, The Cyclops, Medusa and Wallace and Gromit hadn't been possible.

Just as Ray walked in the footsteps of Willis O'Brien and the other pioneers, there are now a dedicated group of artists who want to continue the traditions of the art of stop-motion animation, finding new styles and subjects in which to use the technique and so keep the personal touch that enables their creations to always appear original, real and three-dimensional. As suggested elsewhere in this book, CG is a wonderful thing but the hands-on approach, which led to the computerized imagery, created some memorable films and 'stars' and continues to do so.

Bibliography

Archer, Steve, *Willis O'Brien: Special Effects Genius*, McFarland & Co, 1993.

Cox, Prof. Barry, Savage, Prof. R.J.G., Gardiner, Prof. Brian and Dixon, Douglas, *The Illustrated Encyclopedia of Dinosaurs and Prehistoric Animals*, Macmillan, London, 1988.

Czerkas, Stephen, *Cine-Saurus: The History of Dinosaurs in the Movies*, The Dinosaur Museum, Blandings, Utah, 2006.

Dunn, Linwood G., ASC, 'Creating Film Magic for the Original King Kong', *American Cinematographer*, January 1977.

Frank, Mark, 'The Stop-Motion World of Jim Danforth', *Photon magazine No 21*, 1971.

Gebhard, Nathan, Marriner, Mike and Gordon, Joanne, *Roadtrip Nation: A Guide to Discovering Your Path in Life*, Ballantine Books.

Goldner, Orville and Turner, George E., *The Making of King Kong*, Ballantine Books, 1975.

Grafton, Donald, *Before Mickey: the Animated Film, 1898-1928*, University of Chicago Press, 1982.

Hammond, Paul, *Marvellous Méliès*, Gordon Fraser, 1974

Hartlaub, Peter, 'Phil Tippett a Special-Effects Pioneer', *San Francisco Chronicle*, 19 February 2008.

Hickman, Gail Morgan, *The Films of George Pal*, A.S. Barnes & Co, 1977.

Jones, Stephen, *The Illustrated Dinosaur Movie Guide*, Titan Books. 1993.

MacQueen, Scott, 'The Lost World: Merely Misplaced?', *American Cinematographer*, June 1992,

Méliès, Georges, *Mage et 'Mes Mémoires' par Méliès*, Prisma, Paris, 1945.

Murcury, Miron, *Willis O'Brien: The Oaklander Who Created King Kong*, souvenir brochure for an exhibition of paintings, sculpture and photographs at the Kaiser Center Art Gallery in March/April 1984.

Musser, Charles, *The Emergence of Cinema: The American Screen to 1907*, University of California Press, 1990.

Payant, Felix (Ed), *The Book of Puppetry*, Design Publishing Co, 1936.

Pettigrew, Neil, *The Stop-Motion Filmography (1999)*, McFarland & Co, 1999.

Shay, Don, 'Willis O'Brien, Creator of the Impossible', *Focus on Film. No 16*, Autumn 1973,

Shay, Don and Duncan, Jody, *The Making of Jurassic Park*, Ballantine Books, 1993.

The dates of all film releases given in the text were referenced in the current edition of *Halliwell's Film & Video Guide*, HarperCollins.

Notes

Chapter 1

1 It is usually accepted that 35mm silent film ran at 16 frames per second, although film historian Kevin Brownlow has recently carried out research that possibly shows that some silent films were shot at 24 frames per second. In any event, Ray was told by Obie that it took less time to shoot the animation for *The Lost World* than for *Kong* or *Mighty Joe Young*, which suggests that he was shooting at 16 frames per second.

2 We were forced to make these calculations from the DVD. A television, video tape or DVD often runs at 25 frames per second so these timings may not exactly represent the time it took Ray to complete the animation, but are nonetheless a useful approximation.

3 A matte is simply a sheet of glass on which an area is painted matt black to prevent light from reaching the film stock in the camera. Part of another image, in this case on the rear-projection screen, will later go into the unexposed area to create a composite image.

4 The glass would have a mark on the left-hand side to ensure it was always inserted correctly.

5 A lightbox is a semi-translucent sheet of glass or Perspex that is lit from behind to enable transparencies to be viewed or, in this case, matte glasses to be painted.

Chapter 2

1 Musser, *The Emergence of Cinema*.

2 Just before the completion of this book new evidence came to light that may suggest that Dawley was more important in the history of stop-motion animation than previously thought. Palaeontologist, animator and film historian Stephen Czerkas discovered a cache of films that included one reel (850 feet) of *Along the Moonbeam Trail* (1920), which had previously been thought to be lost. Stephen informs us that the footage contains 'the flying dragon/pterosaur attacking a plane' and a 'stegosaur sequence as well as the battle between the tyrannosaur and the duckbill dinosaur'. These may have been designed and animated by Dawley or, as previously thought, designed and animated by O'Brien for *The Ghost of Slumber Mountain* and not used for that film. In short, we do not know, and as we have not had the opportunity to view the footage we are forced to go with what we have already written about these two films. Stephen concludes his notes to us by writing, 'There are composite shots (all the same setups) in which people in a cave are seen looking out at dinosaurs.' If this is so, then this film combined live-action with model animation several years before O'Brien did so in *The Lost World* (1925). But nonetheless, we would still stick by our view that *The Lost World* was the first commercial film to use composite shots in many different and innovative ways.

3 Pettigrew, *The Stop-Motion Filmography*.

4 Taken from notes and scrapbooks lodged at The Seaver Center for Western History Research at the Natural History Museum of Los Angeles County. The films Roop's grand-daughter mentions - *The Great Glory*, *Black Cyclone*, *Tarzan's Return*, *The Gorilla Hunt* - are likely to be *The Greater Glory* (1926), *Black Cyclone* (1925), *The Revenge of Tarzan* [aka *The Return of Tarzan*] (1920) and *The Gorilla Hunt* (1928).

Chapter 3

1 Letter from Darlyne O'Brien to Don Shay dated 18 January1965.

2 Letter from Darlyne O'Brien to Don Shay dated 12 September 1963.

3 A press release, or at least a draft release, dated 1916 written by The Edison Studios, New York. It was sent to Don Shay by Darlyne O'Brien who had found it among Obie's effects.

4 Just as we were completing this book, prints of various Dawley films, including *Along the Moonbeam Trail* have been discovered by Stephen Czerkas who has seen the film and has advised us that there appears to be a scene or scenes that show a combination of animation and live-action in the same frame. See notes to Chapter 2, note 2.

5 Interview with Marcel Delgado by Don Shay, April 1973.

6 Letter from Marcel Delgado to Don Shay, November 1963.

7 *Cinefex magazine*, January 1984

8 *Cinefex* magazine, January 1984

9 *Cinefex* magazine, January 1984

10 Interview with Marcel Delgado by Don Shay, April 973.

11 Letter from Darlyne O'Brien to Don Shay dated 29 August 1963.

12 Transcript notes of conversations with Darlyne O'Brien by Val Warren dated 1964, loaned to us by Don Shay.

13 Letter from Darlyne O'Brien to Don Shay dated 22 April 1965.

14 Letter from Darlyne O'Brien to Don Shay dated 19 January 1964.

15 Letter from Mario Larrinaga to Don Shay dated 30 June1967.

16 Letter from Mario Larrinaga to Don Shay dated 30 June 1967.

17 From Goldner and Turner, *The Making of King Kong*.

18 Letter from Marcel Delgado to Don Shay dated 12 December 1963.

19 Letter from Mario Larrinaga to Don Shay dated 30 June 1967.

20 Transcript notes of conversations with Darlyne O'Brien by Val Warren dated 1964, loaned to us by Don Shay.

21 Letter from Darlyne O'Brien to Don Shay dated 12 September 1963.

22 *Cinefex* magazine, January 1984.

23 Transcript notes of conversations with Darlyne O'Brien by Val Warren dated 1964, loaned to us by Don Shay.

24 *Cinefex* magazine, January 1984.

25 Darlyne O'Brien quoted in Archer, *Willis O'Brien*.

26 Sent by Darlyne O'Brien to Don Shay on 23 March 1964.

27 Letter from Darlyne O'Brien to Don Shay dated 17 December 1966.

28 Letter from Darlyne O'Brien to Don Shay dated 19 January 1964.

29 Letter from Marcel Delgado to Don Shay dated November 1963.

30 Letter from Merian C. Cooper to Don Shay dated 10 March 1964.

Chapter 4

1 Ray Harryhausen, 2007.

2 The apatosaurus was a member of the diplodocus family.

3 This was made by the British company October Films for the network station Channel 4 and the title was chosen to cash in on the BBC's CGI series *Walking With Dinosaurs*.

Chapter 5

1 The Fleisher Studios were a Disney rival, producing animated cartoon shorts and some features. The company was run by Max Fleisher who had created such popular cartoons figures as Betty Boop, Koko , the *Out of the Inkwell* series and, most famously, Popeye the Sailor. In 1939, the same year that Disney released *Snow White and the Seven Dwarfs*, Fleisher also released their first feature, *Gulliver's Travels*, followed in 1941 by *Mr Bug Goes to Town* [aka *Hoppity Goes to Town*]. Max's brother, Dave Fleisher, was the administrator of the business and the director Richard Fleisher is Max's son.

2 Hickman, *The Films of George Pal*.

3 Hickman, *The Films of George Pal*.

4 Madison, who was uncredited on *The Great Rupert*, had worked for Disney prior to joining the *Puppetoon* team, working on such two-dimensional classics as *The Reluctant Dragon* (1941) and *Bambi* (1942), and would continue animating until the 1980s. It is possible that Madison was not given a credit because Pal wanted to keep the fact that the squirrel was an animated model a secret.

5 Hickman, *The Films of George Pal*.

6 When Pal had left Holland he had sold his studio to Joop Geesink who named it *Dollywood*.

7 Cinerama was short-lived but was one of the largest of the commercial cinema screens, with an aspect ratio of 1: 2.85, and a curved screen that was 146° wide and 55° high (the arcs of human are, respectively, about 180° and 90°). The image seen by the viewer was made up of three projected images with the frame of each of the individual picture-tracks one-and-a-half times the standard height of a normal screen. The celluloid had to be advanced six perforations at a time instead of the usual four in the camera and the projector. The three projected images were intermeshed with a specially designed 'moving comb' arrangement.

8 Pettigrew, *The Stop-Motion Filmography*.

9 Hickman, *The Films of George Pal*.

10 Frank, 'The Stop-Motion World of Jim Danforth'.

11 Publicity handout released by Edward Small Productions.

12 Pettigrew, *The Stop-Motion Filmography*.

13 Transcript notes of conversations with Darlyne O'Brien in 1974, loaned to us by Don Shay.

14 Ray also had problems with the Cinemascope hot spot whilst making *First Men in the Moon*. For more information see page 179 of *Ray Harryhausen - An Animated Life*, Aurum Press/Billboard Books, 2003.

15 Pettigrew, *The Stop-Motion Filmography*.

16 From notes by Dr Rolf Giesen, November 2007.

17 From notes by Dr Rolf Giesen, November 2007.

18 It was never released theatrically in the UK and was only seen on Channel 4 in 1990.

19 The Annecy International Animated Film Festival was begun in 1960 and takes place at the beginning of June in the town of Annecy, France. Between 1960 and 1998 the festival was held every two years but since 1998 it has become an annual event.

20 Frank, 'The Stop-Motion World of Jim Danforth'.

21 Archer, *Willis O'Brien: Special Effects Genius*.

22 Anderson was to have used some of the models constructed for *King Kong* in the film after Jim had rebuilt them into the film's characters.

23 Frank, 'The Stop-Motion World of Jim Danforth'.

24 Frank, 'The Stop-Motion World of Jim Danforth'.

25 Frank, 'The Stop-Motion World of Jim Danforth'.

26 Frank, 'The Stop-Motion World of Jim Danforth'.

27 Frank, 'The Stop-Motion World of Jim Danforth'.

28 Although designed by Jim Danforth, the model of the Loch Ness Monster was constructed by Wah Chang.

29 Hickman, *The Films of George Pal*.

30 In 1967 Muren raised $6,500 to make this 16mm short film and in 1971 producer Jack Harris blew the footage up to 35mm and photographed extra sequences for a theatrical release. More about this in Chapter 6.

31 According to *The Stop-Motion Filmography* by Neil Pettigrew, the producer Aida Young didn't want to use a large carnivorous creature, such as a tyrannosaurus or allosaurus, because she considered their small forearms made them look effeminate. Strange but probably true!

32 Frank, 'The Stop-Motion World of Jim Danforth'.

33 Frank, 'The Stop-Motion World of Jim Danforth'.

34 The BeetleMan was based on an idea by Pete Peterson in the 1950s for an unrealized project.

35 Pettigrew, *The Stop-Motion Filmography*.

36 See *Ray Harryhausen: An Animated Life* by Ray Harryhausen and Tony Dalton Aurum Press/Billboard Books 2003. Pages 261-282.

37 Jim Danforth was uncredited after he left the project and in Neil Pettigrew's book *Stop-Motion Filmography*, Danforth is quoted as saying, 'While I certainly left the project, my credit was always to be Effects Associates, Inc. This is because the Directors Guild *again* prohibited my "Visual Effects Directed by:" credit. My deal memo on *When Dinosaurs Ruled the Earth* specified my credit as "Visual Effects Designed and Directed by Jim Danforth". Warners were forced by the DGA to change it, which is why some reviewers lump all of us – Roger [Dicken], Brian [Johncock] and me – into the same category. The same rules applied by the time of *Caveman*, except more so. The DGA now prohibits co-direction credits (except for partners), so even though my deal was to co-direct the sequences with Carl [Gottlieb], I couldn't get that credit.'

38 'Jim Danforth: Stop-Motion Legend by Ryan Ball' (01/05/2003). *Animation Magazine* [internet web page].

Chapter 6

1 Allen had made several tests of the Taurus model in Griffith Park Zoo.

2 This was a tribute to O'Brien's *King Kong*, a film which Allen adored. There is also another tribute to *Kong* when, in a dream sequence, we see a miniature reproduction of the gate, stairs and walls that appear in the original film.

3 Jones, *The Illustrated Dinosaur Movie Guide*.

4 Pettigrew, *The Stop-Motion Filmography*.

5 Pettigrew, *The Stop-Motion Filmography*.

6 Pettigrew, *The Stop-Motion Filmography*.

7 Chris Endicott has supplied us more information on the involvement of Hammer. 'While Danforth was at Hammer he interested them in *Raiders of the Stome Rings*. Eventually the project seemed too big an undertaking and Hammer suggested limiting the stop-motion portion of the film to just the opening pterodactyl attack and another such fight at the end of the picture. Hammer suggested replacing the race of lizard-men in the story with people 'in strange headgear'. Since it was primarily David's project, he was the one to decide whether to play along with Hammer's changes just to help his career along, or to hold out and keep the project as intended. David took *Raiders* off the table, so he and Hammer parted ways. In Hammer's last communications with David, they mentioned that the new title of the project would be *Creatures the World Forgot* – which, of course, became the title of the [final] sequel to *One Million Years BC* and *When Dinosaurs Ruled the Earth*.'

8 Rick Baker (Richard A. Baker) born 8 December 1950 in Binghamton, New York, is known for his excellent special makeup effects. A six-times Oscar ® winner he, like Ray, had an early fascination with gorillas.

9 Gebhard et al, *Roadtrip Nation*.

10 Gebhard et al, *Roadtrip Nation*.

11 Gebhard et al, *Roadtrip Nation*.

12 In more detail, Go-Motion is an animation system that photographs a model frame-by-frame while allowing both the camera and the models to move during the process. The movements of both are controlled by a computer, which allows for numerous and repeatable passes and blurs the models slightly during photography, which is more natural to the eye than the strobe effects that can be produced by traditional stop-motion animation in which the models remain static while each frame is shot

13 Pettigrew, *The Stop-Motion Filmography*.

14 Dennis Muren in 'The Lightsabre Interview', published on the internet (www.lightsabre.co.uk) (2008).

15 Interview with Dennis Muren on the *Equinox* DVD.

16 Gebhard et al, *Roadtrip Nation*.

17 Interview with Dennis Muren on the *Equinox* DVD.

18 Aupperle states that, 'We had two process projectors, one for rear projection and the other set up for front projection using a 50/50 mirror and 3M Scotchlite. The projector we used for our rear projection was originally used in the RKO Matte Painting Department at least as far back as 1940.

19 The three shots of the planet were, in order of appearance, (1) a photo of Earth, (2) the painting by Danforth on a eighteen-inch plastic sphere and (3) a closer painting, on board, of the planet by Czerkas.

20 A title artist was a pre-computer designer of film and television titles. Stephen's father worked on a large number of films and also did the titles for the television series *Star Trek* and *Mission Impossible*.

21 Aupperle also managed to contact Marcel Delgado, Wah Chang and Linwood Dunn by the same method.

22 He photographed colour tests on front-projected images to see, 'what I could get' and did stop-motion tests with models, but for individual shots or scenes rather than make a whole film. He also built projectors, armatures and animation motors with parts purchase from C&H Surplus in Pasadena.

23 Randy writes, 'I couldn't get enough of television, especially [Jonathan] Winters whose vocal caricatures of surreal character types awakened me to a unique way of imitating, and by extension, commenting upon people through exaggeration and humor. Along with Ray, I idolized and wanted to emulate Winters... but Robin Williams wound up getting *that* job.'

24 DVD Savant website: 'The Hollywood Children of Ray Harryhausen' by Glenn Erickson, 1999.

25 Cook had met Clampett through a friend (Bob Birchard) and he showed Clampett some of his drawings which the latter thought amusing and asked some questions which Clampett must have thought showed some perception, and so the two developed a friendly acquaintanceship'.

26 Jones, *The Illustrated Dinosaur Movie Guide*

27 Jones, *The Illustrated Dinosaur Movie Guide*

28 Pettigrew, *The Stop-Motion Filmography*.

29 The Fleischer studios sometimes used a miniature turntable for tracking shots, and Winsor McKay used elaborate, hand-drawn camera moves in his amazing silent cartoons.

30 'Animatics' were traditional model animation and were used/viewed during filming by Steven Spielberg, actors, and Stan Winston (who built and operated the full-scale dinosaurs).

31 Pettigrew, *The Stop-Motion Filmography*.

32 Front-light, back-light is a technique where two frames are shot for each puppet position. The first frame uses normal, or final, lighting against a black background, a black curtain in this case. For the second frame the 'front' or normal lights are turned off and the black curtain is pulled up, revealing a white card. That screen is lit and the puppet is now in silhouette. The silhouette frames are used as hold-out mattes in the optical printing process while the other frames provide the puppets' final lighting. The final element is then combined with the background element.

33 In Yancy Calzada's notes he also says that Hal Miles 'built a special device for one of the bat gremlins that moved the wings during exposure to create a blur'.

34 This film was also known as *Infested*.

35 Hartlaub, 'Phil Tippett a Special-Effects Pioneer'.

36 This version of *A Sound of Thunder* was made between 1967 and 1970 with non-professional actors.

37 Hartlaub, 'Phil Tippett a Special-Effects Pioneer'.

38 Hartlaub, 'Phil Tippett a Special-Effects Pioneer'.

39 Retro-Junk.com.

40 *RoboCop* also contains a spoof commercial for a 6000 SUX futuristic car, which was created and animated by the Chiodo Brothers and was not supervised by Tippett.

41 VistaVision was a wide-screen process developed by Paramount Pictures in the 1950s. Basically it ran 35mm film horizontally rather vertically, as normal. This created a frame eight perforations across, with an area twice the normal size and an aspect ratio of 1.85.1. Although it offered far better quality than conventionally projected film, Paramount were unable to persuade exhibitors to change their projectors, so prints were reduced to fit normal 35mm stock for exhibition, although the quality was still an improvement.

42 www.robocoparchive.com. Creating ED-209.

43 Pettigrew, *The Stop-Motion Filmography*.

44 Hartlaub, 'Phil Tippett a Special-Effects Pioneer'.

Chapter 7

1 Publicity tag line for the film *Wallace & Gromit: The Curse of the Were-Rabbit*.

2 'Tim Burton Talking about Animation', Tim Burton Dream Site.

3 'Tim Burton Talking about Animation', Tim Burton Dream Site.

4 Pettigrew, *The Stop-Motion Filmography*.

5 'Tim Burton Talking about Animation', Tim Burton Dream Site.

6 Cinema Confidential (www.cinecon.com). Interview with Tim Burton on *Corpse Bride* by Ethan Aames posted on 15/09/05.

7 Cosgrove Hall Films is a distinguished UK-based company that produces 'all three types of animation - drawn / 2D, stop-motion puppet and CGI'. Created by Brian Cosgrove and Mark Hall in 1976. Cosgrove Hall has now become one of the world's premiere animation studios.

8 Jodrell Bank is an astronomical observatory located in Cheshire, NW England that consists of a radio telescope with a steerable parabolic dish.

9 Pixilation or pixillation is a form of animation in which people are used as subjects and are photographed by stop-motion to achieve rapid, jerky and comic movements (the term pixilated means comically eccentric). A good example of this technique can be seen in the Canadian animator Norman McLaren's film *Neighbors* (1952).

10 Shown on the BBC in 1975.

11 BFI Screenonline. 'Aardman Animations' by Sergio Angelini. Reference Guide to British and Irish Film Directors.

12 Ray had adapted the story into his own version, *The Story of the Tortoise and the Hare* (2002). He had begun the project in 1952 and then abandoned it in favour of feature production. It was completed fifty years later.

Acknowledgements

Special thanks to Tim Nicholson for reading the manuscript and for all his research, help, patience and support throughout the writing of the three volumes.

Special mention should also be made to one of the most excellent and meticulously researched books on the subject, *The Stop-Motion Filmography* compiled and written by Neil Pettigrew. The book has been invaluable as a reference guide and we have quoted from it and also used it to check out information given to us from other sources. If the reader wishes to discover more on the subject of model animation then we can thoroughly recommend this volume. Details are given in the Bibliography. We understand from Neil that he has just published a second volume called *The Stop-Motion Filmography: Volume 2. A Critical Guide to 297 Features Using Puppet Animation.*

We would also like to thank the following individuals and organizations that have made the compilation of this book so much more fun and exciting than it would have been without them.

Aardman Animations, especially Peter Lord, Amy Wood, David Sproxton, Ngaio Harding-Hill and Gabrielle Stackpool.

Amblin.

Jim Aupperle who has been so patient in helping us to make contact with numerous technicians and also supplying us with so much information and many images.

BBC.

Jon Berg.

Doug Beswick who has given us so much help and many images.

Sam Buckland for just listening in moments of crisis, and there were a few.

Mark Caballero for all his help in locating Czech contacts and materials.

Canal + Images UK Ltd, especially John Herron who let us access his excellent library at Pinewood Studios and allowed us to use images from *One Million Years BC.*

Yancy Calzada.

Peter Charlton for his expertise on marionettes.

Rob Craig at Kiddiematinee who has been so helpful in securing items for Chapter 5 and who is a self confessed 'greatest' fan of Ray's.

Stephen Czerkas for all his expertise, enthusiasm and willingness to loan us so much from his extensive collection of stop-motion research and images. We owe Stephen a huge debt of gratitude and this credit doesn't somehow seem adequate.

Randall William Cook. Writing Chapter 6 would not been as much fun without his unique input.

James D'Arc the Curator of the Arts and Communications Archive at the Brigham Young University (L. Tom Perry Special Collections).

DN-Images.

Jim Danforth for his permission to use the images of him in the book and for his tireless efforts in promoting the art of stop-motion animation.

The Deutsche Kinemathek Museum Für Film und Fernsehen in Berlin, which has to be the best film museum in the world. Not only because it has displayed a number of Ray's models for a number of years but because it is one of the most comprehensive tributes to cinema we have ever visited. Everyone there was so helpful when we wanted to photograph Ray's models, especially Peter Maenz, the head of the collections, Vera Thomas (exhibitions), Margit Hofmann (3-D collections). Also special thanks to Holger Delfs who built the dioramas and restored Ray's Satyr, Chris Kunzmann who restored Pegasus, Gwangi and several of the other models, Dietmar Linke, a taxidermist who restored the Cyclopean Centaur, the Mooncalf and the Walrus, and finally to Mr Fiebig of the Naturkundemuseum for the superb restoration of the Gryphon.

Randal M.Dutra who supplied us with so much information and images. We were spoilt for choice.

The East Anglian Film Archive (UEA), especially Katherine Mager.

Chris Endicott for supplying us with so many recollections and so much invaluable information and so many images on David Allen.

Glenn Erickson.

Dr Rolf Giesen who has given us so much help in tracing the early history and helping to ensure we include all the really important contributors to model animation.

Diana Harryhausen for her patience and gentle understanding

Vanessa Harryhausen for her support and advice, as always. She probably doesn't realize just how influential she has been in helping to put this book together. She is probably the greatest fan of her father's work and is determined to make sure it endures.

Joel Hart for allowing us to access his research on the Kinex short films.

The Huntley Film Archive.

Andy Johnson - Lord Carnarvon to Tony's Howard Carter during the second 'excavation' of the treasures we found in Ray's London garage - for photographing, recording and helping to find so many 'Wonderful Things'.

The Kobal Collection in London, especially Darren Thomas who along with Cheryl Thomas, is a great fan of Ray's work. They made our work considerably easier.

Kratky Film Praha a.s. – who supplied most of the images in Chapter 5 on Jiri Trnka, Pojar and Karel Zeman. We would like to especially thank Barbora Wohlinova who was so patient and helpful.

Lucasfilm.

Fred MacDonald of MacDonald Associates in Chicago for his help and copyright advice, not only for this book but over the years.

Mark Mawston for his enthusiasm and for his help in the first excavation of Ray's cluttered London garage. Despite the dust being overwhelming he made the task so much easier.

Mrs C. Messenger (nee Melbourne-Cooper).

Dennis Muren who has been generous with his advice and images.

Národni filmovy archive.

Paramount Pictures.

Neil Pettigrew – the world's greatest expert on stop-motion animation.

Barry Purves.

Ray & Diana Harryhausen Foundation.

Tom St Amand.

Seaver Center for Western History Research, Los Angeles County Museum of Natural History, especially Beth Werling and John Cahoon, for kindly allowing us to access their files on Willis O'Brien and Joseph Leeland Roop.

Don Shay for his invaluable help and advice and making available to us so many letters in his collection from Darlyne O'Brien, Marcel Delgado, Merian C. Cooper and Mario Larrinaga.

Sony Pictures.

Tjitte de Vries & Ati Mul.

Phil Tippett for answering so many questions and supplying so many wonderful images.

Tippett Studio, especially Lori Petrini, who have been so helpful in supplying advice, information and images.

Twentieth Century Fox.

Universal Pictures.

Walt Disney.

Harry Walton / vfxmasters.com

Warner Bros.

Ashley Western for his incredible patience and the immense trouble he has taken to understand the subject.

Finally, as this is likely to be the last book in the series, we would like to thank Piers Burnett, Bill McCreadie and Graham Eames at Aurum Press for believing in us and putting up with all the last minute items we wanted to include in this and the previous two volumes.

Picture Credits

1 Ray & Diana Harryhausen Foundation. **2** Ray & Diana Harryhausen Foundation. Photo Andy Johnson. **3** left, Stephen Czerkas. 3 centre, Ray & Diana Harryhausen Foundation. 3 right, Aardman Animations / DreamWorks. **5** Ray & Diana Harryhausen Foundation. Photo Andy Johnson. **11** Photo Andy Johnson. **12** Stephen Czerkas. **13** Stephen Czerkas. **14-15** Jim Aupperle. **16-17** Ray & Diana Harryhausen Foundation. **18** Ray & Diana Harryhausen Foundation. **19** Ray & Diana Harryhausen Foundation. Photos Andy Johnson. **20** Ray & Diana Harryhausen Foundation. Photos 1,3,4,5,6,7,8,11 Andy Johnson. **21** top left, Ray & Diana Harryhausen Foundation. 21 top right, Ray & Diana Harryhausen Foundation/MGM/Warner Bros. 21 centre, Ray & Diana Harryhausen Foundation/Sony Pictures (Columbia). 21 bottom, Ray & Diana Harryhausen Foundation. Photo Andy Johnson. **22** Ray & Diana Harryhausen Foundation. Top three images, photos Andy Johnson. **23** Ray & Diana Harryhausen Foundation, except Satyr on the right which is inThe Deutsche Kinemathek Museum Für Film und Fernsehen in Berlin. All photos Andy Johnson. **24** Ray & Diana Harryhausen Foundation. Photos Andy Johnson. **25** Ray & Diana Harryhausen Foundation. Photos Andy Johnson. **26** Ray & Diana Harryhausen Foundation. Photos Andy Johnson. **27** Ray & Diana Harryhausen Foundation. Photos Andy Johnson. **28** Ray & Diana Harryhausen Foundation. Top, right and bottom, photos Andy Johnson. **29** Ray & Diana Harryhausen Foundation. Top, right and bottom, photos Andy Johnson. **30** Ray & Diana Harryhausen Foundation. Photos Andy Johnson. **31** Ray & Diana Harryhausen Foundation. **32** Ray & Diana Harryhausen Foundation. Bottom three photos, Andy Johnson. **33** Ray & Diana Harryhausen Foundation. Centre right photo, Tony Dalton. **34** Ray & Diana Harryhausen Foundation. **35** Ray & Diana Harryhausen Foundation. Photos Andy Johnson. **36** Stephen Czerkas **37** Ray & Diana Harryhausen Foundation. **38** Ray & Diana Harryhausen Foundation. **39** bottom left & middle images, DN-Images 39 bottom right, The Kobal Collection. **40** East Anglian Film Archive. **41** DN-Images. **42** DN-Images. **43** Ray & Diana Harryhausen Foundation. **44** Ray & Diana Harryhausen Foundation. **45** Stephen Czerkas **46** top left, Stephen Czerkas. 46 top right, DN-Images. **47** top images, Ray & Diana Harryhausen Foundation. 47 bottom images, Dr Rolf Giesen. **48-50** Seaver Center for Western History Research, Los Angeles County Museum of Natural History. **51** top, Ray & Diana Harryhausen Foundation. 51 bottom, Seaver Center for Western History Research, Los Angeles County Museum of Natural History. **52** Ray & Diana Harryhausen Foundation. Photo Andy Johnson. **53** Seaver Center for Western History Research, Los Angeles County Museum of Natural History. **54** Ray & Diana Harryhausen Foundation. **55** Ray & Diana Harryhausen Foundation. **56** Ray & Diana

Harryhausen Foundation. **57** Stephen Czerkas. **58** Ray & Diana Harryhausen Foundation. **59** top left, Stephen Czerkas. 59 top right, Stephen Czerkas. 59 centre, Ray & Diana Harryhausen Foundation. **61** Andy Johnson. **62** Stephen Czerkas. **63** Ray & Diana Harryhausen Foundation. **65** top row, Ray & Diana Harryhausen Foundation. 65 second row - Ray & Diana Harryhausen Foundation. 65 third row: first image, Jim Aupperle; second image, Ray & Diana Harryhausen Foundation; third image, Jim Aupperle. 65 fourth row, Ray & Diana Harryhausen Foundation. **66** left, Ray & Diana Harryhausen Foundation. 66 right, Jim Aupperle. **67** Ray & Diana Harryhausen Foundation. **68** Stephen Czerkas. **69** Ray & Diana Harryhausen Foundation. **70** Ray & Diana Harryhausen Foundation. **71** Ray & Diana Harryhausen Foundation. Bottom image, photo Andy Johnson. **72** Ray & Diana Harryhausen Foundation except bottom right, Stephen Czerkas **73** Ray & Diana Harryhausen Foundation. Top left, photo Andy Johnson. **74** Ray & Diana Harryhausen Foundation. **75** top, Ray & Diana Harryhausen Foundation/RKO/Warner Bros/BBC. 75 bottom, Ray & Diana Harryhausen Foundation. **76** top and bottom left, Ray & Diana Harryhausen Foundation. 76 bottom right, Ray & Diana Harryhausen Foundation/RKO/Warner Bros/BBC. **77** top left and right, Ray & Diana Harryhausen Foundation/RKO/Warner Bros/BBC. 77 bottom left, Ray & Diana Harryhausen Foundation/ RKO/Warner Bros/BBC. 77 bottom right, Stephen Czerkas. **78** Ray & Diana Harryhausen Foundation. **79** top images, Ray & Diana Harryhausen Foundation/RKO/Warner Bros/BBC. 79 bottom, Stephen Czerkas **80** top left, Ray & Diana Harryhausen Foundation/RKO/Warner Bros/BBC. 80 top right, Stephen Czerkas. 80 bottom, Ray & Diana Harryhausen Foundation. **81** Ray & Diana Harryhausen Foundation. **82** Ray & Diana Harryhausen Foundation. **83** Ray & Diana Harryhausen Foundation. **84** top left and centre, Ray & Diana Harryhausen Foundation. Photos Andy Johnson. 84 top right, DN-Images. **85** DN-Images. **86** top left, The Kobal Collection/RKO/Warner Bros/BBC. 86 bottom, The Kobal Collection/RKO/Warner Bros/BBC. **87** top right, Stephen Czerkas/ RKO/Warner Bros/BBC. 87 bottom left, Stephen Czerkas. 87 bottom right, The Kobal Collection/RKO/Warner Bros/BBC. **88** left, Jim Aupperle. 88 top and bottom right, Ray & Diana Harryhausen Foundation **89** top row left, Ray & Diana Harryhausen Foundation. 89 top row centre, Stephen Czerkas. 89 top row right, Ray & Diana Harryhausen Foundation. 89 middle row, Seaver Center for Western History Research, Los Angeles County Museum of Natural History. 89 bottom row left, Seaver Center for Western History Research, Los Angeles County Museum of Natural History. 89 bottom row centre, Seaver Center for Western History Research, Los Angeles County Museum of Natural History. 89 bottom row right, Stephen Czerkas. **90** top left, Ray & Diana Harryhausen Foundation. 90 top centre, Stephen Czerkas. 90 top right, Ray & Diana Harryhausen Foundation. Photo Andy Johnson. 90 bottom, Ray & Diana Harryhausen Foundation. **91** top left, Ray & Diana Harryhausen Foundation. 91 top right, Stephen Czerkas. 91 bottom, Stephen Czerkas. **92** Ray & Diana Harryhausen Foundation. **93** Ray & Diana Harryhausen Foundation. **94-95** Ray & Diana Harryhausen Foundation. **96** Ray & Diana Harryhausen Foundation. **97** top left, Jim Aupperle. 97 top right and bottom, Ray & Diana Harryhausen Foundation. **98** Ray & Diana Harryhausen Foundation. **99** Jim Aupperle. **100-101** Ray & Diana Harryhausen Foundation. **102** Ray & Diana Harryhausen Foundation. **103** DN-Images. **104** Ray & Diana Harryhausen Foundation /Warner Bros. **105** top, Stephen Czerkas/Warner Bros. 105 bottom, Ray & Diana Harryhausen Foundation/Warner Bros. **106-107** top images, Ray & Diana Harryhausen Foundation/Warner Bros. 107 bottom, DN-Images. **108** Stephen Czerkas/Warner Bros. **109** top, Dennis Muren. 109 bottom, Stephen Czerkas/Warner Bros. **110-111** Ray & Diana Harryhausen Foundation. **112** Ray & Diana Harryhausen Foundation. Photo Andy Johnson. **113** Ray & Diana Harryhausen Foundation. **114** Ray & Diana Harryhausen Foundation. **115** Ray & Diana Harryhausen Foundation. **116** Ray & Diana Harryhausen Foundation. **117** Ray & Diana Harryhausen Foundation, except bottom left, Stephen Czerkas. **118** top left, Ray & Diana Harryhausen Foundation. 118 top right, Ray & Diana Harryhausen Foundation/Sony Pictures (Columbia) 118 bottom, Ray & Diana Harryhausen Foundation. **119** Ray & Diana Harryhausen Foundation. **120** Ray & Diana Harryhausen Foundation. 120 bottom left and right, Ray & Diana Harryhausen Foundation. Photos Andy Johnson. **121** Ray & Diana Harryhausen Foundation. Top left, photo Andy Johnson. **122** Ray & Diana Harryhausen Foundation. **123** Ray & Diana Harryhausen Foundation. **124** top left, Ray & Diana Harryhausen Foundation/Sony Pictures (Columbia). 124 top right, Ray & Diana Harryhausen Foundation. 124 bottom, Ray & Diana Harryhausen Foundation. Photo Andy Johnson. **125** Ray & Diana Harryhausen Foundation. **126** Ray & Diana Harryhausen Foundation. **127** Ray & Diana Harryhausen Foundation. **128** Ray & Diana Harryhausen Foundation. **129** Ray & Diana Harryhausen Foundation. Photos Andy Johnson. **130** Ray & Diana Harryhausen Foundation. Photos Andy Johnson. **131** Ray & Diana Harryhausen Foundation. Bottom left, photo Andy Johnson. **132** top left, Ray & Diana Harryhausen Foundation/Warner Bros. 132 centre and bottom, Ray & Diana Harryhausen Foundation. Photos Andy Johnson. **133** Ray & Diana Harryhausen Foundation. Centre and bottom, photos Andy Johnson. **134** Ray & Diana Harryhausen Foundation. Top, photo Andy Johnson. **135** top, Ray & Diana Harryhausen Foundation. 135 bottom images, Ray & Diana Harryhausen Foundation/Sony Pictures (Columbia). **136** top left, Ray & Diana Harryhausen Foundation. 136 top right, Ray & Diana Harryhausen Foundation/Sony Pictures (Columbia). 136 bottom six images, Ray & Diana Harryhausen Foundation/Canal + Images UK Ltd. **137** Ray & Diana Harryhausen Foundation/Sony Pictures (Columbia). **138** Ray & Diana Harryhausen Foundation. Bottom, photo Andy Johnson. **139** top, Ray & Diana Harryhausen Foundation/Sony Pictures (Columbia). 139 bottom, Ray & Diana Harryhausen Foundation. **140** Ray & Diana Harryhausen Foundation. Bottom right, photo Tony Dalton. **141** Ray & Diana Harryhausen Foundation. Photos Tony Dalton. **142** Ray & Diana Harryhausen Foundation. **143** Ray & Diana Harryhausen Foundation. **144** The Deutsche Kinemathek Museum Für Film und Fernsehen, Berlin. Photo Andy Johnson. **145** Ray & Diana Harryhausen Foundation. **146** Ray & Diana Harryhausen Foundation. **147** Ray & Diana Harryhausen Foundation. **148** MacDonald & Associates. **149** centre images, Ray & Diana Harryhausen Foundation. 149 bottom images, MacDonald & Associates. **150** all images, Stephen Czerkas. **151** Ray & Diana Harryhausen Foundation. **152** Ray & Diana Harryhausen Foundation. **153** Ray & Diana Harryhausen Foundation. **154** Ray & Diana Harryhausen Foundation. **155** top left, Ray & Diana Harryhausen Foundation. 155 top right, Chris Endicott. 155 bottom and top left, DN-Images. 155 bottom left, Chris Endicott. 155 bottom right, Chris Endicott. **156** Chris Endicott. **157** Chris Endicott. **158** Chris Endicott. **159** Chris Endicott. **160** top left, Stephen Czerkas. 160 top right, Chris Endicott. 160 bottom, Stephen Czerkas. **161** Chris Endicott. **162** Kratky Film Praha a.s **163** Kratky Film Praha a.s **164** left, DN-Images. 164 right, Chris Endicott. **165** left, Chris Endicott. 165 right –Stephen Czerkas **166** top left, The Kobal Collection/Kratky Film Praha a.s 166 top centre, The Kobal Collection 166 top right, Kratky Film Praha a.s 166 bottom left and middle, Kratky Film Praha a.s 166 bottom right, Národni filmovy archiv. **167** Kratky Film Praha a.s **168** top left, The Kobal Collection. 168 top right, Kratky Film Praha a.s 168 centre right, The Kobal Collection. 168 bottom right, Kratky Film Praha a.s 168 bottom left, The Kobal Collection/ CSF/FILMOVE. **169** top and centre, Kratky Film Praha a.s 169 bottom, DN-Images. **170** Chris Endicott. **171** top left, Chris Endicott. 171 top right, The Kobal Collection/(MGM)Warner Bros. **172** bottom left, The Deutsche Kinemathek Museum Für Film und Fernsehen, Berlin. Photo Andy Johnson. 172 top, right, DN-Images. 172 bottom right, Chris Endicott. 173 top row, DN-Images. **173** second row left, Chris Endicott. 173 second row centre, Chris Endicott. Photo Bill Hedge. 173 second row right, Chris Endicott. 173 third row, DN-Images. 173 fourth row, Chris Endicott. **174** top, Harry Walton / vfxmasters.com 174 bottom left, Jim Aupperle. 174 bottom right, Ray & Diana Harryhausen Foundation. **175** Chris Endicott. **176** Chris Endicott. Photo Paul Gentry. **177** Phil Tippett. **178** Chris Endicott. **179** Chris Endicott. Left centre, photo Larry Bird. **180** top left, Chris Endicott. Photo Paul Gentry. 180 top right, Chris Endicott. Photo Bill Hedge. 180 bottom left, Chris Endicott. 180 top right, Chris Endicott. 180 bottom, DN-Images. 181 top left, Chris Endicott. **181** bottom left, Chris Endicott. Photo Paul Gentry. 181 centre, Chris Endicott. Photo Jim Aupperle. 181 top right, Chris Endicott. Photo Jim Aupperle. 181 bottom right, Chris Endicott. 182 top left, Chris Endicott. **182** top right, Chris Endicott. Photo Paul Gentry. 182 bottom right, Chris Endicott. Photo Paul Gentry. **183** left, Chris Endicott. Photo Paul Gentry. 183 centre top, Chris Endicott. Photo Paul Gentry. 183 centre bottom, Chris Endicott. 183 right, Chris Endicott. **185** Chris Endicott. **186** Dennis Muren. **187** Dennis Muren. **188** bottom left, The Kobal Collection/Lucasfilm/ Twentieth Century Fox 188 bottom right, The Kobal Collection/Walt Disney/Paramount. **189** top left, The Kobal Collection/Warner Bros. 189 top right, Dennis Muren. 189 bottom, The Kobal Collection/Amblin/ Universal Pictures. **191** Jim Aupperle. **192** Jim Aupperle. **193** Doug Beswick. **194** top left, Jim Aupperle. 194 centre left, Stephen Czerkas. 194 bottom right, Jim Aupperle. **195** Jim Aupperle. **196** left, Jim Aupperle. 196 top right, Jim Aupperle. 196 bottom right, Jim Aupperle. Photo James Belochovek. **197** Jim Aupperle. **198** The Kobal Collection/Irwin Yablans Co. **199** left, Chris Endicott. Photo Paul Gentry. 199 right images, Randy Cook. **200** Randy Cook. **201** Randy Cook **202** Randal Dutra. **203** Randal Dutra **204** Randal Dutra **205** top and bottom left, Randal Dutra 205 bottom right, The Kobal Collection/ Amblin/Universal Pictures. **207** Harry Walton/vfxmasters.com **208** Yancy Calzada **209** Yancy Calzada **210** Yancy Calzada. **211** Phil Tippett **212** top left, The Kobal Collection/ Lucasfilm /Twentieth Century Fox. 212 top right, Phil Tippett **213** all images, Phil Tippett except top right, The Kobal Collection/Lucasfilm/Twentieth Century Fox **214** Phil Tippett **215** Phil Tippett **216** Phil Tippett **217** Phil Tippett **218** Phil Tippett **219** Phil Tippett. **220** Aardman Animations/DreamWorks 2005. **221** Barry Purves. **222** The Kobal Collection/Warner Bros **223** The Kobal Collection/Warner Bros **224** The Kobal Collection/Warner Bros **225** Barry Purves. **226** Aardman Animations. **227** top left, Aardman Animations. 227 bottom left, Aardman Animations. Photo Robert Vandenest. 227 centre, Aardman Animations/BBC 227 top right,Aardman Animations/BBC 227 bottom right, Aardman Animations 1991. **228** Aardman Animations/Channel 4 **229** top four images, Aardman Animations 229 bottom left, Aardman Animations/NFTS 229 right top, Aardman Animations/Wallace & Gromit. 229 right bottom, Aardman Animations/Wallace & Gromit. **230** top left, Aardman Animations/Wallace & Gromit 230 top right,Aardman Animations/DreamWorks LLC. Photo Luke Smith. 230 bottom right, Aardman Animations/DreamWorks LLC. **231** top, Aardman Animations. 231 bottom, Aardman Animations/DreamWorks LLC. Photo Luke Smith.

Index

Film titles are in italics.
References to images are in bold.